Why Tanganyika united with Zanzibar to form Tanzania

Godfrey Mwakikagile

Why Tanganyika united with Zanzibar to form Tanzania

First Edition

ISBN 978-9987-16-045-7

New Africa Press
Dar es Salaam, Tanzania

UGANDA

RWANDA

BURUNDI

KENYA

Arusha

Kigoma

TANZANIA

Indian
Ocean

DEM.
REP.
OF
THE
CONGO

Dodoma

Dar es Salaam

Mbeya

ZAMBIA

MALAWI

MOZAMBIQUE

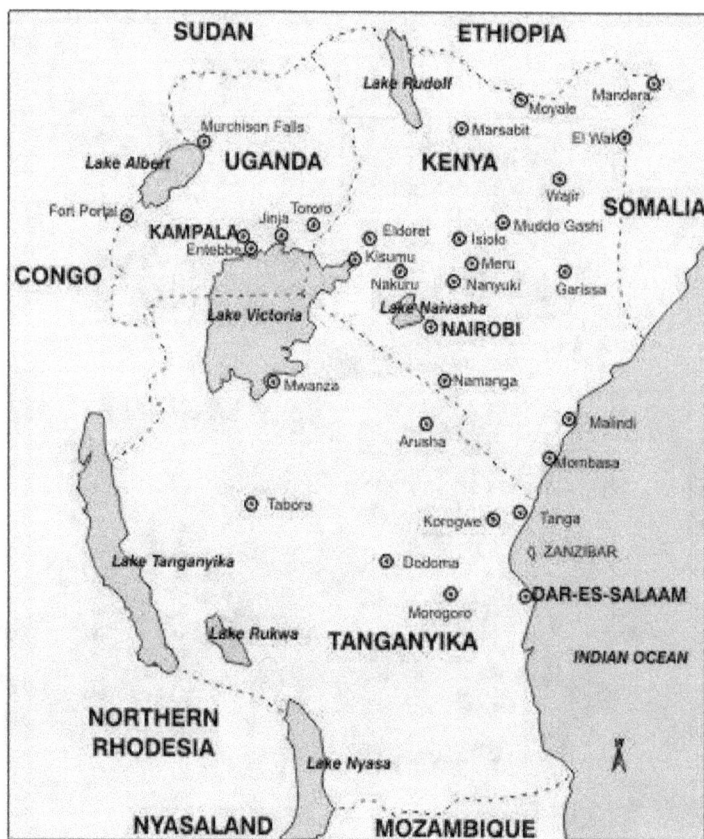

SUDAN　　　　ETHIOPIA

Lake Rudolf
Moyale　　Mandera
Marsabit　　El Wak

Murchison Falls
Lake Albert　UGANDA　　KENYA
Wajir
Fort Portal　　　　　Tororo　　　　　　SOMALIA
Jinja
KAMPALA　Eldoret　Isiolo　Muddo Gashi
Entebbe　Kisumu　Meru
CONGO　　　　　　Nakuru　Nanyuki　Garissa
Lake Victoria　Lake Naivasha
NAIROBI

Mwanza　　Namanga

Malindi
Arusha
Mombasa

Tabora　　　　　　Korogwe　Tanga
Lake Tanganyika　　　　　ZANZIBAR
Dodoma
DAR-ES-SALAAM
Morogoro
Lake Rukwa　TANGANYIKA
INDIAN OCEAN
NORTHERN
RHODESIA
Lake Nyasa
NYASALAND　　MOZAMBIQUE

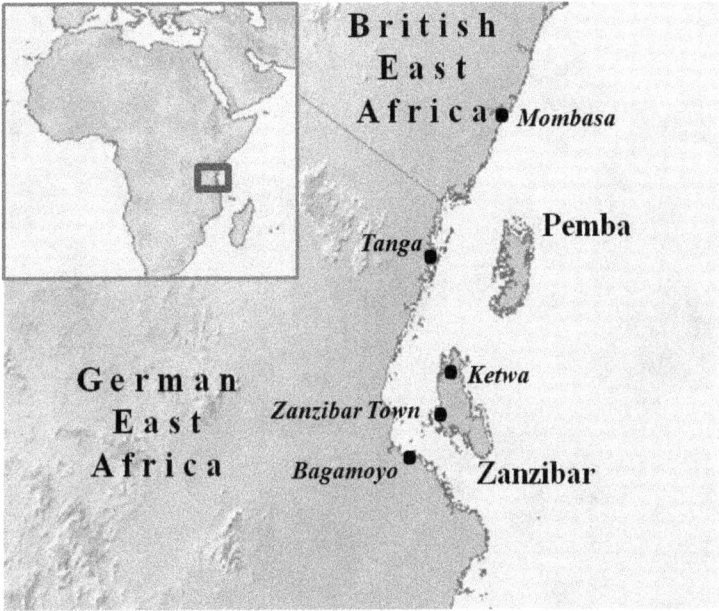

British
East
Africa● Mombasa

Pemba

Tanga●

German
East
Africa

● Ketwa
Zanzibar Town ●
Bagamoyo ●

Zanzibar

Zanzibar and Pemba

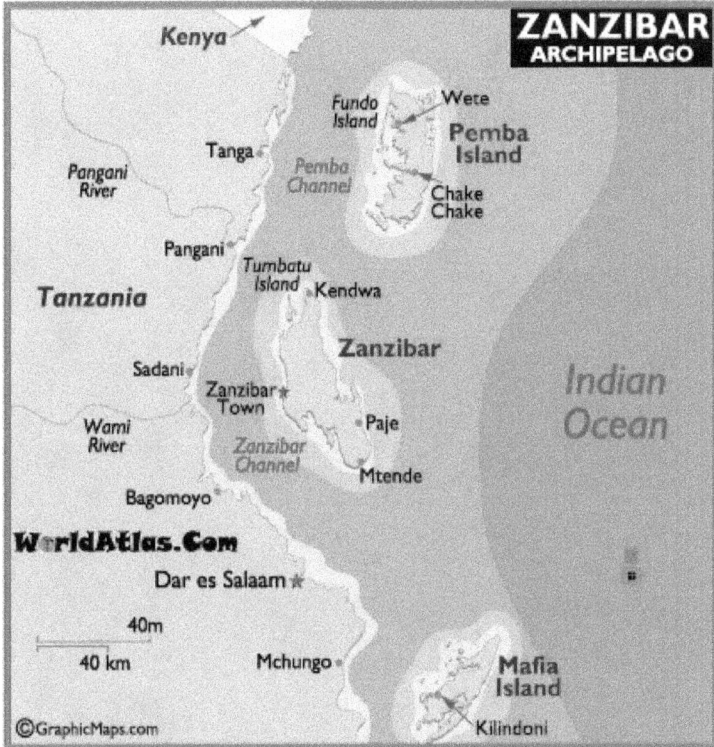

ZANZIBAR
ARCHIPELAGO

Kenya

Fundo Island
Wete
Pemba Island

Tanga

Pangani River

Pemba Channel

Chake Chake

Pangani

Tumbatu Island
Kendwa

Tanzania

Zanzibar

Sadani

Zanzibar Town

Paje

Indian Ocean

Wami River

Zanzibar Channel

Mtende

Bagomoyo

WorldAtlas.Com

Dar es Salaam

40m

40 km

Mchungo

Mafia Island

©GraphicMaps.com

Kilindoni

7

Acknowledgements

I WISH to express my profound gratitude to the sources I have used to document my work. All the sources I have cited are given full attribution. I am very grateful to all of them without a single exception. My work would not be what it is in terms of documentation without them except for the analysis which is entirely mine including its shortcomings.

Special thanks must go to the American diplomats who were accredited to Tanzania and whose interviews, reproduced here, provide some insights into a number of areas including the subjects I have addressed, although what they discussed goes beyond the central thesis of my work. They are vital references, nonetheless.

I am also profoundly grateful to those who conducted the interviews and to the Foreign Affairs Oral History Collection, Association for Diplomatic Studies and Training (ADST) in Arlington, Virginia, USA, www.adst.org, the copyright holder, for permission to use their material in this book.

The material has been very helpful in many ways including providing inspiration to other people who may want to go beyond my work to learn more about my home country, Tanzania, and how things were in those days when Tanganyika united with Zanzibar during the Cold War – to form Tanzania – and what happened in the following years which were some of the most critical in the history of post-colonial Africa.

Introduction

THE unification of Tanganyika and Zanzibar in April 1964 was the first political union between independent countries ever to take place on the African continent in the post-colonial era. And it continues to be a subject of interest among many people more than 50 years after its consummation.

It was preceded by the Zanzibar revolution which took place on 12 January 1964. Three months later, the new nation of Tanzania was formed after the two former independent states of Tanganyika and Zanzibar surrendered their sovereignties to a supra-national entity which came to be officially known as the United Republic of Tanzania. There is no question that the revolution played a major role in encouraging or pushing the leaders towards unification.

The union of Tanganyika and Zanzibar may still have been consummated had the revolution not taken place in the island nation. We will never know. But given the Pan-Africanist inclinations of the leaders involved in the consummation of the union, there was a high probability that the two countries would have united sometime at a later date.

The union was a milestone in the history of post-colonial Africa and in the continent's quest for unity and had an impact that is still felt today, decades after it was formed. It influenced political and diplomatic relations between and among countries and changed the course of history.

It was even a factor in the super-power rivalry between the United States and the Soviet Union during the Cold War. It also became a major subject of intellectual and ideological debates in and outside Africa for many years. And it continues to stimulate debate even today among many Tanzanians and other people.

There are some people in Tanzania including a number of leaders who think uniting the two countries was a mistake. Some people say the union was formed in hurry without seriously considering all the issues involved. Then there are those who say the union should not have been formed at all and that the two countries of Tanganyika and Zanzibar should have remained separate entities with full sovereign status they attained when they won independence from Britain on separate dates.

Tanganyika won independence on 9 December 1961 and Zanzibar on 10 December 1963, although the legitimacy of Zanzibar's government which assumed power on independence day was highly questionable since the black African majority in the island nation were excluded from power by their Arab rulers; one of the factors which played a major role in igniting the Zanzibar revolution.

It has been a bumpy road since independence. And many problems still lie ahead as the two partners continue to find ways to resolve their differences and strengthen the union. In fact, a significant number of Zanzibaris, especially on Pemba island, would like to see the union dissolved and return to the status quo ante.

Only time will tell where the union is headed.

Problems faced by the union of Tanganyika and Zanzibar have also served as a warning to other African countries which may contemplate uniting under one government, although that is a remote possibility on a continent where nationalism transcends Pan-Africanism despite professions to the contrary.

Even within Tanzania itself, Zanzibari "nationalism" is still strong, although Zanzibar is no longer a separate country with sovereign status. It is an integral part of the United Republic of Tanzania. But that has not stopped many Zanzibaris from demanding independence and dissolution of the union.

Some of the union's strongest opponents are members of the Civic United Front (CUF), one of Tanzania's major opposition partie, which has its biggest support in the former island nation, mainly on Pemba Island, and has ties to Oman and other Gulf states.

Opposition to the union also comes from a significant number of people who were supporters of the old Arab regime and are mostly Arab themselves.

The union was a major achievement. But it also has many problems, some of which may not have been anticipated by the architects of this macro-nation.

Why was the union formed, when it was, besides the desire that already existed among the leaders to unite the two countries? Were others forces at work?

Did the United States and Britain exert pressure on Nyerere to unite the two countries as Professor Ali Mazrui and others contend? As Mazrui stated in his article, "Nyerere and I," October 1999, in which he eulogised the former Tanzanian leader:

"My strongest disagreement with Nyerere concerned Zanzibar and Nigeria (when Tanzania recognised the secessionist region of Eastern Nigeria as the independent Republic of Biafra).

Did Tanganyika unite with Zanzibar to form Tanzania

under pressure from President Lyndon Johnson of the United States and Prime Minister Sir Alec Douglas-Home of Britain who did not want Zanzibar to become another communist Cuba?"

Was the merger of the countries a Pan-African initiative by Nyerere and the leader of Zanzibar after the revolution, Abeid Karume and some of his colleagues, to form one country?

Were the two leaders, Nyerere and Karume, equally motivated to unite their countries?

Was it Nyerere who was behind it all? Or was it Karume who first suggested to Nyerere that their countries should unite? As Tanzania's former First Vice President Aboud Jumbe, who had fallen out with Nyerere, bluntly stated at a press conference in Dar es Salaam in January 1998 on the 34th anniversary of the Zanzibar revolution which, among other things, provided an impetus towards unification of the two countries:

"Ask Nyerere, because he is the one who went to Zanzibar. He is the one who wanted the union. He must have had goals. Has he achieved them? I can not speak for mainlanders on the achievement of the union."

Was there an interplay of forces at work when the union was formed? Cold War intrigues and rivalries; Pan-African solidarity and commitment to regional and continental unity under one government by President Julius Nyerere of Tanganyika and his colleagues such as Tanganyika's minister defence and foreign affairs, Oscar Kambona, among other factors.

Was it driven by the imperatives of geography and historical dictates including the "natural" desire by weak countries to work together and even unite and the "inevitability" of regional integration in the East African context, considering the history of the region?

What role, if any, did the Cold War play in inspiring and facilitating the merger of the two East African countries?

Was the union an African initiative by the nationalist leaders of Tanganyika and Zanzibar without any need for encouragement from the United States and Britain? Did Pan-Africanism and pan-African solidarity play a primary or a minor role? Or was it the prime determinant?

Other factors included a passionate appeal by Zanzibari prime minister and vice president, Abdallah Kassim Hanga, to his colleagues in the Zanzibar Revolutionary Council to support the merger of the two countries; fear of a communist regime which could have been established in Zanzibar after the revolution, turning the island nation into what the United States and other Western powers feared would be another Cuba or "the Cuba of Africa"; security concerns by Tanganyika if Zanzibar, so close to the mainland, were to have a hostile regime or became unstable, thus posing a threat to the mainland; fear by Zanzibari leaders especially President Abeid Karume who was worried that his political enemies, especially the Marxist-Leninist Abdulrahman Mohamed Babu, could oust him and the only way he could survive and be secure would be by uniting his country with Tanganyika for protection by a bigger and more powerful neighbour.

What role did all those factors play in the unification process which led to the establishment of of the United Republic of Tanzania after Tanganyika and Zanzibar united to form one country?

Why did Zanzibari leaders such as Kassim Hanga and even Abdulrahman Babu, well-known Marxist-Leninists, support the union with Tanganyika, knowing full well that it would cost them – weaken them politically and deprive them of their power base in Zanzibar and thus make them "allies" of their enemies, the United States and other Western powers, who encouraged the merger of the two countries to neutralise them in order to prevent them from establishing a communist regime in Zanzibar that would pose a threat to Western geopolitical and strategic interests in the region and in Africa as a whole? Why did they support such a union, which amounted to political suicide for them in their native land, Zanzibar, as Marxist-Leninists who ended up being powerless there? And why do the leaders of Tanzania mainland want to maintain the union at any cost although Zanzibar is an economic burden on the mainland?

The union remains a highly contentious subject among many Tanzanians. Many questions are still being asked. And most of them have not been fully answered.

It is not the purpose of this book to answer those questions, whether or not the union should have been formed, or whether or not it was the right thing to do.

The focus of this work is on whether or not Nyerere and his colleagues on the mainland – Tanganyika – and those in Zanzibar initiated the move towards unification.

Cold War considerations are also an integral part of this analysis as a counter thesis to Pan-African initiatives as the driving force behind the consummation of the union.

This work complements my previous one, *The Union of Tanganyika and Zanzibar: Product of the Cold War?*

Why Tanganyika united with Zanzibar to form Tanzania

THE UNION of Tanganyika and Zanzibar was the first merger of independent states on the entire continent and the only one that has ever been consummated. The Ghana-Guinea union formed on 23 November 1958 between the first black African country to win independence from Britain and the first to achieve it from France, and joined by Mali in 1961 to form the Ghana-Guinea-Mali union, was more symbolic than functional.[1]

In the case of Tanzania, both Tanganyika and Zanzibar renounced their sovereignties and submerged their separate national identities in the new macro-nation. The establishment of Tanzania from this merger is also one of the most memorable achievements of the late President Julius Nyerere.

Tanganyika united with Zanzibar on 26 April 1964. For six months, the new country was simply known as the Union of Tanganyika and Zanzibar. It was also officially known by its much longer name as the United Republic of Tanganyika and Zanzibar, and was renamed the United Republic of Tanzania on October 29th in the same year.

17

Dar es Salaam, the capital of Tanganyika, which means 'haven of peace" or "the abode of peace" in Arabic and was founded by the Arab rulers, became the seat of the union government.

The union was preceded by the revolution in Zanzibar which ended Arab hegemonic control of the islands that lasted for hundreds of years since the latter part of the 1600s.

The violent uprising was led by John Okello, a Ugandan who had settled on Pemba Island and who saw himself as a messianic figure on a mission to free his people – blacks in Zanzibar – from Arab domination. And the role this self-styled field marshal played in the redemption of his race on the isles became a sub-text in the unfolding drama that eventually led to the consummation of the union. As Professor Haroub Othman, a Tanzanian of Zanzibari origin teaching at the University of Dar es Salaam in Tanzania, explained:

"Nyerere states that he casually proposed the idea of Union to Karume when the latter visited him to discuss the fate of John Okello. According to Nyerere, Karume immediately agreed to the idea and suggested that Nyerere should be the president of such a union. In a New Year's message to the nation on 1 January 1965, Nyerere implied that even if the ASP (Afro-Sirazi Party led by Karume in Zanzibar) had come into power by constitutional means and not as a result of revolution, the Union would still have taken place."[2]

Even though a convergence of interests – Western (especially American and British) concern that Zanzibar was about to become "the Cuba of Africa," and Nyerere's Pan-African desire to unite with Zanzibar – may seem to have helped create a climate conducive to unification of the two independent African states, the union would probably still have been established on Nyerere's own

18

initiative, even if there was no "communist" threat on the isles and independent Zanzibar – under black majority rule – was a capitalist haven, provided the leaders of Zanzibar also, like Nyerere, had the political will to do so.

Nyerere had just failed, in 1963, to convince the leaders of Kenya and Uganda to unite with Tanganyika and form an East African federation. Now, Zanzibar provided him with an opportunity to realise his Pan-African ambition although on a smaller scale.

American officials themselves who were in government service under President Lyndon B. Johnson during that time did not even claim credit for engineering the union. As Frank Carlucci, who was US consul in Zanzibar and who later became CIA director and then American secretary of defence, stated in an interview in 1986:

"Nyerere had to do something about the Zanzibar problem. I don't know for a fact whether he came up with the idea himself, or whether we gave him the prescription. Whether our urging him to do something about Zanzibar had an effect on him....I do know that the situation in Zanzibar was one of continuing deterioration. In the absence of action from Tanganyika, the place would have been completely controlled by the communists."[3]

The highly volatile situation in Zanzibar during that critical period provided momentum towards unification, but at a tempo influenced even if not dictated by Nyerere – the main architect of the union – and his colleagues in Tanganyika and Zanzibar, since it was they who stipulated the terms for unification. That the events in Zanzibar dictated the pace of this consensus building between the leaders of the two countries which led to the establishment of the union is clearly demonstrated by the short time span in which the entire process was completed.

The two countries united within three-and-a-half

months: the proposal, negotiations and consummation of the union all took place within that short period. And tough negotiations took place because some Zanzibari leaders were opposed to the merger. As Professor Haroub Othman stated:

"Discussions on the Union were conducted very secretively. From the archives, and the statements of those who were in the corridors of power at the time, it would appear that not many people in the Tanganyika Government, or the Zanzibar Revolutionary Council, knew what was happening.

Apart from Nyerere and Karume, the only other people who might have been privy to these discussions were Rashidi Kawawa, Oscar Kambona, Abdallah Kassim Hanga and Salim Rashid.

What is important is that the Articles of Union, signed by Karume and Nyerere on 22 April 1964, were subsequently ratified by both the Tanganyika National Assembly and the Zanzibar Revolutionary Council.

Both Abdulrahman Babu and Khamis Abdallah-Ameir, the two former Umma Party leaders who were in the Revolutionary Council at the time, have confirmed that the matter was discussed in the Council and that, while there were reservations on the part of some members, these were overcome by Abdallah Kassim Hanga who made an emotional appeal in support of the Union.

Presenting the proposal for a Union to the Tanganyika National Assembly on 25 April 1964, Nyerere based his argument on the proximity of the Islands to the Mainland, a common language, friendship between TANU and the ASP (Afro-Shirazi Party in Zanzibar), and common cultural traditions. But the ultimate ground for the Union was, he said, a commitment to the cause of African unity. Nyerere saw the Union with Zanzibar as a step towards federation in East Africa."[4]

With that step, Nyerere made a lasting contribution towards African unity and, after he died, left behind a very peaceful and stable nation; one of the very few on this turbulent continent. That Nyerere left behind such a cohesive entity he skillfully built – first as Tanganyika – and nurtured for more than 40 years is probably his most enduring legacy; yet the least appreciated among his most ardent critics who talk and write about his failed socialist policies more than anything else while ignoring his achievements. But in spite of all that, his influence continued to grow and he remained a towering figure on the national scene and in the international arena throughout his political life.

Even after he voluntarily stepped down from the presidency in November 1985, he remained such a formidable figure on the national scene that he not only provided guidance when needed but influenced the course of events in Tanzania until his death. His choice of his successors, Ali Hassan Mwinyi and Benjamin Mkapa, was easily approved by the ruling party, Chama Cha Mapinduzi (CCM), a Kiswahili name that literally means the Party of the Revolution, or Revolutionary Party.

His opposition to the establishment of a separate government for Tanganyika as demanded in the early 1990s by some members of parliament from mainland Tanzania, and even by some Zanzibaris such as the former first vice president, Aboud Jumbe, was equally supported by the ruling party – against prevailing sentiment within the party itself in favour of a separate government for Tanganyika – and probably saved the union which may not have survived with three governments: one for Zanzibar as has always been the case since the union formed; one for Tanganyika as proposed by some members of parliament in 1993 but rejected outright by Nyerere; and one union government for the whole country which has at the same time also served as the government of Tanzania mainland, hence Tanganyika, although the latter no longer exists as a political entity like Zanzibar still does.

In fact, it is also politically unacceptable in a nationalist context for the people on the mainland to call themselves Tanganyikans, unlike the people of Zanzibar who still call themselves Zanzibaris probably more than anything else when they assert and affirm their identity, express their grievances against the union, and are nostalgic about the halcyon days when they were a separate independent nation.

That Nyerere was able to prevail in these and many other cases was vindication of his status as the most powerful leader in Tanzania even after his retirement. He remained the final arbiter on the national scene until his death. And because of his formidable influence, there was some concern that the union of Tanganyika and Zanzibar would not survive without him. As President Benjamin Mkapa said when he announced the death of Nyerere on national radio in Kiswahili:

"I know the death of the father of the nation will shock and dismay many. There are many who fear that national unity will disintegrate, the union will falter and our relations with our neighbours will deteriorate following the passing of Nyerere. But Nyerere has built a sustainable foundation for national unity, the union and relations with our neighbours."[5]

President Mkapa also issued a stern warning to those who may try to break up the union of Tanganyika and Zanzibar. He said they would be dealt with severely: "(Anyone) dreaming about breaking the unity of Tanzania, generating insecurity or stirring up tensions...will be dealt with ruthlessly and their activities curtailed."[6]

Obviously, the warning was taken seriously despite attempts by the Civic United Front (CUF) – which was then the largest opposition party in Tanzania and whose biggest support still comes from Zanzibar, especially

Pemba Island, its stronghold – and by maverick politicians such as Christopher Mtikila, a Christian fundamentalist minister from the mainland and leader of a small opposition group, the Democratic Party, to destabilise and break up the union.

The union was consummated at the height of the Cold War, and there have been all kinds of speculations, allegations and innuendoes that the merger was externally engineered. The implication of these arguments is that Nyerere would not have formed the union had he not been prompted, prodded, exhorted and manipulated by these external forces to do so. As Professor Ali Mazrui stated in "Nyerere and I":

"Did Tanganyika unite with Zanzibar to form Tanzania under pressure from President Lyndon Johnson of the United States and Prime Minister Sir Alec Douglas Home of Britain who did not want Zanzibar to become another communist Cuba?

Nyerere bristled when it was suggested that the union with Zanzibar was part of the Cold War and not a case of Pan-Africanism."[7]

The argument that Nyerere was coerced by the United States and Britain into uniting Tanganyika with Zanzibar to deprive communists of a base on the island nation is not validated by Nyerere's track record. And as we learned earlier, the American consul in Zanzibar during that time, Frank Carlucci, did not even claim that the United States – or any other Western power including Britain – engineered the union.

Looking at Nyerere's record, we see that throughout his political career, he demonstrated a degree of independence in pursuit of his goals which irritated and sometimes even infuriated both ideological camps, East and West, during the Cold War.

As far back as 1959, before he led Tanganyika to

independence from Britain, he called for a boycott of apartheid South Africa because of her racist policies at a time when both the United States and Britain and other Western powers were giving full and unconditional support to the apartheid regime which was oppressing black people and other non-whites. He was not intimidated by the West and maintained his principled stand against apartheid and other white minority regimes on the continent as was clearly demonstrated when he invited the freedom fighters to establish their bases in Tanganyika soon after the country won independence from Britain on 9 December 1961. He did all that contrary to Western wishes and interests, and in defiance of the West.

He also defied the West when he established strong ties with the People's Republic of China, the Soviet Union and other Eastern-bloc countries soon after independence. But he also annoyed communist nations when he continued to maintain equally strong ties with the West in pursuit of his policy of positive non-alignment. As he sharply responded to critics from the East and the West as far back as 1961: "We have no desire to have a friendly country choosing our enemies for us."[8]

He even publicly criticised the Soviet Union when Warsaw Pact troops, led by the Soviets, invaded Czechoslovakia in August 1968.

Nyerere's commitment to African unity, like Nkrumah's, was well-known. And he lived up to that commitment; which had nothing to do with getting encouragement from the West to advance Pan-African goals.

Those were the very same countries which were intent on perpetuating their domination of Africa and were therefore opposed to any move which would threaten or undermine their hegemonic control of the continent.

A strong, united Africa would naturally not be in their best interest since it would seek to end such domination. And Nyerere was one of the most implacable foes of

24

imperial domination of Africa by both East and West. As he stated in August 1961, about four months before he led Tanganyika to independence:

"I believe the danger to African unity is going to come from...external forces.... The rich countries of the world – both capitalist and socialist – are using their wealth to dominate the poor countries. And they are ready to weaken and divide the poor countries for that purpose of domination....

Whenever we try to talk in terms of larger units on the African continent, we are told that it can't be done; we are told that the units we would create would be 'artificial.' As if they could be any more artificial than the 'national' units on which we are now building!.... Many of them are deliberately emphasizing the difficulties on our continent for the express purpose of maintaining them and sabotaging any move to unite Africa.

The technique is very simple. One power bloc labels a move for unity a 'Communist plot' – not because it is Communist, but because they don't like it. Another power bloc labels another move for unity an 'imperialist plot' – not because it is so, but because they don't like it.

What annoys me is not the use of these slogans by power-hungry nations, for this is something we do expect; but what does infuriate me is that they should expect us to allow ourselves to be treated as if we were a bunch of idiots!"[9]

In pursuit of his Pan-African goals, Nyerere had earlier, in 1960, offered to delay Tanganyika's independence due in 1961 so that the three East African countries of Kenya, Uganda, and Tanganyika would emerge from colonial rule on the same day and form a federation. Yet, no one would seriously suggest – if at all – that Nyerere offered to do so at the behest of the departing colonial masters in order to establish a

25

federation.

Nyerere sought to unite African countries even as far back as the fifties. Therefore, it was not surprising that he wanted to unite Tanganyika with Zanzibar, an island nation that already had long historical and cultural ties with his country.

During the struggle for independence, Nyerere already had a strong desire to unite the East African countries under one government. He had the support of some of his colleagues in Tanganyika and even in the other East African countries. Therefore, there was already a movement towards unity in the region.

In fact, Kenya, Uganda and Tanganyika already had common services which united them as a regional bloc on economic matters even during colonial rule. They even had a common currency and a common market.

The other entities were the East African Posts and Telecommunications Corporation, the East African Harbours and Railways Corporation, the East African Airways and research facilities, all under an umbrella organisation, the East African Common Services Organisation (EACSO) based in Nairobi, Kenya, which virtually functioned as the colonial capital of East Africa. All three countries – Kenya, Uganda and Tanganyika – were under British rule.

Nyerere saw all that as a basis for regional unity and sought, together with the other East African leaders, to transform and strengthen the common bonds shared by the three countries into a vehicle that would form a strong foundation for a political union under one government.

The union of Tanganyika and Zanzibar formed under his leadership was therefore only a part of the Pan-African quest for regional federation and eventually for continental unity; which is what prompted him to say, if two countries (Tanganyika and Zanzibar) can unite, three can; if three can, thirty can.

It was also Nyerere who brought together the political

parties in the countries of East and Central Africa which were fighting for independence in order to coordinate the struggle against imperial rule. He invited the leaders of the parties to a conference in Mwanza, Tanganyika, held from 16 – 18 September 1958, which led to the establishment of an organisation, the Pan-African Freedom Movement for East and Central Africa (PAFMECA), under his leadership.

The organisation was expanded, again under his leadership, in 1962 to include the countries of southern Africa and was renamed the Pan-African Freedom Movement for East, Central and Southern Africa (PAFMECSA). PAFMECSA played a major role in the establishment of the Organisation of African Unity (OAU) in Addis Ababa, Ethiopia, in May 1963.

A few years earlier in 1960 after a PAFMECA meeting in Addis Ababa, Nyerere said the following concerning the imperative need for unity:

"Many of us agree without pretences or inhibitions that the East African Federation will be a good thing. We have stated this, and it remains true, that the borders separating our countries were put in place not by ourselves but by imperialists.

Therefore, we should not allow them to be used against our unity....We must persistently knock at the offices of the colonialists not to demand the independence of Tanganyika, then Kenya and Uganda and finally Zanzibar, but we must do it to demand the independence of East Africa as one political federation."[10]

He pursued the goal relentlessly more than any other leader in the region. Years later, he said failure to form an East African federation was his biggest disappointment. He said that in interview with James McKinley of *The New York Times* in his home village of Butiama in August 1996 after he stepped down from the presidency and more

27

than 30 years after the failure to form an East African federation before the end of 1963 as the the three East African leaders – Nyerere, Jomo Kenyatta of Kenya and Milton Obote of Uganda – had agreed to do at a conference in Nairobi in June 1963. They also said Zanzibar was invited to join the federation and could do so after it won independence. Therefore it would have been a federation of four countries: Kenya, Uganda, Tanganyika and Zanzibar.

But it was never formed. Instead, only two countries out of four, Tanganyika and Zanzibar, were able to unite under one government under the leadership of Nyerere.

Looking back at his political career, Nyerere said his greatest failure was that although he managed to form a union between Tanganyika and Zanzibar in 1964 to create Tanzania, he never succeeded in persuading the leaders of the other countries – Kenya and Uganda – to form a larger entity in 1963, a move that would have made the region a powerhouse. As he put it:

"I felt that these little countries in Africa were really too small, they would not be viable – the Tanganyikas, the Rwandas, the Burundis, the Kenyas. My ambition in East Africa was really never to build a Tanganyika. I wanted an East African federation.

So what did I succeed in doing? My success is building a nation out of this collection of tribes."[11]

When he tried to convince the other East African leaders to form an East African federation, before Kenya, Uganda and Tanganyika won independence, Nyerere stated in June 1960:

"In the struggle against colonialism the fundamental unity of the people of Africa is evident and is deeply felt. It is, however, a unity forged in diversity in a battle against an outside Government. If the triumph in this battle is to be followed by an equal triumph against the forces of neo-imperialism and also against poverty, ignorance and disease, then this unity must be strengthened and maintained.

The feeling of unity which now exists could, however, be whittled away if each country gets its independence separately and becomes open to the temptations of nationhood and the intrigues of those who find their strength in the weakness of small nations.

There is one way to ensure in East Africa that the present unity of opposition should become a unity of construction. The unity and freedom movements should be combined, and the East African territories achieve independence as one unit at the earliest possible moment. This means a Federation of the Territories now administered separately.

But a federation of Kenya, Tanganyika, Uganda and Zanzibar can not and must not be imposed upon the people of these territories. It must be a decision of the people expressed through their elected representatives. Only by this method will the present sentiment of unity become an actuality capable of transforming the economic and social position of our territories. This means that discussions on the question of the establishment of a Federation of East Africa can only come after all the countries concerned have governments which are responsive to the wishes of the people, elected by the people and which have full internal power. This position can be reached early in 1961. I believe it must be reached then so that the four governments have an opportunity to put into political effect the unity now felt throughout our countries.

At the moment Tanganyika is more advanced on the road to independence than any of the other territories; the British government could not refuse a demand from us for independence in 1961. I believe, however, that it is in the best interests of Tanganyika as well as of the other territories that we should unite into a federation. I also

29

believe that the attainment of complete independence by Tanganyika alone would complicate the establishment of a new political unit. If the British government is willing to amend their timetable for the constitutional changes of the other territories and then those territories expressed a desire for federation, I would be willing to ask the people of Tanganyika to join that federation with the others.

Ever since we started discussing this question of a Federation of East Africa, I have not found anybody yet either in East Africa or outside East Africa who is against the principle of federation. Indeed, when the leaders of the PAFMECA Conference met recently in Mbale, they unanimously agreed that the proposed federation was worth supporting and that we should work out the details and how to bring it about. I think it is the details of this federation and how to bring it about on which we are likely to have differences of opinion.

I would like to express my own views, not on the details of ultimately what form of federation we are going to have; those we must leave to the leaders, if and when they decide to frame in more detail the form of federation they would like to see. The views I want to express are how to bring it about.

I believe that if it is desired to bring about this federation, the right moment to do this is not after each country has separately achieved its own independence but before. Already there are people in East Africa who have expressed differences of opinion about this approach. There are people who believe, no doubt sincerely, that in order that the decision to bring about the federation may be, and may appear to be, a free expression of the people of East Africa themselves, we must wait until the separate countries are completely independent. If is argued that if we were to achieve this federation before the countries were completely independent, there is a danger that it might appear that the federation was imposed on us by the colonial power and that it was not a free expression of wishes of the people of East Africa.

It has also been argued that if we do not prepare for the separate independence of the East African territories but were to merge them into a federation before they had separately achieved their independence, the merger might delay the independence of East Africa.

It is true that in order that this federation may be a reality, it must be willed, designed and put into effect by the peoples of East Africa themselves. An imposed federation like the Central African Federation has no chance of succeeding and is completely out of the question. I believe, however, that the expression of the wishes of the people of East Africa does not have to wait until these countries are completely independent.

We in Tanganyika, for instance, have now a form of government which we call Responsible Government. If the Legislative Council of Tanganyika were to seek the independence of Tanganyika, and this is what we are going to do in March, nobody, by any stretch of the imagination, can say that the expression of the Legislative Council of Tanganyika seeking the independence of Tanganyika is not an expression of the people of Tanganyika.

Similarly, if the Legislative Council was to express a view that Tanganyika wanted to to come out of colonial status to independence as part of East Africa, that expression would be an expression of the views of the people of Tanganyika – unless, of course, the people of Tanganyika were opposed to such views.

I realise that at present no other East African country has the same kind of government. It is for this reason that I have suggested that if the people of East Africa want a federation, the right moment to bring it about is after each country in East Africa has reached the same kind of constitutional change as has now been reached by Tanganyika, and that we should insist that the elections which are due to take place in all those countries should result in governments truly responsible to the people.

If after these countries have achieved elected government they decided to achieve their independence separately, that decision would be a true expression of the views of the peoples of those countries. If, on the other hand, they all decided that they wanted to achieve their independence as one political unit and they have the backing of their people, they would equally be expressing the wishes of their countries.

I do not see, therefore, that for the purpose of making sure that the desire to join a federation is the wish of the peoples of those countries, we have to wait until those countries have achieved complete independence.

It has been argued, largely by some of our friends in Uganda, that we must put our separate houses in order first, before we can contemplate federation. I do accept this argument. If we were all in chaos, it would be silly to add chaos to chaos – although one can ask the difference it would make. But when does one satisfy oneself that our house has been put in order? I say after Responsible Government. Some of my friends say after independence. I find it difficult to accept this. Surely, the argument of 'let's put our house in order first' will be made stronger after independence than before independence. As I'll try to show later, federation before independence can help to put each house in order. Federation after independence will not even have this attraction which appears to be so dear to our friends.

If people resist a move now which has every chance of hastening the complete independence of East Africa, during a period when the struggle for independence is our unifying force, how can they help to resist federation after independence has been achieved separately? Surely our friends who argue separate independence first can not have considered the matter seriously.

The argument of 'bado kidogo,' 'you are not ready,' is the same argument the imperialists have always used to delay our independence. Is it not going to be the most curious piece of irony if we, African nationalists, who have always wanted unity, were to inherit and use this argument in order to perpetuate colonial divisions?

There are obvious disadvantages if we wait until all the countries of East Africa have reached complete independence before we begin to bring them together in one federal unit. If each nation achieves independence separately, any move by one of them in the direction of federation is likely to be misunderstood and will certainly be subjected to a campaign alleging imperialistic designs and a search for personal power. For this reason the most honest and least selfish of the leaders will be strongly tempted to avoid the issue. Further, the leaders of each state will become so preoccupied with the immediate problems of their own government that the long-term disadvantages which can come from the establishment of a federation will be crowded out of consideration.

We have to accept, too, that if each of the East African territories is independent, we shall each have to open embassies in the main overseas territories, accept diplomatic offices in each of our capitals, and, because of our close ties, we shall even have to exchange diplomatic representation. All these things are a waste of scarce resources.

But the main danger to the prospects of federation comes from the proliferation of foreign embassies in our respective territories. These embassies will be interested in the strength of their our countries and not in our unity. We shall find ourselves being flattered and filled with false nationalistic pride by reference to our virtues in contrast with the evil habits of our neighbours – or vice versa. We shall find in the fact that the present sentiment of unity gets weaker and weaker.

Further, ones the four nations each have their own representative at the United Nations, have their own flags and foreign representatives, we shall have established centres of vested interests against unity. This is not because we shall be increasing the number of human beings who have a personal interest in disunity; because they are human beings, most of them will be more conscious of the advantages of the present situation and the difficulties of change than of the long-term benefits which could come.

Furthermore, federation after complete independence means the surrender of sovereignty and all the prestige and symbols of such sovereignty. Surely, if it is difficult now to convince some of our friends that federation is desirable, when it does not involve surrendering any sovereignty, it is going to be a million times more difficult to convince them later. As I'll try to show later, federation now has the possibility, even probability, of hastening the independence of our countries, a prospect very dear to all our hearts. Federation after independence does not have this obvious binding force. The appeal of unity is much stronger now than it will be after independence. And yet the need for that strength-in-unity, which will enable us to preserve our hard-won independence, will be at least as great after independence as before. But, and this is very important, unless we emerge out of colonialism as one political unit, separate independence will have made us less united than we are at present, and will at the same time have reduced both the desire for unity and the chances of bringing it about.

We need no visas to cross our boundaries now. Separate independence will almost inevitably impose visas on us. Those unfortunate tribes who now find themselves divided by the present boundaries find it very awkward now. But they will find it more awkward, if awkward is the word, in future, for separate independence will, internationally, make Tanganyika as foreign to Kenya or Uganda, as China or America is. Their cousins on the other side of the border will be foreigners. We trade now without tariff barriers; separate independence may necessitate such barriers.

34

We have a common currency which could easily lead to a common Central Bank. Separate independence will almost inevitably lead to separate currencies and the establishment of national central banks to make separate independence a reality. One could go on almost ad infinitum to show that separate independence will encourage disunity, not unity. Separate independence means in effect that we shall find ourselves less united after colonialism than before colonialism. Independence will have resulted in greater disunity and the more or less permanent balkanisation of our region. The irony of separate independence is as stark as that.

THE BALKANISATION OF AFRICA

The balkanisation of Africa is a source of weakness to our continent. The forces of imperialism and of neo-imperialism will find their own strength in this basic weakness of our continent. Surely, one would have expected that if we have a chance to undo part of the harm that has already been done by this balkanisation of our continent, we would not hesitate in taking that chance. My contention is that our best chance of removing this balaknisation of East Africa is a few months from now, after all countries have got elected governments.

African nationalists who resist this will find themselves in the same bed with the oddest of companions. There is the intelligent imperialist who knows without a doubt that the moment the East African countries have joined forces after reaching responsible government separately, non-one can stop them from naming the date for independence of East Africa. He will resist this obvious strengthening of the forces of nationalism. The same imperialist will know that since the advocates of federation are linking it with the Responsible Government in all the East African countries, the gathering momentum in favour of federation is bound to hasten the achievement of Responsible Government in the remaining two territories of East Africa. This is what happened in the case of British Somaliland. Those who would not like this to happen will resist it and help Africans too to resist it.

The imperialist who knows that the gathering momentum for a voluntary federation will destroy any chance of maintaining an imposed federation in Central Africa, will resist the establishment of a popular Federation in East Africa. This is no conjecture.

When I was in London recently, many intelligent people remarked that the success of an East African Federation voluntarily created by the African leaders themselves would spell the end of the unpopular Central African Federation. It was even bluntly said that I had gone to London to sabotage the Central African Federation. This was not true, but there is not the slightest doubt in my mind that a popular federation can not but hasten the collapse of an unpopular federation next door.

The British Government itself is placed in a most awkward position by this talk of an East African Federation. If several years back we were mad enough to advocate a Federation for East Africa, Britain would have backed it up without any hesitation. Today matters have changed. The Rip van Winkles are not aware of the change.

The United Kingdom Government can not back up a popular federation without destroying or encouraging the destruction of an unpopular one. If we establish a voluntary federation in East Africa, no argument, not even force, could prevent our colleagues in both Nyasaland and Northern Rhodesia from claiming the freedom to join that federation.

This is so obvious, and for that reason alone, the friends of the unpopular federation will resist the establishment of the popular one. But there is an even stronger reason. They, and their friends in South Africa and in Portuguese East Africa, would rather have

Tanganyika alone as their neighbour than than a free and united East and Central Africa with nearly 30 million people. They would encourage us 'to put our separate houses in order first,' not only before, but also after our separate independence. Why should they want a united Eastern Africa? They, together with the many others who would join them in encouraging the balkanisation, would have a better chance of manipulating an East Africa so divided. They will flatter and bribe us and produce even greater arguments for the perpetuation of the balkanisation of East Africa, and exploit our need for technical and financial assistance to keep us divided.

The flattery and corruption of African leaders in order to keep them separated has already started. As I said earlier, it will be intensified a million times when each of our capitals has the embassies of all those countries in the world which find power and prestige in the weakness and disunity of others. Those of us who so innocently produce this sweet argument of delay will find themselves in company with the greatest enemies of the true independence and dignity of our continent.

It has been suggested by some stupid people that I advocate federation because I am a stooge of the British and I want to impose on East Africa a form of government acceptable to my British masters. I believe in the unity of Africa. I do not mind, therefore, what appellations stupid people give me as a result of that belief. But let us examine the true position.

We have always been advocates of unity. In our nationalist organisations, we have constantly warned ourselves against the snares of the imperialists whose policy is 'divide and rule.' Whenever we have asked for our right to govern ourselves, it has been the imperialist who has told us that we are not ready because we still have tribal, religious, communal and other differences. At the same time, it has been the imperialist who has encouraged these divisions in order to continue to rule a weak and

37

divided people. It is the fellow who fell into this snare of the 'divide and rule' apostles whom we rightly regarded as a stooge of the imperialists.

When did this rule change? Are we now going to regard as true African nationalists those who say we are not ready to unite? Are we now to regard them as our true heroes those who join the imperialists and the neo-imperialists in perpetuating the balkanisation of East Africa? Are we going to regard as stooges those who are now carrying the battle for unity beyond those artificial boundaries created by the imperialists to more natural boundaries of our own creation?

The answers to these questions are obvious. It is the apostles of 'bado kidogo' – when they really mean 'never' – and the apostles of balkanisation whom we must ask to produce their membership cards in the imperialist clubs. Those of us who want to see a united East Africa as soon as a free choice can be made are being absolutely consistent. We have nothing to explain or apologise for. If we want to look for stooges and tribalists, we must look into the camp of the 'bados.'

Surely if the advocates of separate independence were consistent, they would, for instance, allow the dismemberment of Uganda now and try to put it together later. The suggestion is as illogical in the case of East Africa as in the case of Uganda.

I know that the advocates of delay will reply that Uganda is different. It is one country already, whereas East Africa consists of different units. Admitted. But we are adjacent countries, governed by the same colonial power, doing many things in common already. The difference is one of degree and not of kind.

Besides, in our pure nationalistic moments, we shout that we do not recognise these artificial boundaries which were drawn by the imperialists without consulting us. Either, we mean what we say or we are a bunch of hypocrites. If we mean it, we should refuse to recognise those boundaries now and demand our independence from the imperialists as one federal unit. I am sure that the moment we do that the forces of imperialism will crumble in no time. If unity can also hasten our independence, what more can we want as African nationalists determined to free our continent from the humiliation of colonial rule? If we have a chance to bequeath to our children a free and united East Africa, should we treat that chance lightly, or take it seriously as all true patriots should?

REASONS FOR FEDERATION

It would be naïve to claim or leave the impression that all those who want federation now want it for purely patriotic motives. Such a claim would be unfounded. Different people join great movements for different motives. In our own separate nationalist movements, we have all sorts of people. Indeed, the imperialists often try to exploit this fact to discredit our nationalist movements. But the case for independence from colonial rule stands on its own merit. It does not derive its sanction from the sanctity of its advocates. If all the advocates of freedom from colonial rule were selfish and evil-minded people, that fact would not destroy the right of every people to govern themselves. Similarly with federation. Among the advocates of federation could be found people motivated by different considerations.

There will be businessmen, capitalist businessmen, imperialistic businessmen, who will see federation offering a large opportunity for profit making, or neo-imperialism on a grand scale. There will be self-seekers who, having failed to make a mark on territorial politics, will want to try their luck on the federal plane. There will be people who will advocate federation because a personal enemy opposes federation; just as there will be people who will oppose federation because an enemy advocates it. There will be all sorts of people on the side of federation and they have all sorts of motives. They can form as strange a mixture as the mixture I have tried to describe of the 'bado kidogo' group.

But, I repeat, the case for a federation freely willed, designed and effected by our own people stands on its own merit. It can not be marred or helped by the motives, the character, the status or colour of its advocates. The value of diamonds does not depend upon the character or motives of those who mine them. A mineral is a diamond or it is not.

If the devil himself appeared in person to support this scheme for federation, that fact would not change my views on the federation or the devil himself. If the devil is not a fool, it is easy to see how his mind would work. He knows exactly what federation means. If he opposes it, he will make it popular. If he supports it, people will begin to have doubts. If he does not want the federal scheme, his choice is quite simple: he will try to give it the kiss of death. Those who would otherwise have supported the scheme but for the 'support' it received from the devil would have fallen into a very simple trap, and the devil would rejoice.

The suggestion that federation can delay the independence of East Africa is almost absurd. I can not see such a possibility. The only country is East Africa at present which is fairly certain of its approximate date of independence is Tanganyika: it is reasonable to assume that if the East African countries are going to achieve their independence separately, Tanganyika is is very likely to be the first country to achieve independence. If, therefore, independence for East Africa was to come much later than the likely date for Tanganyika's independence, it would be Tanganyika which would have to be delayed.

But I can not see how the very fact of the East African countries joining forces in demanding their independence would lead to the possibility of their achieving their independence later than if they had not joined forces in demanding their independence. I can foresee exactly the opposite.

In March, Tanganyika is holding a conference with Her Majesty's Government in the United Kingdom to determine a date for Tanganyika's independence. After that date for Tanganyika's independence has been fixed, all of us in East African countries have three choices. If we decided to demand our independence together, we can demand a date earlier than the Tanganyika date. In all those three choices, no choice is likely to be later than any of the other countries would have achieved its independence separately if we had not joined forces. It appears obvious, therefore, that the decision to demand independence together is likely to hasten and not to delay the independence of any part of East Africa.

We have precedent before us: Somalia was a Trust Territory like Tanganyika: her date for independence had not been fixed, Somaliland was a protectorate under the British: her date for independence had not been fixed. The two countries decided that they should emerge out of colonialism as one unit. This did not necessitate the delay of independence for Somalia whose date had already been fixed; it did not necessitate the delay of independence for British Somaliland. The result in fact was exactly the opposite.

The British Government, in order to meet the desire of the two countries to become one, deliberately hastened the independence of Somaliland which in fact achieved her independence five days before Somalia!

With that precedent before us, surely the East African countries would be in a very strong position to demand that Tanganyika's date for independence should be the date for independence for the rest of East Africa. The argument, therefore, that there is any possibility of the decision to form a federation delaying the independence of any part of East Africa appears to me to be unfounded.

But I believe in the unity of our countries. I do not

want to leave the impression that no price need be paid for such unity. If I go into a shop and I want a packet of cigarettes, I pay the price for it. If we believe that the balkanisation of East Africa is an evil thing; if a price is necessary to remove this evil, then in all honesty to ourselves, we must say that we are prepared to pay the price, if it appears to be a fair price.

Supposing, therefore, that the people of Tanganyika fixed their independence for 1961. Supposing all the people of East Africa wanted a federation. Supposing some devil made it impossible for the federation to achieve its independence in 1961 but fixed a federal independence date for 1962. Supposing my claim is correct, that separate independence would tend to perpetuate the balkanisation of our region, and therefore Tanganyika's separate independence would contribute to this perpetuation of a balkanised East Africa. I, for one, would be prepared to postpone the celebration of Tanganyika's independence for a few months and celebrate East Africa's independence in 1962 rather than take the risk of perpetuating the balkanisation of East Africa.

Nigeria paid a similar price. The two Southern regions of Nigeria could, if they had so desired, have achieved their separate independence much earlier. They did not do so. After achieving internal self-government, they decided to work for a greater Nigeria. Thanks to their vision, we have now on the continent a country that has the potential of protecting its hard-won independence through strength.

But, as I have already indicated, this price on the part of Tanganyika is likely to be a theoretical one and I have tried to answer it theoretically. In actual fact, we do not have to pay it at all.

There are those who argue that an independent Tanganyika will be in a much better position to hasten the independence of both Kenya and Uganda. Thus, it is argued, even if federation before independence is not deliberately designed to delay East Africa's independence,

42

such delay is bound to be its result, if, because of federation, Tanganyika does not take her separate independence now.

This view is very flattering to Tanganyika. But it exaggerates the power of an independent Tanganyika and minimises the forces of nationalism within both Kenya and Uganda. Tanganyika or no Tanganyika, the independence of both Kenya and Uganda is a foregone conclusion.

If we achieved our independence separately, and Kenya and Uganda followed a few months later, I'd certainly be one of the last people to claim that Kenya's and Uganda's independence was due to the influence of an independent Tanganyika. In a very short time, both Kenya and Uganda are bound to become independent. Thus, independence of East Africa is no longer in any doubt except in the minds of nincompoops. What is in doubt, and in the minds of very intelligent people, is our unity, after achieving independence.

One need only to look at what happened in other parts of Africa and the world to see the truth of this. Separate independence did not help the unity of the subcontinent of India. Western Europe has a greater scope for unity than we have in East Africa. But the fact that Western Europe is already balkanised into different sovereign states rules out any prospects of political union.

Western Africa has smaller units than we have in East and Central Africa. But the fact that those units are now sovereign independent states makes the problem of unity much greater than it is for us. This is true not only of the English speaking West African units, but also of the French speaking units.

One could go on multiplying these examples which show that unity is very difficult after sovereign independence has been achieved separately.

One could equally go on giving numerous examples to show that it is easier to achieve such unity simultaneously with the achievement of independence. I have already mentioned the example of the two parts which form the present Republic of Somalia. There are numerous other examples.

The U.S.A. is a federation. But the struggle for freedom from colonial rule and the struggle for unity were combined into one and the same thing. The thirteen original colonies came out of colonialism as a federation. Canada is a federation, but is not a federation which was brought about by merging different sovereign and independent states. Freedom and unity were brought about in the same way.

The Republic of India is a federation which was brought about at the same time as India achieved her independence. The negative lesson of India and Pakistan I have already mentioned. Nigeria, Africa's biggest nation, is a federation brought about in the same way. The Nigerians wisely and deliberately avoided an India/Pakistan situation.

In Africa we have only one exception to this rule. But it is one of those rare exceptions which *truly* prove the rule. There is unity between Guinea and Ghana. This unity was brought about after each country was a sovereign independent state. But it is not the kind of unity which has been achieved by the countries I have cited. It is in fact a strong friendship between two sovereign states. A very desirable thing indeed. Yet these countries are led by two of the most brilliant and far-sighted of the sons of Africa. No-one but a fool could say that their desire for African unity is either half-hearted or selfish. It is neither.

The fact is that there is the right moment for everything, and the right moment for unity is certainly not after the achievement of separate sovereign independence. If separate independence is inevitable, we should certainly not give up trying, but it is going to be a much harder task to unite our countries. But in the case of East Africa, separate independence is not inevitable.

The United Arab Republic is the only true exception I can think of. But if we really want to remedy the balkanisation of our part of Africa, we would be most unwise to act contrarily to the clear lessons of history and assume that we will be another exception to this rule.

I have no doubt in my mind that history has given us East Africans a unique opportunity. Let us use it now and earn the gratitude of future generations. If we really mean business, here's the challenge:

LET US MAKE 1961 EAST AFRICA'S YEAR OF INDEPENDENCE IN UNITY.

'It has been frequently remarked that it seems to have been reserved to the people of this country, by their conduct and example, to decide the important question of whether societies of men are really capable or not of establishing good governments from reflection and choice, or whether they are forever destined to depend for their political constitutions on accident and force.' – Alexander Hamilton in *The Federalist*.

'Men at some times are masters of their own fates. The fault...is not in our stars but in ourselves that we are underlings.'

'There is a tide in the affairs of men, which, taken at the flood, leads on to fortune: omitted, all the voyage of their life is bound in shallows and in miseries. On such a full sea are we now afloat; and we must take the current when it serves, or lose our our ventures.' – William Shakespeare.

People of East Africa, Unite! You have nothing to lose but your chains!

'Behold how good and pleasant it is for brethren to

dwell together in unity.' – Psalmist."[12]

As in the case of Kenya, Uganda and Tanganyika, inclusion of Zanzibar in the envisaged East African federation was an integral part of Nyerere's agenda to unite the region under one government. Therefore, it should not surprise anyone who is familiar with his political career as a staunch advocate of African unity determined to unite countries on regional and continental basis that he pursued unity with Zanzibar and achieved part of his goal, although on a smaller scale, when he united his country with the island nation.

That was not Cold War politics. That was African politics. When as far back as 1960 he talked about forming an East African federation which would include Zanzibar, the Zanzibar revolution which brought the Cold War to the island nation – and to Tanganyika – had not even taken place. It was not even in the planning stage; it was three-and-a-half years away when he wrote the article above in June 1960.

Did the Cold War back then, before the Zanzibar revolution, also push him to pursue federation of the East African countries which would include Zanzibar? Or was it his Pan-African commitment when he said it would be a great achievement if all the countries in the region, including Zanzibar, united before they got independence?

In his article above, he said 1961 would be the best year for the East African countries to win independence together on the same day and emerge from colonial rule as a single political entity and form a federation. That was the year Tanganyika was scheduled to get independence; and it became the first in the region to be attain sovereign status.

Although he did not achieve his ultimate goal of uniting the four East African countries – Kenya, Uganda, Tanganyika and Zanzibar – under one government, he achieved something that was unprecedented in the history

46

of post-colonial Africa and that has not been achieved elsewhere on the continent since then: uniting two independent states.

It was not the Americans or the British who succeeded in uniting Tanganyika with Zanzibar to form the new nation of Tanzania under one government. Consummation of the union can not be attributed to pressure exerted on Nyerere by the United States and Britain to do something he already wanted to do. With or without the United States and Britain, he would have pursued the same goal to unite Tanganyika and Zanzibar, and he did.

The CIA itself conceded the union was initiated by Nyerere, not by the United States or Great Great Britain, and took place under his guidance:

"The idea of a union was not a new one. Nyerere probably had it in the back of his mind when he first became involved in Zanzibar politics, beginning around 1956. For years, he had looked forward to the time when an African government would come to power in Zanzibar, at which time he planned to merge the two countries....

The important point is that the union of Tanganyika and Zanzibar *was a Tanganyikan initiative* (italics added – Godfrey Mwakikagile). Although the idea had occurred to Western officials as the obvious solution to the Zanzibar problem, the subject was never officially discussed with the Tanganyikans. Thus, it appears that the move to form the union was strictly African in origin, without British or American inspiration; the news of the event caught all of the major world powers by surprise.

For more than a month, Nyerere and his representatives had been conducting secret negotiations with Karume and other Zanzibari leaders."[13]

Decades later, in an interview in 2000, Donald Petterson who once served as the American ambassador to Tanzania and who before then was the head of the

American consulate in Zanzibar during the revolution, said the same thing the CIA wrote in its report – that the major powers were caught by surprise when the announcement was made that Tanganyika had united with Zanzibar. As Ambassador Petterson stated: "Their decision (by Nyerere and Karume), when announced, came as a complete surprise."

The United States and Britain would not have been caught by surprise when formation of the union was announced if they were the ones who engineered it.

Also, Helen-Luoise Hunter states in her book, *Zanzibar: The Hundred Days Revolution*:

"Even before the revolution, the affiliation of Zanzibar with Tanganyika had been under discussion in the context of a larger East African federation. Nyerere, Karume, and Hanga were on record as favoring such a federation; Babu was opposed. It had never been a question of a union between Tanganyika and Zanzibar alone, however; that possibility arose as a direct result of the revolution.

As noted earlier, it was Nyerere who initiated the negotiations leading to the union. Much has been written about his reasons for wanting a Tanganyika-Zanzibar union. Press comment in the United States and other Western countries tended to emphasize the cold war aspects of the situation....

The tendency of the United States and other Western press to emphasize the cold war aspects of Tanganyikan-Zanzibar relations complicated Nyerere's efforts to work out a solution within the framework of non-alignment. He said on a number of occasions that he was personally furious with the way the American and British press treated the union....

Among Zanzibari leaders, Hanga was probably the most receptive to the Tanganyikan initiave. He stated privately that he and Kambona agreed that Tanganyika and Zanzibar should unite when they were students together in

48

London. Nyerere also commented that Hanga favored the union even more than Karume. In July, Tanzanian Foreign Affairs Parliamentary Secretary Tambwe claimed that Nyerere was 'particularly pleased with Hanga because he is, above all, an African nationalist who really supports the union.' "[14]

Nyerere himself – without American inspiration – wanted to neutralise radical elements in Zanzibar, especially Babu and his followers of the Umma (people's) party. The most effective way to do that was to deprive Babu of his political base in Zanzibar by uniting the island nation with Tanganyika. Therefore, he did not need encouragement from the West to do that.

He did get such encouragement. But it was unnecessary. And it was not unique. Even fellow African leaders – except Nkrumah – encouraged Nyerere in his quest for regional unity which included uniting Tanganyika with Zanzibar, not just with Kenya and Uganda. They were not asked, encouraged or pressured by the United States and Britain to support Nyerere in his Pan-African quest.

And like Nyerere himself, the biggest supporters of the Zanzibar revolution were Africans themselves – leaders such Nkrumah, Abubakar Tafawa Balewa, the prime minister of Nigeria, and Jaja Wachuku who was Nigeria's minister of foreign affairs. Nyerere's desire to unite Tanganyika with Zanzibar came from within – Africa itself – without external inspiration even is such inspiration may have been "fuelled," somewhat, by external interest, American and British, in the geopolitical dynamics generated by the Zanzibar revolution.

Therefore, even if the United States and Britain and the rest of the West did not exist at all, he would have pursued the same goal. Just because they encouraged the merger does not mean they initiated it; nor does it mean they were the driving force behind it; Nyerere initiated the

49

merger and was the driving force behind it.

It just happened that the West and Nyerere shared the same concern about the island nation's radical shift towards the communist bloc under Babu's influence and had nothing to do with pressure being exerted by Western powers – the United States and Britain – on Nyerere to "absorb" Zanzibar, something he himself wanted to do, and was going to do, anyway, compounded with his Pan-African desire to unite East African countries even if it had to be on a smaller scale first, uniting Tanganyika with Zanzibar, which is what he did.

The West does not deserve any credit for that. Credit goes to Nyerere for initiating and successfully completing the merger of the two countries.

The interests of the West only coincided with Nyerere's interest over Zanzibar and were *not* the primary motive for unification of the two independent states. The driving force was Nyerere as the CIA itself conceded in its classified reports which were later declassified.

But it is true that the revolution did provide an impetus for unification which probably took place sooner than even Nyerere himself had expected or anticipated. The fundamental issue here is that the desire to unite the two countries was in his mind all the time even before the revolution, an interest that did *not* come from the West.

Even if Western powers, the United States and Britain, played a role in facilitating the union because Tanganyika's interests coincided with theirs in terms of neutralising communist influence in Zanzibar, it was only peripheral. Internal dynamics played a far more important role and were the determining factor in the consummation of the union. As Mohammed Ali Bakari, a lecturer at the University of Dar es Salaam, states in his book, *The Democratisation Process in Zanzibar: A Retarded Transition*:

"There has been an extensive discussion on the process

leading to the Union between Tanganyika and Zanzibar with varying emphasis on either domestic factors or external factors. The book by Amrit Wilson (*US Foreign Policy and Revolution: The Creation of Tanzania*, Pluto Press, 1989) has well documented the process leading to the Union. In this book with a lot of documentary evidence, the United States has been portrayed to have played a key role. The main concern of the United States then was geopolitical and strategic; that Zanzibar immediately after the revolution was seemingly heading towards a radical leftist direction to the extent that, it was thought by Washington, it could become a 'Cuba of East Africa.'

Although the influence of foreign forces on the founding of the Union, cannot be underestimated, domestic factors seemed decisive. Had Karume not felt highly insecure, and had Nyerere believed or at least had not been made to believe that strategically he would be insecure in the event of Zanzibar becoming a radical leftist regime, the attempt by Western powers and the US in particular to manipulate them into accepting the Union would have been futile."[15]

Nyerere knew on his own, without being told or manipulated by the United States, that an unstable Zanzibar would be a threat to the security of Tanganyika because of its close proximity to the mainland – only about 20 miles away. That is why he once said if he could move the island nation farther into the ocean, he would. He said that not only before the Zanzibar revolution but even before he led Tanganyika to independence. He said it in 1960. Therefore, he did not need to be convinced – four years later – by the Americans and the British about the danger of an unstable or radical Zanzibar.

Bakari also quotes Nyerere who said at a mass rally in Dar es Salaam on 15 November 1964, about seven months after the union was formed:

"We sent our police to Zanzibar. After overcoming various problems we united. We ourselves voluntarily agreed on union. Karume and I met. *Only the two of us met.* When I mentioned the question of the union. Karume did not give a second thought. He instantly asked me to call a meeting of the press to announce our intention. I advised him to wait a bit as it was too early for the press to be informed. (Emphasis added by Bakari)."[16]

Western interest in Zanzibar tended to overshadow Nyerere, especially in the Western media, as the architect of the union and its driving force from the beginning. The focus was on Cold War intrigues and rivalries in the island nation between the two ideological camps, East and West. But, as Donald (Don) Petterson who was the American consul in Zanzibar when the revolution took place (after Frank Carlucci was expelled) and who later served as ambassador to Tanzania, stated in an interview years later on 30 November 2000:

"Nyerere and Karume decided that they would unify their two countries to undercut Babu. This they did, telling only a very few trusted advisors. Their decision, when announced, came as a complete surprise....Nyerere wanted it and Karume wanted it."[17]

The deputy American ambassador to Tanzania, Robert Hennemeyer who (as DCM – Deputy Chief of Mission) served under Ambassador William Leonhart was also in Tanganyika when Tanganyika united with Zanzibar. He said the union "was not a merger" but a federation. Leonhart was the first American ambassador to be accredited to Tanganyika, later Tanzania.

Hennemeyer also talked about other subjects concerning Tanganyika, later Tanzania, and reflected on the years he was there:

"Q: When you came out (of the University of Oxford), you were really put into a very critical position, weren't you? You went to Tanganyika. How did you get the appointment?

Hennemeyer: I don't know how it happened. I received orders while I was at Oxford that I would be going to Dar es Salaam, which then was still a U.N. trust territory under British trusteeship. Therefore, our post was a consul general. Red Duggan was our consul general, and I was to go there as his number two.

There was one very fortunate thing that happened and one very sad thing that happened. The fortunate thing was that while at Oxford, I met four Tanganyikans who were studying there. All four, within a couple of years, became Cabinet members when they returned, and this gave me a set of contacts that was almost unique, because while at Oxford, we were very close. That was a very positive thing and gave me a leg up in starting at Dar es Salaam.

The sad thing was that Red's eyesight was failing very rapidly, and just after (Tanganyika's) independence in December of 1961, within days, Red's eyesight failed completely. He had glaucoma. He had to be Medevaced. Then I was chargé for an extended period. It would have been better had Red been able to stay on, because he had a wealth of knowledge of the post. He had been there for several years, a very able man. But it didn't work out that way.

Q: Could you describe the situation when you first arrived? This was still colonial in 1961.

Hennemeyer: I got there in July of 1961, and independence came that December. So it was an atypical colonial situation in that it was a honeymoon period. The agreement on the date for independence had been reached. The British were doing their best in a short period of time and in an orderly fashion to phase out. The Tanganyikans were very, very upbeat and happy about the coming independence state. It was a real honeymoon. Nobody was complaining about anything.

The only complaints I heard were from the British, who were grousing a bit about how many positions they would have to continue to staff at the Tanganyikans' request, because they didn't have enough people to take over. So it was not an atmosphere where they would be pushed out at all.

Q: Also, Tanganyika was somewhat different in that it had been a German colony. The British roots, I assume, weren't as deep there as they would have been in Kenya and other places.

Hennemeyer: That's true. The British settler community was minuscule, unlike Kenya. So they were not really a political factor at all. Well, that's an overstatement. They were a minor political factor.

There were times during the inter-war period when British governments in London sought to merge Tanganyika with Kenya and Uganda into a greater East Africa entity on the Kenya model. Some governments wanted to encourage large-scale British settlement in Tanganyika. But interestingly enough, there were British governors-general during that period in Tanganyika who reminded London that this was initially a League of Nations mandate, and subsequently a U.N. trustee territory, and that didn't accord with the conditions of the mandate, and resisted the idea of British settlement.

So there's some unsung heroes there, because rather than a Mau Mau epoch as Kenya experienced, Tanganyika had none of that. The very few British settlers who were there, Derek Bryceson was one who became Minister of Agriculture in the first government, and Lady Marion Chesham, another settler, an American by birth, married to a British subject, who remained after independence and became a member of Parliament. So it was a very amicable transition.

Q: How did the story develop as you saw it and

may have experienced it?

Hennemeyer: The first couple of years of independence, I stayed until July of 1964, exactly three years. The first two years went fairly smoothly, the transition where more and more Tanganyikans took over senior positions.

One noticed that it didn't always work as well as it had in the past, but on the other hand, they were trying to do more difficult things and they were trying to do it with relatively inexperienced people. But it went along fairly well, and relations with the remaining British were quite good, and our relations with the government were excellent.

Q: They didn't have the feeling that the United States was being a bit starry-eyed about this new independence, whereas the British were saying, 'Well, you know, this isn't going to work,' sort of dog in the manger?

Hennemeyer: No. I'm sure that was an attitude in some other places, but I think because of the fact that the colonial civil service (servants) who went to Tanganyika always knew that it was a different set of ground rules, a mandate or a trust territory, and that this did not have a colonial future, I think that was understood.

They were a different breed of cat from colonial civil servants that I had met elsewhere. I admire(d) them. For the most part, they were very good people with a clear understanding that their role was a temporary one, and that their task was really to work themselves out of a job. So I found very little of that. I'm sure some of them thought that the Americans were starry-eyed, but I didn't find the dog-in-the-manger attitude.

Q: Ambassador Leonhart was there.

Hennemeyer: Right.....

Q: Going back to the situation in Tanganyika, it is now Tanzania.

Hennemeyer: It became Tanzania after the federation

with Zanzibar. It never was a merger.

Q: Could you talk about your relations and your observations of Julius Nyerere, who is, of course, a seminal figure in the African scene?

Hennemeyer: First of all, on a very personal level, an extremely likeable man, not pretentious, not full of himself at all, enjoyed a joke, a person who was pleasant to be with. He was also a great political theorist and, unfortunately, economical theorist. I think as a manager he left much to be desired. He was a charismatic figure on the stump, a great leader of his people. I don't believe for a moment that he meant anything but to do the best he could for the wellbeing of his people.

But I guess the best way I could put it is that during early 1962, Nyerere decided that the party, TANU, Tanganyika African National Union, was not functioning the way it was supposed to. It wasn't really mobilizing the masses for new initiatives and so on. So he decided he would give up the premiership and go out in the boonies, revitalize the Party, and he would turn to Rashidi Kawawa to be acting premier. He (Kawawa) was a minister--I've forgotten of what, a very small man but well-known because he had been an actor in Swahili-language films. So everybody in the country knew him.

At any rate, Rashidi Kawawa was no great political figure at all, but within days of Julius' departure for the boonies, one noticed a difference in the way government functioned. You got answers to questions, decisions were made, and it was simply because Kawawa was not [a] theorist, didn't spend hours and hours talking about the future of the world with visitors from other parts of the world, but instead came to his desk promptly early in the morning, looked at his 'in' box, took things out of his 'in' box, made decisions, and put them in his "out" box. It made a world of difference.

Q: Bob, what was the situation with Nyerere? How did you see him?

Hennemeyer: As I mentioned, one could not help but like and respect him as a leader. **Clearly he was a world leader, not just an African leader.** But he was not really one who enjoyed the nitty-gritty of government, and he was not very good at it. He tended not to empty his 'in' box, and that was a complaint I heard from his ministers and so on. That was not his strong suit. The result was, of course, that since this became a one-party state and became highly centralized in his person, when he didn't empty his 'in' box, a lot of things didn't happen.

Q: You saw him as the leader who was going to be around for some time.

Hennemeyer: Oh, yes, no doubt. He was unchallenged.

Q: As the United States representatives there, did you find yourselves being concerned about the fact that he seemed to be off, you might say, on the left-wing socialist side, both for our own political interests, but also for concern about the economy?

Hennemeyer: That wasn't so apparent during the time that I was there. We did have some concern about the speed with which he was trying to develop cooperatives as an alternative to the Indian middle class, which had a monopoly of commerce. Obviously there was a political imperative for him to involve his own people, to involve the local people in the economy. That had to be done. But some of us had some concern about the pace and the method. But that didn't really become an acute problem until after I left, until the Lusaka Manifesto (the Arusha Declaration?) and things like that.

Q: We had no real commercial interests there, did we?

Hennemeyer: Almost none. There was a time some years earlier when the U.S. automobile industry had some major exports to Africa, but by that time we had been displaced largely by Peugeot in East Africa, and I suspect they've been replaced by the Japanese since then.

Q: There are schools that say that American policy is driven by economics and trade and all that, but in many cases there just isn't that much at stake there. You didn't feel anybody breathing down your shoulder on that?

Hennemeyer: No, not at all. No, that was not a major factor at all. I think we started out with a lot of genuine goodwill towards Tanganyika and Nyerere as a leader. I think as time went on, our concern was that the Soviet bloc or the Chinese not acquire undue influence there. We wanted to keep Nyerere basically Western oriented; that was our objective. I think, with minor glitches, that was successful.

He never really went over to the other camp. He flirted, but I suspect some of that was tactical, and some of that, of course, was dictated by the fact that he saw one of his major roles to be a haven for those who were trying to free from colonialism the rest of Southern Africa

So one of the more interesting aspects of my time in Dar es Salaam was the presence there of major Southern African liberation organizations or political parties. ANC was there, PAC, Frelimo. In fact, I knew Eduardo Mondlane quite well. That gave the place certain spice that it would not otherwise have had.

Q: What was our attitude? What were your instructions on how to deal with Frelimo? We're talking about the early sixties.

Hennemeyer: That's right. We maintained close and friendly relations with them. By this time we had on our staff a very, very able first-tour officer, John Blacken, who is now our ambassador in Guinea-Bissau. John and I worked very hard to maintain close personal relations with Sam Nujoma (of SWAPO, Namibia), who was there at that time, and with a great many others. We would invite them to our homes, we would see them in their offices. What some of them wanted very much--they realized soon that that was not in the cards--was military assistance from us.

58

It just wasn't going to happen.

Q: You made that quite clear?

Hennemeyer: Well, that had to be made clear right away that we weren't going to do that. What we did try to provide them were educational opportunities, believing that while eventually they would succeed in governing their own countries, in the interim it might be very worthwhile for some of their better young people to acquire skills that would be useful in an independent non-apartheid South Africa.

So through AID, we contracted with the African American Institute. Pat Murphy was then the director of the program in Dar es Salaam, and we ran an active program of providing scholarship opportunities in the States and elsewhere in the West for exiled Africans, if you will, and we established a small school, also under African American Institute auspices, funded by AID, for Mozambican government. However, at the same time, we were aware, of course, that they were receiving military assistance.

I remember one case where a ship from Algeria came in with a great deal of military equipment for Frelimo and other organizations. So others were doing that, but clearly that was something we could not do, but we felt it was important to maintain contact with these people and, in the area of education, to do something constructive for them for their future. I think even though some of them are rather high-powered in their rhetoric of criticizing us, I think some of them are really aware that what we did at that time was helpful.

Q: How about Nyerere? Back to him for a minute. What was his attitude toward the United States?

Hennemeyer: I think it was very friendly. I thought his attitude toward the United States was generally positive. I think there were times when he felt that we were neglecting Africa, other times that he felt that we were excessively preoccupied with the Cold War, but I felt that, too.

Q: How about the situation in Zanzibar? That became rather volatile while you were there.

Hennemeyer: Yes, it did. That happened in January of 1964. To me it came as a surprise, although, in retrospect, Fritz Picard, who was our consular there at the time, was aware of growing unrest. I don't think any of us predicted what finally happened. Yes, I remember very well.

Then the press descended on Dar es Salaam to try to find out what was going on in Zanzibar. But we had no special brief for the Sultan's Government in Zanzibar. In fact, as you recall, the election, which had confirmed the Sultan's Government in power, was one that was a very dubious affair, and nobody was really happy with the result. It was clear, I think, to most observers that if it was going to survive, it was going to have a lot more representatives, and it didn't have a chance to do that.

A lot of people have forgotten what a bloody affair that was--there were several thousand people killed, Arabs driven down to the beaches and slaughtered at the beaches by the insurgents.

There was an Italian photographer who chartered a plane from Mombasa, flew down there and got some extraordinary footage of the slaughter on the beach.

At any rate, our concern was exactly the same as the Tanganyikan Government's concern, and that was to contain the rebellion on Zanzibar and direct it to a more constructive end. That is, it accomplished its immediate purpose--that is, it brought a black African majority group into power. But then the question arose for Tanganyika's own security: What kinds of relationships would that new government have? As you know, very early on there was a fairly strong East Bloc presence, and that concerned us and the Tanganyikans.

So very quietly and discreetly we worked with the Tanganyikans to help them establish a police presence initially on Zanzibar, and we encouraged Nyerere in his

60

efforts to develop a cooperative federal arrangement with the Zanzibar Government. That succeeded to some extent, although it never worked the way it was supposed to. But in time, the red house on Zanzibar, for whatever reason, calmed down and it never became what **some sensationalists** predicted, the 'Cuba of Africa.'

Q: Did you have any part in dealing with it? At one point, Picard and the others were actually under arrest and they had a problem extracting.

Hennemeyer: That's right. I was involved in the call. There was a U.S. Navy ship in the city. At that time the Navy ran periodic cruises around Africa. I think they were called SoLant Amity at the time. The ship was the USS Manley, I remember very well, was visiting Mombasa at the time of the Zanzibar revolt. Picard and the other Americans there, particularly the Project Mercury people, which was a NASA project, a tracking station for NASA's satellite program, most of them were contract employees of Bendix, as I recall, they were literally trapped on the island. There came the question of trying to get them out. Fritz Picard, with great courage, persuaded Karume and the revolutionary council to agree that the Americans would leave.

Ambassador Leonhart and Jim Rookte, who came down from Nairobi to help us out, and I, we succeeded in getting in tough with the Manley and got approval for the Manley to come down. I believe Jim flew back to Mombasa, boarded the Manley, then went with the Manley into Zanzibar.

Fritz, at great personal risk, succeeded in getting everybody on the ship. He and maybe Dale P____, stayed behind. I can't swear to that. But Fritz stayed behind. I remember Fritz's wife, Shona, and their son came and stayed with us. Fritz came out later, but I've forgotten how. He also came to live with us.

As you know, he was quite ill at the time. He had what seemed to be a kind of nervous breakdown. No sooner did

61

he arrive with us than the Tanganyika Army mutinied. Fritz thought he was back on Zanzibar, and this was Zanzibar happening again. So he was very difficult to control for a few days.

Unfortunately, during some of that time, I was under arrest by the mutineers, and after that, trapped in our embassy, in the chancellory, for a while. So I was unable to assist my wife in trying to manage Fritz. It was a very difficult time for her. Shona and Hoge, the boy, we had gotten out earlier before the mutiny, and they had gone to Nairobi.

At any rate, the mutiny burst on us completely unprepared. We didn't know that was going to happen. I realize now what the immediate causes of it were, and it was one of these unfortunate management glitches which occurred on Nyerere's watch. There was a program for Africanizing the Tanganyika rifles officer corps. The non-commissioned officers and the enlisted personnel were all Africans. This was supposed to be phased in over a period of time; I've forgotten how long it was. It was a three- or four-year period.

In the meantime, Tanganyikan African officer candidates were being sent to Sandhurst, the British military academy, for the short course, and as they returned, one more British officer would return to his regular regiment. In the process, however, not all billets were slated for Africanization in the near future. In a few of those cases, some British officers were being replaced by British officers. This was misunderstood by many of the Tanganyikan non-commissioned officers who thought that meant that Africanization was being abandoned.

The reason they thought that was that Nyerere had made a speech that because they had moved too quickly in Africanization, there were a number of economic activities and other government activities that had suffered in the process, and therefore they were going to have to reschedule this and draw this out. This coincided with three new British officers arriving. Mind you, we're dealing with a fairly small universe. A number of senior non-coms decided this meant that Africanization of the officer corps was being abandoned, and they had pay demands, as well, and so on. Within a couple of nights, the mutiny was plotted.

The first inkling we had of it was when I got a call in the middle of the night from an African officer, Alex S_____, (Alexander Nyirenda) one of the first commissioned officers, later became commanding general, saying that the troops had mutinied, that many of the officers had fled, and that some of the British officers had been captured up at Colito Barracks, north of Dar es Salaam, were being held prisoner, and he was saying, 'You should keep your people off the streets.' That's what his message was.

So I called Ambassador Leonhart. We had a warden system, and he agreed to implement the warden system and tell people to stay home. I agreed I would go down to the chancellory and get a message out. So I started driving down. It must have been about 1:00 or 2:00 in the morning. I decided I would drive by State House to see if anything was going on, or if Nyerere was up, I'd talk to him.

I got there just in time to see a group of soldiers breaking down the front gate, while being resisted by a group of police. So I decided not to stop there, and drove down to Azania Front, which was the street right on the harbor in the center of town, where the old German bungalows were, which housed some of the ministers.

I saw, on the street corner, my British colleague. He was the number two, but was then serving as chargé, Steven Miles, and the Minister of the Interior, Job Lusinde. So I stopped. We were chatting, trying to put together what was happening. Just then an Army jeep Landrover pulled up with a group of soldiers on it, and they grabbed the three of us and threw us in the back of the Landrover and drove off with us, not far, a few blocks away to the post and telegraph building, where they put us up against the wall and held us there.

This group was rather disorderly. Some had been drinking, and some, I think, had been smoking bang, a type of hemp. Some were sort of in bits of pieces of uniforms. All of them had their new British-issued rifles that they had gotten to replace the old Lee Enfield 303s. They had their new SLR NATO-type rifles.

Periodically, several of them would say they were going to shoot us, and they'd level their rifles at us. One, the only who I think was not drinking, a corporal, kept saying, 'No, no, they're not British officers.' Well, they knew who Lusinde was, but they thought Miles and I were new British officers who had come. The others kept saying we were, and we should be shot.

I remember one imaginative young soldier taking the clip out of his rifle, taking the cartridges out of the clip, sharpening them on the sidewalk (in front) of us, reloading, pulling the bolt, and putting the muzzle right up against my nose, and saying, in what English he knew, 'Time is finish. Now is time to kill.'

At any rate, this went on all night. I remember I turned to Job Lusinde and I said, 'What are we going to do about this, Job?' He turned to me and said, 'It's better if we don't know each other.' So we three tried to stay as quiet as we could while this internal debate went on.

I remember sometime during the course of the night, a truckload of soldiers came by and said that they wanted to take us along. Our guys said, 'Go find your own prisoners.' At any rate, it was a long and difficult night.

Q: In a situation like that, all the diplomatic niceties and everything else go by the boards, because there's nowhere to go or to protest or anything else.

Hennemeyer: No, and I tried a diplomatic nicety, but it didn't work. I didn't know how to say I was deputy to the ambassador in Swahili, but I knew how to say 'ambassador.' So I told them I was the ambassador and I was going to my office. One said, 'No, I've seen the ambassador, and you're not the ambassador.' So I just made my case more difficult.

At any rate, this went on in this vein, with them being ugly and calm at intervals, until about 7:00 in the morning, I guess, when they suddenly said to me, 'Kwenda.' 'Go.'

I started to walk down the street, making myself walk very slowly. I turned around and I saw that they had their rifles leveled at me. I don't know if that was to see if I would run or what, but at any rate, I walked down the street, and when I got to the first corner, I ducked around it, only to find two more standing there saying I couldn't go that way, I had to go back out in the same street.

At any rate, I walked down the length of the street, turned the corner, and got over to the chancellory, where Bill Leonhart was waiting and very anxious about what had happened. He asked, and I said, 'Well, the mutineers took me prisoner.' I remember he said, 'Good. You can try to finish this cable.' He handed it to me. He was trying to describe what had happened, and thought that since I had been with them, I could finish it.

I sat down to try to write it. Just then, the reaction set in. I couldn't write, my hand was shaking so. That lasted only about a half-hour or so, but at any rate, we got the word out. That was my little adventure.

Then came the problem of what to do, because some of the mutineers were getting out of hand, there was a little looting. Although in retrospect, I have to say, given what I've heard of since, it was a relatively orderly mutiny.

Q: It wasn't of the scale, say, of the Force Publique, which was full of killing and looting?

Hennemeyer: No, no. There was a little killing and a little looting, but by and large, as I say, in retrospect I have to say that it was a fairly orderly mutiny.

As soon as we could move around a little bit, which took a day or so, in the meantime, the mutineers decided that there might be a landing and that they would take my house as a stronghold to defend against the expected landing. My wife and our two very small children were surrounded by these soldiers, who didn't harm them, but it was frightening for them.

Then came a rather confused several days when we were consulting with our British allies, trying to figure out what to do. Basically, this was Bill Leonhart's responsibility, with the British chargé, to persuade Nyerere to ask for British assistance. That proved to be rather difficult, but eventually he did agree.

At that time, the British aircraft carrier, the HMS Centaur, came in from Adana with the Royal Marine commandos. There were some extraordinary events, some of which I heard about, some of which I saw, of getting Brigadier Patrick S____ Douglas, who was the deposed commander of the Tanganyika Rifles, out to the Centaur to lead the Royal Marine commandos. That was accomplished largely, I think, by the NI-5 man at the British High Commission, a gentleman by the name of Jacobson.

There were a few of us who knew that the Royal Marine commandos were going to come in to Colito Barracks the next morning very early, and as I recall, those of us who knew agreed to stay in the chancellory or at the High Commission that night so there would be no leak.

They did come in. They had a bombardment of blanks first, artillery blanks, over the barracks, then came in with helicopters. Douglas landed first and told them to surrender, identified himself. There were a few shots fired. The Marine commandos then fired a bazooka, shot through the orderly room, killed a few of the mutineers, and then the others ran. They ran to the bush, and the helicopters rounded them up. Most of them were taken prisoner. They were picked up over a period of days.

I think the following day, the Royal Marines flew to the other garrisons. I think there was one down at Iringa

(Nachingwea), one up in Moshi or Arusha, I can't remember where, and one in Tabora. They took their surrender, so that ended it.

Then subsequently there was a Commonwealth arrangement whereby the Nigerians came in and replaced the British. The Nigerians maintained order until Tanganyikans were able to reorganize another force.

Q: Did Nyerere come to you or to our embassy, or did you go to them as being a party off to one side?

Hennemeyer: Nyerere was in hiding during this week. Subsequently, I learned that he was held very closely, and I was not involved with the negotiation with Nyerere, so I didn't have to know. But I've learned later that he was in a convent on the south end of the harbor, the other side of town. But he was reachable. It was, I think, mostly Steven Miles who conducted the negotiations.

There was some criticism of Nyerere at the time for being in hiding. I guess one has to respect his judgment. It was Oscar Kambona, the Minister of Defense, who went out on the streets and tried to get the disorderly elements of the troops to go back to their barracks, and who then went out to the barracks to try to free the British officers who were being held prisoner, for which he was beaten and pretty roughed up by the soldiers.

At the time we thought Kambona showed great courage, and it contrasted with Nyerere's being in hiding. But there may have been more important reasons for that. I'm not suggesting Nyerere should have gotten out on the streets. He might have been killed, and the sole rallying point for the country would have been lost. But I think it hurt him somewhat politically and probably led later to the quarrel with Kambona, which resulted in Kambona being exiled. I believe he's still in exile in London. I think from that time, there was ill feeling, but I'm speculating here. That was the conventional wisdom.

There was considerable disorder and considerable confusion. I remember the chief of protocol was also chief

67

of the secret police. We were friendly. He came to my house to warn my wife that he feared the next day there would be kind of a 'night of the long knives' against the wives. This allegedly because the dock workers' union, the leadership of which had been East German-trained, had made common cause with the police, and they had decided that they would also mutiny.

The police, by the way, had more or less disappeared when the Army came, with the exception of the prison wardens out at Morogoro, who decided to march on Dar es Salaam to combat the Army, which would have been very foolish because they didn't have the weaponry at all. Fortunately, somebody stopped them before they got there. At any rate, these are random bits and pieces.

Q: What was our embassy role at the time? Was it basically one of reporting?

Hennemeyer: It was basically one of reporting, and supporting our British colleagues, who were the ones directly involved in trying to bring some order out of the chaos. We supported their effort to get Nyerere to agree to ask the British to come in, because the alternative was anarchy. So our role was a support role, not a lead role.

Q: That was just before you left?

Hennemeyer: This was January 24th, within a week of the Zanzibar events.

Q: When did you leave?

Hennemeyer: I left in July. The rest of the time following the post-mutiny events in Tanganyika and the negotiations that Nyerere was having with K____ to establish Tanzania, one of the concerns of the Tanganyikan Government, which was initially allowed to send a small police contingent over to help maintain order in Zanzibar, was allowed by the Zanzibari Revolutionary Council, was that compared to the Zanzibar rebels, they did not have the same fire power at all.

So we were of some assistance in getting the place some hardware which they could then give to their force in

Zanzibar. That may or may not have played a role, but ultimately, as you know, the negotiations were successful. I think April was the date when Tanzania was announced.

It was a very, very loose federation, indeed, with a good bit of friction between mainland and island. But it did, I think, mark the high point of what could have been potential disorder from the island to the mainland. From then on, things gradually got under some degree of control."[18]

Hennemeyer was later appointed ambassador to The Gambia.

One of the American diplomats who was in Zanzibar before and after the revolution and when Tanganyika united with Zanzibar was Donald Petterson. He was in Zanzibar from 1963 to 1965. Years later, he served as the United States ambassador to Tanzania from December 1986 to December 1989. He said the following in an interview years later about those days:

"**Petterson:** I had applied for hard language training, specifically for Swahili. That summer of '62, I would say about July, I received notice that I had been accepted for Swahili language training and that my onward assignment after language training would be Zanzibar. Now this was a rare thing, when you had advance notice a year ahead of time –

Q: Yes.

Petterson: Not only of your training, but also of the following assignment.

Swahili language training was to start in November. We left several weeks earlier, Julie and I with our baby, Susan, who had been born in late July and was about two months old when we departed Mexico. We drove to California to see friends and relatives. From there, wee drove across the United States, still in the same VW (Volkswagen) Bug. We arrived just at the height of the Cuban Missile Crisis. I began Swahili training, the second class in Swahili given by the Foreign Service Institute. Julie enrolled in an English course in downtown Washington.

In my class, there were five of us going to various places, including Uganda, Kenya, and, of course, Zanzibar. In time two people peeled off early for their assignments, and we ended with three of us in the class. I slogged through the Swahili and got a three, three. I had been reading all I could about East Africa and Zanzibar. And Julie and I did what a Foreign Service junior officer and his spouse would do in those days to get ready for a Third-World assignment. We had to buy supplies of things we wouldn't find where we were going, and we bought them as cheaply as possible. For example, with another couple, we bought glassware from a restaurant supply store in Washington, D.C....

We didn't get princely salaries, but it was great when I first started working to have a paycheck coming in regularly for the first time since I left the navy. I started out at $5,500 or $5,600 a year. By this time, at the beginning of 1963, I was making about $6,500.

We got reservations on the USS *Constitution*. In those days you could journey by sea if you were going to a place where U.S. lines were traveling. We had a ten-day trip to Genoa, which was wonderful, a wonderful way to travel....

We went to Genoa and visited with our friend Carolyn Kingsley, who was assigned to the consulate there. After two days, we took a train to Rome, where we boarded a propeller aircraft for the trip to Nairobi. It was a long flight, and it was late in the day when landed at Nairobi's airport. We transferred to a DC-3 and flew to Mombasa, Tanga, and finally Zanzibar, arriving in the darkness of night.

Getting out of the airplane, we were enveloped by warm, humid tropical air. We were met by Frederick "Fritz" Picard, the consul, and Dale Povenmire, the vice-consul, and driven over to Fritz's house for dinner. From

70

there we passed through checkpoints manned by British soldiers. The pre-independence elections had just been held, and there was tension on the island. We were taken to our house, a thatch-roofed, whitewashed coral and lime structure that originally was a stable. It would be our temporary home until Povenmire, whom I was replacing, was transferred.

Our life in Africa had begun.

Q: You were in Zanzibar from when to when?

Petterson: From July 1963 until November 1965, over two years.

Q: I wonder, could you explain what the situation was when you arrived, not what happened after, but when you arrived, and what our consulate was doing or expected?

Petterson: The American consulate, the first consulate in Zanzibar, was established in 1837. As a cost-saving measure, it was closed in 1915, but reopened in 1961. The reopening was occasioned by the establishment of a Project Mercury tracking station on Zanzibar Island.

Q: Yes, our space program.

Petterson: Project Mercury was the first manned space effort of the United States, and tracking stations were set up at various places around the world. Zanzibar was one of them. At that time, Zanzibar was moving toward independence. It was a British protectorate under the guidance of British colonial authorities, led by the resident. His title was "resident," not "governor," because Zanzibar was a protectorate, not a colony as such. The protectorate consisted of Zanzibar Island and the island of Pemba, which lay about 45 miles northeast of Zanzibar, and a few very small islands. Arabs had dominated Zanzibar since the end of the seventeenth century, when Omani Arabs seized control of it.

The Sultan of Oman moved his sultanate to Zanzibar in 1832. It became a British possession in 1890, when the Germans, who had gained control of Tanganyika and were on the verge of occupying Zanzibar, agreed to let the British have it in exchange for Heligoland. The British ruled through the Sultan of Zanzibar but retained ultimate power and administered the protectorate.

There had been some turmoil in the years immediately leading up to independence, because of deep antagonism between the black African majority and the Arab minority who continued to dominate Zanzibar politically and, with the Asians, people of Indian and Pakistani origin, economically. The Arabs were a minority, with about 50,000 inhabitants, whereas the Africans numbered some 250,000. The Asians, a community of about 20,000 divided into various religious sects, were mainly businessmen, shopkeepers, and professional people, most of them living in Zanzibar Town. The European community numbered about 500 – the British colonial administrators, some business people, and spouses and children. The sixty or so Americans in Zanzibar were counted as members of the European community.

The elections in 1961 had been accompanied by riots and some killings. So the British, concerned about the '63 elections, brought in troops, Scots Guards, to maintain the peace. The election went off with no violence.

Q: The election had taken place before you arrived?

Petterson: Yes, just before our arrival in July 1963. A coalition of the Arab-led Zanzibar Nationalist Party and a smaller party consisting mainly of people of mixed blood, won the elections. There were accusations that the British had gerrymandered the electoral constituencies so that the African majority would not win. In the event though, it was the divisions among the Africans, their inexperience in politics, and the organizing skills of the Arabs that won the prize for the Arabs and their allies. An Arab named Ali Muhsin led the coalition government.

From the elections until independence, which came on December 12, 1963, although the African politicians voiced strong opposition to the acts of the pre-

72

independence government, there were few overt signs of serious unrest among the Africans. Yet, many worried that after independence there could be some trouble, for the Africans were deeply upset by what had occurred. I remember that a Special Branch police officer, a Briton who was about to leave Zanzibar, told Fritz Picard that there would be trouble, but not until well into the year.

With the arrival of Zanzibar's independence, our small consulate became an embassy. Picard, the consul, was to became the chargé d'affaires. I was the other State Department embassy officer, and Stuart Lillico was the U.S. Information Service officer. Imelda Johnson, was Fritz's secretary. The four of us made up the American diplomatic establishment in Zanzibar. The other Americans on the island, in addition to our families, were associated with the tracking station.

Q: Let me ask you what you have to say about Zanzibar independence.

Petterson: Neither the British nor the Americans knew that for months, almost a year, before independence, a shadowy figure by the name of John Okello was making preparations for an armed revolt. The African majority party, the Afro-Shirazi Party, which had lost the election, had determined that, if necessary, they might resort to arms to take over the country, whose government they believed rightfully belonged to them. Okello, who was from Uganda, had come to Pemba in 1959. Four years later, in early 1963, he came to Zanzibar and began plotting revolution. The handful of people in the Afro-Shirazi Party who became aware of this did not include the party's leaders.

During the independence ceremony, there was an ominous incident that foreshadowed trouble. At midnight, when the British flag was lowered, the lights went out, and when they went back on, the new Zanzibar government flag was raised. There were cheers from among the gathered dignitaries, but the Africans, including the hundreds who were off to the side of the cricket pitch where the independence ceremony was held, were ominously quiet.

On January 12, 1964, a month after independence, the revolution took place. During that month, the Arab-dominated government had done just about everything they should not have done to anger the Africans. They passed legislation that was unfavorable to the African population. In addition, they made it clear that Zanzibar was going to align itself with Egypt and the Arab world, rather than with the sub-Saharan, black African world, as the Africans wanted.

On the night of January 11, I had come home in the evening. There was a well attended dance going on in the African quarter, Ng'ambo, where I had taken the children's nanny home, but I saw no sign of anything untoward. At about 2:30 in the morning, the phone rang. I went to the hall and answered it. While I was walking to the phone, I could hear popping sounds. Fritz Picard, my boss, the American chargé d'affaires, was on the line. He told me that something was up and that I should begin to notify Americans to stay home. The firing became more intense. I could hear it quite distinctly.

Our next-door neighbor was Ali Muhsin, the leader of the government (not the prime minister, but the de facto leader), and armed revolutionaries had come to get him. So we were very close to the action at the time. As the morning wore on, Fritz, Stu Lillico, and I managed to get in touch with most or all the Americans. They hunkered down.

It became apparent that the government was no longer in control. At about seven o'clock, Okello got on the radio for the first time and began a series of broadcasts in which he announced that the radio station had been seized, the government had been toppled, and a new government was taking over under the leadership, Okello said, of Abeid Amani Karume, the head of the Afro-Shirazi Party.

Karume was actually, at that time, in Tanganyika, in Dar es Salaam. Young revolutionaries who had came to his house on the night of the 11th had told him that he should leave the island because it might be dangerous for him. He was taken to Dar on a boat. Two other leading Zanzibari opposition politicians had also gone to Dar. One of those was Abdulrahman Mohammed, "Babu."

The Americans and the British viewed Babu as a Communist who was exerting a dangerous pro-Communist influence. Just before the 1963 elections, he had broken with the Zanzibar Nationalist Party, of which he had been the Organizing Secretary. Much more radical than the party's other leaders, he founded his own political party, the Umma Party. In the first week of January, the government banned the Umma Party, searched its offices and Babu's house. As a warrant for his arrest was being prepared, he fled the island and went to Dar es Salaam.

So the big actors of the opposition were in Dar es Salaam when the revolution took place, which further indicates that they really were not in charge of its inception, as was said later. Okello was. Nevertheless, he announced that Karume would head the government. Karume came back to Zanzibar the day after the revolution, along with Babu and Abdul Kassim Hanga, who would become Karume's vice president.

To get back to the action that morning, about midmorning Fritz said we should all gather near the airport in case we needed to evacuate. He had been trying to get in touch with the government and with the British authorities, who were still there. Although the British had ceded control to the new government, many British civil servants remained, some of them occupying high administrative positions. Fritz did reach some of these officials, but none was well informed about what was happening. He also tried to communicate with Afro-Shirazi Party leaders, but without success. Thus he did not know the degree to which Americans and other foreigners might be in danger. However, he did not determine at that point that we should evacuate.

The firing around our house had subsided by the time that Fritz had called me. So when he said we should go to Stu and Helen Lillico's house, which was not far from the airport, I figured it was no safe enough to do so.

I had gone into town on my bicycle about seven or eight o'clock to see what was going on. I didn't tell Fritz I was going to do this, but I thought it would be interesting. As I approached Ng'ambo, Africans told me I should get out of there because it was dangerous, and indeed, people had been killed in that area earlier that morning. Most of the violence was taking place outside of Zanzibar Town by that time, but it was still dangerous in town.

Julie and I bundled up the two little girls. I guess I neglected to mention that in September, Julie gave birth to our second daughter, Julianne, at the Karimjee Jivanjee Hospital (soon to become the V.I. Lenin hospital). Julianne was the second American ever to be born in Zanzibar.

We put the two little girls in the Volkswagen, and I drove from our house, past Ali Muhsin's, to the road that led to the airport. The prison was close to the left side of the road a couple hundred yards farther down. As we approached, a rebel attack on it was taking place. Suddenly we saw just ahead on the right side of the road a group of twenty or thirty men armed with various weapons. When they saw us coming, they turned and pointed their weapons at us. But when they saw who we were, they yelled at us to get out of there and removed the roadblock they had placed across the road. We chugged by.

Q: You did not turn around?
Petterson: No.
Q: You continued on?
Petterson: I continued driving on, thinking, "Well, that's that," I suppose, if I thought anything! [Laughter]

We came around a corner less than 200 yards after that, and there behind some palm trees was another group of

Africans, another log across the road, and another firefight going on. Once again we were confronted by people with weapons, everything from spears to old rifles. Bullets were actually whizzing over the car, as I stopped it. I could hear them smacking into trees. The rebels, as before, saw that we were foreigners. They told me to drive around the roadblock and get out of there, which I did. [Laughter]

We went on our way. Once we were clear of that area, I had to stop the car for a moment and steady myself, because it dawned on me how close we had come to losing our lives. Julie was extremely scared. Poor little Susie, who was a year and a half old, was very, very frightened. The baby [laughter] didn't have any problems. She was in her basket at Julie's feet. Susie was on Julie's lap.

We proceeded, and drove out to the Lillicos' house. There we gathered with the other Americans who had come together to wait and see what happened. Picard, who lived a little further out, had not arrived yet. I talked to him on the phone, and he said to come over, which I did. It was quiet in that area. He and his wife, Shoana, had been packing. After we had talked for a bit, I took Shoana and their three children to the Lillicos'. Fritz followed later. Once at the Lillicos', Fritz, who had been in contact with the embassy in Dar es Salaam by telephone, called again to inform them of the state of play. Even though the rebels controlled everything by that time, they had not cut international telephone service.

Peering through gaps in the shutters – we had closed the door and shuttered the windows – we watched revolutionaries as they went into nearby Arab houses. We could hear people screaming and saw some killing. It was frightening. The Americans who were gathered with us were very, very apprehensive.

At some point in the early afternoon, Fritz decided that he and I should go to the airport to see if we could arrange for an evacuation. We drove the less than one mile to the airport. As we approached it, a car filled with Africans

77

headed towards us, and as it went by us, the long barrel of a large weapon emerged from one of the windows and blasted a cloud of black smoke and I don't know what else.

They apparently were trying to give us a fright, not harm us. They succeeded, but nevertheless we went on to the airport control tower, where we talked with the two British air traffic controllers. They pointed out some groups of armed rebels who were standing about in the tall grass just beyond the periphery of the airfield. They told that it was too risky for any aircraft to try to land. Fritz and I left and returned to the Lillico's.

Q: Hang on a second.

Petterson: Yes.

Q: Who was in control of the airport at this point, Arabs or Europeans?

Petterson: Europeans.

Q: Europeans.

Petterson: The airport was managed by an Arab professional, Ali Khalifa, and it had a mixed-race staff. The air traffic controllers were British. At this time, when Fritz and I were at the airport, nobody else was around, just the two controllers.

Q: Were there any either East African Airways, the small East African Airways planes, or charter planes around?

Petterson: No, there were no aircraft there. The East African Airways flight that normally would have come in that morning had been diverted. The prime minister of Zanzibar had been trying to get a shipment of weapons in. He had communicated his request through the controllers, who were in radio contact with the mainland. But the weapons never arrived. Shortly after Fritz and I left the airport, the Africans took it over.

Our decision then was whether to evacuate or not. Fritz decided that an evacuation was called for. Because it would have to be done by sea, we would need to go into

Zanzibar Town and congregate there with the Americans who lived to the north of the city. Once together, we would prepare for an evacuation.

Fritz asked me and a fellow named Irv Zolo, who worked for the tracking station, to drive into town to see if the road was safe. We got into my car and headed into town. I was sweating profusely, and not just because it was hot and humid! We both were nervous because we didn't know what would be around each curve in the road. As it happened, we encountered no problem. We saw some results of the revolution. Cars shot up. We saw no bodies. They had been removed already. We went all the way into town. Conditions seemed to be safe enough for the rest of the Americans to make the trip. After we went back, everyone got their things together, and in a convoy of several cars, we drove into town to the English Club, which was right on the beach.

In the meantime, the Americans who lived on the other side of town had gathered together in one of their houses. After hearing from us about the decision to evacuate from the English Club, they drove toward town in several cars. Unlike us, they did encounter rebels, who stopped them, threatened them, and might have harmed them. But someone with authority interceded, and they were allowed to proceed. On their way in, they saw some grisly sights of Arabs who had been killed and had been mutilated in a very gruesome fashion. So they had first-hand experience with some consequences of the revolution's first day, consequences to –

Q: The Africans that threatened those people in those cars, did they know that they were Americans?

Petterson: Yes, well, they knew that the people were Europeans, as all whites were termed.

Q: Europeans? Why would they be sort of angry with Europeans?

Petterson: Well, there was no love on the part of many of these people for foreigners, who led comfortable lives and had all the things that most Africans didn't have. But this was not the problem, for there really was no deep hatred. The rebels carrying weapons were, for the most part, simply ragtag fellows who had no discipline, who had been drinking, or were on something, and they were out of control. They were trying to shake down the Americans.

At one point, a baby began to cry, and one of the rebels said to the mother to shut the baby up, or he would kill it. They were pretty nasty. But then someone more reasonable arrived, someone in authority, and he changed the climate of what was going on there. The Americans were allowed to proceed, and reached the English Club without further incident. There were 60 or 65 Americans at the club, and later some Europeans tourists in town joined us.

Q: So that includes the people from the tracking station as well?

Petterson: That's right. The official American community - the small embassy and USIS staff - along with the tracking station people, and our respective families. With the tourists, there must have been some seventy to eighty people in the hotel as the sun went down. We decided that we would man a command post downstairs. Upstairs, men, women and children got set for the night. Fortunately there was some food in the establishment, and people were able to get something to eat that night. I stayed downstairs and manned the command post all night long, as it turned out, because of an incident that took place in the middle of the night.

Fritz Picard became very concerned about the fate of Stu Lillico's secretary, a young Zanzibari woman whose name was Fathiya. She was an incredibly beautiful woman, and Fritz was having an affair with her, which I mention because it turned out to be quite germane to what could have happened to the Americans.

The revolutionaries were looking for members of the

government. One of her relatives was a cabinet minister, a man named Mshangama. She was at his house, which was not very far from the English Club. Fritz had been talking to her on the telephone, and she told him that rebels were coming.

Fritz came down from upstairs and without telling me and the other fellow who was with me at the command post what he was going to do, he went out into the street and began to make a racket. I didn't know what he was doing. I went out and told him to come back into the English Club, but he persisted. What he was trying to do was to divert the attention of the rebels who might be endangering Fathiya and her family. He wanted to get them to stop what they were doing and come to the English Club instead. He succeeded in doing this because very soon a group of armed men came by and tried to ascertain what he was doing. He bantered with them for a while. Finally they told him to shut up and go back inside, which he did.

At that point, I was simply worried about Fritz. I didn't know what he was doing. He then explained, and I was very angry because he had put all of the people in the English Club at risk. Whether or not his diversion saved Fathiya, I'll never know, but at any rate, the rebels did not go into that house. Later that night Fathiya, her mother, and her two children came into the club. Fritz had telephoned her and told her to come there. He met them at the door and took them inside. She was downstairs, and his wife was upstairs.

Q: Oh, really?

Petterson: Yes. He arranged for her to stay in a place downstairs away from the Americans who were upstairs, including Shoana. In fact, nobody knew about Fathiya until the end of the following day.

In the morning, the embassy in Dar es Salaam informed us that approval of the evacuation had been given, and that an American destroyer, the USS Manley, would be coming in to take the Americans off the island. The Manley had been in Kenya at the port of Mombasa on a ship visit when the revolution occurred. The ship was ordered to steam back and forth off the coast of Zanzibar over the horizon until the decision was made that an evacuation could be carried out.

During the course of that day, Fritz continued to act in a way that disturbed me. For example, when we went out of the English Club onto the beach to talk to rebels, Fritz, at one point, brought his five-year-old son with him. Throughout the day he carried a mug of beer with him, whether he was in the club or outside. It caused a lot of people to raise their eyebrows. It was bizarre behavior. Nevertheless, he showed some very fine qualities later in the day. Certainly his judgment as to the need for the evacuation was not questioned by anyone. The Americans, all of them, were thoroughly frightened and wanted off the island.

The Manley picked its way into the harbor very slowly about mid-afternoon. A small boat came ashore with Jim Ruchti, who was the deputy chief of mission at the American embassy in Nairobi. He had been in Mombasa for the ship visit. The captain had asked him to accompany the ship to Zanzibar and to give him political advice. Jim received permission to do that. He brought with him a Kenyan cab driver, so there would be somebody who could speak Swahili, listen to the radio to hear local broadcasts, and thereby help keep Ruchti and the captain abreast of what was happening in Zanzibar Town.

After the ship had anchored, Ruchti came ashore in the ship's whaleboat with the executive officer and several sailors. They were not permitted, initially, to land until Fritz prevailed upon a group of armed rebels on the beach to permit Ruchti and the executive officer ashore. The sailors had to remain in the boat. Fritz and I took Jim and the exec to the English Club, where we continued to try to contact the revolutionary government.

Q: Let me just ask you a quick question there, interrupt you. Picard and the captain of the ship had not themselves just decided to evacuate the personnel who were at the English Club? Just go ahead and do it?

Petterson: No. The State Department, Defense Department, and White House had approved Fritz's request for the evacuation. But when the executive officer of the ship came ashore with Jim Ruchti, we had not yet received permission from the rebels. It was only through negotiating with the rebels on the beach that were we able to get those two people off the whaleboat, so that they could wait with us to see whether or not permission for the evacuation would be granted.

Q: Permission from the?

Petterson: From the rebels.

Q: Revolutionaries?

Petterson: That's right....

We returned to the English Club. Fritz went off to the hotels to pick up those tourists who were still there. While Ruchti and the executive officer went down to the boat to get the crew ready for the operation and to notify the captain what had happened at Raha Leo, Lillico and I met with the Americans, who waiting for us on the club's upper porch, which overlooked the beach. Earlier, we had stipulated that women and children, regardless of nationality, would go first. However, now a couple of the Americans, tracking station employees, said, "Uh-uh, Americans first, foreigners second." Stu and I said [laughter], 'Not on your life! Women and children first.' And we made that stick. With Fritz now back, everyone who wanted to go was at the club, and the whaleboat and another boat, the captain's gig, began taking the evacuees out to the destroyer. The sun had gone down and it soon grew very dark. I took Julie and the babies down to the boat with the few possessions that she had brought, mainly things for the children and some clothes. We said goodbye, and I kissed her and the two little girls.

She was fearful, as she said later in letters to her parents and to mine, that she would never see me again. I had no such thoughts, myself! [Laughter] I was having too much of an interesting time! Off she and the children went into the gloom. We had set up some portable lights from the ship on the beach, but their beams didn't carry much beyond 30 or 40 yards out to sea. The boats would disappear into the darkness as they went out to the ship. After all the evacuees were aboard, the Manley sailed to Dar es Salaam.

Q: Let me interrupt you again for a second.

Petterson: Yes.

Q: Were personnel from any other consulates taken off, the British for example?

Petterson: No. There were no other diplomatic establishments, just the British and the Americans at that time. The British had not made a decision to evacuate. They considered it, but had not yet decided. There was some criticism of the American decision to evacuate, but Fritz had sound reasons for doing what he did. (1) We had no idea that the word was out not to harm foreigners. (2) We were unable to get in touch with the revolutionaries. We didn't know whether the violence would get worse, or whether it would subside. (3) There had been animosity shown toward the Americans by some of the very people who carried out the revolution. They had protested the presence in Zanzibar of what they termed the American rocket base and demanded its removal. There was a lot of hostile propaganda directed against America in that month after independence.

The Manley arrived in Dar es Salaam harbor that night, but couldn't go in through the channel, which was very narrow.

Q: Including yourself?

Petterson: Oh, no, no! Pardon me! I forgot to mention

that Fritz and I stayed. We had agreed that somebody should stay behind to look after the embassy and the property of Americans. Washington said that if we wanted to stay we could, so that left the two of us on the island. The next day, in Dar es Salaam the Americans disembarked from the destroyer. My family and Fritz's family remained in Dar until a week later.

Q: How about Fritz's girlfriend?

Petterson: She was there. Everybody [laughter] saw her on the Manley.

Q: She went over to Dar as well?

Petterson: Yes.

Fritz and I then went home that night and drank a lot of beer. I had a beer or two, but by that time I'd been up for over 48 hours and was very tired. I went home to my now lonely house. By the way, we were no longer in the stable. We had moved two months earlier to my predecessor's house in another part of town, a much nicer home.

The next day, Fritz and I were told by the revolutionaries not to leave our respective houses, but later in the day we were given permission to go about our business. My Swahili came in to very good use, either that day or the next. We were driving from Fritz's place to the embassy when we came upon a group of armed men, who yelled in Swahili, 'Simana,' which meant, 'Stop!'

Fritz didn't speak Swahili; I did. I said, "Fritz, stop the car" which he did. [Laughter] Otherwise, he would have kept going and we might have been shot at.

By the way, my Swahili (and I'm talking to Nick who studied Swahili with me) –

Q: A classmate.

Petterson: That's right...was very useful....

On the morning of January 16, four days after the revolution, we were at the embassy. Fritz received a telephone call from the British high commissioner, who somewhat testily said, 'Some of your people are causing a problem down at the port, reporters, your people,

Americans.' He said they were a matter of 'grave embarrassment.'

So Fritz told me to go there, which I did. At the boat landing, I encountered several armed men who were gathered at the top of a concrete sea wall from which steps led down to the water. A couple of British colonial port officials also were there. I could see the top of a dhow's mast. After explaining who I was and why I had come, I was allowed go to the edge of the sea wall. I saw that there were seven men in the boat.

We talked, and I learned that they were American, British, and Canadian newspapermen – reporters for *Time*, *Newsweek*, *The New York Herald Tribune*, a Canadian paper, and a British paper – and an Indian photographer for *Life* magazine. So they weren't just Americans, were not, in the words of the High Commissioner, 'your people' only. They had sailed in the dhow from the mainland, arriving in Zanzibar the previous night.

They started asking me questions. Foolishly I answered. At that point a rifle was pointed right at my face, and I was told to "Shut up!" So I stopped talking, [laughter] the better part of valor! Some authorities from the revolutionary government joined these armed people at dockside. They said that the men in the boat were spies and we were going to be taken to revolutionary headquarters. Off we went. I tried to explain to the rebels who I was. They couldn't care less, nor did they accept that these were just newspaper people.

We had been held at Raha Leo for several hours when Fritz showed up. He finally had found out where we were and what the problem was, and had talked to a minister in the government. Karume was away. He had gone to Dar es Salaam that day. The minister said, 'Well, sure. Let these people go.' Fritz told us the good news, and he and I drove the journalists to the Zanzibar Hotel, where they got rooms and then went off about their business.

But suspicions were high about these people. Some of

them had U.S. Defense Department press cards, and they showed them when asked for an ID (identification) card. The name of one of the reporters was Conley, Robert Conley. That sounded like "colonel." So the rebels had this Colonel Robert, and they had Defense Department ID cards. Spies, you know! It really rang a bell with some of these less-than-sophisticated rebels.

When Karume returned late that afternoon, or early that evening, he was told about the reporters and the suspicious about them. He was also given some of their notes, which had been taken from them and which were not too complimentary about the revolution. Karume was angry, and he went to the Zanzibar Hotel to confront them. Picard was with them.

The minister who had allowed these fellows to go about their business happened to be a political enemy of Karume, even though he was in the cabinet. When Karume saw Picard with his political enemy and the correspondents, he was furious. Babu, who was with him, and another government official, who had no love for Fritz, egged Karume on. In essence they said, 'You know, these people are up to no good. Picard has interfered.' Karume bought that and angrily ordered Picard, at gunpoint, to be taken to his house.

I was over at the embassy at that time, composing a long classified cable, using a primitive system of those days called a 'one-time pad,' and as, Nick [laughter], you'd know, it was a very laborious task! It took me a couple of hours to encrypt the message. It was dark outside when I locked up, left the embassy, and started across the square – Kelele Square – to Cable and Wireless to deliver my telegram for transmission. In the darkness, in the middle of the square, I came upon Karume and a gaggle of fellows with weapons. Karume asked me what I was doing.

I said, 'I'm taking a message over to be sent.'

He said, 'No, I can't allow that!' He told me what had happened. He said that he had arrested Picard, that Picard had done something bad and would be expelled from the island, and that I would have to be placed under arrest, too.

He ordered four of the armed men to get in my car, the VW, and accompany me. I drove toward my house with the barrel of a rifle in the back of my neck, not intentionally, but it was a bit disconcerting! They didn't stop at my house, but instead took me to Picard's. There I spent the night with Fritz, who was drinking heavily.

The next day, a chartered plane came over from Dar. Fritz was placed on the airplane, along with some of his possessions and the Lillico's dog, which had been left behind, and off he went. I was at the airport with him and breathed a sigh of relief when the plane left, because I had been worried that his behavior since the onset of revolution might lead to his harm. There were some Chinese at the airport taking pictures of Fritz's expulsion. Babu and some of his people were also present....

I had a number of adventures in trying to protect American property, failing in some cases because looters had come, encountering looters at one property and chasing after them, foolishly, on my bicycle, and capturing one of them, only to find that he was just a kid. If I turned him in he would be executed, so I let him go, and warned him not to do that anymore.

I managed to communicate by telephone with the embassy in Dar es Salaam. I was not given diplomatic privileges. I could send nothing out by diplomatic pouch and could send cables only if they were not encrypted and were approved by a government censor at Cable and Wireless. Now and then, the censor didn't like my choice of words and refused to all the message to be transmitted....

Occasionally I got a classified message out by taking it over to the British, who had been given the permission to use their classified pouch. Twice, at the airport I met American officials who were on a flight from Dar to

Nairobi via Zanzibar. I was allowed to go out and talk to them. I slipped each of them an envelope with a message in it.

My time was largely taken up with looking after the American property, trying to find out what was going on, dealing with the revolutionary government, and reporting as well as I could.

By mid-February, it was clear that the revolutionary government was getting fed up with the lack of recognition from the British and the Americans. Concern about Zanzibar in the American government reached the highest level, President Johnson, and in the British government at its highest level, Prime Minister Alec Douglas-Home. This was extraordinary when you think about it. Zanzibar was seen as a precursor of revolution for Africa, as a Communist foothold could spread into the continent. The Chinese communists, the Soviets, and East Germans had established embassies (which grew to be quite large) and had begun arranging for military and economic aid. Communist diplomats, technicians, and military trainers began to come to Zanzibar in relatively large numbers.

The British were dithering. They didn't want to recognize a government that had come to power by force of arms. Moreover, they didn't like this government's pro-Communist or apparent pro-Communist leanings. So the British waited despite the urgings of Tanganyikan Prime Minister Julius Nyerere that they grant recognition to the new government of Zanzibar. Washington followed the British lead. By a month or so after the revolution, the Zanzibaris were out of patience.

On the 19th of February, I was summoned to revolutionary headquarters, where the British high commissioner had arrived just before me. Karume told us that because the U.S. and UK (United Kingdom) had not recognized his government, we would have to go; otherwise, the people might rise up and do harm to us or to

89

the government. Well, that was an exaggeration, but we were given 24 hours to leave.

From the embassy, I called the American ambassador to Tanganyika, William Leonhart, in Dar es Salaam and informed him of what had happened. Then I went back to burning classified documents, which I had been doing for several days, using a small potbellied stove. Leonhart tried that day to convince Nyerere to influence Karume to postpone my expulsion, but without success. That evening, the ambassador called me. Passing a message from Washington, he said I should see Karume if I could and ask him to delay the expulsion for at least twenty-four hours. I should tell him that a U.S. official from Washington had just arrived in Dar and could come over the next day to talk to him about recognition.

I managed to get through to Karume, who said I could come see him. He didn't agree to the proposal but left the door open. After another exchange between Leonhart and me, and a message from Washington for Karume, which arrived at seven o'clock the following morning, Karume agreed to receive Leonhart and the man from Washington.

At midmorning, Ambassador Leonhart and Frank Carlucci, a Foreign Service officer, came to Zanzibar in a small chartered aircraft. I met them and went with them to see Karume.

Q: What was Carlucci doing in Dar?

Petterson: Frank had been in the Congo, where he had acquired a reputation as an exceptionally able Foreign Service officer. He was the embassy's troubleshooter in the Congo. After the Congo and before coming to Zanzibar, he had a job in the State Department –

Q: Well, when I saw him, he was assistant desk officer for the Congo under Charlie Whitehouse.

Petterson: OK.

Q: That was '63.

Petterson: Yes. Frank was well-regarded by Joe Palmer, the Assistant Secretary of State for African Affairs

90

and by Charlie Whitehouse, and by everybody else. It had been decided that Frank would be the new chargé d'affaires in Zanzibar. He came with a letter from President Johnson that indicated recognition would be coming soon. Frank and Leonhart tried to convince Karume that with recognition just around the corner, it would be much better if he didn't throw me off the island. By the way, the whole Revolutionary Council, which included all the wild men along with some of the more able and moderate Zanzibari Africans who were in the cabinet, were at this meeting.

The discussion went on for a couple of hours, but in the end Karume and the Council rejected the American proposal. Karume, when he said goodbye, said, 'If you come back, if recognition takes place, and you come back, Mr. Carlucci, we'll have a parade in your honor.' So with that, Frank and Ambassador Leonhart returned to Dar es Salaam.

I went back to the embassy to finish burning the classified materials. I had just started when there was a pounding on the front door. Ali Mafoudh, the head of the newly created special police force, demanded to come into the embassy. When I refused him entry, he said he would have to take me in custody. He drove me to State House, the seat of the government. An official there told Mafoudh to take me back to the embassy and not interfere with me.

After I did some burning, I went home for a quick lunch. When I returned, the officer in charge of the soldiers who had surrounded the building said I could not reenter it. When I argued with him, he told me a government official wanted to see me and he drove me to a government office.

I was taken to the office of Abdul Azziz Twala, one of the more militant members of the cabinet. Unbeknownst to me, an argument had preceded my arrival. Some of the people there wanted to kill me. At least that's what a man named Mohammed Ali Foum, who was there at the time and later became a diplomat in Tanzanian diplomatic service, told me years afterward. We met at the United Nations one day, and he told me this. I don't know if it's true, but he swore it was. He said that after some argument, it was decided that killing me would cause too many problems. At any rate, when I got there, Twala simply told me to return to the embassy, then go home and get ready to leave later that day. This was –

Q: You had been summoned over to the Revolutionary Council headquarters?

Petterson: No, to an administrative office –

Q: They'd asked you to come over?

Petterson: Yes, right.

Q: But once you got there, nothing much happened?

Petterson: That's correct.

Q: And then you went back home?

Petterson: No, to the embassy. After using an ax to demolish the code machine, which didn't work and we'd never used, I started burning papers again. I soon realized that I couldn't destroy all the classified papers using just the stove, so I got one of the two or three destruction kits that were stored on the same floor as the walk-in vault, where we kept the classified files. Each kit was a heavy cardboard cylindrical drum, about three and a half feet high and two feet in diameter, the size of a large garbage can. It contained a bag, or bags, I can't remember, of inflammable chemicals in granular form and a magnesium igniter.

I put in papers, threw some of the chemical stuff on them, put in more papers, more chemicals, until all the papers were in the container. With everything now ready, I then dropped in the igniter. It worked like a hand grenade. You pull the pin, drop it in, and whoosh! A sheet of fire shot up. The heat of the fire was so intense that had I not kept the vault door open, I would have been incinerated. The pressure that resulted was so strong that to close the vault door, which I left open, I had to put my feet against of the opposite wall of the narrow hallway outside the vault and use my leg muscles to get the door closed. I began to wonder, 'What the hell have I done?'

Knowing that the troops outside would see smoke coming through the small open barred space in the vault, I went outside and talked to the guy in charge. Sure enough, black smoke could be seen pouring through the opening. He asked me what I was doing. I said, 'Oh, I'm just burning a few papers. It's normal for us to do that, you know.' And he accepted it, and I went back inside. I really thought, 'How am I going to explain [laughter] to Washington that I burned down the embassy?'

Luckily the vault was built of steel-reinforced concrete. Had it not been, the walls would have buckled, and the fire might well have spread. But it was contained in the vault, and I didn't burn down the embassy.

Q: This is all very interesting because your evacuation certainly wasn't the last and won't be the last. But one of the lessons learned perhaps is that when you use these destruction kits, you should use them outdoors?

Petterson: Absolutely!

Q: Or on a roof, or something?

Petterson: Absolutely! They didn't have directions on them. A couple of weeks or so later, I sent what we called an "operations memorandum" to Washington describing in detail what had happened and urging the Department to put a label on the destruction kits, "Do not use indoors under any circumstances!" I'm told that that memorandum made the rounds in the department and [laughter] got a lot of laughs.

I went home, packed a suitcase, and waited to be taken to the airport for the flight to Dar es Salaam.

Q: On an East African Airways flight?

Petterson: Yes, a regularly scheduled flight. I was met at the airport in Dar, taken to the embassy where I was debriefed. I wrote a report before I left the next day for

Nairobi, where Julie and the children were. They had been in Dar es Salaam but had been evacuated from there after a mutiny by the Tanganyikan army had almost toppled the government of Julius Nyerere and had brought considerable violence to Dar es Salaam. During that violence, Fritz began to relive the Zanzibar revolution, and he had to be medically evacuated. He'd been under great stress and was as tight as a drum. After medical treatment in the States, he was medically cleared and resumed his career. It had been damaged, however, and ended after his next overseas assignment had not given him the kind of efficiency report he needed for a promotion.

I flew to Nairobi and spent two or three days there. I had the flu, but didn't feel too bad. I got a call from Frank Carlucci in Dar telling me to come back, that recognition had been granted. He and I would be going over to Zanzibar right away. So I flew to Dar, and, with Ambassador Leonhart, Frank and I flew over to the island. There was no parade to welcome us. Karume, who was visibly pleased, received us at State House, and Frank read to him the formal note of recognition. Leonhart returned to Dar es Salaam. Frank and I opened the embassy.

The first thing we did was clean up the vault, which was covered by a thick coating of slimy dark brown [laughter] soot. While Frank, his secretary, Lynne Derzo, and I were doing that, I almost passed out. I was done in by a bad case of flu, fatigue, and maybe weight loss. I had lost a lot of weight when I was alone on the island, cooking for myself or being fed by friends. Anyway, I was simply....

Q: Exhausted!

Petterson: Yes. So I went back to Nairobi, spent about a week with Julie and the children before going back to Zanzibar to resume my job working with my new boss, the chargé d'affaires of the American embassy, Frank Carlucci.

I began a very good year with Frank Carlucci, one of

94

the most able, dedicated people I've known anywhere, certainly an outstanding Foreign Service Officer. Frank was very generous in giving me free rein to do whatever I wanted to do in the way of political reporting. Under Fritz I had been confined to lower-level officials and labor reporting. But Frank gave me, as I said, free rein.

I learned a lot from him by his example. He was an excellent reporter. He got out, beat the bushes, met people. He was charming. He got people to trust him. He dealt with people who were essentially hostile to us at that time, befriended them, and got a lot out of it. He knew what was going on in Zanzibar before he'd been there very long. A measure of his dedication is shown by the fact that whereas he spoke no Swahili when he got there, one year later, by taking tutoring from an Anglican nun and listening to tapes, Frank got a three-three in Swahili when he was tested at the Foreign Service Institute.

Q: Let me just interrupt you there to say, you know, obviously, you have a lot of respect and admiration for Carlucci. But I think it might be interesting for researchers, as well as journalists and other people who are going to use this interview, for you to describe briefly what the characteristics are, in your opinion, of an outstanding American diplomat. What is it that Carlucci represented, in your opinion?

Petterson: First of all, he had extraordinary intelligence, coupled with very good common sense, and an outgoing nature. He knew how to get along with Africans. He wassensitive to their culture. He had no false pretensions. He was an excellent writer, had superior analytical skills, and was a superb manager. He knew how to delegate.

Q: What makes a good reporting officer, Don?

Petterson: Somebody who's willing to get out of the office, travel around the country, to do whatever is necessary to get information, to establish a rapport with people so they will talk to you. You collect intelligence

95

from people whom you meet and process it through whatever abilities you have. You learn to sift out good information from bad.

I believe, too, that, like Frank, the best officers are very industrious and dedicated. Frank worked long, hard hours and gave a great deal of thought to his work. He also (maybe this isn't a quality of a great reporter or necessarily a successful Foreign Service officer, but to me it's something very important) cared about people, the people who worked with him, and he showed that. He got their loyalty, and he got a lot out of them. He had all the qualities that would later propel him to high offices in the U.S. government, including secretary of defense.

Q: Okay, so there you are in Zanzibar?

Petterson: That's right. We are behind the bamboo curtain, as we said in those days, or the clove curtain, as some joked, cloves being Zanzibar's principal export. Frank set out to meet and establish a relationship with as many people as possible in the government and other areas.

Q: Yes, but this story is about you and not about Frank.

Petterson: [Laughter] Yes, but –

Q: So you were doing the same thing?

Petterson: Yes, I was very happy to be able to start becoming a political reporter because it was what I had wanted to do, and I had not been able to do it either in Mexico or much in Zanzibar before the revolution. I now got out and about, established whatever contacts I could. It was very difficult because we were under suspicion. Sometimes we were under surveillance. People were afraid to see us. We could not entertain Zanzibaris; nobody would come to our house. So we didn't have the usual kind of social opportunities to meet people and get information.

But we could wander around and go to people's offices and other places where we could meet people who might

96

give us information of the kind we needed in order to inform Washington what was happening in Zanzibar, which had become (in the eyes of Washington and London) a bastion of Communism. The Chinese brought in more people - military trainers, agriculturists, and embassy staff - as did the Soviets and the East Germans. The East Germans were delighted to have a diplomatic establishment in Zanzibar. Before getting Zanzibar's recognition, they had not been recognized by any other countries except communist countries.

Q: But those three countries are among the three most difficult countries for a Western diplomat to observe and gather information about.

Petterson: True. We were we trying to report not only on what was happening in Zanzibar among the Zanzibaris, but, more important from Washington's standpoint, on what the Chinese, East Germans, and Soviets were doing. Other communist countries were also represented in Zanzibar. Cuba, for example, the Czechs, the Poles, North Vietnamese, Bulgarians, you name them; they were all there. It was a great place to be as a young reporting officer in the Cold War days.

We set about our work. As I said, I learned a lot from Frank and began doing political reporting. I was also the administrative officer and the consular officer. Our embassy began to grow. Suddenly we were in the front lines of the East-West struggle and a place, at least for some more months to come, considered to be very important in the eyes of the State Department and others in Washington.

Q: When you say that you began to grow, for example, did the USIA (United States Information Agency), USIS send any people? Were there any CIA (Central Intelligence Agency) people there?

Petterson: USIS reestablished their office, and an officer came to run it. The CIA did come in. This was the major factor in the growth of the embassy, as you can imagine. Zanzibar was very fertile ground for the CIA, the KGB (Komitet Gosudarstvennoy Bezopasnosti, Committee for State Security, USSR), and other counterparts of these intelligence services.

So yes, we now have a CIA presence. We had a station chief and his staff, which included communications personnel, an administrative person, and a secretary. The State Department side began to grow a little, too, as we got another secretary and an administrative assistant, who took the admin burden off of me. So from a four-person U.S. mission, we expanded to about a dozen.

Q: Did the NASA tracking station people come back?

Petterson: Momentarily. The Karume government decided in April that the tracking station would have to close down. The decision came despite a report that had been issued just before the revolution by a Swedish diplomat whom the previous government had asked to assess the station. He attested to the peaceful purposes of the manned space program (which indeed they were). Pressure to close the station decision had been building. It was being exerted by Communist diplomats, as well as by people within the government, including but not limited to Babu and other leftists.

Whether they believed it or not, I don't know, but some continued to call the tracking station an American rocket base. Karume summoned Frank and told him the tracking station would have to be dismantled. So a few of the Project Mercury people and the NASA representative came back and very quickly dismantled the station, much faster than Karume had thought it would take. He was pleased by the professional way they did this.

Q: This would be about mid '64?

Petterson: No, we're still in the early part of '64....

Q: Let me ask you, Don. In Tanganyika at the time of independence, there was a small Indian minority as well as a few Arabs. If there were also these minorities

98

in Zanzibar, what happened to them?

Petterson: The population, as I mentioned earlier, included about 250,000 Africans. A high percentage of them were them people from the mainland who had come over to pick cloves and then had stayed and had established their families in Zanzibar. Some of the Africans were longer-term inhabitants, many of whom, especially those living in Pemba, called themselves Shirazis, claiming that they were descended from the Shiraz people of Iran. In addition to the Africans, Zanzibar had 50,000 Arabs, and about 20,000 Asians of Pakistani and Indian origin.

During the revolution, some 5,000 people were killed. Almost all of these were Arabs. That's one tenth of the Arab population. By the time I left the island near the end of 1965, the number of Arabs was less than 25,000. Those who remained had no place in the power structure whatsoever. The Asian population was also down by half or more by that time. As the government of Zanzibar became more and more repressive, Asians wanted out, and those who could, left.

Karume, despite a lot of good qualities, became increasingly dictatorial. I didn't see the worst of it during my time and I got along very well with him, as did Frank. But subsequent to our time there, he became more and more erratic, more and more dictatorial. Eventually he was assassinated, and a more moderate man, Aboud Jumbe, whom I mentioned earlier, became Zanzibar's president.

Frank and I settled down for a long siege of working in the Cold War trenches. Julie and the children came back in March. In April, because of anti-American demonstrations, they went back to Dar for a short time, returning after the demonstrations were ended and any possible threat was over.

We had a wonderful life in Zanzibar when all the hullabaloo was over. We had a small circle of friends – small because we couldn't mix with Zanzibaris. The

Revolutionary Council had become very anti-Western and prohibited Zanzibaris from having anything to do with the Americans and British. Even cabinet members were afraid to associate with us. So our social circle was limited to the small British community that remained, members of the British high commission, the Americans, and a few other foreigners, including some Africans. We had a tight-knit little community. We did a lot of socializing. The beaches were lovely. A number of us took our children to a beach just about every Sunday.

Zanzibar was a nice place to be, from that standpoint, and a very fascinating place to be because of what was occurring there, as we watched the influx of Communists and observed how things were playing out. We tried to influence Karume and others in the government to take a more moderate stance, and to be more truly nonaligned. We finally succeeded in that. Frank made a lot of inroads and a lot of progress before he had to leave the island.

Q: I wanted to ask. This is a good time. Were there any AID (United States Agency for International Development) or Peace Corps people on the island when you were there?

Petterson: No Peace Corps or AID. But we had an AID project, and AID officers from Dar es Salaam came over occasionally, or I would go over there to confer with them. The project was the construction and equipping of a secondary manual arts school that would turn out artisans, technicians, which the island very much needed. Karume looked upon the project with great favor.

A Zanzibari resident, a South African architect, designed the school to our specifications. The project, which cost about a million dollars, was appropriate to Zanzibar's needs and was not at all grandiose or ill conceived. Within a decade, however, it failed. After the school was turned over to the Zanzibari authorities to run by themselves, they didn't handle it well at all, and it deteriorated physically as well as academically.

Q: While you were there, then, this AID project was one of the tools of American diplomacy. Were there any other tools that you had to try to influence the Zanzibari government?

Petterson: Well, the tool of rational discourse with the Zanzibaris. The agency has its own way of making friends, and some money was passed around. Whether that that produced any lasting positive results, I don't know. Our USIS library was very popular with Zanzibaris, especially young people. But its very success as a tool of our diplomacy was its undoing. At different times in the coming year and a half, our opponents succeeded in bringing trumped up charges against two USIS officers and getting them expelled.

Another thing we had going for us was the mistakes made by the communists themselves. The East Germans promised to build a massive housing projects, enough housing for all the Africans in Ng'ambo. We're talking about 40,000 or 50,000 people. In the end the Germans built some apartments that were unsuitable to the culture of the Zanzibari people, who didn't want to live in large blocks of flats. They wanted a house that would be their own. The Chinese imported a lot of commercial goods, some of which were shoddy. For example, they brought in some talcum powder, which sat in a warehouse and congealed in the heat and humidity. The Soviets didn't come through with the kind of aid they promised.

I don't want to give a picture that the Communists really blew it. Because of their mistakes, they may have lost some of the luster they had gained right after the revolution, but overall their aid was welcomed. The Chinese gave a cash grant of one million pounds, which the Zanzibar government sorely needed. Although the Chinese rice production of the communal farms was hardly bountiful, Zanzibar's leaders seemed favorably impressed by it. And the Chinese brought in medical personnel to work in the hospital. Soviet military advisors, as well as Chinese, continued to train Zanzibari soldiers. Both countries provided more arms, equipment and ammunition. And the East Germans brought in technicians of various kinds, and teachers as well. They also delivered an armed patrol boat and some fishing boats.

As for our AID project, we never promised what we couldn't deliver, and I think that set well with Karume. He was impressed by what we did. He wanted to have a balanced relationship with East and West - very hard to do in those days. He seemed to come to the conclusion that we were there not to do him in, but to work with him. Even though he had been very much angered and upset because of the delay of our recognition, in time we developed a good working relationship with him during those years before he became so erratic, eccentric, and dictatorial.

Q: It sounds to me as though Karume, at least for a while, had the same sort of balance among foreigners and foreign interests as Julius Nyerere had in Tanzania with the Russians –

Petterson: To a degree, yes.

Q: And the Chinese that were in Tanzania, as well as the Scandinavians and the Germans and the Canadians.

Petterson: Yes, but the West didn't have as many countries represented in Zanzibar, just the British, a one-man French consulate, and ourselves. So we were really outnumbered by the communist countries, and more so by the number of people they brought into Zanzibar. In the long run, it would not matter, as Zanzibar's importance in the Cold War diminished and both East and West lost interest in it. But that did not happen while I was there.

Q: Okay. So now we're up to '65?

Petterson: Yes, let's put it at the very beginning of 1965. Frank was well in stride running the embassy. All of us were pretty productive. U.S. relations with Zanzibar had improved. So, things were definitely going well when, suddenly, there was an unexpected reverse. On January 15, Frank went to Dar es Salaam. While he was there, Bill Leonhart was summoned to Nyerere, who said that Frank and Leonhart's deputy chief of mission, Bob Gordon, had been involved in a plot to overthrow the government of Zanzibar.

Now this was totally idiotic. It stemmed from a telephone conversation that Frank and Bob had had earlier in the month, a telephone conversation in which they were trying to work out a way to get a high-level American official to attend the celebration of the first anniversary of the revolution. Ambassador Leonhart was against the idea, and there was opposition to it in the State Department. Frank and Bob were developing arguments in its favor. They were speaking guardedly, using code words, because they figured the phones were tapped. Among other things, one of them said something like, 'This will give us ammunition to get the big gun,' the big gun meaning [laughter] Assistant Secretary of State Soapy Williams, G. Mennen Williams, who they hoped would come for the celebration.

Whether the tape was doctored or not, it and some spurious intelligence reports that he had seen convinced Nyerere that Frank and Bob Gordon were concocting a plan to bring down the Zanzibar government. Nyerere foolishly believed it.

His rush to judgement is all the more incredible considering that only two months earlier he had been burned by an equally unlikely fabrication that the American government, in league with Portugal, was plotting to overthrow the Tanzanian government.

The allegation was based on documents that had been sent to Nyerere's foreign minister by the Tanzanian ambassador to the Congo Republic. The foreign minister, Oscar Kambona, had made them public and denounced the United States. This gave rise to a surge of anti-Americanism in the country.

103

Subsequently, a document-authentication expert proved to the Tanzanians that the documents were crude forgeries. Kambona's and Nyerere's readiness to believe the worst of the United States had made them look foolish and must have been embarrassing to Nyerere. But here he was, once again acting precipitately.

Ambassador Leonhart urged him to reconsider, but Nyerere was adamant. Frank and Bob Gordon had to go. Frank was allowed to come back to Zanzibar to be able to pack before leaving. He went to Karume and told him the whole story. Karume was sympathetic, and said that he had no role in the affair. He and Frank parted on cordial terms. The next day, we said goodbye, and off he went. His wife, Jean, stayed on long enough to pack their household effects.

Nyerere, incidentally, finally came to realize, after receiving messages from President Johnson and from Secretary Rusk in which the entire story had been laid out to him, that he had made a mistake. He was contrite, but nothing could be done.

Q: But obviously it had no bad effect on Frank's career. So there you are in Zanzibar, again in charge?

Petterson: Yes. There I was, once again, in charge of the embassy. I was acting consul. By the way, we were no longer an embassy because when Zanzibar and Tanganyika joined to become Tanzania, Zanzibar no longer was the capital, so we were reverted back to consular status. I was acting consul for a larger establishment than when I was acting chargé d'affaires, when I was the only one there. I now had, in some ways, a more challenging kind of a job, certainly from a management point of view.

Before long, Washington, perhaps figuring that if once again they sent someone to be my boss again, he might get thrown out [laughter], decided to let me be consul for the rest of my tour of duty. This was done even though Frank's replacement would come out while I was still there and would be an officer who outranked me. The officer was Tom Pickering, and we worked together for the rest of my tour, which ended in November 1965.

Q: Tom Pickering, another one of the shining stars of the United States Foreign Service!

Petterson: Absolutely.

Q: Yes, you worked with both Frank Carlucci and Tom Pickering.

Petterson: Yes, I tell people that I made Tom's career.

Q: [Laughter]

Petterson: I wrote an efficiency report [laughter] on him. I hope it was a good one! He was an extraordinary guy and a lot of fun to work with. He and Alice, and Julie and I had good times in the months that we were together in Zanzibar continuing to do the kind of work that Frank and I had done. We had some new difficulties. For example, the Zanzibaris accused Harry Radday, who was the USIS officer, of being up to no good. According to the charges against him, he was seeing the wrong kind of people, plotting, doing this or that. It was total nonsense. I went to Karume, and said, in effect, "This is not true; don't do this! He is a good officer, who has done nothing wrong."

But Karume was inflexible. He said the decision had been made by the Revolutionary Council and could not be changed. Harry, who was popular among the Zanzibaris, and, because he was so tall – at least six foot five – was called "Bwana Twiga" (Mister Giraffe), had gotten around town a lot, meeting a wide range of people in the course of doing his job as our cultural affairs and information officer. I'm convinced that either a hostile intelligence service or extreme radicals in the government, or the two working together, had fabricated the reports about Harry. And they had chosen him because he was being effective in countering the anti-American propaganda that was so prevalent and was providing Zanzibaris with information about the United States and the outside world that otherwise was not available to them.

Q: So he was good at his job?

Petterson: He was good at his job.

Q: And making friends for America?

Petterson: Yes. Harry was expelled quietly, which was how Karume had proposed to handle the matter. Another USIS officer, a man named Barney Coleman, whose most recent assignment had been in Nigeria, replaced Harry. Barney eventually ran into the same problem. He was out seeing people and doing his job. Our enemies didn't like it, stories were circulated about him, nasty stories, and Karume said he had to go. Again, I remonstrated with him. Karume could be reasonable on some things, but he dug his heels in, and Barney Coleman had to go. So we didn't have complete easy sailing, to say the least. There was always some kind of battle going on.

Q: So what it sounds then, Don, a little bit sort of like Stalin, you know. Karume is a man with great strengths, but also very deep suspicions, because this makes, I think, three American diplomats who have been quietly or otherwise pushed out of Zanzibar in a year!

Petterson: That's right, and before that, of course, Fritz Picard. Karume did have definite weaknesses. He was a very suspicious man, and with reason as time went on because he had enemies within his own establishment. Some of those people came to grief later on and were executed. Othman Sharif was. He was the minister I mentioned when Fritz Picard got expelled, the one who had authorized the release of the American reporters and before the revolution had been a political enemy of Karume.

After the union of Tanganyika and Zanzibar, he became a minister in the Tanzanian government, serving in Dar es Salaam. Later, he went to Washington as ambassador. On a return trip to Zanzibar, Karume imprisoned him. Nyerere got him out, and he went back to the mainland. But later on, the government of Zanzibar accused him treason. He was brought back to the island and was executed. Abdul Kassim Hanga, the vice president of Zanzibar, was also executed, along with some others.

Q: More and more like Stalin?

Petterson: Yes, he became, unfortunately, more and more –

Q: Paranoid?

Petterson: Paranoid, erratic and dictatorial as time went on. My own relationship with him, and again, this was before he really got bad, was quite good because of the friendship we had established when I was a vice consul, and because I continued to deal with him in his own language, and, of course, treated him with a proper measure of respect.

Q: So, Don, in terms of the career Foreign Service, this is another really good argument for language training?

Petterson: Oh, absolutely.

Q: Would you say, in retrospect, that the Foreign Service should be doing more in terms of training officers in languages?

Petterson: Yes! The Foreign Service at different times placed greater emphasis on foreign language training, but in general the focus was on training as many people as possible, but not training enough in depth. Many officers, as a result, would gain a superficial working knowledge of a language, but far short of excellence. The Service did not, and still does not, have enough officers possessing a grasp of languages approaching bilinguality, especially in difficult, important languages such as Arabic, Chinese, and Japanese. We have some, but not nearly enough.

Q: So that sort of wraps up Zanzibar?

Petterson: Zanzibar, almost. Our second and third children, Julianne and John, were born while we were in Zanzibar. Julianne was born on the island in 1963 and John in Dar es Salaam in 1965. Julie had gone to the

107

mainland to have John because the hospital in Zanzibar had deteriorated so much by 1965. In September we had our first and only vacation while we were in Zanzibar. We spent four days in game parks at Ngorongoro Crater and Lake Manyara and had a wonderful time. She and the children left Zanzibar near the end of September, and I followed in November, ending my assignment in Zanzibar and turning the reins over to Tom Pickering.

Let me interject here, that if whoever reads this account would like more details on what happened in Zanzibar, I have written a book entitled *Revolution in Zanzibar* that will be published by Westview Press in April 2002.

Q: Okay, so that's then –

Petterson: The end of 1965. Julie had gone before me so she could spend several weeks with her parents and family in Mexico. After I rejoined her and the children there, we went to California. I had a lot of home leave, and we spent December in San Luis Obispo.

Q: Sixty-five.

Petterson: After New Year's Day, we went to Washington before going off on our next assignment. En route to Mexico from Zanzibar, I had stopped in Washington for consultations and to see about an assignment.

My personnel officer was Charlie Whitehouse. He didn't think much of my request to go to the Congo or Vietnam, or some such interesting place. He said, 'You know, Frank's example shows that if you stay with your neck out on the block long enough, it's going to get chopped off.'

He thought a less volatile country would be in order and that I needed a political officer job in a large embassy, since I had had a consular job in Mexico and had just come from a tiny post. He said, 'Nigeria would be a good assignment for you – Lagos, Nigeria.'

So I was assigned as the number two officer in a three-person political section in Lagos. We left Washington in

108

January 1966 and flew on a Pan Am flight to Lagos. Pan Am then had a flight from the U.S. to Africa.

As we approached the airport in Lagos, announced, 'Ladies and gentlemen, I'm sorry to tell you that there's been some trouble. The airport has been seized by army troops. The government has just been taken over by the military.'

Let me give a little background. Nigeria had been independent for a several years. Its coalition government was led by Abubakar Tafawa Balewa, a northerner and a very remarkable man. There was political friction in Nigeria, especially between the larger tribes, the Yoruba in the west, the Ibos in the south, and the Hausa-Fulani in the north. The northerners, the more numerous people in the country, were somewhat dominant. The frictions were causing unrest, and some violence had broken out.

Before I arrived in Nigeria, I knew there was some political turmoil, but I didn't know how bad it was. The embassy was not sending political officers out of town enough to comprehend the full scope of the violence that was taking place not all that far from Lagos. They really did not have a handle on the full extent of the dissension and violence."[19]

Another American diplomat who was in Tanzania during the Zanzibar revolution and when Tanganyika united with Zanzibar was Robert Gordon. He was in Tanzania from 1964 – 1965 and left after being declared *persona non grata*. As he stated years later in this interview on a number of subjects:

"Q: You left Khartoum in 1961 and then went to the War College in 1964.

Gordon: Personnel in 1961 to '63, two years. Head of European Personnel.

Q: I would like to move to your appointment as Deputy Chief of Mission, the DCM in Dar es Salaam.

109

Was it called Tanzania in those days?

Gordon: It became Tanzania while I was there.

Q: In the first place, what was the country called at the time?

Gordon: It was Tanganyika and Zanzibar. Tanganyika had been its name clear back in the 19th century. I agree with you, we're way over the time, but probably the most fascinating, important work I did was in Personnel, the three or four tours I had in it. But it's nothing, basically, for overseas.

Q: I thought we would come back to Personnel a little later.

Gordon: Fine. Anyway, I went to the War College. And like all the FSOs at the War College, we all knew that we were going to have to have new assignments at the end of the War College.

While I was at the War College, I was promoted to class two and so I became eligible for a DCM job by the criteria then existing. When Dar es Salaam came open they asked me if I was interested. I said I was, very much so, because it sounded like an interesting post. Although I had been in the Sudan and while they are both in Africa, they are quite different countries. Just like Morocco and Zambia are in Africa, but there's no comparison. And so I said I would be interested in that job and I got it. And within a month after the War College I was in Dar es Salaam as DCM.

Q: Who was the ambassador?

Gordon: It was William Leonhart.

Q: How would you describe him as an ambassador?

Gordon: He was a very hard driving man who felt that if the embassy hours were 7:30 to 2:30, but if he wasn't there until 7 o'clock at night, he felt he hadn't put in a full day. And he liked people around writing reports, and recommendations, and analyses. He was very demanding on himself and his staff and, at times, he was a difficult man to work for. He probably didn't think so.

Yet, I can remember one time later I was being inspected. And the inspector was a very senior inspector. I can't remember his name. He asked me, 'Well, how was it working for Bill Leonhart? I've understood from several sources he's a very difficult guy to work for, very demanding.' I said, 'Well, after all, I only worked for him six months.' Because I was declared *persona non grata*, I only had a six-months tour with him there.

As I say, every time anybody would take anything to him, he would have to completely rewrite it. I didn't mind that, that's the prerogative of the ambassador. But the fact that eight out of ten times he improved what I did, I didn't like that at all.

Q: What was the situation in Tanganyika at the time?

Gordon: As I say, in the spring of 1964 it had become Tanzania and had united with Zanzibar. And we had an office in Zanzibar comprised of two officers, Frank Carlucci, who has gone on to great fame since then. And the other one was a fellow by the name of Donald Petterson, who is the current ambassador to Dar es Salaam. That was a subordinate post since it was a consulate reporting through Dar es Salaam.

I arrived there in June and was out in January, and also out three weeks in the London Hospital for Tropical Diseases, so I didn't spend an awful lot of time there. I just barely got myself oriented where I started producing something when the ambassador was called in by the President who told him that Frank and I were declared *persona non grata* and we had 24 hours to get out of town. Never gave any reason or anything, which you don't have to do.

And one of my ambitions has always been to find out exactly what the reason was. We found out through a quirk that they had tapped the telephones and were listening to conversations I had with Carlucci. He would phone me or I would phone him back and forth just keeping in touch on things. And we had a long discussion a couple days before we were declared PNG. He had called me and said the Independence Day Anniversary of Zanzibar was coming up. I said yes. He said, 'I'd like to do something. Some message of some kind.'

I said, 'Don't forget it's now Tanzania. It's no longer Tanganyika and Zanzibar. It's Tanzania.' I said, 'I want to move fairly slowly on this.' I said, 'Let's wait and see what Nigeria, Ghana, Great Britain, Members of the Commonwealth, let's see what the members of the Commonwealth countries do about this type of thing, whether they are going to send a message or not. And if they do, then that will give us the ammunition we need to go back to Washington and maybe get a message out of Soapy Williams or somebody.' Now at that time we weren't aware that our lines were being tapped. Now, a few days later we were declared PNG and no reason given.

Many theories of why. One was the fact that I had used the word 'ammunition' with Frank and, theoretically, it was interpreted that Frank and I had plotted against the Government of Zanzibar behind the ambassador's back through direct contacts with CIA. Joe Palmer at that time was Director General and he sent a big rocket around to every post in the Foreign Service saying to be very, very careful when using slang. This and that could be misinterpreted and so forth. Giving credence to the fact that that was the real reason.

Well, baloney. I never had believed that. I still don't know. I can remember when I was going out as ambassador to Mauritius. I went over to CIA for the usual briefings. Frank Carlucci, at that time, was Deputy Director of CIA. I went up and had a cup of coffee with him. I said, 'Frank, now that you've got this job, find out what the hell was the reason.' He said, 'I've never been completely satisfied, either. And I can tell you there's not much here because one of the first curiosity files I poked into was that one.'

112

About two years ago, three years ago, I got a letter from Frank telling me that he had met a very high Soviet official at a reception. And this Soviet official told him that they had set us up on this and that they had fiddled with the tape of what we said and didn't say. I remember Nyerere, the President of Tanzania, said to our ambassador, 'Well, they used a word which I think is a very insulting word and they think I wouldn't know that word.' And the word was -- whatever the word was. I couldn't repeat the word now and it had no meaning to us. So that made me feel that those guys had been fiddling with the tape, too. Anyway, this may be the answer, that the Russians set us up.

Q: A disinformation campaign.

Gordon: Yes. The early days of it.

Q: What was your impression of President Nyerere?

Gordon: Of course, when we were there he was the great intellect in both the African independence movement and the movement of 'we will correct all of our ills with a well-organized socialist-directed society.' And, of course, we see that that brought him to no good. It helped ruin what agricultural base they had in the first place. I didn't have too much of an impression except I knew he was very highly thought of.

He was a great pain in the neck already to the United States. But he was somebody we had to work with and he could be very helpful because he had an enormous amount of influence with other black African leaders. He was so revered as the great father and so on, and so forth.

And I understand that he at one time was trying to be very helpful as one of the front line states in the Namibia-Angola-South African negotiations that have just come to fruition in the last months or so."[20]

Frank Carlucci, who was based in Zanzibar when the revolution took place, an event that helped to facilitate the unification of Tanganyika and Zanzibar, also recalled in an interview years later what happened during those days:

"**Q: You went from the Congo, were you assigned directly to Zanzibar?**

Carlucci: No. I came back and I was in effect Congo desk officer during the Katanga secession. Then I had a brief tour in Personnel. When Zanzibar broke – that is to say, when they expelled our consul and closed our consulate – and a few months later, I was asked to go out there.

Q: So you went to Zanzibar. You were there from when to when?

Carlucci: I arrived 1964 and I was there just about a year. So it would have been probably – I think I would have gone out in early '64 and I think I was expelled in January 1965.

Q: What had been the situation in Zanzibar that led to the previous expulsion?

Carlucci: Zanzibar had become independent in 1963. We had a consul, Fritz Picard was his name, who has since died. The Africans rose up and slaughtered the Arabs because the Arabs had been running the place. They drove a number of them right into the sea. They took over but they had a decided communist tinge. A lot of the Africans had been trained at the Patrice Lumumba University.

Q: Which is in Moscow?

Carlucci: Moscow. Now there were a couple of Arabs involved with them. Babu and Ali Sultan Issa, who had been trained in Moscow and Beijing respectively. By the way, they have since both become capitalists.

At the time, I remember shortly after I got there, the hospital was named the V.I. Lenin hospital and the stadium became the Mao Tse-tung stadium. All land was nationalized. In effect, all the Westerners were kicked out. There was a good deal of hostility toward the Americans and our consulate was shut down. Fritz Picard was marched out of the country, I think, literally at gun point.

114

A long, intensive effort began to reopen our consulate, then turned embassy.

A number of us in the State Department favored reopening the embassy as soon as possible. The upper levels of the State Department wanted us to play a secondary role to the British. The British were more cautious. They didn't want us to open and their embassy had been closed down, too. It was quite a long negotiation getting back in. Actually I went to Dar Es Salaam and worked on the issue with then Ambassador Leonhart. We struggled to try to get me over there. Eventually the Zanzibaris agreed and I went.

Q: Now what was the situation in between Zanzibar and Tanganyika at that time?

Carlucci: They were independent countries.

Q: Two independent countries.

Carlucci: Two independent countries. It was later, in fact it at least partly our design, I think it was Bill Leonhart's idea as a matter of fact, that Tanganyika swallow up Zanzibar as a way of getting rid of the communist influence in Zanzibar. And eventually that proved to work, but it took time.

Q: Well, why were we pressing to develop or resume relations with this rather small, little island nation?

Carlucci: There was a lot of the focus on it. It was being called the African Cuba. But we also had a NASA [National Aeronautics and Space Administration] tracking station in Zanzibar which NASA at least thought was quite important. When I got to Zanzibar, I concluded that it was hopeless and we would have to dismantle the tracking station.

Q: What was it that in your estimate... In the first place, how did these negotiations go with Zanzibar? What was your role, what were the contacts like?

Carlucci: Well, the contacts, there were multiple channels. Basically, sometimes using the British, sometimes working with other African countries, or

115

sometimes using Tanganyika to get in touch with the Zanzibaris. Eventually, Amani Abeid Karume, who was president, agreed that we could come back in.

Q: What was the rationality from their point of view to bring us back in?

Carlucci: I can't really answer that. I assume they didn't want to be totally isolated from the western world. Karume himself was not a communist. The government under him was basically communist and Karume was not a very sophisticated man (He was later assassinated.). He had a certain amount of goodwill toward the west. I assume that eventually he prevailed, allowing us to come back in.

One of the reasons that I think I got kicked out was that I managed to develop a good relationship with Karume. Karume spoke very little English and at one point I asked him what I could do to develop better relations with Zanzibar. He said learn Swahili, so I set to work and learned it. I was the only senior
diplomat on the island who could converse with him in Swahili and he loved that. So we had a very good relationship.

Q: Well when you arrived there in early '64, what was the situation from your perspective on the island?

Carlucci: It was pretty chaotic. People would be thrown in jail left and right. Asians sometimes literally were whipped in the streets. Mosques had been invaded and people killed. All land had been nationalized. The British club became the people's club, which was advantageous to me because tennis balls then became free and I was the only westerner left who played tennis. I found [locals] who could play with me.

There was just a lot of hostility toward the West. The Soviets and the Chinese flooded the place. There were well over a 100 Soviets attached to their embassy and the East Germans had a very significant presence. All doctors had fled except one female Asian doctor. The only doctors

116

on the island were East German.

We had a North Vietnamese embassy. We had a North Korean embassy and a very substantial Chinese communist presence, hardly matched by a very small British and American presence. I think there were three of us, a vice consul, one other officer, and a secretary or two. A very small British presence and that was it as far as the West was concerned.

Q: To me, one of enigmas is the large Chinese, at that time called Communist Chinese, presence in Africa which seemed to often have quite large missions and they were doing things, and yet I haven't heard anybody say it had any particular influence as far as getting involved. What was your impression in Zanzibar?

Carlucci: My impression was that the lead country for the Communists was East Germany. They had the most influence. They had a young, attractive ambassador, although the Soviets sent one of their most senior ambassadors. He had been ambassador to Canada. I think clearly the Soviets and the East Germans exercised more influence than the Chinese.

Q: Were the East Germans heavily into the security side as far as secret police and that sort of thing, because that seemed to be their specialty?

Carlucci: Yes, they got into that and they got into the media and the education system. They were building houses. Some of their projects turned out to be disasters. I managed to get one small aid project going. I built a school which I'm told is still functioning in Zanzibar today.

Q: With the expulsion of the Arabs, I would have thought that this would have been a disaster for the economy in Africa. Had the Arabs been sort of the merchant class and that type of thing?

Carlucci: The economy essentially was closed-tourism and some small trade. The economy spiraled down, such as it was. It wasn't a very significant economy to start with. They just planned to live on aid from the then Soviet Bloc.

Q: Did you have any problems getting the small aid project rolling?

Carlucci: Oh, yes. I had difficulty getting it accepted. Once again the President had agreed to it and he actually, as I recall, came out and dedicated the school which was fairly major event because we couldn't get anybody even to attend our Fourth of July party. One of my neighbors, a minister named Jumbe, who later became vice president, had a tendency to drink a bit and one night he came over to my house. No sooner did he come in than the police arrived and essentially told him to get out.

We were pretty much isolated. We were socially ostracized. Virtually every Sunday there would be a demonstration against me. I would get my tear gas [mask] and my beer and I'd go to the embassy and watch the demonstrators. They would go around the block about three or four times to exaggerate the numbers. Sometimes I'd go down and mix with them as they were getting ready to demonstrate.

Q: Was there any focus or was there just...?

Carlucci: Anti-American. It got serious when the Belgians sent paratroopers into Stanleyville.

Q: This is Dragon Rouge?

Carlucci: Yes. That's the one time the demonstration got quite serious. By then we had had some Tanganyika police on the island. They managed to keep the demonstrators from breaking into the embassy. I guess it was then a consulate general because technically we had merged with Tanganyika. That demonstration by the way was led by the chief of protocol.

Q: How did this...Let's talk first about the NASA station. It was a space monitoring station was it? Had it been running during the time that we had no relations with the country?

Carlucci: No, I think it had been shut down temporarily. There were some NASA people-I'm not even sure if the NASA people stayed, they may have been evacuated. It was essentially dormant when I got there. To get back to the aura of your question, the only reason Zanzibar was important was U.S. domestic politics. I can remember before I left, Averell Harriman, who was Under Secretary of State, called me in and gave me essentially two instructions; get the NASA tracking station back in operation and to make sure that Zanzibar was not a political embarrassment to President Johnson during the campaign. Those were two difficult tasks.

Q: Was Zanzibar at all on the political map? Did you have correspondence coming in?

Carlucci: Oh, yes. There was quite a bit of press about the 'African Cuba.' It had become, I don't want to say it was a major story, but it had become at least a significant story in the U.S. press.

Q: Were you able to do anything about that or...?

Carlucci: Well, there was eventually, as I said, we merged with Tanganyika and the situation moderated, but that was over a period of time. During the first year, it was pretty chaotic. We didn't manage to score any major victory, I guess I'd have to say although it was clear that our influence was increasing as time wore on. To the extent that our influence increased, the Soviets and Chinese influence decreased and I was warned that they were going to try and get me.

Q: Was there a Soviet fleet presence there? If I recall, about this time, this was not too long after the Cuban Missile Crisis which was '62 and the Soviets really didn't have a very major fleet.

Carlucci: No, there was no Soviet fleet there.

Q: I mean it was really in the '70s when the Blue Seas Navy was developed.

Carlucci: No, it was really a civilian presence but they would spread scare stories. I can remember one time being called off the tennis court by the President of the country who said to me, 'There's an American submarine surfacing in our waters. Get it out of here.' Of course there was no American submarine.

Q: How would you conduct...What would a day's work be there for you when you say you were pretty well quarantined against most contacts?

Carlucci: The ministers would receive me in their offices and I had pretty good access to the President. When I asked to call on the President, invariably they would agree and I used to have some fairly good and lengthy conversations with him. Essentially, my time was spent providing political analysis, observing what was going on, establishing as many contacts as I could, talking to my colleagues in the British embassy, talking to the Israeli consul general, seeing what they had found.

I also had some contact with the Soviets. The Soviet ambassador became quite friendly. I remember he brought my daughter one of those Soviet dolls. And I spent a fair amount of time, at least in the early portion of my stay, learning Swahili.

Q: When you were having these conversations with the President, what were the subjects?

Carlucci: Trying to reassure him of our desire for a mutually beneficial relationship and to convince him that a lot of the stories that he'd been reading about us were not accurate. I talked to him about ways in we could help Zanzibar, working with him on the school project. Essentially, trying to regain their confidence because there were a lot of misleading and inaccurate stories that had been spread about the United States.

Q: What about relations with Tanganyika? Did you go over there fairly frequently?

Carlucci: Yes, I did. I never looked forward to the trip because the only way of getting over was a 1930, I think it was a '30s DeHavilland aircraft, which could hold about four or five people. The pilot, I remember, would pull out

120

his novel the minute the wheels got off the ground, which was always a bit disconcerting.

Q: We're talking today, the 30th of June and on the 26th of June, Ambassador (William) Leonhart died. Unfortunately, I never interviewed him.

What was your impression of his support and how he ran his embassy?

Carlucci: His support as far as I was concerned was absolutely outstanding. He and I had an extremely good relationship. Bill Leonhart was a brilliant man. I'd have to describe him an intense man, a workaholic who spent hours and hours and hours in the embassy. No cable left his embassy unless it was perfect. He worked it over. I think he ran a really tight embassy. But he was always receptive to ideas from me and would take them and make them better if they were good ideas. He'd come up with a lot of ideas himself. I had such high regard for him, that when I later became deputy director of the CIA, I brought him over to the CIA and put him on a review panel for our analytical shop.

Q: Did you play any part, or our embassy in Tanganyika play any part, in this merger of Zanzibar and Tanganyika into Tanzania?

Carlucci: The answer to that is yes. I'm not sure exactly how Bill Leonhart did it, but clearly he played a significant role in it. Whether he convinced Julius Nyerere on a one to one basis or whether there were other channels that were used, I can't say because I was not party to those conversations. But I knew that Bill broached the idea to me long before it happened so there's something that was germinating at least through our embassy in Tanganyika.

Q: What were you reporting from the Zanzibar side as far as you saw through receptivity of the people on Zanzibar to this greater merger?

Carlucci: I think it was a mixed bag. The Communists were not favorable to it. They saw it as loss of authority for them. Karume was very much in favor of it. I think it was seen as a threat by the Revolutionary Council. Those were the days where African unity was very important. You could not argue with the idea of African unity. It was a hard concept for them to argue against.

Q: As far as being in Zanzibar itself, was this a subject you could raise at all or was this something that almost better if you didn't raise this?

Carlucci: I can't recall whether I actually raised it. If I did, the only one that I could have talked to about it would have been the President. Certainly none of the Communist ministers had any kind of dialogue with me on that subject.

Q: What about the Soviets and the Chinese? Were they involved in this trying to stop this thing or were they...?

Carlucci: Not overtly. What they did behind the scenes I can't say. Clearly they were involved in getting me and Bob Gordon expelled.

Q: Bob Gordon was your...?

Carlucci: He was the DCM in Dar Es Salaam.

Q: The DCM, okay. Did you find that the East Germans, for example, were following you or harassing you or anything like that?

Carlucci: No. To the best of my knowledge nobody followed me or harassed me. The East Germans and I never talked because we didn't have relations. We would frequently be standing near each other in ceremonies. Everybody would gush all over him and ignore me.

Q: It must have been a little awkward on a small island with the diplomatic corps. You had the East Germans that we didn't recognize, the Vietnamese who we didn't recognize and the North Koreans that we didn't recognize?

Carlucci: The only people at ceremonies I could talk to were the Brit, the Israeli, and the Soviet. I'd have to listen to all the diatribes. In one of the more humorous incidents, I decided to visit the neighboring island of

Pemba, which was being run by a Commissar, named Ali Sultan Issa, a man who was trained in Beijing. He was so indoctrinated that he insisted we even share the same bed. 'This is the way we do it in the People's democracy.'

He took me around the island with people chanting and singing since it was in the 'workers paradise.' Then he had a rally and meeting and I could see during the rally, this was in the early stages of my stay, that he would point at me and the crowd would applaud and yell and scream. So I asked someone what he was saying and he told me he was saying, 'There's the enemy. Why don't you applaud or don't you think we ought to throw the Americans out?' Right then and there, I decided that learning Swahili was essential.

Q: I would have thought that you would have been up against all these groups and you being sort of the butt of their attacks and speeches and all that at any ceremony you went to, you could almost stand up with a target painted on you or something like this. You must have had to make the decision, do I just stand here and smile or keep a stern face or what do you do?

Carlucci: Just smile and roll with the punches. There was one other African that I could talk to. He was the Chairman of the Afro-Shirazi party, Thabit Kombo, who was probably in his 70s or 80s at the time, and was such a revered figure in Zanzibar that he could talk to me without fear of retaliation. He and the President were essentially the only two that I could talk to.

Q: Turning again to the NASA station, they opened it up, reopened it while you were there?

Carlucci: No. Well I can't recall, to be honest with you, whether it was open for a brief period or not. I doubt it. We had to negotiate its removal and of course we stalled for time. Time was an issue because the government was demanding that we remove it within a matter of weeks and NASA said that just couldn't be done. It was very valuable equipment, which they wanted to get out. So I spent a lot of time trying to negotiate a reasonable period for dismantling the station.

Q: Was there any feeling about NASA one way or the other?

Carlucci: Of course, the communists had thoroughly planted the idea that this was a spy station; it was all run by the CIA and so the situation was almost hopeless. Everybody believed that it was a spy station.

Q: What about the Soviets, because if I recall, although space flight was in its early stages in those days, yet we had made offers that if the Soviets had a space problem they could use our space facilities and vice versa. Did they play any part in it?

Carlucci: I'd have to assume that the Soviets were behind the campaign to force us to remove our tracking station. That the attacks came from the communists, there is no question.

Q: How about the press. Is there anything to report on the press?

Carlucci: It was entirely government controlled. Anything the government wanted they'd give to the press. There was no free press. The only way that I could know about the real world was through tuning in VOA [Voice of America] on my radio.

Q: Did you notice any difference when Zanzibar and Tanganyika became Tanzania? You were there during the initial stages of the amalgamation?

Carlucci: Yes. I went from being chargé to being consul general.

Q: Did you notice how the amalgamation was working at that point?

Carlucci: Well, very slowly. We virtually couldn't feel any effects in Zanzibar, other than as I mentioned earlier we finally negotiated getting some Tanganyika policemen into Zanzibar. This was the first tangible presence. The island was very unwilling to give up its de facto independence.

Q: Could you do a little compare and contrast between the way things were run in Zanzibar while you were there and what you'd seen in the former Belgian Congo?

Carlucci: Well, there was a certain similarity obviously. There was initial hostility toward the west but in the case of the Congo, there had not been the kind of thorough Communist penetration that you'd had in Zanzibar. The Congolese didn't know what communism was, although some of our politicians, particularly Senator Dodd, called them Communists – Senator Tom Dodd, not Chris Dodd, the son.

The Zanzibaris, a lot of them, had been to school in Moscow or in Beijing. They were much more sophisticated in their approach. Both situations were chaotic of course. I suppose the Congo might have been slightly more dangerous. We regarded Zanzibar as not particularly dangerous, although some people were killed. Of course during the revolution, a great number were killed.

Q: The similarity is the extreme nationalism and the anti-western overtones.

Carlucci: They were more explicit in Zanzibar than they were in the Congo. Zanzibar at least had a resolution. The Congo has never found its resolution.

Q: You were seeing the products of the Soviet training of Communists. Did you find that the people coming out of then named Lumumba University in the Soviet Union were pretty fairly indoctrinated?

Carlucci: Oh, yes. The big thing was the young pioneers, which was East Germany. I can remember large numbers of Zanzibaris being taken to East Germany and coming back as young pioneers in uniforms. Indoctrination was pretty thorough. Lumumba University hadn't really been established when I was in the Congo. By the time I got to Zanzibar, it was in full swing and there were large numbers of Zanzibaris, way out of

125

proportion to their population, going to places like East Germany and Moscow and Beijing to study.

Q: Did you find any, were there any, Tanganyikan officials starting to drift over that you could talk to?

Carlucci: No. Not outside of the police. Even then I didn't have much contact. There was a Zanzibari police chief that I could talk to. He was not totally hostile to the West, but he was subsequently removed. While I was there, you could not feel much Tanganyikan presence.

Q: How did you expulsion come about?

Carlucci: Bob Gordon and I were having a phone conversation. This is about January of '65. We were discussing a message of congratulations on the second anniversary of the revolution. We did something very foolish.

Q: Where were you calling from?

Carlucci: I was in Zanzibar. And Bob Gordon was the DCM in Dar Es Salaam, Bill Leonhart's deputy. We started to double talk, which you should never do; it's easily decipherable. We started talking about the anniversary of the revolution and shouldn't we send a message, meaning a message of congratulations. Bob said, "Well, they are very reluctant in Washington and you will need more ammunition" meaning a stronger argument to make our case. I said, "I want to come over and discuss this." I flew over and I was at the home of Jack Mower, one of our embassy officials. He had the radio on and the radio announced that Bob Gordon and I had been expelled.

Bill Leonhart went to Nyerere and said, 'What's this all about?'

Nyerere said, 'We have a tape of this conversation.' And when Nyerere described it, it was obvious the tape had been doctored in some way to make it appear that we were plotting to overthrow the government of Zanzibar.

I went to see Karume, who even under those circumstances received me. He said this was wrong and should not happen. It was the Tanzanian government now that had expelled me, not the Zanzibar government. He said he'd call Nyerere, but there was nothing much more he could do. There seemed to be no alternative, so I left. A number of years later, I was at a reception at the State Department. A big Russian came up and almost swept me off my feet and said, 'Don't you remember me?'

I said, 'I'm not sure.'

He said, 'Well, I'm so and so. I was the Tass correspondent in Zanzibar when you were there.'

I said, 'Then maybe you can satisfy my curiosity. Who was it that plotted my expulsion and doctored the tape. Was it you Soviets or the East Germans?'

He said, 'Oh, we were all in it together.'

Q: It's interesting though that Nyerere got into this because he certainly must have...

Carlucci: Well, apparently somebody took the tape to the cabinet and played it for the entire cabinet. Of course the more radical members of the cabinet, insisted that we be expelled. What position Nyerere took in that cabinet meeting I don't know to this day. Don Peterson, who was my vice consul, later became ambassador to Tanzania. He told me that he had a conversation with Nyerere, this is years later, and Nyerere said they had made a mistake and that I was welcome to come back. But I don't know what transpired in that Cabinet meeting. I thought my career was at an end that day."[21]

After the two American diplomats – Frank Carlucci and Robert Gordon – were expelled from Tanzania, relations between the two countries soured and Nyerere himself once publicly addressed the subject.

Although Nyerere had profound philosophical and ideological differences with the United States, American diplomats in Tanzania did not question his integrity and commitment to his people and to the causes he espoused and acknowledged he was a man of deep intellect.

In addition to the interviews with American diplomats

reproduced in the main text, interviews with others – American diplomats as well – constitute Appendix XII of this work. Presented below is a sample of the views of some American ambassadors –Democratic and Republican – about President Nyerere.

Deputy American ambassador Robert Hennemeyer who was in Tanganyika, later Tanzania, from 1961 – 1964 described President Nyerere as "a great political theorist,...a charismatic figure,...a great leader of his people. I don't believe for a moment that he meant anything but to do the best he could for the wellbeing of his people....He had an enormous amount of influence with other black African leaders. He was so revered as the great father.... Clearly he was a world leader, not just an African leader."[22]

Ambassador Claude G. Ross described Nyerere as a leader who was "full of good intentions and the epitome of integrity."

In the words of Ambassador John W. Shirley:

"I enjoyed the fact that during my tenure in Dar es Salaam Julius Nyerere was still President of Tanzania. I found him an interesting and extremely intelligent man. And since South Africa was in turmoil at the time, and because Nyerere was, to say the least, not particularly sympathetic to the policy of constructive engagement, my meetings with him were frequent, animated, sometimes sharp, but never acrimonious. It was as intellectually stimulating to deal with him, as it was to deal with Prime Minister Salim Salim." – (Ambassador John William Shirley, Appendix XII).

. Ambassador W. Beverly Carter described Nyerere in the following terms:

"Julius Nyerere was...one of the early heroes, political heroes, of mine and of many other Africanists....(He) was an extremely popular person....(Other African) countries tended to look to Tanzania for leadership, and Nyerere was never hesitant about offering it and giving it and doing it well..He is probably one of the most principled men I ever met in my life....

I talked earlier about my Government's ambivalence about Tanzania....Nyerere should have been treated more like the world leader that he is and that everyone recognized him to be....Just unheard of for a man of his... Nyerere's worldwide leadership being treated, I felt, as, not as well as other people who didn't come nearly up to his size. It's sort of symptomatic of the problem I had in dealing with my own Government....

You didn't think of (President) Tolbert (of Liberia) as being ... a Kenneth Kaunda or Julius Nyerere. He didn't have that capability, was not an intellectual giant. He did not even have quite the quality that Botswana's Seretse Khama had, who was not a giant intellectually the way I think Nkrumah was or Nyerere is.....With Nyerere it was the kind of relationship that you have in a dormitory at night when you're engaging in a good debate (laughs)." – (W. Beverly Carter, Appendix XII).

Ambassador James W. Spain described Nyerere this way:

"Nyerere's rule was relatively benign. I am quite sure he never ordered anybody killed. There were a few people in jail but not many. Some were from Zanzibar, under sentence of death there but kept alive on the mainland....People didn't get killed. They might get relocated under the ujamaa system of farming, but Nyerere never even thought of 'liquidating the kulaks'....

Nyerere's great aim was to bring education and medical facilities to his people. That was pretty hard to do when they were scattered like that. So he set up the idea of ujamaa, the family village....and Nyerere did bring educational and medical facilities to the villages, far better than those in rural Kenya.... He was a hopeless socialist. Still, he was clearly a very sincere and humane man.

If I did anything useful, it was to convince Washington that Nyerere was not a brutal African dictator and a Communist stooge....

I found Nyerere fascinating. He had an MA from Edinburgh University and loved word play. I never read a book that he hadn't read. He translated Shakespeare into Kiswahili....I am very fond of Julius Nyerere....

Most Western development aid to Tanzania came from Scandinavia, particularly the Swedes. They liked the intellectual socialist, the benign father of his people who didn't kill or imprison people, while trying to create a new way of life with better prospects. The fact that it all didn't work very well didn't bother them....

For one thing, unlike other parts of Africa, no one was starving or dying of uncontrolled disease in Tanzania. For another, despite Nyerere's close identification with radical socialist theory, I don't think he cared much about economics. He was basically a humanist with a keen sense of both tribal traditions and modern politics, a social science type....

The fact was that Nyerere certainly wasn't on our side, but he wasn't a tool of the Chinese or the Russians either....

(On Uganda)...Nyerere replaced Amin with Milton Obote, a previous Ugandan prime minister who had been in exile in Tanzania for some years. He ran the grocery store (in Dar es Salaam)where we bought our food supplies. He was another intellectual socialist but without Nyerere's charm, humanity, or intelligence.

I was personally very fond of Nyerere--not necessarily a good thing for a diplomat. He was a very remarkable man and, I think, a very constructive element in the peaceful solutions to the problems of Southern Africa that eventually emerged." – (Ambassador James W. Spain, Appenx XII).

130

Ambassador Richard N. Viets said the following about Nyerere:

"At that time in mid-1979, the so-called front-line states in Southern Africa, I think there were five of them...the organization was chaired by Julius Nyerere, the President of Tanzania, a very remarkable gentleman. Nyerere really towered over the other four heads of state and this organization in many respects was a one-man operation. Because of his long association with the independence movements in East Africa and throughout Southern Africa he was highly respected.

Nyerere is an intellectual of very considerable dimensions, an extraordinarily articulate person. So the leadership of this group was essentially his without any challenge. He was offering almost daily advise to the Zimbabwean leadership on tactics, strategy, etc. in their negotiations with the British and the Americans and the others involved....

I decided I needed to know more about Julius Nyerere than anybody else on the face of the earth.... He is a very shrewd man.

He was...a most remarkable figure in contemporary African political history. I always said, and others who knew him well I think shared this view, that if Nyerere had been born in Western Europe or the Far East or even in North America, he would have been an exceptional figure in public life. He was a superb politician.

He had an acute brain, the memory of an elephant, intellectual horsepower that was second to none.

He was cunning. He could be warm-hearted one moment and cut you off at the legs at the next if it met his political or personal needs. He had, of course, been the principal political figure behind the Tanzanian independence movement in the 1950s....

Nyerere... remains as far as I know the principal

translator of Shakespeare from English into Swahili and one of the most gifted orators I have ever heard in English, and a marvelous drafter of the English language....

I can remember listening to him rail hour after hour against the IMF and the prescriptions the IMF was demanding of Tanzania that he argued would send it further into poverty, etc....

Nyerere regime's record is...in the human rights arena when one is talking about imprisonment and torture, or loaded legal shenanigans against opposition, I think his record is remarkably good. If human rights includes the right to a job, an education, hospitalization, etc., then you have to give him pretty good marks." – (Ambassador Richard N. Viets, Appendix XII).

Ambassador David C. Miller, a staunch Republican, said the following about Nyerere:

"He was on his way to the Cancun summit, the only head of government from Africa among the 13 presidents at Cancun. He was the leader of the frontline states in the negotiations over Resolution 435, which was the Namibian independence resolution passed by the UN. In terms of national power at home, he was at quite a peak. Physically, he was old enough to be wise and young enough to be vigorous. He was a great guy to work with....

Nyerere had been a world leader of the non-aligned movement for a long time. His economic policies were well-known and the impact of his economic policies had been apparent for some period of time. In a nutshell, on the domestic front, Tanzania had succeeded in integrating itself as a political entity. At independence, there was Zanzibar and there was Tanganyika.

But there was also Julius Nyerere's belief that it was important for every citizen of Tanzania to move forward roughly together economically and to integrate themselves socially and that over a period of time his approach to the economic management of Tanzania would produce a more coherent, unified country than, as he was fond of pointing out, Kenya, his nextdoor neighbor, which was our favorite country. So, domestically, he had succeeded with a single party approach to governing Tanzania and thought that that had worked well for him...

Wonderful, warm, friendly, smart, honest, brave, humble. He was as great a head of government as Africa has seen as evidenced not by his ability to do the little day-to-day things of running a country but on the big accounts, the most important being his lifestyle, which remained humble throughout his whole time as head of government. Most remarkable, was his retirement from the presidency at a time when he was perfectly capable of going on physically.

Then, of course, he returned to his village upcountry as one of the few heads of government in Africa who behaved the way George Washington behaved here and said, 'We do not need presidents for life in Africa and I don't intend to be one.'

Frankly, he was probably happiest when he was back home in Butiama with his wife and grandchildren in a very humble home. It was hard to get to by vehicle. So, for me, he stands out in stark relief to the failed public leadership in Africa that can be found in almost every country....

Julius Nyerere because of his global leadership – and this is the thing that you have to remember: nobody in their right mind today can tell you who was president of Burundi or Rwanda 20 years ago – Julius was an international author, an international statesman, and used that effectively as a head of government to gain support for Tanzania well beyond either its objective importance or its internal economic performance. To a great degree, that's what a head of government in a developing country ought to be trying to achieve. Julius achieved that.

So, did the economy ever work perfectly? No. Did it achieve what he wanted? Yes, it did. It produced a level economic base that is now producing a solid Tanzanian economy without the disasters that befell Kenya. If Julius were here today sitting with us, he would say, 'I told you, David. Kenya turned into a corrupt mud hole. Tanzania is now slowly taking off the ground with responsible leadership in a country that's socially unified.' I'm happy to make that argument for him....

It was an outstanding diplomatic world simply because of Nyerere's presence and who he was and the importance of having Julius' support when he was head of the Non-Aligned Movement, of having Julius' support when he was running the Frontline States. When Julius Nyerere spoke or traveled, people listened to him. So, countries that were playing in that environment wanted to have a good mission in Dar es Salaam....

He had a position on the world.... He was first and foremost an intellectual and an ideologue.... Julius Nyerere was an intellect. He wanted to talk to people about his ideas and what worked and didn't work." – (Ambassador David Charles Miller, Appendix XII).

John H. Burns who served as the American ambassador to Tanzania from January 1966 to June 1969, not long after the Zanzibar revolution and the unification of Tanganyika and Zanzibar, had this to say in interview about Tanzania and Nyerere:

"Tanzania...had a highly intelligent and cultivated president, Julius Nyerere...
Q: Why did you want to go to Tanzania?
Burns: It was a very interesting time in East Africa. Tanzania had been independent only a few years and had recently experienced the much publicized revolution in Zanzibar--from which emerged the name Tanzania following the union of Tanganyika and Zanzibar. The country had a President, the remarkable Julius Nyerere, unique—then and ever since--in Africa.

The time in the CAR (Central African Republic) had stimulated in me a real interest in Africa; and then, from a personal point of view, I loved that out of doors life and Tanzania offered the best, Mt. Kilimanjaro, the Serengeti, the Selous and all. It is not that I am a hunter but I am a dedicated camper, animal watcher and all that.

Q: When you went out to Tanzania did you have any sort of brief? What were American interests and what were you doing?

Burns: Here I will say something that I have never recorded before. But that does not matter as no one would be interested this many years later. It harks back, perhaps, to Bill Blocker's telling me that if I followed the Foreign Service Regulations to the letter I would be a poor officer. Maybe I harked back to that counsel more often than I should have during my Service years but if so I have no regrets.

Tanzania placed a limit on the number of its own nationals each Embassy could have accredited. It was 14 or 15, as I recall, and applied to every country except the United Kingdom, which had, of course, many British citizens seconded at various functions throughout the Tanzanian government. During the briefings in Washington, before leaving for Dar es Salaam, both the CIA and the Department of Defense made it very clear to me that increasing the number of their personnel there (CIA) and opening an attaché's office (Defense), were, in their own words, 'their top priorities in Africa.'

I assured them that I would do my best but my fingers were mentally crossed. The Department never gave me actual specific instructions to present formal arguments for the removal of the American personnel limitation but it was clear that that was favored by most everyone.

I look on my three and one half years as what I might term the most 'singing' assignment of my entire career. And that was directly attributable to there being such a small staff.

We had one officer for each function: one political officer, one economic, one administrative, one consular (who also worked for CIA, as did the code clerk).

No one had to look for anything to do and we had little time for things like staff meetings; we'd have one every two weeks or so.

I have always thought meetings, generally, a terrible waste of time. I have also always thought that the more time officers spend out of the office the better and the staff at Dar, especially the Swahili speakers, did a lot of traveling around the country, as I did myself.

We had an old 4-wheel drive Land Rover and it was on the road most of the time. Not only did this add to the substance—and I might say validity--of our reporting, it was a practice extremely well received by the Tanzanian government. Because of our mandatorily limited staff, the Department was careful to send out the best qualified individuals. For instance Tom Pickering was DCM, followed by Jack Matlock.

Q: Both Ambassadors to the Soviet Union later on.

Burns: Yes. George Roberts was a witty, brilliant political officer and Earl Belinger the quietest, most efficient administrative officer I ever had the pleasure to work with. Roberts spoke fluent Swahili as did Pickering and Matlock. President Nyerere once said to me, 'Your Mr. Pickering speaks better Swahili than half the members of my parliament,' which was true.

The result of all that was an operation of which I was immensely proud and, as I have noted, the most satisfying assignment of my entire career.

Before leaving I had a long, sort of retrospective, conversation with President Nyerere, sitting on the terrace of Government House, just harking back, with many laughs (President Nyerere had a fine sense of humor) over events of the three and one half years.

Just before leaving I said to him, 'Mr. President, there is one thing I'd like to say. As long as I have been here I have

136

been urged by my government to try to persuade you to raise, or remove, the limitation on the number of Americans who can be assigned to this Embassy. As you know, I have never mentioned the subject to you and if I can bespeak anything in behalf of my successor, whoever that might be, it is that you never raise it.'

Laughing, he said, 'Of course I won't. What country could have an interest in little Tanzania to justify the diplomatic presence here of more than fifteen persons?'

And, of course, he was exactly right.

I recall a book written by Ambassador Ellis O. Briggs, who held, I believe, seven different missions, in which he said that the most efficient, and effective, of all seven had been Prague because the Czech government limited the number of Americans who could be stationed there.

Were I asked what single action would most improve everything about the Foreign Service I would without hesitation say, 'Reduce all staffs by a minimum of 25%.' Of course the chance of anything like that happening, or even winning measurable support, is about the same as that of Death Valley experiencing a snowstorm.

Q: Well, could we talk about, during the '65 to '69 period that you were there what the situation was in Tanzania?

Burns: There were no real political problems. Nyerere had essentially no political opposition. When, years later, he finally left the presidency he did so entirely voluntarily. His problems were economic.

Tanzania is a miserably poor country, with no basis for hope of much change in the situation. Nyerere, realizing that, consistently worked to lower public expectations--which naturally soared after independence--or even hope of rapid economic advancement and stressed, rather, the importance of work and efforts to improve agricultural production and housing, simple advancements in living standards.

Although he attracted an immense amount of foreign

137

aid, there was something about the idea of aid that was alien to him and he was anything but a petitioner. He, himself, lived very simply and he insisted that members of his government do likewise. There were no Mercedes limousines assigned to his ministers--or to himself. He resided in his own house, not a Government House, the old British palace, and it was by no means as grand as the average embassy residence.

He not only established diplomatic relations with communist China but paid a visit there. This agitated Washington tremendously, much more so than it did the British, Tanzania's erstwhile 'principal.'

I was frequently instructed to protest this or that action of Tanzania, which Washington found insufficiently 'pro-West' and, of course, there was the constant run of pressure about Tanzanian votes in the UN. I found this difficult when dealing with a man as innately sophisticated as Nyerere.

Once he laughingly said to me, 'Mr. Ambassador, we can't let our friends choose our enemies for us.'

He never showed the slightest resentment when, to tell the truth, he often had reason to do so.

Q: What was your impression of Nyerere during this period?

Burns: I have rarely known anyone more dedicated to what he saw as his purpose in life. I once said that the song 'The Impossible Dream' could have been written for him.

He was a remarkably educated and cultured man, a graduate of the University of Edinburgh. One of his hobbies was translating Shakespeare into Swahili and one or two of them --Julius Caesar was one--were performed at the University of Dar es Salaam, an institution in which Nyerere, not surprisingly, took great interest.

His problems were, as I have said, economic and they were beyond his solution. I wonder if they, and the economic problems of Africa as a whole, do not defy solution.

It was frustrating to try to bring Washington to understand Nyerere. The first African chief of state invited to Washington by the Johnson administration was Colonel Mobutu of Zaire, who cooperated--one might almost say slavishly--with the United States in return for which he received untold millions in military and economic 'aid.' He is today one of the world's wealthiest men.

Incidentally, the week before he arrived in Washington on a state visit, he publicly executed several of his political opponents.

We could never even arrange to have Nyerere received on a personal call at the White House, when he went to the United States to address, at their invitation, the Council on Foreign Relations. This was all because he had established diplomatic relations with communist China.

Q: Did you find that he was open to you when you came there?

Burns: Completely. Originally I had feared that he might be tempted to refuse agrément to one coming direct from the office of the Supreme Commander Allied Powers Europe, and that at least that might inhibit our relationship. Not at all. He is a much bigger man than that. And, as I have noted, he was blessed with a most engaging sense of humor.

Q: Was he going through the, I don't know what the term was, but it was the creation of all those small village communes. I heard some remarks to the effect that this really broke up what was a viable agricultural system and did not help.

Burns: I don't believe that would be a fair contention in that, in my opinion, there was not a viable agricultural system to begin with. The country had not altogether emerged—if that is the proper word--from tribalism and the program called 'Ujamaa,' a sort of communal village scheme, was something of an expansion of the tribal arrangement based on an organized plan. I don't know how

139

it turned out but I never believed it would work, anymore than planned economies have ever worked in any country. I don't think our own governmental farm programs really "work", however much they may benefit certain segments of our agricultural economy.

Q: This brings up an interesting situation. Nyerere was being accused of being too much of a devotee of the British Fabian Socialists and...

Burns: I have never known how Fabian socialism differs from plain socialism. I do know that Nyerere believed in socialism for Tanzania, a country with no capital foundation, other than land and that not very productive.

I believe that he thought that the introduction of large amounts of foreign capital into Tanzania would be simply a reversion to another form of colonialism.

His idea was to discourage great economic expectation among his people while endeavoring to raise the simple standards of their day-to-day lives, through work and education. For instance, during the years that I was in Tanzania there was no television; none at all. It was Nyerere's view that 1) they could not afford television in the first place, 2) it would keep people from the work they should be doing and 3) it would promote discontent by acquainting the mass of Tanzanians with a way of life they could not hope to equal, at least not any time soon.

As I said, Nyerere had an 'impossible dream.' One interesting sidelight of the no television situation was that almost every officer of the Embassy requested an extension of duty at that so-called 'hardship post.' They all had several children of school age--one had seven--and they found a life with no television to have many advantages; not to say that that was the only consideration affecting their desire for longer duty. There were many agreeable features about life in Dar es Salaam.

Q: Were you able to contribute anything to the educational thing through exchanges or...

Burns: Not to any great degree, no. We couldn't attract much attention from Washington for Nyerere. He was regarded by certain influential circles of the Johnson administration as a dangerous thinker. Despite the best efforts of Bill Leonhart, my predecessor, myself and Tony Ross, my successor, we could never persuade any of that particular group otherwise.

Q: You were there during some of the major periods of the civil rights movement in the United States. How did that play or not play, or was it...

Burns: It was of course of a certain amount of interest, mostly limited to university circles, journalists, etc. Nyerere, who, as I have said, was a sophisticated thinker, was very--but quietly--interested. He was deeply disturbed by Robert Kennedy's assassination. Kennedy had visited Tanzania about a year earlier, a visit which even anti-American elements of the Tanzanian press called 'a triumph.' Nyerere was deeply pleased by Kennedy's coming to Tanzania (it was Kennedy's own proposal) after his trip to South Africa and grieved--and I might say embittered--by his murder.

Q: Kennedy was assassinated about June of 1968, I believe.

Burns: Around that time. A few months later Robert Kennedy, Jr. came out to East Africa with Lemoyne Billings, who had been probably John Kennedy's closest friend, and stayed a few days with me at Dar es Salaam. Nyerere was very gracious to him, receiving him in his office, talking seriously with him about wildlife preservation etc. and posing for pictures with him. Of course Nyerere was a gracious man by nature.

Q: Did you deal with Robert Kennedy when he came? How did that go?

Burns: It went as perfectly as anything like that can go. He and Mrs. Kennedy, as well as others accompanying him, stayed with me and of all the official visits with which I was involved over thirty years--and there were

141

many--none equaled this one for its positive effect so far as US interests were concerned. Senator and Mrs. Kennedy charmed everyone and displayed sincere interest in everyone they met and everything they saw.

Q: Well, was there any problems...was Zanzibar pretty well in Tanzania at that time?

Burns: Zanzibar was legally a part of Tanzania but day-to-day governmental operations and politics were handled exclusively by a group headed by Sheik Karume, on Zanzibar. Karume held the title of First Vice President of Tanzania but his role on the mainland (where I do not recall his appearing while I was there) was essentially non-existent, as was Nyerere's on the island.

Nyerere early made it clear, in so many words, that he did not want the Embassy bothering his administration about questions concerning Zanzibar. It might be interesting to note that three successive Consuls at Zanzibar were Frank Carlucci, who later became Secretary of Defense, Tom Pickering, who went on to six subsequent embassies including the UN and Russia, and Jack Matlock, who also held several embassies, including the Soviet Union.

So Zanzibar, a post which was later closed, helped spawn three highly successful careers.

Zanzibar was regarded by Washington as a fermenting problem when Tom Pickering arrived. Carlucci had been 'PNGed' not long before. Within a short time Zanzibar disappeared from the 'pending problems' lists in Washington offices and from the agenda of 'meetings.'

I don't know how familiar you are with Tom Pickering's career but that has happened wherever he has gone. For instance when he was moved from Nigeria to El Salvador--with Secretary Shultz saying, 'We are sending our best,' the 'media' was reporting explosive stories on a daily basis from that country. Within a month El Salvador had disappeared from the US headlines, or even the front pages. For some reason or other this has happened

142

wherever Pickering has gone. Some officers have a talent--
if not actually the intention--of calling attention to their
activities. Tom Pickering is the exact opposite."[23]

After John Burns left Tanzania in 1969, he was
replaced by Claude Ross who served as the American
ambassador from from December 1969 to June 1972.
When Ross arrived there, the union of Tanganyika and
Zanzibar was still in its infancy but stable. As he stated
years later in an interview about his service in Tanzania
and on a number of subjects including Nyerere and the
country as a whole:

"**Ross:** I got a call from John Burns, who had just left
Tanzania and was now Director General, asking me if I
would go to Tanzania.
Q: That was the second time he'd called.
Ross: Yes. I must say in all fairness, I wasn't that keen
about it. I had rather hoped at that stage to go to another
Latin American assignment at a larger embassy. As it
turned out, there was one in the works that I didn't know
about until I got back to Washington.
I got there to sit on a selection board in August or
September of 1969, and the ARA executive director,
Findley Burns, said, 'You know, Secretary Meyer wants to
send you to Venezuela. Would you have any objection? I
said, 'No. I told John I would go to Tanzania, but sure, if
Meyer wants me to go to Venezuela, of course.' It's a class-
one embassy. Maurice Bernbaum had come out sometime
earlier. He'd come out through Haiti, and I'd seen him. I
didn't know anything about this until Findley Burns tried it
out on me.
Anyway, they sent the Under Secretary, to the White
House, to see if they could undo what had been done
regarding Tanzania and put me in for Venezuela.
Q: I think it was probably Elliot Richardson.
Ross: It might very well have been. Maybe it was

143

Elliot. Anyway, no go. Over there they said, 'No, we've already processed it for Tanzania, so that's where he's going to go.' So that's where I went.

Q: That was a hell of a big country, but also another difficult one.

Ross: As I found out later, Venezuela might have been offered to me earlier on, but they had tried originally to send Ambassador Hurd there, and then it was discovered, belatedly, that he had all of those oil company connections. So his nomination was withdrawn. When I didn't go, Rob McClintock eventually did. I went to Tanzania and President Nyerere. That was an interesting experience, I must say.

Q: He's always been a fascinating person.

Ross: He was fascinating. There again, I had a very good personal relationship with him, although there were some issues on which we were on opposite sides of the fence. Vietnam was at its height then, and we were on opposite sides of that. He didn't think we were moving fast enough or firmly enough in Southern Africa to work changes in South Africa or in the Portuguese territories. Then, of course, as you know, he was a Fabian Socialist and had his own ideas about how the Tanzanian economy should develop. That didn't keep him from accepting a substantial amount of aid from us, and that aid being used fairly well.

On the fiscal side, there was very good accountability, because they had a Tanzanian, an Indian who had been born in Tanzania, as their Minister of Finance (Amir H. Jamal). He was very good and had very good standing in the international financial community, which helped them out over a long period, when otherwise they might not have had as much.

Q: Did the Indians have the same trouble there that they had in other parts?

Ross: It came before I left. It started coming in 1971, I guess. Yes, they changed a lot of the local laws. You

144

couldn't own rental property after a while. If you lived in it, okay. But you couldn't have apartment houses or apartments for rent, etc. Also they clamped down on foreign exchange available for Tanzanian children to go abroad for study. Lots of the Indians, the ones who could afford it, had sent theirs to Britain or elsewhere.

Q: Ambassador Ross, we were talking about the problem of the Indians, particularly in Tanzania.

Ross: As I say, there were a number of measures that were, on the face of them, not discriminatory, but in the practical effect, only affected the Indian element of the population. So these people began pulling up and going out, and in the process, the Tanzanians lost a very productive element of their population--doctors, for example, merchants of one kind or another--because most of the merchants were Indian.

Q: In fact, it was the middle class, almost.

Ross: That's right. There were some relatively well-to-do Tanzanians, particularly up in the north in the coffee areas.

Q: Probably more in Tanzania than Uganda?

Ross: I don't know. I really don't know. There were a few Africans, but not very many. Of course, the whole thrust of Nyerere's policies was to make a kind of classless society, and he used this device of Ujamaa villages, where he hoped he was going to be able to develop centers of productivity throughout the country, establishing villages where, in effect, everybody worked for the common cause, and at the end of the harvest season, you all shared and shared alike, that kind of thing.

Well, that didn't go very well, because, as you might suppose, there were those who worked very hard and those who sat around. Obviously, they weren't about to share equally when that kind of thing existed. He tried, too, to convert to Ujamaa some things like coffee-producing areas, which would have been a real disaster.

He decided he wanted to move the capital out of Dar es

Salaam to a place called Dodoma, in the middle of the country. He wanted to have a more centrally located place, and I think to get the government away from whatever foreign influence that came from being on the coast. They still haven't achieved this, although I gather technically the move is still on the books. It was obvious that there were going to be all kinds of problems.

I went up to Dodoma and there wasn't any water there. I mean, it was a very dry part of the country, and one wondered how you were going to support any kind of a population or put the capital there with all that entailed. That was just one overriding problem. But he was full of good intentions and personally the epitome of integrity. I don't think any kind of financial scandal was ever attached to him.

Q: And a man you could talk to.

Ross: Oh, yes, yes.

Q: You might not reach any conclusion, but you could talk.

Ross: That's right. But he was a very interesting man, very articulate, you know, and had a better education. He'd gone to Edinburgh and had advanced training, not a doctorate, but advanced training, and I think it during his British sojourn that he came under the influence of Fabian socialists and took a turn in that direction.

Q: Was his advanced training in economics?

Ross: I can't remember whether it was that or in the education field. Because he was a teacher. The Tanzanians all called him, in Swahili, Mwalimu, which means 'teacher.' That's what he was early on.

Q: What did we have there basically in the way of programs? Did we have a Peace Corps there?

Ross: We did not have a Peace Corps there.

Q: At no time?

Ross: No. We had had a Peace Corps, and it had been pulled out at the request of the Tanzanian Government the year before I was posted there. I think it was late 1968 or

146

early 1969. It was not reinstated in my day. There again, you know, the idea being, I guess, that there was too much American influence out in the countryside.

Q: Corruption?

Ross: That's right. I was there at the time when, back here in the States, Afro hairdos were in style and things like that. Nyerere wouldn't have any of it. No Afro hairdos in Tanzania. There were several other things which he just didn't want.

Q: He was a conservative?

Ross: Yes. He wanted to keep his people free from this. But it was a fascinating place, and the relationship between Tanganyika and Zanzibar was an interesting one, because we had two vice presidents one from Zanzibar and one from Tanganyika. The vice president from Zanzibar who was assassinated shortly before I left, a man named Karume, was, in effect, the dictator of Zanzibar. Zanzibar was a big foreign exchange earner for Tanzania, because it is an island that grows cloves.

Q: And other spices.

Ross: Other spices, too, but cloves are the big crop, both on Zanzibar proper and on Pemba, which is part of the Zanzibar geographical entity. However, under Karume those revenues were kept by the Zanzibaris for their own use. They didn't come over as part of the total Tanzanian revenue. I think eventually this may have changed, but in my day it didn't.

Q: In other words, they ran their own foreign exchange.

Ross: Yes, and they had, as a carryover from the time they were independent before the union with Tanzania, consular posts there that Nyerere might not have authorized. The East Germans were there, the Czechs were there, etc. They gave assistance directly to the Zanzibaris without going through the Tanzanian apparatus. I don't think that sat terribly well, but I guess there were limits on what Nyerere could do.

147

Q: You said that he might not otherwise have authorized these things. Was he that strong a leader?

Ross: I think he would want to keep control of this, you see. We had a consulate there, a holdover from the old days, too. The Brits no longer had a resident consul there but the British High Commissioner used to visit periodically. I don't recall that otherwise there was much in the way of a Western presence there on Zanzibar.

Q: I never got into Tanzania at all when I was there, because there was always friction between Kenya and Tanzania.

Ross: Yes. They broke up their common market.

Q: Common services.

Ross: Yes. East African common services.

Q: That happened while I was there, and it was a great loss, I think.

Ross: It was. That happened while I was there, too, the termination of one common service and then another.

Q: The Ugandans got out very early, I think.

Ross: Yes.

Q: That was a great loss, because that was a good operating thing.

Ross: It was. Yes, they had a lot of good things.

Q: Of course, it was something installed by the British.

Ross: It was. It did tend to work much more efficiently than three separate entities would and probably less costly.

Q: The currency was an important thing, too.

Ross: That's right, as we've had occasion to note in other places, the various vested interests in a country.

Q: I think it was each one with national pride.

Ross: That's it.

Q: And the fact that Kenya was going well economically.

Ross: Yes. It was always a point of great resentment and dissatisfaction among the Tanzanians that all of the safaris from Europe and America and elsewhere came into

Nairobi and then fanned out from there.

Q: They collected much of the foreign exchange.

Ross: That's right. Even to the point, you see, that the people on safari didn't know when they were in Tanzania. As you say, most of it was collected by the tour groups that were either headquartered abroad or in Nairobi. So that was another reason for the dissatisfaction.

But I must say, when the Tanzanians were handling it themselves, they never succeeded in really accomplishing a great improvement in the situation, at least during the time I was there. They would get tour groups, but they were all pre-paid, pre-packaged tour groups, so that the individuals who came would go to one of the beach resorts near Dar es Salaam. They might come into town once or twice, but for the most part, they were out there. It was all pre-paid. They spent very little money in the country.

Q: The hotel bills and so on, which were group rates.

Ross: Exactly. So one wonders. They had a few souvenirs that they may have bought, but one wonders how much the Tanzanians did get out of it.

Q: What were their principal sources of revenue and foreign exchange besides the spices?

Ross: There were the spices, there was tourism, and there were some gemstones. Just before I went out there, as a matter of fact, a stone called Tanzanite came on the market, a blue stone, semi-precious, really, which Tiffany's had the lock on. As I remember, when I went out through New York, I went to Tiffany's to see this. But Tanzania didn't have alluvial diamond fields as they did in the Central African Republic. That was one of the American interests there.

In Tanzania, diamonds were found in 'pipes' as they are in South Africa. In Tanzania they weren't all that extensive or important. Sisal and cotton had been important, but the markets for these had slumped as I knew from Haiti. For a little while, it looked like sisal

149

might come back. Remember paper dresses? We had a period for things like that. But that never really developed. Coffee and tea were other foreign-exchange earners. The tea was in British hands on southern highlands, British companies.

Q: Was there any great American commercial penetration?

Ross: No, not a great deal.

Q: My experience is that eastern Africa is just too darn far away.

Ross: That's right. Then you ran into all kinds of difficulties. For a time the Lykes Lines used to come in, you know, and then they stopped, because the port was so congested that you'd have to stand off maybe for two weeks. What American freighter could do that? I think they were figuring it might be something like $30,000 a day. They weren't about to stand for that. So we stopped having American bottoms turn up there.

I only got one American naval vessel there, and that was near the end of my tour. We got one of them from the force in the Persian gulf, a destroyer. That took a lot of doing. It went off all right, no harm done. The U.S. Navy were very keen on doing it. They were always looking for ports of call.

Q: I had a very dichotomous attitude on that where we were, but I had them come in, and it worked all right.

Ross: I had an unfortunate experience in that regard in Guinea, which I neglected to touch upon, which perhaps I'll add later on. I wasn't all that keen to have them come in, in the face of what I could see was, at best, a lukewarm attitude.

Tanzania, as you know, has Mozambique on its southern border, and Dar es Salaam was the center from which Eduardo Mondlane, the head of Frelimo the Mozambican independence movement, operated. He was married to an American. He was assassinated shortly

150

before I got there, but the Mozambicans were a presence there, as were, of course, groups from Rhodesia and South Africa.

Q: What was the relationship with Malawi? Was that significant?

Ross: Not really. I think the Tanzanians all thought that Banda was a bit of an Uncle Tom. Relationships were all right. They shared the lake together, you know.

Q: And the transportation came through, I suppose, to Dar es Salaam, didn't it?

Ross: Not really, no. A lot of things from Zambia came through, yes, but not from Malawi. That was one reason that the Tanzanians got the Chinese in there to build that railroad to Zambia. They were hoping to eliminate Zambia's having to use the railroad that ran through Rhodesia and Mozambique. The Chinese came and built the railroad.

There was great suspicion and fear in Washington that the Chinese would never leave, having come in. I was at considerable pains to try to get some sense of balance on that question in my reporting, because we could find no evidence of this, or that the Chinese were having much of an impact on the Tanzanians. I'm sure they were grateful for the assistance, yes, but the Chinese weren't imparting any particular political philosophy, and certainly not any work habits, on the Tanzanians.

The Tanzanians were quite prepared to sit there and watch the Chinese work, but they weren't about to work the way these coolies were working on the railroad.

Q: You couldn't say that we did anything except have the Chinese build our railroads across the country anyway.

Ross: Yes. We were engaged in road building. That is to say, we had an American Company called Nello Teer, building a road from Dar es Salaam to Morogoro.

Q: Was this an actual paved road?

Ross: It was to be.

Q: Our road building in Somalia was mostly what they called "stabilized earth," which you mixed a little cement in with the soil.

Ross: Yes. They weren't finished by the time I left, so I don't know how it all turned out. But the first stages were paved. Incidentally, it might interest you to know that one of the other road-building outfits in Tanzania, particularly in the north of Tanzania, was the Frederics Company, owned by in-laws of Henry Tasea. They were also involved in building the international airport that was put up between Arusha and Moshi in the north, presumably for travelers to come in and go directly into the game areas of Tanzania. Whether that ever worked out or not, I don't know. Shortly before I left Tanzania, I went to the inauguration of the airport. But up to the time I left, there was very little traffic in and out, and I don't know if there were any scheduled flights.

Q: Does that pretty well wind up Tanzania?

Ross: I think so. When I knew that I was coming out, there was that chiefs of mission conference in Addis shortly before, in April of 1972, and David Newsom asked me if I would come in to be the senior deputy of the bureau. In anticipation of that, after that conference, I went first to Morocco to visit my son. Andrea went with me.

Then I went up to Lisbon, took a plane, and flew from Lisbon to Luanda and did a tour of Southern Africa, in preparation for my Departmental job. I went to Angola first and flew to South Africa--Pretoria, Johannesburg, Durban, and Cape Town. In Cape Town I had an hour's conversation with Forster, one on one, in the course of which his comments and attitude showed me how intractable the South African stand on apartheid really was. I then went to three former High Commission territories--Botswana, Lesotho, and Swaziland, and to Mozambique. It was all extremely useful.

When I got to Washington, Rogers was still secretary. I

think we probably got a little more attention in the African bureau from him than we subsequently did from Kissinger, except perhaps as South African questions came up. We got his attention for them, but not for run-of-the-mill African things. For a few things in North Africa, yes. We still had the office of North African Affairs in the African Bureau and we were negotiating liquid-gas contracts with Algeria, which the seventh floor was interested in. But in general, we didn't receive a great deal of interest in the day-to-day operations.

One big problem that we had was the Ugandan flap when Idi Amin was there causing all that trouble. We pulled our Ambassador out and Bob Keeley ended up being chargé. Then it became a question of whether we were going to leave anybody in or whether we were going to wind up the operation."[24]

The preceding interviews with senior American diplomats including ambassadors who were accredited to Tanzania provide an American perspective or perspectives on Tanzania and on Nyerere as a leader during one of the most critical periods in the history of post-colonial Africa when some of the most important events on the continent took place: the Zanzibar revolution and formation of a union of two independent countries unprecedented in the history of the continent since the advent of colonial rule.

Some of the diplomats were there during the revolution and when the union of Tanganyika and Zanzibar was formed. Others were there when the union was going through a transitional phase of consolidation, adjustments and readjustments to prevailing conditions, domestic and external, especially during the Cold War when Tanzania and many other Third World countries were pursuing a policy of non-alignment.

The union of Tanganyika and Zanzibar featured prominently in discussions and in many debates during that time as President Nyerere kept it non-aligned between

153

the two contending ideological camps: East and West. It is a union that continues to generate debate even today more than 50 years after it was formed.

Although the interviews featured here do not exclusively focus on what led to the consummation of the union of Tanganyika and Zanzibar, they have been included in this work almost in their entirety where they focus on Tanzania because because they cover other subjects vital to a better understanding of what is the largest country in East Africa and one of the largest on the continent with a potential to be a major player in continental affairs once its potential is fully harnessed. For example, years later, it was no coincidence that three American presidents – President Barack Obama and former presidents Bill Clinton and George W. Bush – as well as the American secretary of state, Hillary Clinton, visited Tanzania around the same time within a two-year period; Obama and Bush were in Tanzania during the same time. Hillary Clinton went to Tanzania at least twice; Bush also, at least twice, including once when he was president.

One of the main reasons Tanganyika, now mainland Tanzania, drew the attention of world powers during the Cold War was its strategic significance; nowadays because of its abundant natural resources including a dazzling array of minerals, vast reserves of gas, and great potential for oil discovery; it is also still strategically significant.

Almost centrally located on the East African coast, Tazania is the gateway to the heart of Africa, now the Democratic Republic of Congo, a treasure trove and potentially the richest country on the continent, and to the countries of southern Africa which are also endowed with abundant natural resources including strategic minerals vital to the industrial economies of the world.

Tanzania also shares borders with more countries than any other country on the continent besides the Democratic Republic of Congo which is bordered by nine countries;

Tanzania is bordered by eight. But it also borders the Indian Ocean (another strategic asset), a total of nine boundaries like Congo's.

And that made mainland Tanzania an important potential client during the Cold War, probably even more than Zanzibar was, an outpost in the Indian Ocean, isolated, without being surrounded by other countries like Tanganyika was.

And while it is true that the United States and Britain wanted Tanganyika to unite with Zanzibar in order to prevent the island nation from falling into communist hands, it must also be conceded that uniting the two countries was a goal Nyerere always wanted to pursue. It is something that he had in his mind as far back as the mid-fifties. Because of the indissoluble ties which had existed for centuries between the people of the mainland and the isles, Nyerere – other people as well – had always considered Zanzibar to be an integral part of the mainland divided only by colonial boundaries.

Therefore, uniting the two countries was simply reuniting the people who had always been one. Unification was inevitable, sooner or later. He would have pursued it even if the United States and Britain did not exist on the face of the earth; hence his contention: "It is an insult to Africa to read cold war politics into every move towards African unity."

No amount of external pressure would have been enough to make his pursue the goal of uniting the two countries if he was not interested in doing so; if it was not in his best interest to do so, and if conditions within Tanganyika and Zanzibar – not only during that time but even before then – were not conducive to unification. Common bonds between the two countries – cultural and historical – were a major factor in the quest for unification although they were not given due prominence in the context of Cold War rivalries between the East and the West during that period.

Decades later about one year before he died on 14 October 1999, Nyerere again expressed his disappointment about his failure to form a larger union, the East African federation, in an interview with Ikaweba Bunting of the *New Internationalist*:

"I respected Jomo (Kenyatta) immensely. It has probably never happened in history. Two heads of state, Milton Obote and I, went to Jomo and said to him: 'Let's unite our countries and you be our head of state.' He said no. I think he said no because it would have put him out of his element as a Kikuyu Elder....

Kwame Nkrumah and I were committed to the idea of unity. African leaders and heads of state did not take Kwame seriously. However, I did. I did not believe in these small little nations. Still today I do not believe in them. I tell our people to look at the European Union, at these people who ruled us who are now uniting.

Kwame and I met in 1963 and discussed African Unity. We differed on how to achieve a United States of Africa. But we both agreed on a United States of Africa as necessary. Kwame went to Lincoln University, a black college in the US. He perceived things from the perspective of US history, where the 13 colonies that revolted against the British formed a union. That is what he thought the OAU should do.

I tried to get East Africa to unite before independence. When we failed in this, I was wary about Kwame's continental approach. We corresponded profusely on this. Kwame said my idea of 'regionalization' was only balkanization on a larger scale. Later African historians will have to study our correspondence on this issue of uniting Africa."[25]

If the British, who were the colonial rulers, wanted to form an East African federation, they would have done so a long time ago. They had plenty of time, decades, to do that: at least since the end of World War I when Tanganyika, the last territory in the region to be colonised by Britain, came under the League of Nations mandate ruled by Britain after Germany lost the colony in the war; Tanganyika later became a UN Trusteeship.

The British did, in fact, attempt in the 1930s to establish a giant federation stretching from East Africa all the way down to South Africa composed of all the British colonies in the region: Kenya, Uganda, Tanganyika, Zanzibar, Nyasaland (now Malawi), Northern Rhodesia (renamed Zambia), Southern Rhodesia (now Zimbabwe), Bechuanaland (today Botswana), Swaziland, Basutoland (renamed Lesotho), and South Africa.

But they wanted to form such a federation for a different reason: to consolidate imperial domination of Africa. The plan was strongly opposed and resisted by African nationalists in those countries.

In pursuing unification, Nyerere's intention was not to perpetuate imperial domination of East Africa by the British colonial rulers when he strongly advocated formation of an East African federation before independence and even offered to delay Tanganyika's independence if such a move would help to achieve that goal. And the British as well as other Western powers definitely had more influence on Jomo Kenyatta than they did on Nyerere, if at all. Yet Kenyatta was the least enthusiastic of the three East African leaders about forming a federation. It was also reported in 1977 – 1978 that Kenyatta was on the CIA payroll together with Mobutu Sese Seko and a number of other African leaders. Nyerere was not one of them.

Had Kenyatta and Milton Obote been as enthusiastic as Nyerere was, about regional unity, the East African federation would have been formed before the end of 1963 as the three leaders had agreed to do in the declaration they signed in June in Nairobi, Kenya, the same year.

Although the failure of the three East African leaders

157

to form a federation in 1963 was one of Nyerere's biggest disappointments, he remained undaunted in his quest for unity and went on to form the union of Tanganyika and Zanzibar the following year; not because the Americans and the British asked him to do so.

His track record in pursuit of African unity and independence contradicts that line of reasoning. And consummation of the union was one of his greatest achievements in the Pan-African context and in the area of foreign policy. It was also clear vindication of his non-aligned position in the bipolar world of the Cold War.

The new nation of Tanzania went on to forge strong links with the Eastern bloc – the nemesis of the West, which supposedly inspired the union in its ideological war against the communist bloc – and continued to maintain equally strong ties with the West contrary to the wishes of the Russians and the Chinese. In fact, Tanzania got more financial and technical assistance from the West than she did from the East, mainly because of historical ties.

It is also worth remembering that if Nyerere was subservient to – or took orders from – the West as supposedly was the case when he formed the union of Tanganyika and Zanzibar, he would not have been able to expel American diplomats from Tanzania in 1964 when they were accused of trying to overthrow him; and they would not have tried to undermine his government since he was their "ally."

Also, he would not have broken diplomatic ties with Britain in December 1965 over the Rhodesian crisis, the first African country to do so; nor would he have curtailed ties with West Germany when the latter objected to diplomatic representation of East Germany in Tanzania. The West German ambassador was shown the door, and the Canadians came in to train Tanzania's fledgling air force after the Germans threatened to withdraw their aid for the training programme. Nyerere told them to withdraw all their aid in all fields.

All those cases clearly show that Nyerere was an independent-minded leader who also demonstrated a degree of independence in his policy pursuits and initiatives rarely seen among Third World leaders.

Yet, in spite of all this evidence, the litany continues that the union of Tanganyika and Zanzibar was a product of Cold War intrigue, and not of Nyerere's own initiative in pursuit of his Pan-African goals. If the communist threat prompted Nyerere to unite Tanganyika with Zanzibar at the behest of Britain and the United States in order to stop communists from establishing a base in Zanzibar, why did he go on to establish strong ties with communist countries after the union was formed – instead of avoiding them? It seems he didn't pay very much attention to the British and the Americans who "told" him to form the union and avoid communists.

The union never served as a bulwark against communism – it did as a socialist state against capitalism – because it was never intended to be one; nor did it serve as a launching pad for communist penetration of Africa from the east coast – it was never intended for that either. And communism never penetrated Tanzania in spite of the strong ties the country had with the Eastern bloc. It remained a non-aligned nation; hence Nyerere's contention that we are not going to allow our friends to choose enemies for us. As he stated in a speech, "Policy on Foreign Affairs," 16 October 1967:

"We shall not allow any of our friendships to be exclusive; we shall not allow anyone to choose any of our friends or enemies for us. It should also be clear that we shall not allow anyone – whether they be from East or West, or from places not linked to those blocs – to try and use our friendship for their own purposes."[26]

Also, if Nyerere formed the union to neutralise communists in Zanzibar, and in Tanganyika itself, he not only would not have established strong ties with the People's Republic of China and other communist countries; he would also have tightened his grip on Zanzibar, the potential base for communist subversion; and he would not have appointed to cabinet posts Zanzibaris who were known to have communist leanings. The president of Zanzibar who formed the union with Nyerere, Sheikh Abeid Karume, wanted a complete merger, hence a stronger union. But Nyerere refused to go that far. He preferred, instead, to have a weaker union in which Zanzibar would continue to have its own government and enjoy considerable autonomy virtually as a sovereign entity in a number of areas except foreign affairs, defence, immigration, and others specifically placed under the jurisdiction of the union government.

He was concerned that if a complete merger of the two countries and governments took place, the people of Zanzibar would feel that they had been swallowed up by Tanganyika, a much bigger country. It would not be a union of equals since as a sovereign entity, Zanzibar was entering the union as an independent country, not as a junior partner.

Another Zanzibari leader who was strongly in favour of a much stronger union was Kassim Hanga who served as prime minister and vice president under President Karume and was one of the leaders on the isles known for his communist sympathies.

Another leader from Zanzibar with known communist leanings was Abdulrahman Mohammed Babu, leader of the Umma (The People's) Party, who became minister of defence and external affairs under President Karume. Yet, in spite of his communist ties and ideological orientation, he was later appointed to cabinet posts in the union government by President Nyerere and went on to become one of the most distinguished and influential leaders in Tanzania whose influence as a scholar and Marxist theoretician extended beyond Tanzania. He held key ministerial posts serving as minister of economic planning and minister of commerce and industries between 1964 and 1972. He was also one of the strongest supporters of the union and African unity in general, despite his earlier misgivings about the union which took place in his absence.

Nyerere's approach to unity between the two countries probably saved the union more than anything else. Had Zanzibar not been allowed to have its own government and its own president who also served as the first vice president of the united republic – the second vice president automatically came from the mainland – the union would probably have collapsed.

Even soon after it was formed, there was strong opposition to the merger by some elements in Zanzibar who argued that their smaller country had been swallowed up by Tanganyika in what amounted to annexation, as Professor Ali Mazrui has erroneously characterised the merger.

Had Zanzibar indeed been swallowed up, without allowing it to have its own government, secessionist sentiments in the former island nation – which have existed since the union was formed – would have grown to be much stronger, providing momentum to a separatist movement which could even have led to an insurgency on the islands plunging the country into chaos.

But the secessionists were robbed much of this momentum by allowing Zanzibar to continue having its own government, under its own president, and under its own constitution, enabling it to enjoy extensive autonomy.

Although it was intended to maintain the union by being fair to Zanzibaris, even such extensive devolution of power, if not properly managed, could have had unintended consequences by encouraging people opposed to the union to demand even greater autonomy, progressively leading to a return to the status quo ante: restoration of Zanzibar's full sovereign status, hence dissolution of the union.

Yet it was skillfully managed by Nyerere under a unique arrangement, what was essentially a unitary state – with some federal features as a concession to Zanzibaris – which did not allow such extensive devolution of power to the regions on mainland Tanzania except to the former island nation of Zanzibar.

Nyerere's consummation of the union was criticised even by some of his fellow socialists although of the Marxist bent; Nyerere was not a Marxist. As Ann Talbot, a Trotskyite, stated in "Nyerere's Legacy of Poverty and Repression in Zanzibar":

"The late President Julius Nyerere, the first president of independent Tanganyika,...formed a union with Zanzibar to create Tanzania in 1964.

Nyerere remains an icon of the Pan-Africanist movement and the limited welfare measures that he introduced in Tanzania are still held up by some as an example of the benefits of what was known as African socialism. To many he remains as saintly a figure as Nelson Mandela has become....

Nyerere formed the union with Zanzibar when a spontaneous popular uprising had just overthrown the government of large estate owners that Britain had given power to on independence. Neither of the two opposition parties, the Afro-Shirazi Party (ASP), or the Umma Party, were in control of the uprising. Power fell into their hands because the movement lacked a programme that represented the interests of the dispossessed estate workers or the workers on the docks....

Nyerere recognised that the uprising was a threat to his own position. In the weeks following it... encouraged by the events in Zanzibar, his army mutinied against its British officers.... The ease with which the mutiny had taken place revealed the weakness of his regime to popular opposition. Nyerere realised that if he could not control the political aspirations of the mass of his population, he would be of little use to Britain or any other imperialist power....

Nyerere had an object lesson close to hand in what happened to an African leader who could not control popular movements. Only four years before President (sic) Patrice Lumumba had been assassinated by Western agents because he could not maintain control of the volatile situation in the Congo.

Lumumba had appealed to the Soviet Union for military aid and in doing so had threatened to tip the balance of the Cold War in Africa. Now the new Zanzibar government had established relations with the Soviet bloc, allowed East Germany to open an embassy and accepting their help to train the army.

Nyerere was looking at Lumumba's fate when he initiated the union with Zanzibar. He knew that he would not survive if he allowed the movement in Zanzibar to continue and could not demonstrate his usefulness to imperialism by bringing Zanzibar into a union with Tanganyika.

For his part Zanzibar's President Abeid Karume, who led the Afro-Shirazi Party, saw the union with Tanganyika as a means of undermining his opponents in government. His particular target was Abdulrahman Mohammed Babu, leader of the Umma Party, who favoured close links with the Soviet bloc and Cuba. Babu, whose power base was on Pemba, as the CUF's (Tanzanian main opposition Civic United Front's) is today, was forced to take refuge on the mainland as Karume arrested or killed his opponents. In 1972 Karume was assassinated, probably at Babu's instigation."[27]

Factual errors aside – the army mutinies in all the three East African countries of Kenya, Uganda and Tanganyika took place in January 1964, therefore within days, not after weeks as Talbot says, following the Zanzibar revolution

163

which took place on January 12th; the first mutiny was in Tanganyika on January 20th and lasted for six days; Patrice Lumumba was prime minister, not president, of Congo; and Babu's political base was on Zanzibar, not on Pemba Island – there is a distinct ideological line, Trotskyite, Ann Talbot is pursuing in her deeply flawed analysis of Nyerere instead of focusing on objective inquiry regardless of one's ideological oorientation. It is these ideological blinders which have thrown her off track in what should be a scholarly pursuit involving dispassionate analysis. And Babu, of course, differs with Talbot on the role of the Umma Party in the Zanzibar revolution. As he stated in "The 1964 Revolution: Lumpen or Vanguard?":

"Although the Umma Party did not fire the first shot of the uprising, it nevertheless rose to the occasion with revolutionary zeal and skill. It helped to transform a wholly lumpen – in many ways apolitical – uprising into a popular, anti-imperialist revolution, which, left to its own momentum, and without the external intervention that followed, would undoubtedly have opened up a new path – the road to socialism."[28]

The revolution itself was an indigenous expression of mass discontent, not a foreign-inspired uprising as some still maintain. And to contend, as Ann Talbot does, that Nyerere was an imperialist agent at the beck and call of the British and other imperialist powers – presumably the United States and other Western nations as well, since as a Trotsykite socialist, she would never conceive of a scenario in which she would see the Soviet Union, now dead, acting as an imperialist power – is, once again as I argued earlier, to deliberately ignore Nyerere's record of independent domestic and foreign policy initiatives which irritated and even infuriated both ideological camps at different times during his long political career; not only as a Tanzanian or as African leader but also as a Third World leader and one of the most influential world leaders in the twentieth century.

Yet, as a Trotskyite, Talbot is obsessed with "proving" in every conceivable way that Nyerere was "wrong" because he didn't toe the Trotskyist party line; he didn't the Maoist either. Any socialist – including Nyerere – who deviates from this or does not toe this party line is considered to be an apostate or a traitor. And I don't use the term Trotskyist – as opposed to Trotskyite – in a disparaging way in this context, as it is normally used in the description and analysis of trotskyism by some of its critics.

Nyerere's independence from Marxism-Leninism – and unimpressed by Marxist-Leninist dogma – did not earn him endearment in the socialist camp anymore than it did in the West for his relentless criticism of Western imperialist policies towards Africa.

Trotskyites, like other Marxist-Leninists who include Maoists, see themselves as the standard-bearers of Marxism-Leninism even though it is a discredited ideology as has been validated by experience and by the collapse of communist regimes around the world since the end of the Cold War. Even some of the most hardline Marxist-Leninist states have renounced the ideology.

There is no question that Nyerere was independent-minded. He demonstrated such independence even during the Congo crisis as the leader of Tanganyika before uniting with Zanzibar and after the two countries were united under his stewardship to form Tanzania, at a time when the East and the West were locked in the most bitter and intense rivalry on African soil right in the heart of the continent in the turbulent sixties.

In spite of Tanzania's weakness, Nyerere openly supported the Congolese nationalist forces – followers of Lumumba – against the Western puppet regime in Leopoldville installed and supported by the CIA and other

Western interests including French and British. He also allowed Cuban troops led by Che Guevara to use Tanzania as a conduit to enter Congo and even allowed them to have a rear base in western Tanzania to support the Congolese nationalists fighting the CIA-backed Congolese government.

Kigoma, a town on the eastern shore of Lake Tanganyika, was used by Che Guevara as his rear base. Fidel Castro did not sneak Cuban troops and Che Guevara into Congo through Tanzania. He sent hundreds of Cuban troops, and Che Guevara, to Congo through Tanzania with the full knowledge and permission of President Nyerere and his government. And the CIA knew this; so did the British and other Western intelligence services, as did their governments, from Washington to London, Brussels and the rest. They also knew that Nyerere allowed the Russians and the Chinese to send weapons to the nationalist forces in the Congo through Tanzania.

This does not seem to be the kind of leader who was a servant of Western imperialism, as Ann Talbot contends, or as someone who took orders from the United States and Britain – the very powers he fought against – to form the union of Tanganyika and Zanzibar as others claim.

And it is worth remembering that even after the Congolese nationalist forces failed to dislodge the CIA-backed regime in Leopoldville, Nyerere never changed his position. He continued to oppose Western domination and exploitation of Congo – and the rest of Africa – and supported the Congolese pro-Lumumbist nationalists and liberation movements in other parts of the continent. And when Che Guevara failed in his Congo mission, he retreated to Tanzania and stayed in Dar es Salaam, the nation's capital, for many months from October 1965 to early March 1966, during which he wrote his famous book, *The African Dream: The Diaries of the Revolutionary War in the Congo*, before returning to Cuba. As Jorge Castañeda states in his book, *Compañero: The*

"His secretary during those crucial months in Tanzania...was...Colman Ferrer....During the time he spent with Pablo Ribalta, the Cuban ambassador to Tanzania and his old comrade-in-arms, in the Tanzanian capital, Che made two crucial decisions: he would not return to Cuba, and his next destination was Buenos Aires....His wife arrived in Dar es Salaam. They were staying at the Embassy....

Che spent his free time writing – his favourite activity, apart from combat and literature.

Working from notes taken in Congo, he began drafting...*Pasajes de la guerra revolucionaria (el Congo)*. Colman Ferrer, a young secretary at the Cuban Embassy in Dar-es-Salaam, served as his assistant. Che dictated his text, Ferrer transcribed it, then Guevara revised and corrected the final manuscript. In the words of Ferrer, Che basically spent the days 'marking time, preparing the conditions for a change of scenery.' As Oscar Fernandez Mell recalls it, 'One of Che's great virtues was the way he enjoyed reading, though he also had more exacting tastes and ways of spending his time. He could read for hours; he had a good time even when he was alone.'

He was extremely meticulous in his work. In Ferrer's words, 'he was careful in the things he was going to write, avoiding any mistakes. He took great care, he analyzed and reread the transcription repeatedly.' The book left little time for other activities. 'He wrote day and night. His only distraction was an occasional game of chess with me. One day when I was about to checkmate him, he looked at me as if he had not realized what was happening; it was obvious that he wasn't really in the game.'

Finally, at the end of February or beginning of March 1966, Che agreed to leave....'Everybody returned to Cuba and he stayed on alone in Tanzania, and then I decided to get him out of Tanzania and take him to a safe place until he decided what he was going to do,' Ulises Estrada, (in) interview with the author (Castañeda), Havana, February 9, 1995."[29]

The CIA and other Western intelligence agencies knew Che Guevara was in Dar es Salaam, Tanzania, for months, after the failure of his Congo mission. He settled in Dar es Salaam in October 1965. And they knew when he left. Much as they hated him for spreading revolution to other parts of the Third World, they would have pressured Tanzania to expel him from the country if President Nyerere was their stooge as Ann Talbot claims. And if they tried, then they failed to speed up his exit.

Che Guevara left Tanzania when he was ready to do so. And he stayed in Tanzania for as long as he did because he was allowed to. Yet one can't think of him staying, even for one day, in a country whose leader was subservient to the West. He would have been expelled the same day, let alone allowed to have an operational base, as Che Guevara was, to support anti-Western nationalist insurgents in a neighbouring country.

That Nyerere allowed the Cubans to operate from Tanzania, and communist powers to funnel weapons through Tanzania to support nationalist forces in Congo, demonstrated a degree of independence and his commitment to non-alignment one would hardly characterise – if at all – as a sign of weakness and subservience to the West.

And his opposition to American involvement in Vietnam during the Vietnam war, and to the invasion of Czechoslovakia in 1968 by the Warsaw Pact forces led by the Soviet Union, once again demonstrated his independence and commitment to positive neutralism without taking orders from either side of the Iron Curtain.

It is in this context that Nyerere's establishment of the union of Tanganyika and Zanzibar must be viewed as a realisation of his policy objectives, a triumph of Pan-

Africanism, and a rejection of imperial domination by any of the world powers regardless of their ideologies. Yet, because of his modesty, even his adversaries underestimated him. As Gamal Nkrumah, son of the late president of Ghana, Dr. Kwame Nkrumah, stated in the obituary he wrote about Nyerere, "The Legacy of A Great African," in *Al-Ahram*:

"Nyerere's presence at political rallies, remote poverty-stricken villages, academic conferences and international forums where he pleaded the case of the South always lit up the occasion. He had a way with the words....He was the philosopher-king, intellectual, enlightened, the polar opposite of the despotic ruler so common in the Africa of his day. But he was also a man of the people....

Two years ago, at celebrations marking the 40th anniversary of Ghana's independence, I met and spoke to Nyerere for the last time. I would never have guessed that he was ill....

He was not only a man of integrity, but he also had the courage and modesty to admit to past mistakes.

I have heard him speak in London, at the Commonwealth Institute, in several forums in the United States and at the United Nations, as well as in many an African setting.

To me personally, Nyerere was always the attentive father figure, never missing an opportunity to remind me that my own father's vision for a united Africa was the only way forward.

With his wit, humour, sharp intellect and disarming sincerity, Nyerere was always a winning personality. But, to say that he was an uncontroversial character would be a grave mistake. From the beginning of his political career, Nyerere was widely seen as a moderate, and that at a time when more militant African leaders prevailed. As early as the late 1950s and early 1960s, official US documents, now declassified, interestingly reveal that America's Central Intelligence (CIA) regarded him as the only 'responsible' African leader. Nyerere himself was clever enough to realise that such a revelation was no compliment....

His greatest achievement is undoubtedly the successful unification of mainland Tanganyika with the Indian Ocean island of Zanzibar (and Pemba). The United Republic of Tanzania was born in 1964 out of that union with an overwhelmingly Muslim island-nation whose closest historical, economic and political ties were with Oman in particular and the Arab Gulf countries in general. Zanzibar was for two centuries the Omani official seat of government and the official residence of the Sultan.

In contrast, Tanganyika...had a more mixed population, equally divided between Christians and Muslims.

It was to Nyerere's credit that he managed to unite this most ethnically, linguistically and religiously diverse of nation-states and make it one of Africa's most politically stable countries."[30]

It is true that the United States denounced Zanzibar as "the Cuba of Africa"[24] after the January 1964 revolution led by John Okello who toppled the Arab-dominated regime and transferred power to the predominantly black majority and their allies including a number of Arabs, Iranians (originally from Shiraz in Iran), and others. But it is also true that the people who led the revolution were not interested in substituting one master for another – capitalist or communist – and their uprising was not communist-inspired. It was an expression of indigenous aspirations triggered by the racial injustices the black majority suffered at the hands of the Arab-minority regime to whom the British transferred power at independence on December 10, 1963.

The communist threat in Zanzibar was overly exaggerated. Even the leaders who could have established communism on the isles dismissed this threat. They were explicit in their intentions and would not have shied away from acknowledging that they were going to establish communism in Zanzibar – which would been an open secret, anyway, sooner rather than later. They included Abdulrahman Mohammed Babu, the most prominent leader with communist leanings on the islands and whom the CIA followed closely, as it did all the other leaders. According to one of the declassified documents in the US Archives written by Averill Harriman – the American roving ambassador to Nigeria – to President Lyndon B. Johnson and Secretary of State Dean Rusk on 25 March 1964:

"In long talks with Prime Minister Abubakar (Tafawa Balewa) and Foreign Minister (Jaja) Wachuku,...both minimized concern I expressed for Communist takeover in Zanzibar, assured me that Karume was sensible and Babu was primarily African nationalist and would not permit Communist takeover. When I pressed Wachuku, he firmly insisted he could guarantee Babu whom he had personally known a long time."[31]

The preceding telegram was followed by other reports on the potential for communist penetration of Africa during the early years of independence in the sixties. Ambassador Harriman himself in another report to President Johnson on 28 October 1964, about nine months after the Zanzibar revolution and just one day before the Union of Tanganyika and Zanzibar was renamed Tanzania (on October 29, 1964), conceded: "Not a single new African nation has succumbed to Communist domination."[32]

Officials in the Johnson Administration were convinced that communists had played an active role in the Zanzibar revolution on 12 January 1964, according to released documents contained in the 850-page volume of

Foreign Relations of the United States 1964 - 1968. As one US State Department background paper, 7 February 1964, asserted: "There was obvious communist involvement in Zanzibar."[33]

Yet, the same officials admitted that disturbances in other parts of East Africa – the army mutinies in Tanganyika, Kenya, and Uganda in January 1964 – around the same time did not appear to be communist-inspired. In fact, President Nyerere himself resolutely maintained that there was "no evidence whatsoever to suggest that the mutinies in Tanganyika were inspired by outside forces – either Communist or imperialist."[34]

But there was a common logic that linked the mutinies to the Zanzibar revolution. The revolution was an African uprising against Arab domination and had a distinct racial component (it was also a class conflict between dispossessed blacks and the merchants and landowners who were mostly Arab and Indian), as was clearly demonstrated during the revolution in which hundreds of Arabs and Indians, but mostly Arabs – probably no fewer than 2,000 – were massacred. Some estimates put the death toll at 13,000 – 25,000. But they mostly come from the supporters of the old Arab regime, especially Arabs, who are also strongly opposed to the union of Tanganyika and Zanzibar.

The army mutinies in Tanganyika and in the other two East African countries (Kenya and Uganda), partly inspired by the uprising in Zanzibar, also had a racial dimension. In addition to demanding an increase in salary, the mutineers also demanded the replacement of British army officers with African ones to Africanise the armed forces in a true spirit of independence by eradicating the last vestiges of colonialism. But the mutiny in Tanganyika almost ended up as a military coup, according to the evidence gathered from an analysis of records and documents contained in the archives of the East Africana Collection at the University of Dar es Salaam, Tanzania:

"(The) abortive military mutiny on January 20, 1964, (was) motivated by demands for higher pay and the replacement of British officers by Africans.

The six-day mutiny, which began at Colito Barracks (renamed Lugalo Barracks) in Dar es Salaam and spread to troops stationed at Tabora (and Nachingwea), appears to have been well planned.

After arresting their British officers, soldiers built roadblocks at strategic points throughout the city, seized the State House (the president's official residence, although Nyerere did not live there but in a simple house on the outskirts of the city in Msasani, and used the State House, popularly known as Ikulu, only for official functions), police stations, airport, radio station, and railway station, and placed guards at critical postal, telegraph, and bank buildings. The Tanganyikan mutiny sparked similar uprisings in the Ugandan and Kenyan armies as well as the looting and pillaging of Asian shops in Dar es Salaam.

Hundreds of people were arrested during the looting in the commercial areas of the capital. Local forces of order were weakened by the government's earlier decision to send the Dar es Salaam Field Police (known by the acronym FFU - Field Force Units), a contingent of 300 men, to Zanzibar to help restore order on the troubled island.

The fear that racial violence might escalate was linked to the revolution in Zanzibar, which took place in the preceding week and was accompanied by race riots, the murder of hundreds of Arab and Asian shopkeepers, and the mass exodus of Asians to the mainland.

Field Marshal John Okello, who had seized power in Zanzibar, declared: 'We are friends of all Europeans and other foreigners. It is only the Ismailis and certain other Indian groups and people of Arab descent we do not like.' (*Tanganyika Standard*, January 17, 1964).

173

The racial antagonisms behind the army mutiny were evident in the behavior of the mutinous soldiers stationed in the town of Tabora, who beat up all Europeans and Asians who crossed their path. (Listowel, 1965: p. 433). During the looting of Asian shops in Dar es Salaam, 17 people were killed and 23 seriously injured. (*Tanganyika Standard,* January 22, 1964).

Rumors spread throughout the capital that Nyerere had fled the country and a general strike was imminent. Nyerere, while still hiding, broadcast a radio message on the second day of the rebellion, to reassure the country that he was still in power.

Had they moved quickly, the mutineers could probably have seized control of the government, but the rebellious army units had no plans to launch a coup d'etat. Rebellious soldiers negotiated with Minister of Defence Oscar Kambona and agreed to release the 30 captured European (British) officers, who were quickly flown out of the country. Kambona had offered to replace all European officers with Africans and discuss wages, provided the troops release the officers and return to their barracks.

Nyerere's first public act, after he emerged from hiding on January 22, was to tour the city on foot, visiting the areas of looted Asian shops to express his condolences to Asian shopkeepers who had been targets of violence. (*Tanganyika Standard*, January 23, 1964).

Only after the mutineers began to negotiate with militant leaders of the trade union movement did the government reluctantly ask the British to intervene (the British were soon replaced by Nigerian troops at Nyerere's request at an urgent OAU summit he called in Dar es Salaam to deal with the crisis). Trade union leaders hoped to take advantage of the situation and turn the mutiny into a coup d'etat.

The two most prominent proponents of Africanization, trade union leaders Christopher (Kasanga) Tumbo, who had returned from Kenya, and Victor Mkello, met in

Morogoro to plan a new government. (Listowel, 1965: pp. 437 - 38). On January 25, British troops quickly took control of the barracks and disarmed the rebels, killing five African soldiers in the confrontation.

The army mutiny proved to be a great embarrassment for the government, which was forced to call on troops of the former colonial power to restore public order. Yet the uprising also provided the occasion to move decisively against those who had continued to press for Africanization.

After the abortive mutiny, the government arrested 50 policemen implicated in the uprising, reorganized the military (while Nigerian troops sent to Tanganyika by the Nigerian Federal Government provided defence for the country), and replaced British officers to defuse the issue of Africanization. It used Preventive Detention Law, rarely invoked since its passage in 1962, to order the arrest of more than 200 trade union leaders, many of whom were released after questioning. Fifteen soldiers were sentenced to prison for their role in the mutiny.

The trade union movement was brought firmly under the control of the government by the dissolution of the Tanganyika Federation of Labour (TFL) and establishment in its place of the TANU-controlled National Union of Tanganyika Workers (NUTA).

Several days after the suppression of the mutiny, on January 28, 1964, Nyerere announced the appointment of a presidential commission to pursue the plans that had been announced earlier to create a single-party state, subsequently instituted in the constitution of 1965."[35]

Therefore, from all available evidence, it is clear that communism – or any form of external involvement or manipulation – was not a factor in the army mutiny in Tanganyika or those in Kenya and Uganda; three inter-related incidents in a chain reaction that almost plunged the three countries into chaos during those fateful days in

January 1964.

Probably more than anything else, even more than salary demands, the mutinies were inspired by black nationalism and were a military expression of indigenous political aspirations; so was the Zanzibar revolution, although it transcended race and included some Arabs and Persians in the vanguard in the quest for racial justice.

But since the oppressive regime which was overthrown was Arab, oppressing and exploiting black people more than anybody else, the revolution assumed a racial dimension as an indigenous expression of the political and economic aspirations of the black majority – who did not need communism to wake them up to reality and show them that they were being oppressed and exploited by the Arabs because they were weak and black. Experience is the best teacher.

Although it is true that American policy towards Africa during the Johnson Administration (as well as preceding and future ones) was one of communist containment, there was little evidence to show that communism was gaining ground anywhere on the continent; hence Ambassador Harriman's observation as early as 1964 that – "not a single new African nation has succumbed to Communist penetration"; and the conclusion, in the same year, by the US State Department that: "There is no hard evidence at this time that the trouble in East Africa (the army mutinies) was part of an inter-related communist plot to take over the area."[36]

A plausible explanation for American involvement in "facilitating" the establishment of the union of Tanganyika and Zanzibar may lie in the fact that the interests of the United States with regard to Zanzibar coincided with those of Julius Nyerere who had always wanted all the countries in the region (including Zanzibar) to unite, and therefore the American government – at best – did not interfere and try to block the union from being formed; but not in the fact, the erroneous fact, that the union was conceived and

176

engineered by the United States and Britain.

Whereas the United States may have been concerned about the potential for the establishment of a communist regime in Zanzibar which could serve as a beachhead for communist incursions into the African continent and threaten her geopolitical and strategic interests on the continent and in the Indian Ocean as a world power – since the island nation would be turned into a communist satellite dominated by the Soviet Union or the People's Republic of China; Nyerere, on the other hand, saw the establishment of the union as a step towards African unity and a realisation of his Pan-African ambition to unite countries in the region; an ambition he had always cherished long before the "communist-inspired" revolution in Zanzibar took place, and even long before Tanganyika and other countries in the region won independence.

But even if the Americans thought that by uniting Zanzibar with Tanganyika, communists would be deprived of a base in the island nation under a radical regime, they were not very comfortable with Nyerere himself under whose leadership Zanzibar's radicalism was supposed to be contained or neutralised; thus raising a number of question including – why would they help such a leader to unite his country with Zanzibar in the first place.

Therefore, the legitimacy of the fundamental assumption – or argument – itself that Nyerere united Tanganyika with Zanzibar at the behest of the United States and Britain, and not on his own initiative, loses credibility.

In fact, recently declassified documents show that President Lyndon Johnson and members of his administration, as well as many – if not most – members of the United States Congress, were not comfortable with Nyerere's socialist beliefs and policies. According to a memo written by a National Security Council staff member, Ulric Haynes, on 8 June 1966:

177

"Under the mercurial and fiery independent leadership of Nyerere, Tanzania is the bastion of radicalism in East Africa.... Soviet and Chicom influence is considerable, especially in Zanzibar."[37]

According to the documents released, the Central Intelligence Agency (CIA) was actively involved in covert operations in East Africa in the mid-sixties (and later, of course), although they don't specifically say what the activities were; no one expects them to, given the clandestine nature of their operations. But such explicit admission by the CIA of its activities in East Africa only corroborated some of the accusations made against the United States in her attempts to sow dissension in the region.

It also confirms the accusation by President Nyerere that the United States tried to undermine his government, leading to a deterioration of relations between the two countries and prompting the expulsion of American diplomats from Tanzania. As Nyerere himself stated in 1966:

"We have twice quarrelled with the US Government; once when we believed it to be involved in a plot against us, and again when two of its officials misbehaved and were asked to leave Tanzania....

The disagreements certainly induced an uncooperative coldness between us, thus suspending and then greatly slowing down further aid discussions. A comparison of American aid to Tanzania and other African countries supports the contention that at any rate our total policies (including support of the African liberation movements) have led to a lower level of assistance than might otherwise have been granted."[38]

It was later said the expulsion of the two American diplomats from Tanzania was based on false intelligence

178

provided by the Russians – KGB agents based in Dar es Salaam – who worked with the Tanzanian authorities on the case which had been initiated by the Russians themselves.

But that does not change the fact that Nyerere did not flinch from making hard decisions – expelling American diplomats – and from taking a firm stand against the United States, or against any other power, if he had to; nor does it change the fact that the CIA did, at different times, try to undermine his government. The two diplomats, Frank Carlucci and Robert Gordon, were given 24 hours to leave Tanzania.

The United States itself, the most advanced country in the world and in the entire history of mankind, with highly sophisticated intelligence-gathering capabilities, has on a number of occasions taken decisive and even lethal action against its perceived enemies on the basis of false – even deliberately falsified – intelligence as happened in the case of Iraq when it invaded that country and became embroiled in a war which cost tens of thousands of lives to destroy "weapons of mass destruction" which did not even exist. It was later verified that Iraq never had those weapons which the United States used to justify its invasion.

If the United States, a major world power, can make such a "mistake," what about a small and underdeveloped country like Tanzania making a mistake involving a case that required intelligence-gathering capabilities it did not even have? It is in that context that President Nyerere's decision should be looked at, as a rational decision any responsible leader would have taken in the best interest of his country involving national security.

His decision was nothing to be ashamed of. It was based on the intelligence that was provided to him an his cabinet. He made an honest judgement based on the information he believed to be correct and which came from a credible source on a case that involved national security. Therefore, for anyone to suggest that his decision was hasty and irrational is to make an irrational judgement of what he did. And there was reason to be suspicious of the activities of the United States in Tanzania even with regard to the union of Tanganyika and Zanzibar.

Obviously because of his policies, the United States did not see Nyerere as an ally in the region and therefore had no reason to help him establish and consolidate a union – of Tanganyika and Zanzibar – except in strategic "partnership" to thwart communist advances, of which there were actually none, and about which Nyerere was not worried as he clearly demonstrated when he forged strong ties with Communist China and, to a lesser degree, with the Soviet Union and her satellites. If the United States had no strategic interests in the region, it would not have supported the union even if she knew formation of such a union would not militate against her interests.

In many fundamental respects, his policies were the exact opposite of those of the United States. He was a socialist, opposed to capitalism. The United States was and still is capitalist, opposed to socialism. He was an implacable foe of apartheid South Africa and other white minority and colonial regimes on the continent – the Portuguese colonies of Angola, Mozambique, Guinea-Bissau and Cape Verde, and Principe and Sao Tome; Rhodesia (Zimbabwe); and South West Africa (Namibia) ruled by apartheid South Africa in defiance of United Nations resolutions which terminated its mandate to rule the former German colony. The United States, on the other hand, supported apartheid South Africa, Rhodesia, and Portugal as geopolitical and strategic allies during the Cold War and as a bulwark against communism in Africa – a red herring to perpetuate Western domination of the continent.

The United States also supported Portugal, a fellow NATO member, and refrained from criticising her policies in her African colonies because the Americans were allowed to maintain a military base on the Portuguese-controlled Azores islands in the Atlantic Ocean northwest of Africa. The United States and other Western countries also supported apartheid South Africa, Rhodesia, and Portugal for racist reasons, taking sides with their kith-and-kin regardless of the immorality of such a stance. As Nyerere bluntly stated in his article, "Rhodesia in the Context of Southern Africa," published in *Foreign Affairs*:

"The deep and intense anger of Africa on the subject of Rhodesia is by now widely realized. It is not, however, so clearly understood. In consequence the mutual suspicion, which already exists between free African states and nations of the West, is in danger of getting very much worse....

Successive Western governments have declared their hostility to apartheid, and their adherence to the principles of racial equality. They have frequently made verbal declarations of their sympathy with the forces in opposition to South African policies. But they have excused their failure to act in support of their words, on the grounds of South Africa's sovereignty. Africa has shown a great deal of scepticism about this argument, believing that it masked a reluctance to intervene on the side of justice when white privilege was involved. Now, in the case of Southern Rhodesia, legality is on the side of intervention. What is the West going to do? Will it justify or confound African suspicions?

So far the West has demonstrated its intentions by the gradual increase of voluntary economic sanctions; there has been a refusal even to challenge South African and Portuguese support for Smith by making sanctions mandatory upon all members of the United Nations. And there have been repeated statements by the responsible authority that force will not be used except in case of a break-down in law and order – which apparently does not cover the illegal seizure of power! What happens if the economic sanctions fail to bring down the Smith regime is left vague.

The suggestion therefore remains that, despite legality, the domination of a white minority over blacks is acceptable to the West....It is time...for Britain and the United States of America to make clear whether they really believe in the principles they claim to espouse, or whether their policies are governed by considerations of the privileges of their 'kith and kin.'"[39]

Therefore, whatever help Nyerere got from the United States and Britain to form the union of Tanganyika and Zanzibar – and there is no tangible evidence of that – it did not have any moderating influence on his Pan-African militancy. He continued to criticise the West, as he did the East, when he deemed it appropriate to do so. And his criticism was not confined to their policies towards Africa. For example, when the Warsaw Pact forces led by the Soviet Union invaded Czechoslovakia in August 1968, claiming they had been invited, Nyerere sharply responded: "Call an invasion, an invasion, not an invitation."[40]

The Tanzania government also issued a formal statement on 21 August 1968 condemning the invasion. According to Colin Legum and John Drsydale in *Africa Contemporary Record: Annual Survey and Documents 1968 – 1969*:

"The violation of Czechoslovakia's sovereignty by the Warsaw Pact countries evoked from Tanzania one of the strongest protests made by any African government. Expressing its 'profound shock,' the Tanzanian Government said that 'this act constitutes the betrayal of all the principles of self-determination and national sovereignty which the governments of these countries had claimed to support and uphold.'

The statement added that Tanzania opposed

182

colonialism of all kinds, whether old or new, in Africa, in Europe or elsewhere.

A week before the invasion of Czechoslovakia, the Tanzanian Government issued an unexpected warning to Communist countries not to interfere in Tanzania's internal affairs or external policies. *The Nationalist* (the daily newspaper of the ruling party TANU) said in an editorial that Tanzanians would not allow such interference just because their relations with some Western countries were strained. 'Let those Eastern countries who think they can do as they like in Tanzania take note of the fact that this is a free and independent nation, and it is determined to remain so'....

A protest note handed to the Soviet embassy in Dar es Salaam after a demonstration by TANU youths on August 21st demanded an immediate and unconditional withdrawal of the 'aggressive troops of the Soviet Union and her four satellite states from the territory of the Socialist Republic of Czechoslovakia'....

The demonstrators later went to the Czechoslovak embassy, where they expressed their sympathy at the suffering which the Czechoslovaks had been forced to endure under the oppressive hands of friends who have now turned against them."[41]

On American involvement in Vietnam, Nyerere had this to say:

"We are told that great principles are involved, and that the richest nation on earth is defending those principles against attack.

What are these principles? There is the principle of self-determination for the people of Vietnam. For twenty years, with unparalleled courage and determination, the people of Vietnam have been fighting for a chance to implement this principle – first against the French, and now against the Americans....(And) if this is a civil war, what are outside nations doing in that conflict?

Again, we are told that democracy is being defended, and only last month (September 1967) there were some 'elections' in South Vietnam. But these elections only covered the 'pacified areas,' and no candidate could stand on a clear platform of opposition to the war! And in any case these were the first elections since 1956, when South Vietnam came into existence, and no one could possibly call the governments of Mr. Diem, or his military successors, democratic.

Or we are told that the outside power responded to a request for assistance from a legitimate government, which was threatened by aggression. One can only look at the figures of soldiers operating in South Vietnam and ask whose aggression?...

The USA must recover from the delirium of power, and return to the principles upon which her nation was founded. Those millions of Americans who are now opposing their government's policies in this matter, and calling for peace, are working for the honour of their country."[42]

On Britain:

"We have quarrelled with the British Government on a number of issues, e.g. when we refused to associate ourselves with the Commonwealth communique on Rhodesia in June 1965; when we refused to support the proposed Commonwealth Peace Mission to Vietnam on the grounds that it was neither practical nor genuine; and when we received a Chinese offer to help with the building of the railway to Zambia while still discussing the possibility of British and American help on the same project."[43]

Tanzania was also the first African country to break diplomatic relations with Britain over Britain's

184

unwillingness and refusal to take decisive action, including the use of military force, to end the rebellion by the white minority regime which illegally declared independence in Rhodesia on 11 November 1965.

On relations with West Germany, Nyerere stated:

"East Germany wanted Tanzania to give diplomatic recognition to her, and West Germany wanted us to ignore the existence of the German Democratic Republic and pretend there is no such administration over the Eastern part of Germany.

In fact we refused recognition to the East German authorities but accepted an unofficial Consulate General from them – a formula which had been accepted in one other African country.

As a result of our decision West Germany withdrew some types of aid – unilaterally breaking a five-year air training agreement – and announced that other aid was under threat if Tanzania did not change her policies. Tanzania refused to do this and told the West Germans to withdraw all their federal government aid."[44]

Nyerere continued to pursue an independent, non-aligned, foreign policy throughout his tenure as president of Tanzania just as he did when he was president of Tanganyika before the union with Zanzibar in April 1964. The union only widened the scope of his activities because of the merger itself as a subject of major interest in diplomatic circles and other international forums; also because it was the first union of independent states on the African continent, setting a precedent; and because of the controversy over Zanzibar as a potential communist outpost, and the revolution itself as a phenomenal event in the history of African decolonisation hailed across the continent for its Pan-African militancy.

And despite Nyerere's own commitment to African unity which inspired him to unite Tanganyika with

185

Zanzibar, the political dynamics in the island nation itself also played an important role in facilitating the establishment of the union.

Therefore, even if Tanganyika did not have a leader of Nyerere's calibre and depth of Pan-African commitment, the unstable situation in Zanzibar only a few miles from the mainland – 24 miles or so – would perhaps have encouraged or compelled another leader to seek such a merger himself, even if it was just for the security of the mainland without any concern for African unity.

And there is concern for security. Even today, in the minds of many Tanzanian leaders on the mainland, of paramount importance in consummation of the union was security for the mainland. Many of them, even Nyerere himself, may not have explicitly said so. But there is no question that in addition to Nyerere's quest for Pan-African solidarity in pursuit of regional and continental unity, security of the mainland and the entire region was also a major concern.

A radical or an unstable state just a few miles offshore which could destabilise the mainland and may be even spread chaos to other parts of East Africa, but especially to what was then Tanganyika, could not be tolerated by any leader on the mainland.

What if the island nation were to be torn by civil strife? What if it degenerated into chaos? Where would the people flee? Where would the islanders seek refuge?

What if an independent Zanzibar had a radical government and radical leaders across the spectrum – social and political – who wanted to spread their brand of radicalism and teachings to the mainland to upset the social order in order to have leaders who shared their social and political beliefs? What would the mainlanders have to do to ensure their own security, that they were safe from such upheavals, considering Zanzibar's close proximity to the mainland?

The best way to contain and even neutralise such

186

radicalism, any form of radicalism coming from Zanzibar, was to unite the two countries, and continue to maintain the union even today.

Had Zanzibar been 300 miles away in the Indian Ocean, it would have been an entirely different story. You could see the boats coming, after getting advance warning from the mainland's surveillance of her territorial waters that they were on the way, giving the mainland's authorities ample time to stop or intercept them. As Joseph Warioba who concurrently served as prime minister and vice president of Tanzania from 1985 to 1990 said in an interview in 1996, the mainland wanted to maintain the union for security reasons even decades after it was formed. According to Mohammed Ali Bakari in his book, *The Democratisation Process in Zanzibar: A Retarded Transition*:

"Joseph Warioba, former Prime Minister, for example, was asked as to why the Mainland is not willing to part with Zanzibar given the fact that the latter has on some occasions violated the agreements of the Union, and economically, it is a burden to the Union government for its failure to pay its share of costs in the running the Union government? And he categorically responded:

'Even if economically we do not gain anything from the Union, we are highly concerned with security implications. We cannot afford to dismantle the Union. Zanzibar is just a few miles from the mainland – the security of the mainland may be destabilized.'

A supplementary question was posed by another participant (in a discussion in Hamburg, Germany) as to how he could justify such fear when Zanzibar is a very small country with a population of only 800,000 and Tanganyika has a population of 27 million. Again, he responded: 'it might be that our fear cannot be justified,

187

but certainly we have that perception."[45]

Perception is reality even if it does not correspond to reality. But in the case of the mainland and Zanzibar, concerning fear among some mainlanders for the mainland's security if Zanzibar were to become an outpost of instability and insecurity, that is the reality. One Tanzanian scholar, Mwesiga Baregu, went even further by being more explicit:

"It is quite clear to me that Tanganyika would not feel secure with an offshore Zanzibar controlled by Oman (where the former rulers of Zanzibar came from) or hosting a U.S. Naval or airforce base. Neither would Zanzibari indigenous nationalism – which precipitated the 1964 revolution – tolerate such a situation. The result would likely be chaos and internecine conflicts which would inevitably engulf at least both countries, if the ten-mile strip on the East coast of Kenya does not become an issue!!"[46]

What Professor Baregu calls "indigenous nationalism" is a euphemism for black African nationalism on the former island nation which is overwhelmingly black. The Zanzibar revolution can not be justified without them because of the social, political and economic injustices they suffered at the hands of the Arab rulers who were overthrown during the 1964 upheaval.

Although Tanganyika united with Zanzibar to form one country, the union was not a complete merger in all areas. Zanzibar retained its status as a separate entity, with its own identity, while Tanganyika lost hers and no longer exists as a political entity – not even as a geographical region. What was once known as Tanganyika is now simply known as mainland Tanzania or Tanzania mainland. But both countries lost their sovereignties when they united to form Tanzania. Their sovereignties were

188

submerged in a larger entity, the macro-nation of Tanzania, although Zanzibar still exists as a political and geographical entity.

But Zanzibar is semi-autonomous only because it does not enjoy international recognition as a legal sovereign entity. In reality, it is autonomous. It enjoys great autonomy, which is not equivalent to being semi-autonomous. It has its own government with complete jurisdiction in many areas. It has its own president who is not subordinate to the union president in many areas. It even has its own flag, and its own constitution which differs from the union constitution in many respects including its definition of Zanzibar as a separate country, not a part of another country.

Even Zanzibaris who support the union have, together with their brethren who are against it, always insisted on maintaining their separate identity as Zanzibaris. They also contend that Zanzibar is still a separate country even if it is an integral part of the United Republic of Tanzania. And there are those who want to break up the union. They want to return to the status quo ante when Zanzibar was an independent nation enjoying full international recognition because of its sovereign status.

Zanzibaris will *never* give up their identity as Zanzibaris. Many of them don't even want to call themselves Tanzanians, an identity they contend was imposed on them when they were forced into a union with Tanganyika.

But there are those who support the union. One of them is Ali Karume, a son of Zanzibar's first president, Abeid Karume. He is a vocal supporter of the union and is resolutely opposed to the restructuring of the union which would lead to the establishment of three governments: a union government, a government for Zanzibar which already exists, and a government for Tanganyika, all separate with distinct jurisdictions. Like Nyerere who was also strongly opposed to the three-tier government system

189

for Tanzania which he said would signal the end of the union, Ali Karume contends that creation of three governments will lead to dissolution of the union which will not last even five years if the three-tier government structure is adopted.

He reiterated that position in July 2013 in an interview with the *Guardian*, Dar es Salaam, and in other forums. He articulated the same position together with many other Tanzanians on the union's 50th anniversary in April 2014.

During his presidency, Benjamin Mkapa issued probably the strongest warning ever given by a Tanzanian leader to those who want to disrupt the union. He emphatically stated that the government will do everything it can to protect the union even if it has to be ruthless. There will be no mercy for those who are trying to destroy it.

His strong warning was directed at the opposition, especially the Civic United Front (CUF) which is opposed to the union, and others who are against it.

The CUF also refused to recognise his victory after he won a second term in 2000.

He hailed the union as "a symbol of unity in the whole of Africa."[47]

There is no question that there is strong opposition to the union itself and to the two-government structure on both sides of the union. But the strongest opposition comes from Zanzibar. Therefore something must to done to resolve the matter.

In order for the union to continue to exist as a stable entity, there is an imperative need to make major concessions to Zanzibaris.

Give them what they want, short of total independence, by granting them extensive autonomy in many areas – except vital ones such as security (intelligence services, police, and the military), immigration, foreign affairs, and monetary policy under which they can not have their own currency and their own central bank. There must be one currency, and one central bank, for the whole country: the United Republic of Tanzania.

That is probably one of the best ways to neutralise secessionist sentiments in the isles.

The union government, especially mainland leaders, must face this reality. Without extensive devolution, expect agitation and even unrest to continue in Zanzibar with some spillover on to the mainland.

The key is greater autonomy for Zanzibar. If that does not work, form a confederation as a last resort, but with a strong central government, and a constitutional provision which allows secession – only if wishes to secede have been determined in an internationally supervised plebiscite to be the expression of the majority of Zanzibaris. Mainlanders should be accorded the same right. That is the only way the union can be dissolved on amicable terms.

But for their own security, mainlanders should do everything they can – never to allow Zanzibar to secede. Zanzibar is not the Seychelles, Mauritius or the Comoros separated from the mainland by vast expanses of water of the mighty Indian Ocean. It's next door. It takes only simple canoes to get to the mainland from Zanzibar. Should the isles degenerate into anarchy or become an incubator and breeding ground for subversive elements bent on spreading chaos to the mainland in pursuit of their agenda or whatever agenda they want to implement, the mainland will be in danger. Subversive elements can easily get to the mainland and cause trouble.

However, denying Zanzibar greater autonomy through extensive devolution of power can only radicalise those elements even further and fuel secessionist sentiments in the isles. And, as a last resort, the only way they can be contained or neutralised is by military occupation of Zanzibar – a prospect too ghastly to contemplate – which in the end will mean the end of the union itself. Not only will it destroy the union; the mainland would have to be

191

prepared to face more enemies from the isles who have been radicalised by the injustices they have suffered as a result of the military occupation of their homeland by the union forces.

So, listen to Zanzibaris. They know what they want. Give them what they want – but within prescribed limits, taking into account security concerns by the mainland which were also major concerns on the part of Tanganyika when the union with Zanzibar was formed. But they were not the only reason Nyerere decided to unite the two countries.

However, there is no question that the revolution in Zanzibar was a major catalyst towards unification. But the revolution itself must be looked at in its proper context from an African perspective and without being blinded by ideological biases.

The Zanzibar revolution took place in the midst of the Cold War. Therefore, the communist threat could not have been ignored anymore than a threat from the West could have been: penetration and domination of the island nation by the United States and other Western powers after the revolution to secure their geopolitical and strategic interests in the region and keep the Russians and the Chinese out.

A threat to independence from the West is no more benign than a threat from the East; a "subtle" distinction that still seems to elude many Westerners, including political pundits, who think the West is a paragon of virtue and had the right to control Zanzibar to make sure the island nation was not dominated by the Russians or the Chinese and their local communist stooges.

Western domination of Africa was not a blessing. Otherwise African countries would have been happy to remain under colonial rule and would never have fought for independence.

It is also important to look at Zanzibar from another African perspective on why the union was important for black Zanzibaris who constituted the vast majority of the population in the island nation.

There was a racial element in the quest for unity between Tanganyika and Zanzibar. Black people in Zanzibar had been oppressed by the Arabs for centuries. The oppression included outright enslavement of blacks not only on the islands but also on the mainland which was the source of slaves who were taken to Zanzibar and beyond. Indigenous blacks themselves, in Zanzibar, trace their origin to the mainland from where they migrated many centuries ago.

The January 1964 revolution won them freedom. But with freedom was the residual fear that their former masters could reclaim the islands one day and re-institute tyranny with the help of the Arab states, especially the Gulf States, Oman in particular where the majority of the Arabs in Zanzibar including the sultanate came from.

Their only hope for security was a union with Tanganyika, a country much bigger and stronger than Zanzibar, and with more than 20 times the population, also mostly black just like the vast majority of the Zanzibaris themselves.

Security was undoubtedly a factor when the black leaders of Zanzibar promptly agreed to the merger, with Zanzibari President Abeid Karume calling for total unification; a formula rejected by Nyerere who felt that total renunciation of sovereignty by Zanzibar, without retaining extensive autonomy, would destabilise the union and even lead to its dissolution.

Therefore, the union was a product of a combination of factors, internal and external, but mostly internal. As Samir Amin said in the First Babu Memorial Lecture in honour of the late Abdulrahman Mohammed Babu (22 September 1924 – 5 August 1996), one of the architects of the Zanzibar revolution and the union of Tanzania, in London on September 22, 1997:

193

"For me, speaking about Babu is speaking, not only of a comrade and an elder but of a personal friend whom I knew right from the post-war period – the whole of our generation in Africa. Babu was someone with whom I shared most political views for something like 40 years....

It was in London, in 1952, that we first met. Babu was then, like me, a young student, he was elder to me by a few years which at that point of time seemed a considerable difference – later of course the difference lost most of its meaning.

We were both very active among African students in Britain and France trying to start a unified movement.... Babu was connected to the East African anti-colonialist committee....

Babu did better than I (did in Egypt) because he was able... to participate in the creation of objective forces in his country – Zanzibar – which led to a revolution in January 1964, which potentially at least could go beyond nationalist populism.

I knew of course what Babu thought of all this. We had been on the board of a magazine, *Revolution*, which was published in 62/63 i.e. just before the Zanzibar revolution.... We worked, both of us, with others on that magazine, to look at precisely this question. Is it possible and if so under what conditions for nationalist populism to move to the left?... provided the popular classes organised independently go into conflict with the system and go ahead. Babu tried to do this in Zanzibar with some success.... (The) merger...(of) Zanzibar with Tanganyika to form Tanzania...partly...was for reasons internal to Tanzania (Tanganyika) and Zanzibar."[48]

Even without external forces, internal factors alone – "reasons internal to Tanzania (Tanganyika) and Zanzibar," as Samir Amin put it, which also led to the merger of the two countries – constituted sufficient ground for the establishment of the union. But without the Zanzibar

194

revolution, which was an expression of the collective sentiments of frustrated and downtrodden blacks, especially the young, the union of the two countries would probably not have taken place when it did.

The revolution provided a powerful impetus to the merger of the two predominantly black nations, and the leader of the revolution, self-styled Field Marshal John Okello originally from Uganda, provided an equally powerful rallying point for the frustrated black masses groaning under Arab oppression.

The ouster of the oppressive Arab regime was carried out by only a few hundred men – figures range from 300 to 600, but it probably was 300 – led by John Okello.

But after they seized the radio station and other vital installations including the police station where they seized more weapons, and Okello went on the air to announce the takeover, the majority of the African population welcomed the change and rallied behind the freedom fighters giving overwhelming support to the revolution.

Although the Afro-Shirazi Party (ASP) which represented African interests did not participate in the initial phase of the revolution, including its actual planning and launching, it immediately gave full support to the uprising and acted as the official organ articulating the sentiments of the downtrodden black masses. It was joined by the Umma (People's) Party of Abdulrahman Mohammed Babu with which it went on to form a coalition government.

Thousands of supporters of the revolution and the Afro-Shirazi Party (ASP) struck back at their former oppressors, attacking landowners and merchants – who were mostly Arab and Indian – and their property including private homes. The killings spread further to include ordinary Arabs and Asians by virtue of their position as members of the oppressive races. In addition to the hundreds killed, thousands fled the islands and sought refuge elsewhere in Arab countries, Europe, Asia, and even in Africa itself. Many fled to Tanganyika as well, as they did to Kenya. In fact, the sultan of Zanzibar himself and his family and others fled to Dar es Salaam, Tanganyika, after they were denied entry into Kenya, at Mombasa, where they first sought refuge. Many other people also fled to the Comoro Islands.

Many of those targeted in the uprising were also originally from the Comoros, an island nation which has had historical ties with Zanzibar – and even with mainland Tanzania, formerly Tanganyika – for centuries. The Comorians are mostly of mixed Arab-Malay-African ancestry. And in the racially stratified society of Zanzibar, they were also, together with the Arabs and the Asians – mostly Indian – above blacks.

Also, in addition to the historical ties between the Comoros and Zanzibar, there are also racial ties, especially Arab, and linguistic ties. The main languages spoken in the Comoros are Shikomori and Arabic. Shikomori is heavily influenced by Arabic. It is also influenced by Kiswahili which is itself heavily influenced by Arabic, just like in Zanzibar. French is also spoken in the Comoros and is one of the official languages since the islands were once a French colony.

But in spite of the fact that many Comorians have African ancestry, they did not in general sympathise with the plight of black people in Zanzibar since they were members of a different "racial stock," or ethnic group, a confluence of three tributaries: Arab, Malay, and African. And because of their higher status in Zanzibar, as well as contempt for blacks they shared with the Arabs and the Indians, they were some of the primary targets during the revolution.

Estimates of the number killed vary. Some put it even as high as 20,000. But after some extrapolation, it was obviously in the hundreds; may be no fewer than 2,000.

It was virtually a one-sided conflict, with black Africans having the upper hand after Okello and his men

196

seized weapons from the police station they had overtaken. Most of those killed were Arab. Although Indians, Comorians and other minorities were some of the victims, they did not perish in large numbers as the Arabs did.

It was one of the bloodiest conflicts in the history of colonial Africa and one of the most well-known. But out of this bloodshed emerged a new nation, born out of a merger of two countries, Tanganyika and Zanzibar, a union that would probably not have been formed when it was, had the revolution not taken place, prompting the Zanzibari Africans to seek immediate protection from Tanganyikans for their newly won freedom by uniting with them; lest their former oppressors launch a counter-attack some time in the future and re-impose tyranny on the islands.

Concern for security by blacks in Zanzibar; a deteriorating economic situation in the island nation; willingness – after some heated debate – of their leaders to unite with Tanganyika; the unstable political situation on the isles; Nyerere's desire to eliminate any threat to Tanganyika that may come from an unstable, economically non-viable and weak neighbour whose weakness would have provided an opportunity for external forces to intervene and dominate the island nation – and that included possible intervention by the West, not just by the East; and his desire to unite all the countries in the region, probably more than anything else; all these factors combined to facilitate the unification of Tanganyika and Zanzibar on 26 April 1964, only three-and-half months after the revolution on January 12th, leading to the establishment of the first union of independent states in Africa, a feat that has not been duplicated anywhere else on the continent.

After the union, Tanzania also became one of the most stable and peaceful countries in Africa under the leadership of Julius Nyerere. Before the union, he had also presided over the establishment and growth of Tanganyika, one of the most ethnically diverse countries on the continent, yet which became one of the most cohesive states in the history of post-colonial Africa.

But in spite of all these achievements, most of Nyerere's critics give him little credit for them, focusing, instead, on his failed economic policies he pursued along socialist lines.

There is no question that his socialist policies were a failure in many cases, good intentions notwithstanding; something even his admirers should admit, as many of them indeed do. There is evidence of that. There is also evidence of his achievements in many areas including economic, not just social.

He did his best – which he himself once said would be a fitting epitaph for him after he died – and definitely meant well, as clearly demonstrated by his deep concern for the wellbeing of the masses which even had a saintly dimension in spite of all his flaws as a mere mortal like the rest of us, including hallowed saints, and one of the most humble, unlike most.

But his achievements must also be acknowledged and not overlooked or deliberately ignored because of what his critics consider to be his failed socialist policies. As Professor Ali Mazrui stated in his tribute to Nyerere at Cornell University in October 1999:

"Julius Kambarage Nyerere's radical thought was multifaceted. He began as an anticolonial African nationalist on his return home, seeking the independence of Tanganyika....

Linked to Nyerere's nationalism from quite early was his Pan-Africanism, a commitment to the pursuit of African unity and the adoption of the principle of African solidarity whenever possible. Sometimes he put his Pan-Africanism ahead of his Tanganyika nationalism, as when in 1960 he offered to delay Tanganyika's independence if this would help achieve the creation of an East African federation of Tanganyika, Kenya and Uganda. In the end, there was not enough political will in the other two countries – Kenya and Uganda – to achieve such a union. African researchers need to investigate why it has been so difficult to achieve regional integration.

Nevertheless, Tanganyika played host to other major Pan-African activities. It became a frontline state for the liberation of southern Africa from Portuguese rule and from white minority governments. Politically the colony for a while hosted the Pan-African Freedom Movement for Eastern, Central and Southern Africa (PAFMECSA). Tanganyika subsequently established major training camps for southern African liberation fighters.

Much later, Nyerere's Tanzania hosted the sixth Pan-African Congress (in 1974 at the University of Dar es Salaam, in Nkrumah Hall, named after another ardent Pan-Africanist leader), an attempt to re-establish the solidarity of Africa and its diaspora worldwide. This was the first of the Pan-African Congresses actually to be held in Africa. The fifth was in Manchester in 1945, with participants who included Kwame Nkrumah, Jomo Kenyatta, W.E.B. DuBois, and George Padmore. The Dar es Salaam Congress of 1974 was in a great Pan-African tradition....

Domestically in Tanzania he inaugurated three reforms – a political system based on the principle of the one-party state, an economic system based on an African approach to socialism – what he called ujamaa, or familyhood – and a cultural system based on the Swahili language.

The cultural policy based on Kiswahili was the earliest and most durable. Tanganyika – and later Tanzania – became one of the few African countries to use an indigenous language in parliament and as the primary language of national business.

Kiswahili was increasingly promoted in politics, administration, education, and the media. It became a major instrument of nation-building, and nation-building became the most lasting of Nyerere's legacies. Yet,

Africana researchers have done little work on Nyerere's best contribution....

Why did ujamaa fail? Was it domestic factors? Was it external pressures? Was Nyerere building socialism without socialists? We need a postmortem on ujamaa....

(Also) Nyerere's Tanganyika did form a union with Zanzibar. This remains the only case in Africa of previoulsy sovereign states uniting into a new country – and surviving as one entity more than three decades. What used to be sovereign Tanganyika and Zanzibar became the United Republic of Tanzania in 1964.

Nyerere strengthened the union when he united the ruling Afro-Shirazi Party of Zanzibar with the ruling party of Tanganyika (TANU – Tanganyika African National Union – in 1977) to form the new Chama Cha Mapinduzi, the Party of the Revolution.

Will this union of Zanzibar and Tanganyika survive Nyerere's death? Once again have Africana scholars done enough to find out why Africans find it so hard to unite?

Has Nyerere's political behaviour sometimes reflected his upbringing as a Roman Catholic?

One school of thought explains his recognition of the secessionist Biafra in 1969 as a form of solidarity with fellow Catholics against a Federal Nigeria, which would have been dominated by Muslims. This was in the middle of the Nigerian civil war. The Igbo of Biafra were overwhelmingly Roman Catholic. It seems much more likely that Nyerere recognized Biafra for humanitarian reasons.

What about the assertion that Nyerere's military intervention in Uganda in 1979 was motivated by a sectarian calculation to defend a mainly Christian Uganda from the Muslim dictator, Idi Amin? In reality, Nyerere might once again have been more motivated by a wider sense of humanitarianism and universal ethics. He was also defending Tanzania from Idi Amin's territorial appetites.

Most Western judges of Julius Nyerere have concentrated on his economic policies and their failures. Ujamaa and villagisation have been seen as forces of economic retardation that kept Tanzania backward for at least another decade.

Not enough commentators have paid attention to Nyerere's achievements in nation-building. He gave Tanzanians a sense of national consciousness and a spirit of national purpose. One of the poorest countries in the world found itself to be one of the major actors on the world scene.

Nyerere's policies of making Kiswahili the national language of Tanzania deepened this sense of Tanzania's national consciousness and cultural pride. Parliament in Dar es Salaam debated exclusively in Kiswahili. Government business was increasingly conducted in Kiswahili. The mass media turned away from English in favour of Kiswahili. Newspapers had not only letters to the editor but also poems to the editor in Kiswahili. And the educational system was experiencing the stresses and strains of the competing claims of English and Kiswahili.

Nyerere's translation of two of Shakespeare's plays into Kiswahili was done not because he 'loved Shakespeare less, but because he loved Kiswahili more.' He translated Shakespeare into Kiswahili partly to demonstrate that the Swahili language was capable of carrying the complexities of a genius of another civilization.

Above all, Nyerere as president was a combination of deep intellect and high integrity...(and) was in a class by himself in the combination of ethical standards and intellectual power. In the combination of high thinking and high ethics, no other East African politician was in the same league."[49]

That is probably an understatement. Hardly any other politician on the entire continent was in the same league with Nyerere in terms of high ethical standards and intellectual prowess; a rare combination. As Professor Mazrui himself stated – almost ten years after Nyerere died – in an interview with *The Gambia Echo* in July 2008:

"Intellectually, I admired Julius K. Nyerere of Tanzania higher than most politicians anywhere in the world. Nyerere and I also met more often over the years from 1967 to 1997 approximately.

I am also a great fan of Nelson Mandela. By ethical standards Mandela is greater than Nyerere; but by intellectual standards Nyerere is greater than Mandela."[50]

Nyerere's most enduring legacy is the nation he left behind as a united, stable entity; a phenomenon rare on the continent.

It all started with Tanganyika. He built Tanganyika into a cohesive state out of more than 126 different tribes and racial minority groups including Arabs, Asians, and Europeans. And he went on to create a larger nation, Tanzania, by uniting Tanganyika with Zanzibar during some of the most tempestuous times in Africa's post-colonial era.

By the time he died, the union had survived 35 years. And it will always be remembered as one of his biggest achievements. Yet, as Nyerere himself conceded:

"My greatest success is also my greatest disappointment. We have established a nation – Tanzania – that is some achievement. Stable, united, proud with immense clarity of what it wants to do, committed to the liberation of our continent. It has played an immense role, poor as it is, in the liberation of our continent and it will continue playing it.

So that is what I think is our greatest achievement. But it is also our failure. I never wanted a Tanzania. I really do not believe that these African countries should establish different sovereignties. They are artificial creations, all of them."[51]

Africa is a natural entity. Achieving African unity is a goal to which he dedicated his life. As he said in Accra where he was invited by President Jerry Rawlings in 1997 to celebrate the 40th anniversary of Ghana's independence: "We are all Africans trying very hard to be Ghanaians or Tanzanians."[52]

He made that remark in a country whose founding father, Dr. Kwame Nkrumah, was one of the most uncompromising advocates of African unity and independence – twin Pan-African goals – and an ideological compatriot of Nyerere. As the first black African country to win independence since the partition of Africa at the Berlin Conference in 1885, Ghana set a precedent and became a source of inspiration to other African countries in their struggle to end colonial rule.

Liberia was, of course, the first black African country to attain republican status, but in name only, and remained a virtual American colony throughout its history, as it still is even today: a client state, or America's "51st state" like Puerto Rico.

While Nkrumah blazed the trail for the African independence movement by being the first leader of the first black African country to attain sovereign status, Nyerere also set a precedent by being the first leader on the continent to unite two independent countries to create one nation, Tanzania; and the first East African leader to lead his country to independence. And while Nkrumah preceded Nyerere in political activism and in the struggle for independence – born on 22 September 1909, and Nyerere on 13 April 1922, he was his senior by almost 13 years – the two became peers in the post-colonial era and two of the most influential African leaders in the twentieth century besides Nelson Mandela; with Nyerere also earning the title, "The Conscience of Africa."

Yet, characteristic of his humility, he paid great tribute to Nkrumah when he visited Ghana after he stepped down as president of Tanzania. According to a Ugandan newspaper, *The Monitor*:

"Mwalimu Julius Nyerere paid a visit to Ghana shortly after his retirement in 1985 and reportedly berated the leadership of that country for the shabby way in which the republic's founder, Kwame Nkrumah, had been treated: 'This man is one of the greatest Africans that has ever lived. If you in Ghana don't respect him, the rest of us in Africa do. Independent Africa owes its liberty to this man. The least you can do is...give him a decent burial.'"[53]

Nyerere also acknowledged the inspiration he drew from Nkrumah when he was still a student at Edinburgh University in Scotland earning his master's degree in economics and history, while Nkrumah was leading the independence struggle in Ghana. And in one of his last interviews in December 1998, about a year before he died, Nyerere remembered Nkrumah and talked about the relationship they had in the quest for African unity and independence. He also talked about his attempts to form an East African Federation with Mzee Jomo Kenyatta and Dr. Milton Obote. The interview was published in *The New Internationalist*:

"It was events in Ghana in 1949 that fundamentally changed my attitude. When Kwame Nkrumah was released from prison, this produced a transformation. I was in Britain and, oh, you could see it in the Ghanaians! They became different human beings, different from all the rest of us! This thing of freedom began growing inside all of us. First India in 1947, then Ghana in 1949. Ghana became independent eight years later.

Under the influence of these events, while I was at

university in Britain, I made up my mind to be a full-time political activist when I went back home. I intended to work for three years and then launch into politics. But it happened sooner than I planned....

For me liberation and unity were the most important things. I have always said that I was African first and socialist second. I would rather see a free and united Africa before a fragmented socialist Africa. I did not preach socialism. I made this distinction deliberately so as not to divide the country. The majority in the anti-colonial struggle were nationalist. There was a minority who argued that class was the central issue, that white workers were exploited as black workers by capitalism. They wanted to approach liberation in purely Marxist terms. However, in South Africa white workers oppressed black workers. It was more than class and I saw that....

Even now for me freedom and unity are paramount.... I respected Jomo (Kenyatta) immensely. It has probably never happened in history. Two heads of state, Milton Obote and I, went to Jomo and said to him: 'Let's unite our countries and you be our head of state.' He said no. I think he said no because it would have put him out of his element as a Kikuyu Elder....

It seems that independence of the former colonies has suited the interests if the industrial world for bigger profits at less cost. Independence made it cheaper for them to exploit us. We became neo-colonies. Some African leaders did not realize it. In fact many argued against Kwame (Nkrumah's) idea of neo-colonialism....

Let us create a new liberation movement to free us from immoral debt and neo-colonialism. This is one way forward. The other is through Pan-African unity....

Kwame Nkrumah and I were committed to the idea of unity. African leaders and heads of state did not take Kwame seriously. However, I did. I did not believe in these small little nations. Still today I do not believe in them. I tell our people to look at the European Union, at

205

these people who ruled us who are now uniting.

Kwame and I met in 1963 and discussed African Unity. We differed on how to achieve a United States of Africa. But we both agreed on a United States of Africa as necessary. Kwame went to Lincoln University, a black college in the US. He perceived things from the perspective of US history, where 13 colonies that revolted against the British formed a union. That is what he thought the OAU (Organization of African Unity) should do.

I tried to get East Africa to unite before independence. When we failed in this way, I was wary about Kwame's continental approach. We corresponded profusely on this. Kwame said my idea of 'regionalization' was only balkanization on a larger scale. Later, African historians will have to study our correspondence on this issue of uniting Africa.

Africans who studied in the US like Nkrumah and Azikiwe were more aware of the Diaspora and the global African community than those of us who studied in Britain. They were therefore aware of a wider Pan-Africanism. Theirs was the aggressive Pan-Africanism of W.E.B. DuBois and Marcus Garvey. The colonialists were against this and frightened of it.

After independence, the wider African community became clear to me. I was concerned about education; the work of Booker T. Washington resonated with me. There were skills we needed and black people outside Africa had them. I gave our US Ambassador the specific job of recruiting skilled Africans from the US Diaspora. A few came, like you (the interviewer, Ikaweba Bunting, who had lived in Tanzania for 25 years when he interviewed Nyerere in his home village of Butiama where he returned in 1985 after stepping down from the presidency and buried in 1999). Some stayed; others left.

We should try to revive it (Pan-Africanism). We should look to our brothers and sisters in the West. We should build the broader Pan-Africanism. There is still the room –

and the need."[54]

The Pan-Africanism Nyerere talked about embraced people of African descent in the diaspora, as did Nkrumah's. It also assumed another dimension when the Organisation of African Unity (OAU) was replaced by the African Union (AU) in 2001, which was formally launched in 2002; the diaspora was represented in the OAU as it is in the AU.

The transformation was intended to facilitate continental unification, and strengthen institutions of regional cooperation and Pan-African integration, leading to the establishment of a common market, a common currency, a continental parliament, a Pan-African court and an executive body as an enforcement mechanism responsible for implementing decisions binding on all countries across the continent which the OAU never had.

And although the Ghana-Guinea union and later the Ghana-Guinea-Mali union – formed by Kwame Nkrumah, Sekou Toure, and Modibo Keita – were more symbolic than functional, they served to inspire other Africans across the continent to pursue regional integration and keep the dream of African unity alive.

The most successful of these efforts was, of course, the union of Tanganyika and Zanzibar formed by Julius Nyerere after he failed to convince the leaders of Kenya and Uganda – especially Kenya – to unite with Tanganyika and establish an East African Federation.

And even if the union were to collapse, if secessionist elements (especially with ties to Oman and other Gulf States) in the former island nation of Zanzibar are not neutralised through extensive devolution of power and formation of coalition government or some other institutional arrangements but without unconditional accommodation for separatists, it will still be remembered as one of Nyerere's biggest achievements; and one of the most ambitious experiments in regional integration on the

African continent and in post-colonial history anywhere in the world. As he said in an interview with the *Black World*, an African-American journal, in the early seventies when he was asked how he would like to be remembered after he died, he hoped that people would say: "He did his best."

Julius Kambarage Nyerere

Nyerere

Abeid Amani Karume

John Okello

Abdulrahman Mohamed Babu

John Okello after the revolution

Front row, from left to right,
Abdallah Kassim Hanga and Abeid Amani Karume

Julius Nyerere and Abeid Karume signing the Articles of the Union of Tanganyika and Zanzibar. Second from left on Nyerere's right handside is Oscar Kambona. Third from left, behind Nyerere and Karume, is Kassim Hanga in glasses.

Oscar Kambona

Nyerere with Babu

Babu in the union cabinet

Nyerere with Karume

Nyerere with Karume

Milton Obote

Jomo Kenyatta, Nyerere, Obote, and Tom Mboya

Obote and Nyerere

Obote, Kenyatta, and Nyerere

218

Kenyatta with Nyerere

Nyerere with Kwame Nkrumah

Nyerere with Fidel Castro

The Zanzibar Revolution and the Union of Tanganyika and Zanzibar Revisited in 2014

This is the fiftieth anniversary of the Zanzibar Revolution. It is an important milestone not only in the history of Tanzania but of the entire continent.

The Zanzibar revolution was one of the most significant events in the history of post-colonial Africa.

It was a victory in the struggle for African liberation; it brought fundamental change in Zanzibar; and it helped pave the way for the political union between Tanganyika and Zanzibar which was a major political transformation in the history of the continent.

On 12 January 1964, the Arab rulers of Zanzibar were overthrown in a revolution which went down in history as one of the bloodiest conflicts up to that time in Africa since the end of colonial rule, involving change of government by unconstitutional means.

The armed uprising was led by John Okello, a self-styled field marshal originally from Uganda who had lived in the island nation, on Pemba island, since 1959. He was born in Uganda in 1937 and also lived in Kenya for a few years.

After he moved to Pemba, he became a policeman and joined the Afro-Shirazi Party (ASP) led by Sheikh Abeid Amani Karume. He moved from Pemba to Zanzibar in 1963 where he started preparing secretly for a revolution to end Arab rule.

During the revolution, Okello led a group of about 300 men to seize power from the Arab rulers and overthrew Sultan Sayyid Jamshid bin Abdullah. Jamshid Abdullah, 35, ascended the throne after his father died. Okello was 26.

The people he recruited for the revolution were young men who were also members or supporters of the Afro-Shirazi Party which resented Arab domination. He had been meeting with some of them secretly for some time to prepare for the revolution. And they made history the following year.

When I was writing one of my books, *Nyerere and Africa: End of an Era* in 2002, I got in touch with one of the people who used to live in Zanzibar and who witnessed what happened on the island when the revolution took place. I asked him some questions and he sent me some information. He did not tell me back then exactly who or what he was when he was in Zanzibar until I found out later. He said he was not a Zanzibari or a Tanzanian but an American – that is all he said to me in terms of his identity – and explained the following in "The Zanzibar Revolution" which he also made publicly available:

"On the night of January 12, 1964 a band of some 300 people violently seized the Island of Unguja. They were led by a little known man named John Okello, who had lived on Pemba, having come to the islands some years earlier from Uganda.

In Zanzibar he developed a popular following among a core of young, tough men, many of whom were the Stevedores and Porters who worked the ships coming in

224

and out of Zanzibar Harbor.

His group met in secret. He promised changes to these men, fellows long used to working together, in sometimes dangerous settings, and ready to follow orders of any 'captain' who could pay their fee. Theirs became a rebellion looking for a home.

Political unrest had been increasing on Zanzibar and Pemba since the death of Sultan Khalifa in 1960. He had reigned in Zanzibar for almost 50 years, since 1911.

After much jockeying for constituencies and coalitions the main political parties had narrowly split the two general elections of 1961 to the satisfaction of none. The British were leaving, their troops, including a contingent of Irish Guards, stationed near the golf course at the edge of Stone Town, pulled out in early 1963.

When the new Sultan, Jamshid, hoisted the flag of the independent nation of Zanzibar, on December 10, 1963, he marked the departure of the last British Resident, (Governor) of Zanzibar and the end of the colonial period.

Another election in late 1963 had given a slim majority to a coalition of two political parties, the ZNP (the Zanzibar Nationalist Party) and the ZPPP (the Zanzibar and Pemba Peoples Party). The ASP (the Afro-Shirazi Party) was to be in the minority in a British style parliamentary system with the sultan serving as the reigning but not ruling 'monarch.'

This nation, a full member of the British Commonwealth and a newly enrolled sovereign member of the United Nations was destined to last only 33 days.

Political debates raged and street demonstrations were not uncommon in those days.

I remember bicycling to school through crowds chanting the names of political leaders and traveling in the country past road-blocks manned by British soldiers.

The various factions debated everything; rights versus privileges, new-comers versus old-established families, capitalism vs socialism, merchants vs landowners,

225

Zanzibaris vs Pembans, Asians vs Arabs, Swahilis vs Mainlanders, and all this against the backdrop of the Cold War and the other nationalistic and de-colonial movements abounding in Africa at that time.

John Okello didn't have answers to these thorny issues, but he did have the insight to realize that all of these competing interests presented an opportunity for a man of action like himself. After all, a few hundred determined men might be able to seize the few local centers of communication and the three police barracks.

Once he had those under his control and possessed the weapons stored there, who on the islands could throw him out?

Would the politicians join together to denounce and oppose his illegal actions? Or as he hoped, would they continue to distrust each other, to suspect that one or another of themselves must have put him up to it?

Would not they want to make a deal with him, quick, before someone else did? On that January night he rolled the dice.

The ASP leaders, though surprised by Okellos' actions, (many were not even on the island at the time) moved quickly to embrace the rebels.

Hundreds of party followers were whipped into a frenzy by those eager to seize this opportunity to cut the Gordian knot of democratic debate and go straight to the prize of ruling. They sought to gain the chance to remake society in accordance with their own ideals. Ideals were a dime a dozen in those days. Humanity was to become a much more costly item.

Having seen just how vulnerable a government could be, and not trusting their own mixed record in open elections, it was clear to some ASP leaders that drastic measures were warranted to secure the survival of what was now being called 'The Revolution.'

The mobs were unleashed. Law and order disappeared from the streets of Zanzibar. Landowners and merchants

226

were dragged from their houses and shops, looting and killing spread throughout Stone Town. The city literally sacked itself.

Arabs and Asians, who had supported the other parties in large numbers, were killed indiscriminately. In a single night uncounted lives were lost and over the next few days thousands more fled the islands with only what they could carry.

John Okello established for himself the rank of 'Field Marshal' and, with his mob-battalions, established a reign of terror on the islands. He broadcast bizarre threats and promises of death to all who might oppose him....

When the dust settled the multi-cultural diversity of the islands was radically altered. A one-party state was decreed. Still nervous regarding the possibility of resurgent opposition from their now exiled opponents, the 'revolutionaries' further secured their positions by signing an agreement of confederation with mainland Tanganyika. This would allow thousands of mainland political allies to intervene in any future struggle.

The police forces on the isles were virtually replaced by mainland police loyal to the party and an isolationist curtain fell over the isles which was destined to persist for more than 20 years."[55]

Although the revolution was carried out by only a few hundred people, it had popular support among the majority of black Africans. Thousands of Arabs were killed and thousands more fled the island nation. Sultan Jamshid Abdullah first sought refuge in Mombasa, Kenya, but was denied entry.

He sailed back and went to Dar es Salaam, Tanganyika, where he and his family and others on the vessel were allowed into the country. He later left Tanganyika and went to live in Britain.

The exact number of the people killed in the Zanzibar revolution has never been officially acknowledged but estimates put the figure at least in the thousands. Some say about 17,000 – 20,000 people, mostly Arab, were killed. Other sources, including an American diplomat, Donald Petterson who was in Zanzibar during that time, say 5,000 Arabs were killed. As Donald Petterson stated:

"The population (of Zanzibar) included about 250,000 Africans....In addition to the Africans, Zanzibar had 50,000 Arabs, and about 20,000 Asians of Pakistani and Indian origin. During the revolution, some 5,000 people were killed. Almost all of these were Arabs. That's one tenth of the Arab population. By the time I left the island near the end of 1965, the number of Arabs was less than 25,000....The Asian population was also down by half or more by that time. As the government of Zanzibar became more and more repressive, Asians wanted out, and those who could, left.

Karume, despite a lot of good qualities, became increasingly dictatorial. I didn't see the worst of it during my time and I got along very well with him, as did Frank (Carlucci)....My own relationship with him, and again, this was before he really got bad, was quite good because of the friendship we had established when I was a vice consul, and because I continued to deal with him in his own language, and, of course, treated him with a proper measure of respect."[56]

Probably the most controversial figure in the Zanzibar revolution was John Okello. He played the most important role in the upheaval in spite of attempts by the main leaders of Zanzibar to write him out of history. He was the one who launched and led the revolution. He was the one who was directly responsible for the downfall of the Arab regime in the island nation. And he was the one who announced to the world that the Arab rulers had been overthrown and that the black African majority would be the new rulers. The revolution was not led by Karume,

Babu or Hanga. They were not even in Zanzibar when the revolution took place. They were in Dar es Salaam, Tanganyika.

When I was growing up in Tanzania, it was John Okello who was the most well-known leader of the Zanzibar revolution. He was acknowledged as the leader of the uprising. The revolution took place when I was 14 years old. And as Petterson explained:

"As the afternoon wore on, a phone call from the rebels finally came. It was from Aboud Jumbe, one of the ministers in the new government, who said that he wanted to come over and take Picard to the revolutionary headquarters. In due course he arrived in an open Land Rover with armed people in it. Jumbe himself was heavily armed.

Fritz and I, along with Jim Ruchti and the executive officer, got into the Land Rover and were driven to Raha Leo (about a mile away), the site of the radio station and the African community center. Raha Leo was now the command headquarters of the revolution. There was electricity in the air when we neared Raha Leo. Hundreds of Africans who were in a very fierce mood ringed the place, many or most armed with everything from sticks to old swords; an occasional rifle was seen.

As we approached the headquarters, better-armed revolutionaries came into sight. They carried police rifles, and a few had automatic weapons. We saw Arab prisoners, some of them bloodied, some lying near the entrance to the revolutionary headquarters, all looking despondent. The crowd was so excited because they knew that at that moment, or soon thereafter, Ali Muhsin, whom they hated, would be brought in....

It was so tense as they began to swarm toward the Land Rover, that Aboud Jumbe yelled at them in Swahili (he had a bullhorn) to get back or he would open fire. They obliged, and a way was cleared for us. We got out of

229

the Land Rover and waited for somebody to come out of revolutionary headquarters.

After a while, a figure emerged, a man dressed in a semi-military uniform. He had on dark shorts and a dark blue shirt, a peaked cap, knee socks in the British style. He approached us, went up to the executive officer, pulled a revolver out of his holster, stuck it right at the exec, either in his ribs as I remember it, or in his face as Jim Ruchti remembered it, and said, 'How do you do? I'm John Okello.'

With that, he put his revolver back in the holster and said there was going to be some target practice behind revolutionary headquarters. Would we like to join in? Well, figuring that the targets might well be some of the captured Arabs, we declined.

He escorted us into Raha Leo. We went up the stairs into a meeting room, where after another wait we were ushered into the room.

Sitting there behind a table with Okello were Abeid Karume, leader of the Afro-Shirazi Party and now the president of the new government, Babu, Hanga, and several others.

Back from Dar es Salaam. Karume had come back to Zanzibar by boat early that morning with Babu and Hanga. The British high commissioner had met with them just before we did, and as he left we entered.

The discussion began. Fritz, first of all, told Okello (who had put his revolver on the table with the barrel pointing at Fritz) that we would not negotiate at gunpoint. Okello made no reply, but picked up and reholstered his weapon. He didn't say much during the ensuing discussion, in which Fritz made the request for an evacuation.

Babu replied angrily, so did Hanga; Karume was uncomfortable. They were angry that the Americans had brought in this warship. And it seemed to us, as we thought about it a bit later, that they didn't know whether the Manley might open fire. In any case, they really didn't

230

care for the evacuation. They didn't want to see it happen, but they agreed to it, fearing there might be consequences otherwise.

Finally, Karume indicated that he would not oppose the request. Then he turned to Okello and said, 'It's your decision.'

Okello sort of shrugged and said, 'All right.'

This made it clear to us there that Okello was indeed of great importance. I say this because later on there were those who belittled Okello's role in the revolution. In fact, the official history of the revolution barely mentions him. But he was the force that pulled it off. Weeks later, others with more political sagacity took control...."[57]

Petterson went on to state:

"I formed a friendship with Karume as a result, because I was the only American who spoke Swahili and my Swahili was getting better and better all of the time. We carried out our conversations in Swahili. I was very deferential to him; Fritz was not. Fritz, unfortunately, was a bit patronizing with Karume....

Now Babu was a factor to be reckoned with. He was not an African. He didn't belong to the Afro-Shirazi Party, but his followers, many of whom had been trained in Cuba or other Communist countries, had automatic weapons. They had more firepower than Okello's people, and therefore were a factor to be reckoned with. Babu was the Zanzibar government's foreign minister. I chatted with him, and we agreed we would talk later on. I was told to go back to my own house, which I did.

That began a period of five weeks, during which I was the only American in Zanzibar, pretty heady stuff, a junior Foreign Service officer in charge of the embassy!....

I formed a relationship...also with Babu, who was a very charming guy, a militant left-winger, to say the least, and very shrewd, very intelligent.

231

Karume was a stolid man, not nearly as bright as Babu, but a man of very real native intelligence. I don't mean to use that term in a derogatory sense at all. He was a very able man in many ways, but impressionable and unsophisticated. As time would go by the results of that would be harmful to Zanzibar...."[58]

Petterson further stated:

"In the early part of '64,...by this time, Okello had been eased out of power. He was simply not up to the skills of people like Babu and Karume. He had embarrassed them during the revolution. He had been on the radio giving very inflammatory announcements about who would be killed and who would be boiled in oil and all sorts of grisly comments, which embarrassed some Zanzibaris and terrified others.

But as much as Karume and others in the Afro-Shirazi Party leadership and Babu and his followers feared Okello for a time, they must had known that they would be able to get rid of him at some point. He had no political base. All he had was some mainly very unsophisticated people with weapons. Okello was not clever enough to see that disarming these people, which Karume had inveigled him into doing, and putting them into new military units would remove his base of power.

Sometime in March, he went over to the mainland, and when he came back to Zanzibar, Karume met him at the airport and said, 'You can't get off the plane.' Karume flew with him back to Dar es Salaam, where he stayed for a while before being ejected from Tanganyika.

He was a Ugandan who had gone to Kenya when he was a young man, worked as a laborer, then as a mason, and learned construction skills that he took with him to Pemba in 1959....

He ended up in Uganda. From Dar es Salaam, he went to Kenya, where he was expelled. Nobody wanted this man around. He had a fearsome reputation. People were afraid that wherever he went, he might foment a revolution. He had trouble with immigration authorities and was either expelled from places or put in jail.

Finally he returned to Uganda, where he was imprisoned. In 1971, he was seen with Idi Amin shortly after Amin came to power. Then John Okello disappeared from the face of the earth, no doubt killed by Amin."[59]

Petterson went on to say:

"In the meantime, Karume was concerned about Babu and his people, who had close relations with the Chinese and who were very well armed. Karume feared that they wanted to take over the revolution. So did Julius Nyerere on the mainland.

Nyerere and Karume decided that they would unify their two countries to undercut Babu. This they did, telling only a very few trusted advisors. Their decision, when announced, came as a complete surprise.

Babu was out of town. As Zanzibar's foreign minister, he was in Pakistan on an official visit. When he heard about the union, he was furious. He later denied that he was upset and said, untruthfully, that he knew in advance about the plan for union. When he came back, he found a new political dispensation. The government of Tanzania, the name chosen for the country later, was in the process of being formed.

Babu was given a post in the Tanzanian government, which was located in Dar es Salaam, since it was the new country's capital. In time, other Zanzibaris who were deemed as possible security threats were transferred to mainland jobs or sent off as diplomats. Babu was effectively stripped of his political power. From then on, he was bitter toward Karume and, especially, Nyerere. With Babu's departure from Zanzibar, Karume's power increased.

233

The marriage between Tanganyika and Zanzibar was a marriage of convenience. It had strains from the very beginning. As time went on the relationship became more strained as Zanzibar wanted to run its own foreign affairs, have its own military, and control its own foreign exchange. But the union continued. Nyerere wanted it and Karume wanted it, if on his own terms."[60]

There are those who contend that the union was a product of the Cold War, formed at the behest of the United States and Great Britain, especially the United States, to contain or neutralise communist elements in Zanzibar who supported the Zanzibar revolution.

What is deliberately ignored or overlooked by the proponents of this view is Nyerere's commitment to African unity. More than any other East African leader, he relentlessly sought to unite the countries in the region and even offered to delay the independence of Tanganyika so that the three countries of Kenya, Uganda and Tanganyika would emerge from colonial rule on the same day and form a federation under one government.

Just months before the Zanzibar revolution, the leaders of Kenya, Uganda and Tanganyika – Jomo Kenyatta, Milton Obote and Julius Nyerere – met in Nairobi, Kenya, and signed a declaration on 5 June 1963 which explicitly stated that the three countries would form a federation before the end of the year and invited Zanzibar to join the union after the island nation won independence. They issued the following statement, "Declaration of Federation by the Governments of East Africa":

"We, the leaders of the people and governments of East Africa assembled in Nairobi on 5 June 1963, pledge ourselves to the political Federation of East Africa.

Our meeting today is motivated by the spirit of Pan-Africanism and not by mere selfish regional

234

interests....Within this spirit of Pan-Africanism and following the declaration of African unity at the recent Addis Ababa conference (from May 22 – 25, which led to the establishment of the Organization of African Unity – OAU), practical steps should be taken wherever possible to accelerate the achievement of our common goal. We believe that the East African Federation can be a practical step towards the goal of Pan-African unity...and wish to make it clear that any of our other neighbours may in future join this Federation."[61]

The federation was never formed. Nationalism won over Pan-Africanism. An even bigger federation including Ethiopia, Somalia, Zanzibar, and Nyasaland, was also discussed. But it also got nowhere.

But that did not discourage Nyerere from pursuing unity on a smaller scale with Zanzibar.

Some observers have questioned why Nyerere did not inform his colleagues – the leaders of Kenya and Uganda – about the impending union or invite them to join the merger since he was so determined to unite the countries in the region.

Informing them or inviting them to join the union would not have served any purpose in terms of regional unification. The three East African countries of Kenya, Uganda and Tanganyika had failed to unite just the month before, December 1963, which they had set as the deadline to form a federation that year when the leaders of those countries met in Nairobi in June and signed a declaration of intent, stating that they would unite their countries before the end of the year.

Therefore, inviting his colleagues to join the smaller union would not have convinced them of the merits of unification anymore than the earlier attempt to do so – which failed – did. They were simply not interested; not as much Nyerere was in forming an East African federation.

So, Nyerere made the next move, which was to pursue a merger of Tanganyika and Zanzibar.

It is also worth remembering that even as far back as the mid-fifties, Nyerere worked closely with the leaders of Zanzibar in the quest for independence and in order to bring the two countries even closer than they already were. Prominent leaders of the party in Tanganyika – the Tanganyika African National Union (TANU) which was campaigning for independence on the mainland – also went to Zanzibar to help the Afro-Shirazi Party (which came into power after the revolution) to mobilise the masses for the independence struggle in the island nation. One of those prominent figures was Bibi Titi Mohammed, a fiery campaigner and an effective mobiliser of the masses even in Tanganyika itself.

The two – TANU and the Afro-Shirazi Party – were already sisters parties even before the revolution. Therefore it was only natural that their leaders went a step further and decided to unite their countries which were already bound by historical, cultural and linguistic ties; in fact, Africans in Zanzibar were inextricably linked to the mainland. That is where they originated.

All those ties, which facilitated unification of the two countries, had nothing to do with the Cold War or pressure exerted on Nyerere by the United States and Great Britain to force him to form the union.

Even without pressure from the United States and Britain on Nyerere to form the union in order to eliminate a communist threat from the island, Nyerere would have pursued the goal, anyway, to unite the two countries because of the indissoluble ties between them and his Pan-African commitment in pursuit of African unity. As early as the mid-1905s, he already had an ambition to unite Tanganyika with Zanzibar.

The United States and Great Britain may indeed have wanted the two countries to unite in order to prevent communist leaders in Zanzibar from turning the island nation into a communist state or into "another Cuba" in collusion with Eastern-bloc countries. But Nyerere also wanted to form the union for his own reasons in pursuit of African unity.

Therefore, a more compelling argument is that the interests of the United States and Great Britain – to prevent a communist regime from assuming power in the island nation by placing Zanzibar under the control of Tanganyika – coincided with the interests of Nyerere who wanted to unite the two countries in fulfillment of his Pan-African commitment even if there was no such threat; a goal he had been pursuing long before the Zanzibar revolution.

Pan-Africanism was not a product of the Cold War. It preceded the Cold War. As a philosophy and ideology of decolonisation and unification, it started way back in the 1900s. It did not start after World War II, although it found concrete expression during that period, especially in the fifties and sixties, which became the era of decolonisation on the African continent.

The Cold War argument, competition between the East and the West as the driving force behind the merger of Tanganyika and Zanzibar to protect Western interests in the region and in Africa as a whole, is refuted even by the CIA itself which was active in Zanzibar – and in Tanganyika – according to some of its declassified documents.

While it is true that the United States and Britain wanted to contain Zanzibar to make sure it did not fall into communist hands, hence the imperative need for unity with Tanganyika which would enable Nyerere and his colleagues on the mainland to control radical elements on the island nation, there is no question that Nyerere pursued unification of the two countries on his own initiative.

He already had a track record of trying to unite African countries, first by forming an East African federation of Kenya, Uganda and Tanganyika, which would have become a reality had his colleagues in Kenya and Uganda shared his passion for unity. According to a CIA declassified report on the Zanzibar revolution, "Zanzibar: The Hundred Days' Revolution," 21 February 1966:

"Toward the end of 1956, Julius Nyerere, Tanganyika's foremost African nationalist and the founder of the Tanganyika African National Union (TANU), is reported to have come to Zanzibar t o urge Africans and Shirazis to stand against the Arabs and to form a political party based on pan-Africanism. On hisi initative, the Afro-Shirazi Party (ASP) was formed in 1957....

In late 1963 Mohammed Shamte, the leader the ZPPP (Zanzibar and Pemba People's Party) and the Chief Minister of Zanzibar's coalition government, stated privatelty that Nyerere and Kambona were basically unfriendly to the present government of Zanzibar 'including Zanzibar Africans like myself.' He expressed bafflement, saying he could not figure out what 'I or any Zanzibar Shirazi had ever done to the Tanganyikans.'

TANU leaders themselves usually advanced two basic reasons for their support of the ASP; first, their close feeling of kinship with the African element in Zanzibar and, second, their fear of Communisin or proto-Communism in the ZNP (Zanzibar Nationalist Party), especially people like Babu. Although there was no talk of alliance or annexation, it no doubt was even then the view of the Tanganyikan leaders that Zanzibar ought to be associated closely with Tanganyika.

Three other non-bloc countries, besides Tanganyika, are known to have supported the ASP (Afro-Shirazi Party) before the revolution in 1964.

Ghana was, perhaps, rather slower than Tanganyika in coming out openly in favor of the ASP, but by at least 1961 the die was cast. In that year, the Ghana Bureau of African Affairs sent over $15,000 to assist the ASP in the election; later that year, Ghanaian legal assistance was afforded the ASP in defense of individual Africans accused of offenses committed during the election riots; at the end of 1962 the ASP opened an office in Accra; and in early 1963 the High Commissioner of Ghana in Uganda held private discussions with ASP leaders on the subject of financial assistance for the ASP.

Prior to the independence of Zanzibar, the Ethiopian Government also provided financial assistance to the ASP, on the grounds that it represented the majority and was the only predominately (sic) African political party. Haile Selassie, who was under considerable pressure from Egypt, was particularly sympathetic to the ASP's concern about Arab influence in Zanzibar. He was reportedly delighted when the coup ousted the Arab-dominated government in January 1964, and the Ethiopian Government was among the first to recognize the new regime.

While the ASP maintained liaison with these several ruling African parties and with Israel, the ZNP (Zanzibar Nationalist Party) found its major international ally in Egypt....

Sometime in mid-1963, probably soon after the June elections, a group of ASP leaders, including Hanga, went to Tanganyika to ask for money and arms in support of their revolutionary plan. Tanganyikan complicity with the ASP has been well established. Although President Nyerere may not have been aware of the extent to which Tanganyikan Defense Minister Kambona was involved in supplying arms and money to the Zanzibar revolutionaries, he obviously knew and approved of the general plan for the revolution.

Apparently, the coup was planned for March or April 1964. The most important figure in the plot was Hanga; Karume personally was never involved; it is doubtful that Othman Shariff knew of the plan....

Although Zanzibar's union with Tanganyika was in his interests – inasmuch as it got Babu off the island –

Karume apparently was not initially enthusiastic about the idea; certainly, he was not as strongly in favor of the union as Hanga, who claims that he and Kambona agreed when they were students together in London that Tanganyika and Zanzibar should be united one day.

The idea of a union was not a new one. Nyerere probably had it in the back of his mind when he first became involved in Zanzibar politics, beginning around 1956. For years, he had looked forward to the time when an African government would come to power in Zanzibar, at which time he planned to merge the two countries. His feeling of urgency about the union in March and April 1964 was probably a reflection of his concern that Babu was well on his way to consolidating his position in Zanzibar and his belief that only decisive action taken in time could save Zanzibar's African revolution from Arab control.

There is evidence that Nyerere was concerned about the excessive degree of Communist influence in Zanzibar, but press and other comment in the West was probably wrong in emphasizing this as Nyerere's chief concern. It seems that the Tanganyikan President deliberately exeaggerated his fears that Zanzibar was falling under Communist control; it was an argument that he could use most convincingly in the West to win support for his move to absorb Zanzibar into Tanganyika.

Whereas in private conversations with Westerners, Nyerere has always emphasized the anti-Communist line as the main rationale for the union, in public he has taken the position that the the union was simply a natural step toward African unity.

The important point is that the union of Tanganyika and Zanzibar *was a Tanganyikan initative*. Although the idea had occurred to Western officials as the obvious solution to the Zanzibar problem, the subject was never officially discussed with the Tanganyikans. Thus, it appears that the move to form the union was strictly

African in origin, without British or American inspiration; the news of the event caught all of the major world powers by surprise.

For more than a month, Nyerere and his representatives had been conducting secret negotiations with Karume and other Zanzibari leaders. Although they had suceeded in convincing several of them – including Hanga and Twala – that it was in their best interests to follow the Tanganyikan guidance, Karume was not immediately persuaded.

Finally, Nyerere's threat to recall the Tanganyikan police contingent had the force of an ultimatum. Faced.with the prospect of being deprived of the support he needed against Babu, Karume agreed to the union.

As an independent nation, Zanzibar had lasted just one hundred days. In its brief and turbulent career as a sovereign state, it had faced a bitter internal struggle for power, near economic collapse, and an intensive Communist offensive. It is not surprising that its new African leaders should have found it impossible to preserve their independence against these odds. Zanzibar was not really equipped for independence. To preserve the integrity of the African revolution they had just won, its leaders had to sacrifice the independence they had just been given. Zanzibar's future had always seemed in the long run to lie with Tanganyika. It was only surprising that this should have been realized so quickly....

During March and April Nyerere frequently invited Karume to Dar es Salaam for private talks, where he would be away from the influence of Babu and Hanga. Reportedly, the Tanganyikan President **was** very worried about what was happening in Zanzibar and was anxious to bolster Karume. In their, Nyerere first broached the subject of a Tanganyika-Zanzibar merger to Karume. Although it was not his sole reason for the union, he definitely believed that a merger would strengthen Karume's power position in Zanzibar. His feeling of urgency about the matter was probably due to his concern to ensure

241

Karume's dominance as soon as possible.

Before the union, the main thing that kept Karume in power was the Tanganyikan police force contigent, which Nyerere s e n t to the island as a measure of protection for Karume against Okello and his armed followers. After Okello's departure, Karuine kept the police as protection against Babu and the pro-Communist elements that were attempting to secure position of power in the government. Although they were nominally under the control of Karume, they took their orders from Nyerere. Without such concrete support from Nyerere, Karume would probably not have been able to stay in power in Zanzibar....

Even before the revolution, the affiliation of Zanzibar with Tanganyika had been under discussion in the context of a larger East African Federation. Nyerere, Karume and Hanga were on the record as favoring the Federation; Babu was opposed. It had never been a question of a union between Tanganyika and Zanzibar alone, however; that possibility arose as a direct result of the revolution.

As noted earlier, it was Nyerere who initiated the negotiations leading to the union. Much has been written about his reasons for wanting a Tanganyika-Zanzibar union. Press comment in the U.S. and other Western countries has tended to emphasize the cold war aspects of the situation....He has said on a number of occasions that he was personally furious with the way the American and British press treated the union....

On the question of the 'African revolution' Nyerere is deeply emotional. The possibility that Babu and his Arab followers might come to dominate the Government of Zanzibar was anathema; to Nyerere, it would have been a repudiation of the Zanzibar revolution.

By late March or early April, Babu had consolidated his position to the point where a take-over by the Arabs appeared imminent. Nyerere could have been expected to do anything and everything in his power to prevent such

242

an eventuality. His solution was the union. As the best way to guarantee the integrity of the Zanzibar revolution, he decided on a union of the two countries in which the Zanzibar Arabs would be absorbed by an overwhelming African majority.

In the case of Zanzibar, Nyerere's natural concern to safeguard the 'African revolution' everywhere in Africa was closely bound up with Tanganyikan national interests. For years, Tanganyikans, including Nyerere, had had the idea that Zanzibar was really a part of T anganyika. They had looked forward to the time when an African government would come to power in Zanzibar, at which time they planned to merge the two countries. It may well have been his interest in a Tanganyika-Zanzibar union that prompted Nyerere to become involved in Zanzibar politics in the first place, beginning in 1956....

Besides Nyerere, Defence Minister Kambona is reported to have long believed that Tanganyika should absorb Zanzibar. Although the union was reportedly a Nyerere initiative and Nyerere remained in full control of the negotiations, this is one instance in which Kambona worked in complete harmony with the President....

Hanga was probably the most receptive to the Tanganyikan initiative. He has stated privately that he and Kambona agreed that Tanganyika and Zanzibar should unite when they were students together in London. Nyerere has also commented that Hanga favored the union even more than Karume. In July URTZ (United Republic of Tanzania) Foreign Affairs parliamentary secretary Tambwe said that Nyerere was 'paticularly pleased with Hanga because he is, above all, an African nationalist who really supports the union'....

The U.S. Government did not have any earlier indication that a union between Tanganyika and Zanzibar was being negotiated....

By all reports, Karume and Nyerere are determined to see the union through.

Nyerere and Kambona and other Tanganyikan officials have said that they will never, under any circumstances, accept its dissolution, that they are prepared to maintain it at all costs – even to the point of armed intervention. So far, they have avoided anything resembling a showdown with the Zanzibaris, but apparently they are prepared to do everything, including intervene (sic) with force, before they see the union crumble. All indications are that the union is here to stay."[62]

In forming the union, Nyerere emphasised the imperative need for unity among African countries, even on a small scale as happened in the case of Tanganyika and Zanzibar. Even a communist like Kassim Hanga, prime minister of Zanzibar under Abei Karume, who strongly supported the union from the beginning did so for the same reason. Had he wanted to establish and consolidate a communist base for himself and fellow Marxist-Leninists in Zanzibar, he would not have made an impassioned plea to unite Zanzibar with Tanganyika. And had the union been a product of Western powers to neutralise communists in Zanzibar, he would not have supported a merger which was deliberately intended, by Westerners, to destroy him politically.

Hanga was widely known as an uncompromising African nationalist and gave an emotional speech in the Zanzibar Revolutionary Council urging his compatriots to approve the merger of the two countries. He supported the union, not to serve Western interests but to advance the cause of Pan-Africanism and the wellbeing of Africa. If he committed political suicide by supporting the union, he did so for the sake of Africa, not the West. Western powers did not exert pressure on him to support a union that would undermine him.

If the West wanted a union to undermine him and other Marxist-Leninists in Zanzibar, Hanga would not have supported it. His support for the union demonstrates the merger was an African initiative. If the West wanted the union for their own reasons, then their interests coincided with the objectives of the leaders of Tanganyika and Zanzibar who wanted the merger for their own reasons as well, mainly in pursuit of Pan-African goals to unite African countries and establish strong governments on regional basis and eventually unite the continent under one government.

Hanga was not a Russian stooge; nor was he manipulated by the West to serve the interests of the United States and her allies. He made it clear he was an African nationalist more than anything else and made that known to the Russians who were considered to be his allies but who expressed displeasure with the union; so did his friend Oscar Kambona who was Tanganyika's minister of foreign affairs at a meeting with the Soviet chargé d'affaires in Dar es Salaam:

"Tanganyikan Foreign Minister Kambona summoned Soviet chargé Ustinov in Dar es Salaam in the early morning hours of 23 April to tell him of the union agreement, a few hours ahead of the public announcement. Ustinov is reported to have received the news glumly, for the most part, in silence; he was obviously displeased. His only comments of substance were an oblique reference to Tanganyika's interference in the internal affairs of Zanzibar and a reminder that the Bloc countries were giving considerable material assistance to Zanzibar. He did not press either point, but the implication was clear that Tanganyika should think twice before jeopardizing the continuance of Bloc aid.

Kambona answered that since Tanganyika was a non-aligned nation, the union would be also, and that assistance would be received gratefully from any quarter as long as that nonalignment was not disturbed.

The Soviet ambassador in Zanzibar is also known to have tried to convince Karume that the union was not in

Zanzibar's interests. Hanga was present at the meeting and he reportedly answered the ambassador: 'Better to be exploited by our own brothers than by the West or East.'

The incident is interesting in that it was the pro-Soviet Hanga, and not Karume, who was the more forceful in resisting Soviet pressure. It is good evidence that Hanga is, first and foremost, an African nationalist – a communist and a Soviet sympathizer, to be sure, but not a mere instrument of the Soviets in Zanzibar."[63]

The Cold War context was clearly emphasised by the Western media, although in some of the analyses, African nationalism was also highlighted as a driving force behind the merger, not just cold-war politics. As Robert Conley stated in hi article, "Tanganyika Vote Completes Union," in *The New York Times*, 26 April 1964:

"DAR ES SALAAM, Tanganyika., April 25—The decision of Tanganyika and Zanzibar to unite as a single state was ratified by the two East African countries tonight with a visible sense of urgency.

Tanganyika's Parliament met in an emergency session to approve the merger in an attempt to protect African nationalism from Communist subversion.

Zanzibar's Revolutionary Council gave its assent at almost the same time. The way thus was open for the two countries to be joined tomorrow as the United Republic of Tanganyika and Zanzibar.

Tonight's ratifications meant that Tanganyika had succeeded in carrying out what amounted to a 'counter - revolution' to prevent tiny Zanzibar from becoming Africa's Cuba.

Island Saved for Nationalism

Tanganyika pressed the merger to break the island, lying 24 miles off her Indian Ocean coast, away from

246

increasing penetration by the Soviet Union, Communist China and their allies and to bring it back into the mainstream of African nationalism.

She also pressed it as a means of rescuing Zanzibar's President, Abeid Amani Karume, who is regarded as an uncommitted African nationalist, from domination by the Marxist faction around him. This faction is led by the Foreign Minister, Abdul Rahman Mohammed, called Babu, an advocate of Peking's theory of violent revolution.

The merger will make Zanzibar and her northern island of Pemba, with a combined population of about 310,000 and an area of less than 1,100 square miles, part of Tanganyika, which has a population of 9.2 million and is the largest country in East Africa.

Action Follows Sultan's Fall

The action comes three and a half months after Cuban-trained guerrillas led Zanzibar's African majority in overthrowing the Sultan, its traditional monarch, and his Arab minority Government.

Tanganyika's President, Julius K. Nyerere, has been openly apprehensive about the way Babu's Marxist faction seized almost every seat of real power in the revolutionary government, so that Mr. Karume was reduced to little more than a figurehead, giving an African image to the revolution while the Marxists solidified their gains.

Dr. Nyerere was known to be fearful that the Marxists would use Zanzibar as a starting point for penetration into the heart of Africa, a staging area for subverting African nationalism on the mainland.

Karume a Vice President

Dr. Nyerere will be the President of the combined republic and Mr. Karume a Vice President of the new state and executive head of Zanzibar.

Zanzibar will have a Parliament whose authority will be about equivalent to that of a provincial administration.

Tanganyika will take charge of Zanzibar's foreign affairs, defense, police, emergency powers, citizenship and immigration. She also will take charge of the island's foreign trade, communications, aviation, harbors, taxes and customs.

Dr. Nyerere sought to minimize the anti-Communist intention of the merger when he made a personal appeal to Parliament to ratify the articles of union. He said the merger had been agreed upon solely in the interest of African unity:

'Unity in our continent does not have to come via Moscow or Washington,' he said to cheers and applause. 'It is an insult to Africa to read cold-war politics into every move toward African unity. Africa has its own maturity and its own will.'

Babu and his faction, in the opinion of a number of influential sources, were left with almost no choice but to accept the merger and a reduced role on Zanzibar.

'If they try to oppose the merger or even fight it,' said one source, 'they will isolate themselves from the African nationalists.'

The decision of Dr. Nyerere and Mr. Karume to join forces appeared to have been timed to coincide with Babu's absence from Zanzibar.

Babu returned tonight from a visit to Pakistan and Indonesia. No Zanzibar officials met him at the airport.

In Nairobi, Babu said at a news conference that he thought the merger would help toward creation of an East African Federation of Kenya, Uganda, Tanganyika and Zanzibar and said that he had been 'in on the planning of such a merger.'

Asked what his position might be in the unified Government, he said: 'I do not know. It is not important."''64

Besides Nyerere and Kassim Hanga, as well as Karume for his own reasons of survival, other leaders who strongly supported the union included Oscar Kambona who was Tanganyika's minister of foreign affairs and defence and a close friend of Hanga since their student days in Britain.

Babu may have accepted the union as a *fait accompli.* But he also understood its significance in a Pan-African context in the quest for regional federation and continental unity and supported it after the merger was announced in his absence when he was in Indonesia.

He initially had misgivings about the union because it derpived him of his power base in Zanzibar. He felt he would not be as influential in the new country – of the United Republic of Tanganyika and Zanzibar, renamed Tanzania on October 29th the same year – as he was in his homeland, Zanzibar.

He was also uncomfortable with the merger because he felt that by uniting with Tanganyika, Zanzibar had been robbed of its revolutionary momentum in its quest for a radical transformation of the the island nation into a socialist state which he eventually hoped or intended to lead. He was already the leader of the radical elements in Zanzibar who wanted to establish a socialist state. But in spite of all that, he supported the merger of the two countries soon after it was announced. Support for the union by Marxist-Leninists such as Hanga and Babu clearly shows the merger was not just a product of Western pressure to unite the two countries. As Professor Ronald Aminzade states in his book, *Race, Nation, and Citizenship in Post-Colonial Africa: The Case of Tanzania*:

"On April 24, 1964, Tanganyika joined with the islands of Zanzibar to create the new nation of Tanzania. The creation of this nation must be understood within the broader global context of the Cold War among Russia, the

249

United States, and their allies....

There is considerable disagreement among scholars about why Tanganyika chose to unite with the residents of a relatively small island off its coast. One compelling account highlights the role of foreign powers, especially the United States, which was worried about communists in Zanzibar's government and feared a 'Cuba off the coast of Africa' that would spread revolution throughout the African continent.

The Union did take place at the height of the Cold War, amid rumors of a Cuban presence on Zanzibar....There is considerable evidence of U.S. State Department efforts to persuade Great Britain to intervene in Zanzibar to prevent a communist takeover and of subsequent U.S. Pressures on Nyerere to create a union with Zanzibar to reduce the influence of communist leaders on the island....

For President Abeid Karume, a union with the mainland nation-state was not the fulfillment of any ideological commitment to African unity, but a response to his own worries that the Marxist-Leninist elements within Zanzibar, especially Babu and his supporters, threatened his rule....

An alternative account of the creation of the Union was that it was a victory for African unity and pan-African solidarity....This view is forcefully argued by Godfrey Mwakikagile, who contends that the Union was an African initiative and an expression of Nyerere's pan-African commitment rather than a product of Cold War pressures....

When Nyerere urged the Tanganyikan Parliament to approve the Union, he emphasized it was a first step toward a united Africa. It demonstrated that 'a single Government in Africa is not an impossible dream, but something which can be realized....If two countries can unite, then three can; if three can, then thirty can.'

In justifying the Union as part of an effort to promote Pan-Africanism, Nyerere emphasized commonalities

250

between the mainland and the islands, including a common language and historical and cultural ties....Nyerere further portrayed the union as a product of 'the overall desire for African unity,' arguing that 'those who welcome unity on our continent must welcome this small move towards it'....

Support for the merger with the mainland from Abdulrahman Babu and Kassim Hanga, the two Marxist-Leninists who generated the most concern on the part of Western governments, suggests that the Union was also not simply the product of a Western anticommunist conspiracy engineered by the United States and Great Britain. Although these leaders may have accepted the Union as a fait accompli, there is evidence to suggest they saw it as an opportunity to gain a larger forum in which to pursue their goal, a United Republic that would be more immune from Cold War interventions."[65]

Nyerere himself, the driving force behind the union, stated in his speech to a special session of the Tanganyika National Assembly on 25 April 1964 concerning the merger:

"The union between Tanganyika and Zanzibar has been determined by our two Governments for the interests of Africa and African Unity. There is no other reason.

Unity in our continent does not have to come via Moscow or Washington. It is an insult to Africa to read cold war politics into every move towards African Unity. Africa has its own maturity and its own will.

Our unity is inspired by a very simple ideology – unity. We do not propose this Union in order to support any of the 'isms' of this world. We propose it in order to support and strengthen Africa, and our particular part of Africa....

We shall work for African Unity and African Freedom, and we shall remain non-aligned in world power struggles which do not concern us. Each international issue will be

251

determined on its own merit and our friendship towards all nations will be affected only by their actions towards us. We shall not allow our friends to choose our enemies for us."[66]

There is no question that the Zanzibar revolution provided an impetus for unification of the two countries: Tanganyika and Zanzibar. But is was not the sole or even the prime determinant, as demonstrated above. It only facilitated the merger, and at a faster pace than would otherwise have been the case involving gradual consummation of the union of the two countries.

The successful revolution led to the establishment of Zanzibar as a republic under the leadership of the Afro-Shirazi Party (ASP). Sheikh Abeid Amani Karume, leader of ASP, became president; Kassim Hanga became prime minister and vice president, and Abdulrahman Mohamed Babu, minister of defence and external affairs.

Babu was the leader of Umma, meaning the Party of the Masses, whose members defected from the Arab-dominated Zanzibar Nationalist Party (ZNP) to whom the British transferred power on attainment of independence on 10 December 1963.

The People's Republic of Zanzibar and Pemba, as the new nation was officially known, was ruled by a Revolutionary Council composed of 30 members. It was the new government. Zanzibar became a one-party state. Land and other assets including major means of production were nationalised in pursuit of socialist transformation of the country.

The Zanzibar revolution was hailed as a victory for the oppressed masses who had endured oppression including slavery under Arab domination for centuries and was supported by many people across Africa and in other parts of the world, especially in the Third World and in socialist countries.

Among African leaders who were the strongest

252

supporters of the revolution were Nyerere and Nkrumah. Other African leaders who supported and defended the revolution included Emperor Haile Selassie, Nigerian Prime Minister Abubakar Tafawa Balewa, and Nigerian Foreign Affairs Minister Jaja Wachuku.

Castro also supported the Zanzibar revolution, as did East Germany, the People's Republic of China and the Soviet Union.

One of the leading figures in the Zanzibar Revolutionary Council, Sheikh Thabit Kombo, stated years later in one of his speeches to the members of Tanzania's ruling party – Chama Cha Mapinduzi (CCM) which means the Party of the Revolution or the Revolutionary Party – that besides Nyerere, Nkrumah also helped to finance the Zanzibar revolution. As Andrew Nyerere, President Nyerere's eldest son, stated in his letter in 2004 in response to a number of questions I asked him when I was working on the second edition of my book, *Nyerere and Africa: End of an Era*:

"As you look at the history of Mwalimu Nyerere and his contemporaries, you see that they were like a team who were born at the same time for the purpose of liberating the country from British imperialism.

So we do well to find out the truth about what these men did. We see, for example, that there is evidence that Kwame Nkrumah financed the Zanzibar Revolution.

In a speech to the Party, Sheikh Thabit Kombo gives an account of it. He explains how during the election in Zanzibar, there had been great carnage and many Arabs were killed. And Nkrumah had financed this. He says it was not the fault of the Arabs that the disturbances started. They had masterminded it, and started the trouble.

But it is just modesty to say that the Arabs made no mistakes because this was a government which was based on slave trading.

So, during this election, there was a lot of trouble and

253

many Arabs were killed, and Thabit Kombo and Mr. Karume fled to Dar es Salaam. They decided that they should go to Nyerere to discuss this with him, to find out what was his opinion.

And when they met Nyerere, they discussed this and he told them to go back, and said, 'I will send you money, I will send you guns.'

They went back and there was a trial. A white judge came from London. And Karume was asked by the prosecutor, 'Do you know, Mr. Karume, when you started that fracas, 75 Arabs died?' And Mr. Karume made a very memorable statement. He spoke out in exasperation. He asked, 'Who did you want to die?'

This is a statement which all the oppressed people of the world should remember. It is all on tape. I made copies of it and sent it to quite a few people."[67]

Tanganyika under Nyerere provided both financial and material support including security forces to restore order soon after the revolution. About three months later, Zanzibar united with Tanganyika to form Tanzania, the first union of independent states ever formed on the continent and which still exists today more than 50 years later.

One of the most dramatic pictures from that period shows Abdulrahman Mohamed Babu rowing a canoe reportedly from Zanzibar to Dar e Salaam, Tanganyika – although that was never confirmed. The new government under the Zanzibar Nationalist Party (ZNP) to whom power had been transferred by the British was getting ready to arrest him before he fled to Dar es Salaam, reportedly in a canoe. He later became one of the most prominent members in the union cabinet and one of the most influential leaders in Africa and in the entire Third World.

He died in London on 5 August 1996. He was 72. The government of Tanzania under President Benjamin Mkapa paid for the funeral and to bring his body back home from London. He was given an official burial – not a state funeral – in spite of the fact that he had not been a cabinet member since 1972.

He was buried in Zanzibar at a funeral attended by many Tanzanian leaders and others. And he will always be remembered as one of the main architects of the Zanzibar revolution in terms of formulating a radical agenda after the upheaval.

It is a revolution that had an impact beyond Zanzibar and the rest of East Africa. In some fundamental respects, its impact was continental in scope in terms of ideological influence and political re-alignment of allies. And as the former Zanzibar resident, Donald Petterson, whom I cited earlier and who was in the island nation during the revolution stated elsewhere in "Nine Hour Revolution":

"Zanzibar is well known for it's 'Shortest War in History.' A 19th Century battle that lasted only about 45 minutes but served to demonstrate for all time the Iron fist beneath the pre-colonial European domination of East Africa.

What is less well known is the 20th Century record Zanzibar set for similar brevity in the Zanzibar Revolution of 1964.

In this Revolution a government with over a century of continuity was toppled in less than a day. Essentially a settler society, with well-defined Arabic, Indian, Swahili, Comorian and indigenous elements, and ruled by an hereditary sultan, the newly independent nation of Zanzibar vanished in astounding suddenness.

That night was full of suspense and surprise, courage and despair. It began at 3 a.m. on the day just before a large religious holiday.

The holiday prompted large numbers of people to congregate in and around Stone Town. They set up tents or just sleep under the palms while awaiting the opening of

255

the festivities in the morning. Among the crowds were large numbers of young men; some of these men were followers of a minor politician named John Okello.

Just how many men actually followed Okello into revolutionary battle is of some dispute.

It is clear that by the end of that fateful day thousands had joined the revolutionaries but this was after the results were known.

It's also true that Field Marshal Okello talked of having had 4 'battalions' in the field against the government forces that night, but how men many were really there when it counted?

Okello reported that the revolution began when he marched in the dead of night on the Ziwani Police Barracks (and Armory) at the head of the 250 men of his '4th Battalion.' At 3:00 a.m. he ordered his men to cut the wire surrounding this fortified compound.

That was the first real revolutionary act and it served to 'separate the men from the boys.' Okello said of his men at the time, 'The enormity of our predicament was suddenly obvious to them: we, armed with pangas, spears and a few motor car springs were going to face the risk of close combat with men armed with automatic rifles...' All but 40 men deserted or refused to crawl through the wire.

These 40 men seized the island of Zanzibar and toppled a dynasty that had ruled the islands through 12 Sultans for over 133 years.

The revolutionaries crawled to within 25 meters of the Barracks building. Inside, asleep were scores of paramilitary police. However like most sensible people on Zanzibar they slept on the upper floors of the building, where cooling ocean breeze could ventilate the hot tropical nights. Only two men were awake and on guard duty below.

John Okello and his men rushed at these guards. Automatic fire rang out and three of the 4th battalion men went down. However one of sentries also fell, downed by an arrow shot by a revolutionary named Albert. By then Okello had closed on the remaining sentry. It was here that the deciding moment of the revolution occurred. The two crashed together. The Field Marshall tells us that 'I got hold of the gun, we fought and I managed to hit him in the cheek with the gun butt.' The firing stopped.

His men were now at the gates of the armory where hundreds of modern weapons and thousands of rounds of ammunition were locked up. The police above, who were unarmed, (in keeping with standard peacetime practice, all weapons were locked away 'for safekeeping' when the officers were off duty), attempted to storm down the single exterior staircase and enter the fray.

However, the 4th Battalion men unleashed a rain of spears, arrows and stones on the stunned troops and they piled up upon themselves on the narrow staircase. Okello's liberated rifle, which had only three bullets left, decided the issue with a short burst of fire. The police retreated back upstairs to look for ropes to lower men out of the windows.

It was too late. The doors of the armory gave way and the 4th Battalion rushed in. Soon every man was armed with a modern automatic rifle. The 'Freedom Fighters' who had started the night armed with sharpened automobile springs now were the best equipped force on the island. They poured a fuselage of fire into the upstairs rooms and very shortly the surviving police surrendered.

The sultan's forces made one serious attempt to counter attack the rebels. The 'flying squad' arrived on the scene about an hour after the defeat of the Ziwani garrison. These 75 or so men had only light duty firearms and were no match for the now heavily armed Battalion ensconced in the fortified Armory.

The rebels allowed the sultans' paramilitary police to approach and then poured an overwhelming storm of fire into them. The firing was so intense that the surrounding bush caught fire and the police retreated in despair.

257

With their new base secure, guns were distributed to the other three battalions (who had encircled but not yet attacked other key sites). In short order the few other police posts and the communications centres were overrun and captured. The most serious resistance was offered by the Malindi Police Station, where firing could still be heard in the late hours of the morning.

However, by noon, the Sultan had fled. The rest is history."[68]

There are many conflicting reports about what actually happened on that day. But there is no question that neighbouring Tanganyika supported the revolution; so did Ghana under Nkrumah according to the testimony of one of the leading figures in the Zanzibar Revolutionary Council, Sheikh Thabit Kombo, which became the government after the revolution.

Regardless of the different interpretations of what happened in Zanzibar during that period, and why the revolution took place, what is clear to black Africans in Zanzibar and to many other Africans elsewhere, and to thoughtful non-African observers, is that the revolution was not a spontaneous uprising. It was a product of cumulative suffering blacks had endured for centuries under Arab domination.

It was a powerful response to such oppression and exploitation, as clearly shown by the overwhelming support the revolution got from the vast majority of black Africans in the island nation. The revolution was also an integral part of the nationalist tide sweeping the continent during the era of decolonisation.

A lot has been said about the Soviet Union, the People's Republic of China, East Germany, Cuba and other socialist countries and their involvement in Zanzibar during those turbulent times. What is overlooked or deliberately ignored in all this is the nationalist aspirations of the black African majority in the island nation. They

258

wanted to be free.

And it was not just the socialist countries which got involved in Zanzibar. The United States also had a strong interest in what was going on and looked at Zanzibar from an American perspective influenced by the Cold War to secure American geopolitical interests in the region and neutralise Soviet and Chinese influence.

The policies of both ideological camps were dictated by Cold War imperatives with regard to most parts of the Third World. And Zanzibar was no exception. Before the revolution, Zanzibar was not high on the American agenda of Cold War politics. But the revolution changed all that, prompting American officials to draw up contingency plans on what to do in case they had to intervene in Zanzibar.

Unfortunately, their perception of Zanzibar was refracted through the prism of the Cold War to the exclusion of any other interpretation which would have been more rational and realistic than what they had.

Declassified documents from the US State Department that were made available in 1999 a few years after the end of the Cold War precipitated by the collapse of the Soviet Union shed some light on what American leaders thought should be done about Zanzibar because of the revolution that had taken place in the island nation.

According to those documents, on 7 February 1964, the US State Department prepared a report for President Lyndon Johnson which stated:

"The crux of the Zanzibar matter is to prevent its takeover by the Communists. The new regime is an uneasy coalition of African nationalist and pro-Communist elements, each struggling for power. We are gravely concerned that the role of the nationalists may be deteriorating.

The elements of preventing a Communist takeover include:

259

1. Elimination or control of 'Field Marshal' Okello and armed thugs, who represent a continuing threat to order and stability.

2. Development of an independent nationalist government probably built around President Karume, leader of the Afro-Shirazis.

3. Political containment of any pro-Communist force, including Babu and Hanga, if they are unwilling to work with Karume. Babu and Hanga have had strong ties with Peiping and Moscow. Nevertheless Nyerere believes in the showdown they are African nationalists who can be and must be worked with. This is questionable.

4. Support and strengthening of Nyerere in Tanganyika and Kenyatta in Kenya.

...The U.K. has a military capability in the area to disarm Okello and his followers and to maintain order. It would do this on its own initiative if British nationals were endangered. Otherwise, understandably, it would desire a written GOZ request from Karume. Only the British can act militarily with adequate effectiveness.

...Every effort must be made to induce the British to take effective action. Since any definitive U.S. action would be based on the extent and type of action by the British, alternative measures the U.S. might take diplomatically, covertly or through economic or technical assistance would best be considered in light of the British program.

Despite the short-term stability which the U.K. military presence probably will insure, basic problems will remain, making British disengagement extremely difficult. Dependable African security forces cannot quickly be developed.

At the same time, East Africa's leaders will be under mounting domestic pressure to seek early U.K. withdrawal. Domestic and general African pressures could lead to a British withdrawal before internal security forces have been adequately strengthened."[69]

Because of the revolutionary nature of the Zanzibar regime which was perceived to be anti-West, the United States assumed a more active role in African affairs and did everything it could to contain the revolutionary elements in Zanzibar. When Zanzibar united with Tanganyika, American officials hoped that President Nyerere would have a moderating influence on the revolutionary government in Zanzibar.

However, he did little to please the West. Tanzania under his leadership was non-aligned and went on to establish strong ties with many countries in the socialist camp – while also maintaining ties with the West – and adopted policies for socialist transformation of the country along African lines in pursuit of African socialism; what Nyerere called *ujamaa*, a Kiswahili term meaning "familyhood," based on the traditional African communal way of life.

The revolutionaries in Zanzibar had, of course, already embraced socialism although of a more radical kind with some of them espousing Marxist principles.

Although the Zanzibar revolution had an impact beyond Zanzibar, it was not engineered, orchestrated or manipulated by external forces and elements. It was an indigenous phenomenon and a military expression of the political aspirations of the oppressed black African majority.

Arabs and other non-blacks who supported the revolution also wanted a new society restructured along egalitarian lines in which rule by an oligarchy of whatever stripes would have no place under the new dispensation. And that is what gave the revolution its transcendent and nationalistic character as a non-racist uprising, getting full support from some Arabs like Abdulrahman Mohamed Babu who was a nationalist more than anything else.

Whatever happened in the island nation, and regardless of the different interpretations which are still being given

261

today by many people including politicians, scholars and laymen alike, there is no question that the revolution was a momentous upheaval of cataclysmic proportions in the context of Zanzibar and changed the island nation forever. Zanzibar has never been the same again.

The revolution also played a critical role in the consummation of the union of Tanganyika and Zanzibar on 26 April 1964. Both leaders, Nyerere of Tanganyika and Karume of Zanzibar, wanted their countries to unite. But the union would probably not have taken place when it did had it not been for the Zanzibar revolution.

The revolution provided an impetus towards unification for a number of reasons. Black Africans in Zanzibar were afraid that their former Arab rulers would try to come back and re-institute Arab domination of the island nation. To prevent that, they sought protection from Tanganyika, a much bigger country that was also predominantly black, by forming a union under one government.

Nyerere and other leaders of Tanganyika were also concerned that instability in Zanzibar – possibly leading to anarchy – would have a direct impact on the mainland and negative consequences which should be avoided before it was too late. Unification of the two countries would be the best way to avert such a catastrophe. It would also enable Nyerere to control some of the far more radical elements in the government of Zanzibar.

Some observers *still* contend that the union of Tanganyika and Zanzibar was a product of the Cold War. They argue that the United States wanted to neutralise communist influence in the island nation. And a union with Tanganyika would provide such a solution.

Frank Carlucci, who was the American consul in Zanzibar during the revolution and who later became director of the CIA and US secretary of defence, said he was not sure whether motivation for the union came from Nyerere or the American government. But he admits that there was concern in the American government that if the situation in Zanzibar was not contained, the island nation would become a communist stronghold.

A number of American officials said they feared Zanzibar would become another Cuba or the Cuba of Africa. And the Zanzibari leader who was feared the most as the spearhead of such communist penetration was Abdulrahman Mohamed Babu.

Babu was a subject of discussion in many circles. For example, in Nigeria, American Ambassador Averill Harriman asked Nigerian leaders what they thought about Babu. Nigerian Foregin Minister Dr. Jaja Wachuku assured Harriman that he had known Babu for many years and that Babu was an African nationalist more than anything else.

It is true that the United States denounced Zanzibar as "the Cuba of Africa" after the January 1964 revolution led by John Okello who toppled the Arab-dominated regime and transferred power to the predominantly black majority and their allies including a number of Arabs, Iranians (originally from Shiraz in Iran), and others. But it is also true that the people who led the revolution were not interested in substituting one master for another – capitalist or communist – and their uprising was not communist-inspired.

The communist threat in Zanzibar was overly exaggerated. Even the leaders who could have established communism on the isles dismissed the threat. They were explicit in their intentions and would not have shied away from acknowledging that they were going to establish communism in Zanzibar – which would have been an open secret, anyway, sooner rather than later.

They included Abdulrahman Mohammed Babu, the most prominent leader with communist leanings on the islands and whom the CIA followed closely, as it did all the other leaders including Abdullah Kassim Hanga. According to one of the declassified documents in the US

263

Archives written from Nigeria by the American diplomat and statesman Averell Harriman (he was a trip to Nigeria as a special envoy) to President Lyndon B. Johnson and Secretary of State Dean Rusk on March 25, 1964:

"In long talks with Prime Minister Abubakar (Tafawa Balewa) and Foreign Minister (Jaja) Wachuku,...both minimized concern I expressed for Communist takeover in Zanzibar, assured me that Karume was sensible and Babu was primarily African nationalist and would not permit Communist takeover. When I pressed Wachuku, he firmly insisted he could guarantee Babu whom he had personally known a long time."[70]

The dispatch from Nigeria by Harriman was followed by other reports on the potential for communist penetration of Africa during the early years of independence in the sixties.

Ambassador Harriman himself in another report to President Johnson on 28 October 1964, about nine months after the Zanzibar revolution and just one day before the Union of Tanganyika and Zanzibar was renamed Tanzania (on October 29, 1964), conceded:

"Not a single new African nation has succumbed to Communist domination."[71]

The report is one of the declassified documents published in *Foreign Relations of the United States 1964 – 1968*. The document has also been been cited by other people including Kevin Kelly, "How Communism Affected US Policy in East Africa," in *The East African*, Nairobi, Kenya, 6 December 1999, the same year the declassified documents from the US State Department were released.

Officials in the Johnson Administration were convinced that communists had played an active role in the Zanzibar revolution on 12 January 1964, according to released documents contained in the 850-page volume of *Foreign Relations of the United States 1964 – 1968*. As one US State Department background paper, 7 February 1964, asserted:

"There was obvious communist involvement in Zanzibar."[72]

Yet, the same officials admitted that disturbances in other parts of East Africa – the army mutinies in Tanganyika, Kenya, and Uganda in January 1964 – around the same time did not appear to be communist-inspired. In fact, President Nyerere himself resolutely maintained:

"(There was) no evidence whatsoever to suggest that the mutinies in Tanganyika were inspired by outside forces – either Communist or imperialist."[73]

The army mutinies started in Tanganyika on 20 January 1964 and spread to Kenya and Uganda within two days. The mutineers demanded higher salaries and expulsion of British army officers whom they said should be replaced by African officers. But there was also potential for a military coup in each of those mutinies.

In Tanganyika, the involvement of union labour leaders Christopher Kasanga Tumbo and Victor Mkello who had close ties to the mutineers created strong suspicion that the mutiny was an attempt to overthrow the government.

There was also a common logic that linked the mutinies to the Zanzibar revolution. The revolution was an African uprising against Arab domination and had a distinct racial component (it was also a class conflict between dispossessed blacks and the merchants and landowners who were mostly Arab and Indian), as was clearly demonstrated during the revolution in which many

Arabs and Indians, as well as some Comorians, but mostly Arabs, were massacred.

The highest figures of those who were killed – 13,000 to 20,000 – come mostly come from the supporters of the old Arab regime who, even today, are still opposed to the union of Tanganyika and Zanzibar.

The army mutinies in Tanganyika and in the other two East African countries (Kenya and Uganda), partly inspired by the uprising in Zanzibar, also had a racial dimension. In addition to demanding an increase in salaries, the mutineers also demanded the replacement of British army officers with African ones to Africanise the armed forces all the way to the highest level in a true spirit of independence by eradicating the last vestiges of colonialism.

The mutiny in Tanganyika was not only the first one among the three in East Africa; it was also the most successful in terms of "usurpation" of power as the only mutiny that almost ended up in a military coup, according to the evidence gathered from an analysis of records and documents contained in the archives of the East Africana Collection at the University of Dar es Salaam, Tanzania. As Professor Ronald Aminzade states in "The Politics of Race and Nation: Citizenship and Africanization in Tanganyika":

"(The) abortive military mutiny on January 20, 1964, (was) motivated by demands for higher pay and the replacement of British officers by Africans.

The six-day mutiny, which began at Colito Barracks (renamed Lugalo Barracks) in Dar es Salaam and spread to troops atationed at Tabora (and Nachingwea), appears to have been well-planned. After arresting their British officers, soldiers built roadblocks at strategic points throughout the city, seized the State House (the president's official residence, although Nyerere did not live there but in a simple house on the outskirts of the city in Msasani,

266

and used the State House, popularly known as Ikulu, only for official functions), police stations, airport, radio station, and railway station, and placed guards at critical postal, telegraph, and bank buildings.

The Tanganyikan mutiny sparked similar uprisings in the Ugandan and Kenyan armies as well as the looting and pillaging of Asian shops in Dar es Salaam.

Hundreds of people were arrested during the looting in the commercial areas of the capital. Local forces of order were weakened by the government's earlier decision to send the Dar es Salaam Field Police (known by the acronym FFU - Field Force Units), a contingent of 300 men, to Zanzibar to help restore order on the troubled island.

The fear that racial violence might escalate was linked to the revolution in Zanzibar, which took place in the preceding week and was accompanied by race riots, the murder of hundreds of Arab and Asian shopkeepers, and the mass exodus of Asians to the mainland.

Field Marshal John Okello, who had seized power in Zanzibar, declared: 'We are friends of all Europeans and other foreigners. It is only the Ismailis and certain other Indian groups and people of Arab descent we do not like.' (*Tanganyika Standard*, January 17, 1964).

The racial antagonisms behind the army mutiny were evident in the behavior of the mutinous soldiers stationed in the town of Tabora, who beat up all Europeans and Asians who crossed their path. (Listowel, 1965: p. 433). During the looting of Asian shops in Dar es Salaam, 17 people were killed and 23 seriously injured. (*Tanganyika Standard*, January 22, 1964). Rumors spread throughout the capital that Nyerere had fled the country and a general strike was imminent. Nyerere, while still hiding, broadcast a radio message on the second day of the rebellion, to reassure the country that he was still in power.

Had they moved quickly, the mutineers could probably have seized control of the government, but the rebellious

267

army units had no plans to launch a coup d'etat. Rebellious soldiers negotiated with Minister of Defence Oscar Kambona and agreed to release the 30 captured European (British) officers, who were quickly flown out of the country.

Kambona had offered to replace all European officers with Africans and discuss wages, provided the troops release the officers and return to their barracks.

Nyerere's first public act, after he emerged from hiding on January 22, was to tour the city on foot, visiting the areas of looted Asian shops to express his condolences to Asian shopkeepers who had been targets of violence. (*Tanganyika Standard*, January 23, 1964).

Only after the mutineers began to negotiate with militant leaders of the trade union movement did the government reluctantly ask the British to intervene (the British were soon replaced by Nigerian troops at Nyerere's request at an urgent OAU summit he called in Addis Ababa, Ethiopia, to deal with the crisis). Trade union leaders hoped to take advantage of the situation and turn the mutiny into a coup d'etat.

The two most prominent proponents of Africanization, trade union leaders Christopher (Kasanga) Tumbo, who had returned from Kenya, and Victor Mkello, met in Morogoro to plan a new government. (Listowel, 1965: pp. 437 - 38). On January 25, British troops quickly took control of the barracks and disarmed the rebels, killing five African soldiers in the confrontation.

The army mutiny proved to be a great embarrassment for the government, which was forced to call on troops of the former colonial power to restore public order. Yet the uprising also provided the occasion to move decisively against those who had continued to press for Africanization.

After the abortive mutiny, the government arrested 50 policemen implicated in the uprising, reorganized the military (while Nigerian troops sent to Tanganyika by the

Nigerian Federal Government provided defence for the country), and replaced British officers to defuse the issue of Africanization.

It used Preventive Detention Law, rarely invoked since its passage in 1962, to order the arrest of more than 200 trade union leaders, many of whom were released after questioning.

Fifteen soldiers were sentenced to prison for their role in the mutiny. The trade union movement was brought firmly under the control of the government by the dissolution of the Tanganyika Federation of Labour (TFL) and establishment in its place of the TANU-controlled National Union of Tanganyika Workers (NUTA).

Several days after the suppression of the mutiny, on January 28, 1964, Nyerere announced the appointment of a presidential commission to pursue the plans that had been announced earlier to create a single-party state, subsequently instituted in the constitution of 1965."[74]

Professor Aminzade of the sociology department at the University of Minnesota conducted his research in Tanzania, published on 2 December 1998.

Reports on the mutiny in Tanganyika were also published in the *Tanganyika Standard*, Dar es Salaam, 22 – 23 January 1964.

In spite of all the speculations about the spectre of communism looming over East Africa, especially Tanganyika and Zanzibar, we see that from all available evidence, it is clear that communism – or any form of external involvement or manipulation – was not a factor in the army mutiny in Tanganyika or those in Kenya and Uganda; three inter-related incidents in a chain reaction that almost plunged the three countries into chaos during those fateful days in January 1964.

Probably more than anything else, even more than salary demands, the mutinies were inspired by black nationalism and were a military expression of indigenous

269

political aspirations; so was the Zanzibar revolution, although it transcended race and included some Arabs and people of Persian origin in the vanguard in the quest for racial justice.

But since the oppressive regime that was overthrown was Arab, oppressing and exploiting black people more than anybody else, the revolution assumed a racial dimension as an indigenous expression of the political and economic aspirations of the black majority – who did not need communism to wake them up to reality and show them that they were being oppressed and exploited by the Arabs because they were weak and black. Experience is the best teacher.

Although all three governments – under Nyerere in Tanganyika, Jomo Kenyatta in Kenya, and Milton Obote in Uganda – survived and remained in power, there is no doubt that the mutinies had a profound impact across the continent and helped change the course of African history during the post-colonial era.

The mutinies not only demonstrated the power of the armed forces to extract concessions from national leaders and governments; they also showed, probably more than anything else, that soldiers in any African country had the power to overthrow governments without fear of retribution or any kind of punishment against them. Governments were too weak to stop or punish them, except in cases of abortive coup attempts.

Within a few years, military coups became a continental phenomenon, although not all of them could be attributed to the mutinies in East Africa. The coup in Togo is a good example. It took place in January 1963, almost exactly one year before the army mutinies in East Africa.

But like their counterparts in the three East African countries who mutinied in January 1964, soldiers in other parts of Africa knew on their own that they could storm out of the barracks, force national leaders to bow to their demands, and even overthrow them at will.

They knew the military was the strongest institution in Africa. Civilian governments were at their mercy and remained in power because soldiers allowed them to. The people were powerless to stop such intervention even if some of the governments which were being overthrown were popular and had been democratically elected.

The army mutinies in the three East African countries not only helped inspire military coups on the continent when soldiers in other countries saw how they could use guns to extract concessions from civilian governments and even overthrow them if they wanted to; they were also some of the earliest manifestations of the intrusive power of the military in African politics as a continental phenomenon, and of what was yet to come in an even more violent way: coups and assassinations spanning four decades.

The events in Tanganyika and Zanzibar in January 1964 – the Zanzibar revolution and the army mutiny on the mainland – were soon followed by another major development unprecedented anywhere else in Africa: formation of a political union of two independent states, Tanganyika and Zanzibar, to create Tanzania on April 26th in the same year.

One of the best analyses of the consummation of this union came from the late Professor Haroub Othman (he died on 28 June 2009 at the age of 68) of the Institute of Development Studies, University of Dar es Salaam, Tanzania. A Tanzanian from Zanzibar, his analysis was published in three parts from April 26th – 28th in 2004 in the *Guardian*, Dar es Salaam, Tanzania, on the union's 40th anniversary, entitled "Tanzania: Forty Years of the Union: Is it Withering Away?"

Appendix I:

Tanzania: Forty Years of the Union:
Is it Withering Away?

**Haroub Othman, a Zanzibari, and professor at
The Institute of Development Studies
University of Dar es Salaam, Tanzania**

"If I could tow that island out into the middle of the Indian Ocean, I'd do it." – Julius Nyerere.

At a dinner party in Dar es Salaam a year or two before independence, Nyerere had remarked that he thought one of Tanganyika's biggest problems in later years would be Zanzibar:

No, I'm not joking....I fear it will be a big headache for us.

Historical Links

In the last forty years, Tanzanians have prided themselves in having the only union of independent states in Africa; and even though no other states have followed their example, they have not been discouraged by this lack

273

of interest in forging larger units in Africa; nor do they think there were any lessons to be drawn form the failures of such attempts elsewhere.

But now cracks are appearing, without any obvious prodding form outside. The international community is bound to raise eyebrows, and to ask itself what is happening.

Situated a few miles away in the Indian Ocean, Zanzibar is mainland Tanzania (Tanganyika)'s closest neighbour to the east. The two countries have had a close relationship that dates back to several centuries before Christ.

It is believed that the indigenous population of Zanzibar, consisting of Wahadimu and Watumbatu, must have originated from the mainland.

The Persian and other explorers and merchants who visited these parts in the 7th century A.D. made Zanzibar their main centre among the city states in the East Coast of Africa. The Arab rulers who came to these areas in the early 18th century extended their rule and influence on the mainland through Zanzibar; and European explorers and missionaries, who appeared on the scene in the 19th century, used Zanzibar as a base to launch their penetration into the African hinterland.

The slave trade made Zanzibar an important centre of this human merchandise. Thousands of people captured on the mainland were sent to Zanzibar to be sold before they were shipped to Mauritius, Reunion, Arabia and other places as slave labour.

And when the clove plantation economy replaced the slave trade as the main economic activity of the islands, it was farm hands acquired from the mainland that came to the islands to open up virgin lands, till them and plant clove trees. Until the late 1950s, people form Tanganyika used to come to the islands in large numbers for seasonal employment in clove picking.

Political Relations

The two countries of Tanganyika and Zanzibar were administered separately during all the time of the colonial rule. When Tanganyika fell into German hands as a result of the Berlin Conference of 1884 - 1885 that carved up Africa amongst the European powers, Zanzibar had already fallen under Arab rule.

Sultan Said of Oman moved his capital to Zanzibar in 1832 and established the Al-Busaidy dynasty in the islands. As a result of the inter-imperialist rivalry in the region, Seyyid Said's son, Seyyid Ali bin Said, accepted British protection, and so the islands formally became a British protectorate on 4th November, 1890.

When Germany was defeated in the First World War, its colonial possessions were divided amongst the victor powers, and Tanganyika became a British-administered territory under the League of Nations mandate (and later the United Nations Trusteeship System).

But even when the two countries were ruled by the same colonial power their administrations were different. The British Governor in Tanganyika was reporting directly to the Colonial Office in London, and periodically the British had to make a reporting to the League of Nations (and the United Nations). In the case of Zanzibar, even though the British Resident was answerable to the Colonial Secretary in London, in his decisions he had to take into consideration the sensitivities of the Arab Sultan.

This in no way indicates, as has been suggested by some writers, that Zanzibar during this period was under dual power. Britain was the ultimate colonial power.

A number of ethnic and cultural organizations were established by the peoples of the two countries to deal with their social, religious and cultural concerns. In 1929 an African Association was founded in Tanganyika mostly as a social and cultural organization of the African elite in Dar es Salaam and other urban areas. A branch of this

Association was established in Zanzibar in 1934 with its membership mostly Zanzibaris of mainland origin.

The struggles for national independence raging throughout Africa did not fail to affect East Africa as well. In Kenya nationalist agitation had already started, culminating in the formation of the Kenya African Union (KAU); and when the demands for independence were not having any effect on the white settler community and the colonial authorities, the Kenyans took up arms in the Mau Mau uprising.

In Uganda nationalist organizations had already begun to form. Tanganyika African National Union (TANU), an organization that was to be the political vehicle of the people in voicing their demands for independence, was founded on 7th July 1954.

In Zanzibar, the Zanzibar Nationalist Party (ZNP) was founded in December 1955 and the Afro-Shirazi Party (ASP) was established on 5th February 1957.

Prior to the formation of these nationalist parties in Tanganyika and Zanzibar, semi-political organizations and trade unions had already been operating: the Tanganyika Territory Civil Servants' Association was established in 1922, and a decree legalizing the formation of trade unions was passed in Zanzibar in 1931. The ports of Dar es Salaam and Zanzibar had experienced their major dockworkers' strikes in 1947 and 1948 respectively.

Unlike in other colonial possessions outside Africa where nationalist movements did not form continental or regional organizations to coordinate their struggles against colonialism, in Africa most nationalist movements, especially those founded after the Second World War, recognized the need for waging common struggles.

Starting with the 5th Pan-African Congress held in Manchester in 1945, and attended by Kwame Nkrumah of Ghana and Jomo Kenyatta of Kenya among others, the African peoples have focused their struggles not only on the independence of their own individual countries but also the complete eradication of colonialism in the continent and for the achievement of total African unity.

It was no wonder, therefore, that nationalist organizations in Eastern and Central Africa came together in September 1958, at the invitation of TANU, in the lake city of Mwanza, to exchange views and experiences and to forge unity. The ZNP and ASP from Zanzibar were also there.

It was at this conference that the Pan-African Freedom Movement for East and Central Africa (PAFMECA) was founded. Later the organization was to include nationalist movements from Southern Africa, and its name was changed to the Pan African Freedom Movement of Eastern, Central and Southern Africa (PAFMECSA).

The nationalist organisations of these three regions of Eastern, Central and Southern Africa in December of that year attended an All-African Peoples' Conference that was held in Accra, Ghana, at the invitation of Kwame Nkrumah's Convention People's Party (CPP).

One of the recommendations at the Mwanza Conference was that in an area where more than one nationalist organization existed, they should try and merge, and if that was not possible, then they should at least coordinate their activities. Zanzibar was one case in point.

The ZNP and ASP agreed to coordinate their activities, and a coordinating body was formed. This point was also stressed at the Accra conference at a meeting of Zanzibari leaders especially convened by Kwame Nkrumah.

These efforts succeeded for a time; but soon tension flared up again, because, as TANU President Julius Nyerere pointed out at the time "... politically the (Zanzibar) parties all agreed to one objective but they opposed each other because of race". Kanyama Chiume of Malawi and Francis Khamisi of Kenya were dispatched to Zanzibar by PAFMECA to help, to no avail. Things became more unsatisfactory when in 1959 the ASP split, and a new organization, the Zanzibar and Pemba People's

277

Party (ZPPP), emerged.

Independence of Tanganyika: The 'Mecca' of Africa's Liberation Emerges

Tanganyika was the first country in Eastern, Central and Southern Africa to gain its independence, on 9th December 1961 (African nationalists and most of progressive humanity had never recognized the "independence" of South Africa). Like Ghana before it, Tanganyika felt that its own "independence was meaningless until the whole of Africa was free".

It therefore helped, with all the resources available, other peoples in the region to gain their independence: it opened its borders to patriots from other areas running away from persecution; it allowed its territory to be used for the training of freedom fighters who would launch armed struggles to end colonial rule in their countries; it made possible the establishment of offices by the nationalist organizations so that they could reach the international community for support; and it gave its diplomatic and political support to all those fighting racism and colonialism everywhere.

It was no doubt this commitment to Africa's liberation together with its geographical position at the time vis-à-vis the colonial territories of the region that won Tanganyika the honour, in 1963, of becoming the headquarters of the OAU Liberation Committee, a body that was to coordinate Africa's and international support for the nationalist movements fighting colonialism, racism, apartheid and white settler supremacy in Africa.

Zanzibar presented TANU and its government with a dilemma. There was the Afro-Shirazi Party (ASP), claiming to represent the indigenous and migrant African population of Zanzibar, who were the majority, and at whose founding Mwalimu Julius Nyerere was present. (And it should be remembered that the ASP was a merger

278

of the Shirazi Association and the African Association that was established in 1934 in Zanzibar as a branch of the Tanganyika African Association - the very association that transformed in 1954 into TANU).

On the other hand, there was the ZNP, which in rhetoric, seemed to challenge the colonial regime, and was very radical in its demands and programmes. But it was preaching non-racialism: would this ensure an African majority government in Zanzibar? ZNP was also embracing the monarchy: would an Arab Sultan be able to survive African nationalism in the area? TANU, in any case, decided to give its full support to the Afro-Shirazi Party (ASP).

Tanganyika as A Political Issue in Zanzibar: The Mainlanders Are Coming

The decision of the TANU leadership to give its full support to the ASP became an issue in Zanzibar politics. This support was not only political but material as well. Some children of ASP members in Zanzibar (including the former Zanzibar President Dr. Amin Samour) were sent to Tanganyika for education; ASP had an office in Dar es Salaam; and several ASP leaders who could not get travel documents to travel abroad used to sneak to Dar es Salaam where they were provided with travel documents.

At times of Zanzibar elections, TANU leaders such as Bibi Titi Mohamed and Ali Mwinyi Tambwe went to Zanzibar to campaign openly for ASP. This was the background against which the Zanzibar Nationalist Party (ZNP) made the accusation that should the Afro-Shirazi Party (ASP) win the elections it would sell Zanzibar to Tanganyika. ASP, of course, retorted by saying that a NZP victory would bring back the slave trade into those islands, given the fact that a number of prominent ZNP leaders were of Arab origin and the party had fully identified itself with the royal family and maintained strong ties with the

279

Arab world.

Zanzibar's Independence:
Arab Dynasty Legitimised?

Zanzibar's road to independence was a bumpy one. While in Tanganyika TANU enjoyed overwhelming support of the population, in Zanzibar the two major political parties had almost even support. In the 1957 elections, the first of its kind in Eastern and Central Africa, ASP stormed through, winning five out of six seats in the Legislative Council; but in the subsequent elections of January and June 1961 and July 1963, the party maintained the lead in the number of votes it captured, but was unable to translate that into a majority of seats in the Legislative Council.

In Tanganyika the struggle for independence went on peacefully, in Zanzibar the June 1961 elections were disrupted by explosive riots that resulted in 68 deaths, 400 injured and 1,000 arrests. A year later, a prominent Zanzibari politician, Abdulrahman Babu, who was at the time secretary-general of the Zanzibar Nationalist Party (ZNP), was sent to jail after a libel case. Certainly the June riots were an indication of what was to come: the 1964 Zanzibar Revolution. Violence was being accepted as a way of solving political conflict.

When the dust had settled, physical wounds healed and tempers cooled, a constitutional conference was held in London between 19th March and 6th April 1962, attended by all the political parties in the Legislative Council, with the Colonial Secretary chairing. At the conference the ZNP/ZPPP alliance and the ASP showed very divergent views on future constitutional development. While they both reaffirmed their loyalty ot the Sultan and the throne and their desire that the dynasty should continue, they had different ideas on the programme of taking Zanzibar into internal self-government and independence.

On 24th January 1963 Zanzibar became an internally self-governing territory, and new elections were held. It was clearly understood by all that these were to be the last elections before independence, and that the government that was to be formed would lead the country to independence.

The elections were held from 8th to 15th July 1963 for a legislature of 31 members. The ZNP/ZPPP alliance won 18 seats, and the ASP 13. As indicated above, the ASP won the majority of votes cast but not a majority of seats. While the ZNP had a fall in in the percentage of votes cast from 35.0% in 1961 to 29.8% in 1963, the ASP increased its share of the votes from 49.9% in 1961 to 54.3% in 1963. The ZNPPP made an increase from 13.7% in 1961 to 15.9% in 1963.

Once more the ASP and its supporters felt cheated in the whole election exercise. After all in the January 1961 elections as well, the party had won 10 seats against ZNP's 9 and ZPP's 3.

ASP could not understand why the British Resident did not call upon its leader to be the Chief Minister, given the fact that with the three ex-officio British civil servants, namely the Chief Secretary, the Financial Secretary, and the Attorney-General, in the Legislative Council, the party would have had a working majority. But the British argued that a party must have its own majority before counting on the support of the ex-officio members. Meanwhile, the ZPPP split itself, with one member joining the ASP and the other two allying themselves with the ZNP.

Thus new elections had to be called in June; and meanwhile, a coalition government of all the parties with the Chief Secretary acting as the Chief Minister operated in the interim period.

Independence was attained on December 10th, 1963, with the Sultan as the head of state, with power also to nominate his successor. Thus, as Michael Lofchie stated, Arab rule had not only survived the introduction of representative institutions, but had acquired a degree of legitimacy under constitutional democracy.

The Revolution:
Class Struggle or Racial War?

What surprised many people outside the islands was how there could occur a 'sudden' revolution barely one month after Zanzibar attained its 'flag independence.' James Cameron, writing on Zanzibar in 1960, said: "Today this sleepy place holds little to help us in our search for the African Revolution." But hardly four years after those words were written, Zanzibar experienced a revolution that not only overthrew the ZNP/ZPPP coalition government, but immediately abolished the monarchy.

With the establishment of a republic and a new coalition of classes in power, a radical change of circumstances occurred. Indeed, it has been remarked that "with the possible exception of (Sekou Toure's) Guinea, no country in tropical Africa changed so radically in so short a time."

The first action of the revolutionary government was to abrogate the Independence Constitution of 1963 and proclaim a 'Constitutional Decree No.5' that provided for "Constitutional Government and Rule of Law." Although the revolutionary government allowed itself a period of one year to call a Constituent Assembly to adopt a constitution, such a body was never called, and Zanzibar only came to have a written constitution 15 years later, in 1979. In fact the first President of Zanzibar, the late Abeid Karume, no doubt remembering how ASP had suffered in elections in the past, had warned that there would be no elections for sixty years!

The revolution has been consistently described as a racial one and as a culmination of the struggle between the minority Arabs and the African majority. But that is only half the truth, and a distorted one as well. If we accept

282

Lenin's definition that every political struggle is a class struggle, we can see that behind the 'racial revolution' there was a class war. The point about pre-revolution Zanzibar is that racial differentiations went parallel with class differentiations.

The 1964 upheaval can be characterised as a revolt of the landless peasantry and the labouring masses against the landed aristocracy and political oligarchy. As Duggan has remarked, the revolt appeared to be a classic one, having been staged "in an area where political, economic and social conditions favoured its institution and guranteed its success." And as Michael Lofchie observed in his book *Zanzibar: Background to Revolution*:

The revolution set as its objective to transform Zanzibar into a wholly egalitarian society...[and] undertook measures to bring about a fairer distribution of the arable land. [It] also sought to eliminate from Zanzibar all symbolic vestiges of racial clubs and organizations and sosught to infuse the society with radical socialist methods stressing class and national solidarity rather than race.

Union of Tanganyika and Zanzibar: African Initiative or Cold War Rivalry?

Since the 1920s the countries of East Africa, namely Kenya, Tanganyika, Uganda and Zanzibar, had developed common services and joint institutions. Matters such as posts and telecommunications, harbours, railways and currency were run jointly. There was also a body to coordinate the development of Kiswahili.

This, no doubt, was easy in view of the fact that all the four countries were neighbours and under one colonial power. The white settlers in Kenya had at one time pressed the British Government for a federation of the East African countries on the lines of that of Central Africa (Northern Rhodesia, Southern Rhodesia, and Nyasaland).

But people in Tanganyika and Uganda feared that if that was to happen it would throw their countries into the hands of white supremacists in Kenya, in the same way that the peoples of Central Africa found themselves under the white supremacists of Southern Rhodesia at the time of the Central African Federation (whose capital was Salisbury, now Harare). And so this idea was opposed at the time.

But as the countries were approaching independence and because of the close cooperation among the nationalist organizations, the idea of federation re-emerged.

Nyerere, in a statement made in Addis Ababa when Tanganyika's independence was imminent, said that he was prepared to delay his country's independence if the four countries of East Africa could come to independence at the same time and form a federation.

But with independence each country retreated into its own national shell, and what was agreed was the formation of the East African Common Services Organisation that later in December 1967 was transformed into the East African Community.

When, therefore on 26th April, 1964, the People's Republic of Zanzibar and the Republic of Tanganyika announced that they had merged to form a Union, the international community felt that Zanzibar and Tanganyika had succeeded where the four East African countries together had failed. But was it the ideals of Pan-Africanism that brought Zanzibar and Tanganyika together?

Was the Union the result of an African initiative or was it propelled by cold war rivalry? The circumstances in which the Union was formed raised a lot of questions, many of which are still unanswered, and some have been at the centre of continuing debates and controversies in Tanzania in the last twenty years. Have the fears of ZNP that Zanzibar would be 'taken over' by Tanganyika been proven true?

In later years, the Union was to haunt the Zanzibar politicians for a long time, with each of them playing the "Union card" either for legitimacy on the mainland or for support at home.

Nyerere stated that he casually proposed the idea of the Union to Karume when the latter visited him to discuss the fate of John Okello. According to Nyerere, Karume immediately agreed on the idea and suggested that Nyerere should be the President of such a Union.

In a New Year message to the Nation on 2 January 1965, Nyerere implied that even if the ASP had come into power through constitutional means and not as a result of a revolution, the Union would still have taken place.

But Amrit Wilson's research has revealed that there was a very strong Western pressure, especially from the United States, for the Zanzibar Revolution to be contained because it was felt that it held the threat of the spread of communism in the East African region.

The United States, Britain and the then West Germany, which Tanganyika was heavily dependent on at the time, viewed the revolutionary government in Zanzibar as either a surrogate of the communist powers or dancing to their tune.

The international press had already started to characterize Zanzibar as the 'Cuba of Africa', though to be fair to Duggan, he had referred to Zanzibar as "Tanganyika's Cuba" far back in July 1963 when he had interviewed Nyerere in Washington during the latter's state visit to the US.

In a cable message to US embassies in Dar es Salaam, Nairobi and Kampala, the US Secretary of State Dean Rusk instructed his diplomats to urge Nyerere, Kenyatta and Obote to explain to Karume the dangers involved in his dependence on Babu and:

The danger Babu represents... to the security of Zanzibar and East Africa generally... they should recognize here that the big problem is that Karume himself has great confidence in and dependence on Babu... also that Nyerere has said that Karume needs Babu who, despite his background, can and must be worked with.

Kenyatta and Joseph Murumbi on the other hand appear to regard Babu as undesirable and the chief threat to Karume.

Would it be useful to liaise with Nyerere, despite his previous objection, the idea of a Zanzibar-Tanganyika Federation as a possible way of strengthening Karume and reducing Babu's influence? Such action at this time may also help Nyerere's own position.

In an interview with Amrit Wilson in 1986, Frank Carlucci, the US Consul in Zanzibar at the time of the Union who was later thrown out of Zanzibar because of CIA activities (and who later rose to become the Director of CIA and US Secretary of Defence), confessed that there was United States' pressure on Nyerere. Susan Crouch in her book *Western Responses to Tanzanian Socialism 1967-1983* reveals that:

To this end the American Central Intelligence Agency was active in trying to create the conditions for union, fanning antagonisms among Zanzibar's revolutionary leaders, and creating a fear of Zanzibar as a communist threat among East African leaders.

Was the Union then, as is indicated in U.S. State Department papers, dictated by cold war considerations first and the questions of pan-African ideals of unity were secondary to ideological factors and questions of personal survival?

It has also been suggested that Karume wanted a Union with Tanganyika as a means of warding off his Marxist and left-wing colleagues. What seems to be the case is that after the electoral defeat of July 1963 Karume's leadership

286

within the ASP parliamentary group was shaky.

There was a schism in it, with Karume being challenged by Othman Shariff, and some of the party's MPs calling for a government of national unity that would bring together in government all the political parties in parliament.

After the revolution, Umma Party radical elements in the government (Babu, Khamis Abdalla Ameir, Ali Sultan Issa, Ali Mahfoudh, Salim Rashid, Badawi Qullatein, etc) were forging links with the ASP leftists (Abdallah Kassim Hanga, Abdulazizi Ali Twala, Hassan Nassor Moyo, etc.), and this might have scared Karume and other moderate elements within the regime.At the same time, the radical way in which the revolution was surging ahead might have alarmed the regime in Dar es Salaam.

It should not be forgotten that within days of the revolution in Zanzibar, an army mutiny took place in Tanganyika (later repeated in Kenya and Uganda); and even though we know now that there was no link between the revolution and those mutinies, it was difficult to see it that way at the time.

As a result of the army mutiny in Dar es Salaam, Tabora and Nachingwea, there was virtually no government in Tanganyika for three days, anarchy prevailed, and Nyerere was forced to request British military intervention to bring the country back to normalcy.

The West, particularly the Untied States, perceived developments in Zanzibar in the context of East-West rivalry, and given the leftist credentials of the Umma Party and some of the ASP leaders that were prominent in the Revolutionary Council, it was assumed that a Cuba-type situation was evolving.

The best way of averting it, short of direct military intervention a la Playa Giron (though this was thought of and preparations made), was to try an "African initiative'. And it worked.

287

Legitimacy of the Union: The 'Absence' of the Attorney-General and The Question of A Referendum

Many questions continued to be raised regarding the legal basis of the Union: whether the two presidents on their own had the powers to sign such a Union Agreement; why the Zanzibar's Attorney-General, as the principal legal advisor to the government, was not consulted; why there was no referendum; and whether in joining such a union Zanzibar was not in fact 'swallowed' and 'annexed' by Tanganyika.

Discussions on the union were conducted very secretively. From the archival materials and the statements of those who were in the 'corridors of power' at the time, it would appear that not many people in the Tanganyika government or the Zanzibar Revolutionary Council knew what was happening.

Apart from Nyerere and Karume, the only other people who might have been privy to those discussions were Rashidi Kawawa, Oscar Kambona, Job Lusinde, Abdallah Kassim Hanga, Abdul-Aziz Ali Twala and Salim Rashidi.

When these discussions were at an advanced stage, Nyerere is said to have called in his Attorney-General at the time, British expert Roland Brown, and asked him to draft a Union Agreement without anybody knowing.

In the case of Zanzibar, the Attorney-General, Wolfgang Dourado, is said to have been sent on a one-week 'leave' and instead a Ugandan lawyer, Dan Nabudere (accoding to his own account which was corroborated by Babu), was brought in to advise Karume on the draft submitted by Tanganyika. Both Brown and Nabudere were present in the Karume-Nyerere discussions.

One can speculate that one reason why Dourado was not involved was because he was 'inherited' from the previous ZNP/ZPPP regime and the revolutionary government was hesitant to involve him in such a sensitive matter.

Under both the 1962 Republic of Tanganyika Constitution and the Zanzibar Presidential Decree No.5 quoted above, the two Presidents had the powers to enter into international agreements on behalf of their governments.

What is also important is that the Union Agreement was ratified by both the Tanganyika Parliament and the Zanzibar Revolutionary Council. Contrary to what some writers have said, the Nyalali Commission was satisfied that the Revolutionary Council met to ratify the 'Articles of Union'.

Both Abdulrahman Babu and Khamis Abdallah Ameir, the two former Umma Party leaders who were in the Revolutionary Council at the time, have confirmed that the matter was discussed in the Council, and while there were reservations on the part of some members, these were 'quashed' by Abdallah Kassim Hanga who made an emotional intervention to support the Union.

Once the 'Articles of Union' had been ratified by the two legislative bodies in Tanganyika and Zanzibar, there was no further requirement in law to make them enforceable. The question of referendum would not have arisen because under the Commonwealth legal tradition, in which the two countries were brought up, the notion of a referendum was unknown.

The referendum was introduced as a legal requirement under British law in the 1970s during the heated debate in the United Kingdom on the question of its entry into the European Economic Community.

To have also expected the Zanzibar revolutionary government to call a referendum on the Union, four months after it came into power through unconstitutional means, was like expecting the French revolutionaries of 1789 to have invited King Louis XVI for dinner after they had overthrown him.

Should ASP have conducted a referendum to ask

Zanzibaris whether or not to stage a revolution? In law, therefore, the Union Agreement, as both Prof Issa Shivji and Dr Kabudi have pointed out, is valid.

Articles of Union: 1 + 1 = 3

The Union Agreement, signed by Karume and Nyerere in Zanzibar on 22 April 1964, is known as the 'Articles of Union'. When this agreement was announced the following day many people inside the two countries, and outside too, were taken by surprise.

The strong feeling was that the West had won in their intention to containing the Zanzibar Revolution; in fact there were military preparations by both Britain and the United States in case there was a violent reaction in Zanzibar against the Union.

What the Tanganyika leadership wanted at the time was to play down the whole event. In a cable message of 23 April 1964 to the U.S. Secretary of State, the U.S. Ambassador in Dar es Salaam, William Leonhart, informed:

Mbwambo, Chief protocol, has just telephoned a personal request ..... that, to the maximum extent, any US public statements on Tangovernment -Zanzibar union be avoided. Situation over the next few days in Zanzibar could be very critical and both the Soviet and Chinese reaction is undetermined.

In an address later to the National Assembly requesting the ratification of the 'Articles of Union', Nyerere insisted that the move was inspired by the ideals for an African unity. "Unity in our continent does not have to come via Moscow or Washington", he insisted.

The 'Articles of Union' have been given different interpretations and characterised as federal, quasi-federal,

290

an interim arrangement towards one government, etc. Some have seen the Union as similar to the relationship between the United Kingdom and Northern Ireland.

Those who were close to the scene at the time also differ as to what type of relationship it is.

The U.S. Ambassador in Dar es Salaam, in a cable message to his government on 22nd April, 1964, the day the 'Articles of Union' were signed by Karume and Nyerere, stated:

Like the relationship between Northern Ireland and Britain, the union of Zanzibar and Tanganyika gave the island limited regional administrative autonomy ... but ensured overall power ... was held by the centre at Dar es Salaam.

But Frank Calucci, reporting from Zanzibar the next day, said that Karume was "still under the impression that he is agreeing to a federation of two autonomous states, not a centralised union envisaged under the present articles".

Attwood, the U.S. Ambassador in Kenya at the time, says he was informed by Dustan Omari, Nyerere's Permanent Secretary then, "that the major power would rest in the centre ... but that Zanzibar would retain its own internal governmental affairs"

While I have difficulty in accepting some of the assertions of some of the writers on the character of the Union for reasons that I will advance later, I would only want to agree with the notion that the 'Articles of Union' are the Grundnorm, the fundamental law of the United Republic, on which the Constitutions of Tanzania and Zanzibar, and other laws, have to be based and from which they derive their legitimacy. Like any supreme law in any other legal system, no other law or constitutional act can be in conflict with it.

'Articles of Union' provide for matters that would be under the Union arrangement. From the original 11 items

291

in 1964, the list has now expanded to 23. Some people question the validity of such an expansion, though one must admit that there was nothing that was added into the list unconstitutionally.

The 'Articles of Union' also provide for the existence of two governments: One for the whole Untied Republic for all Union matters and for non-Union matters in Tanganyika, which, under the 1977 Union Constitution is referred to as Tanzania Mainland, and one for Zanzibar in all matters that are non-Union.

According to Nyerere, Karume wanted a total union, but he (Nyerere) cautioned against it, saying that such a move might be construed by Zanzibaris and others as meaning that Zanzibar had been swallowed up, annexed, incorporated into or taken over by Tanganyika. He insisted that Zanzibar's identity must be maintained.

There is no way one can construe the 'Articles of Union' as a basis for a federal set-up. Nor can they be seen as an interim arrangement towards one government. They intended to create a single state with two authorities, but with one of those authorities having a limited geographical jurisdiction. The intention was to retain the identity of the smaller unit.

By this event, Tanganyika has not been lost; in fact it has been enlarged. Even if it is accepted that the Union was a Western conspiracy against the Zanzibar Revolution, the effect of the intention was to deny Zanzibar the capacity to be an international actor, not to interfere with what was happening inside the country. To be able to change the internal course of events would have entailed changing the regime.

What might have confounded some of the law experts looking at the relationship between Zanzibar and Mainland Tanzania was the fact that no such example existed in the Anglo-Saxon legal system. The closest they could think of then was that of the United Kingdom and Northern Ireland.

The Consolidation of the Union: Popular Approval of the "Swallowing Up"

At the time of the union, Zanzibar and Tanganyika were ruled by different political parties, ASP and TANU respectively. The 'Articles of Union' did not require the formation of a single political party for the whole United Republic.

Thus in the period 1964-1977 each party operated within its own geographical area, though at the approach of every general election, the two parties held a joint congress where they nominated a join presidential candidate for the elections. Only in 1977, after a national survey of members of both parties, did the two parties merge to form Chama Cha Mapinduzi (CCM) with authority over the whole country.

But why did Zanzibaris agree to such a merger? Nyerere had always expressed surprise when recalling the radiant faces he saw and the jovial mood of the Zanzibaris the day CCM was proclaimed at the Amani Stadium in Zanzibar.

The fact is that Zanzibaris were celebrating not only the birth of CCM but also the demise of ASP. By that time the general feeling in the islands was that the ASP had outlived its usefulness.

The revolution which it had championed had stooped so low as to devour its own sons: most of the leaders were busy amassing wealth; prison and death were the only options open to political dissent; and political thugery was a virtue.

One matter that was added in 1984 to the list of Union items was that of national security. This happened at the time when Ali Hassan Mwinyi was President and Seif Shariff Hamad the Chief Minister of Zanzibar in 1984-85, commonly known as the Third Phase Government.

Not having much confidence in the security personnel

they inherited, who might have had personal allegiance to Jumbe and Seif Bakari, the new Administration sought the extension of the National Security Act of the Mainland to Zanzibar. In that case it was possible to transfer the security personnel in Zanzibar to the Mainland and vice versa.

So from the above one can see the following: First, Zanzibaris wanted a merger of the parties, and for the united party to have authority all over the country, in the hope that it would rescue them from a regime that was no longer able to inspire confidence and instil enthusiasm; and second, a 'consolidation' of the Union in this regard was necessary for one faction of the leadership to ward off any possible challenge by the other.

The long-term effect of the parties' merger was to have matters that were entirely within Zanzibar's jurisdiction, and that were not Union matters, decided by a pan-territorial political party where Zanzibari representation was not decisive.

This became clear in 1984 when Aboud Jumbe was forced to resign as Zanzibar President: it was the party's NEC which appointed Ali Hassan Mwinyi as an Interim President and later nominated him for election as the President of Zanzibar.

Since NEC's Zanzibari membership is no more than a third of the total, this means therefore that a Zanzibar President could be chosen by a forum which is predominantly non-Zanzibari. And this was further evidenced with the nomination by CCM's NEC of the present President of Zanzibar.

A number of other measures were taken to consolidate the Union, particularly in the constitutional realm. A permanent constitution was put in place in 1977 instead of an interim one that had been in existence since 1964.

Zanzibar's Identity in the Union

In the 'Articles of Union', Zanzibar is allowed to retain its autonomy and pursue its own policies in all matters other than those stipulated as Union matters.

In this case, the power to decide is left to the Zanzibar organs such as the House of Representatives, the Revolutionary Council and the President of Zanzibar and Chairman of the Revolutionary Council.

The Union Constitution stipulates that constitutional amendments require the approval of two-thirds of Zanzibaris sitting in the Union Parliament and the same proportion of Mainlanders.

In order to avoid a clash in the legislative functions of the two sides of the Union, it has been provided that if the House of Representatives enacts any law which should be under the jurisdiction of the Union Parliament that law will be null and void, and also if the Union Parliament enacts a law on any matter under the jurisdiction of the House of Representatives that law will be null and void.

The Constitution also provides for effective Zanzibari representation in the Union Parliament. It also guarantees a separate judiciary system for Zanzibar which has jurisdiction over Zanzibar alone. Even though the Court of Appeal of the United Republic is a Union organ, it has no power to decide on a case involving a dispute between the Union Government and the Zanzibar Revolutionary Government.

However one might view the circumstances that made Zanzibar merge with Tanganyika in 1964, the fact of the matter is that Zanzibar was not annexed or forcefully incorporated. It agreed on the Union out of its own free will and as a result of decisions made by its own organs. The argument that within the Union Tanganyika has lost its identity has no basis.

If anything it has enlarged its territory. It is Zanzibar's autonomy and identity that must be maintained lest, as Nyerere himself has pointed out several times, an impression is created that the larger and more populous

Tanganyika has swallowed Zanzibar.

Such a situation is not new even in the most centralized states. In China, despite the fact that the country has a centralized authority and no federal traces of any kind, yet because of certain historical, political or cultural reasons, certain areas are conferred autonomy, and are constitutionally given the status of autonomous regions.

As will be pointed out later there are entities in present-day Europe that enjoy full autonomy within one state. To entertain the thought that the 'Articles of Union' are a temporary arrangement, and that ultimately the intention should be to create one government is to manifest 'big brother chauvinism.'

Debates on the Union: The Polluted Political Atmosphere

In 1983/84 and 1990/92 extensive political and constitutional debates took place in the country that deeply probed the question of the Union. The debates of 1983/84 resulted in major amendments to the 1977 Union Constitution and the formulation of a new Zanzibar Constitution in 1984.

But they also resulted in the forced resignation of Aboud Jumbe from all his state and party positions, the sacking of a Zanzibar Chief Minister and the serious warning given by the ruling party to a number of prominent Zanzibar figures.

The debates of the 1990/92 period resulted in the Nyalali Commission making major recommendations on the structure of the Union. In between the two periods also another Zanzibar Chief Minister was sacked, and several leading Zanzibar politicians were dismissed form the ruling party.

As stated above, the question of Zanzibar being 'sold' to the Mainland was an issue in pre-revolutionary Zanzibar. And if one remembers that the political parties

296

were almost evenly divided, then one can assume that almost half of the Zanzibar population was already biased against the Mainland even before the Union.

The post-revolution politics in the islands did not help matters much. Karume went into a Union to save himself from his Marxist and left-wing colleagues; and since Jumbe was not considered to be the 'heir apparent' before Karume's assassination in 1972, he was not thought of as the natural successor when he took over.

It has been speculated that the Revolutionary Council had Col. Seif Bakari in mind, but Nyerere advised that since Karume was killed by an army officer, Seif Bakari taking over might be construed as a military coup. Jumbe, feeling that he had not much support within the Revolutionary Council, depended very much on Nyerere's and Mainland's support.

It is no wonder then that it was during his presidency that much of the consolidation of the Union took place, with the most items added to the Union list. It is significant too that the merger of the parties took place then. But this dependency on the Mainland was costing him much popular support at home.

Either as a way of outflanking his opponents or because of genuine problems he found in the Union (after all he was for a long time a Minister for Union Affairs before he became President of Zanzibar), he first raised the question of restructuring the Union in a speech seven years before the 1983/84 debates.

Other politicians in Zanzibar too have used the Mainland as a trump card either to crush their opponents or to climb the political ladder. Seif Shariff Hamad, Khatib Hassan, Shaaban Mloo and others accused Jumbe in 1984 of planning to break up the Union, and thus forced Jumbe to resign from his political posts then. They in turn faced the same accusation from their opponents in 1988 and were dismissed from the party.

The issues that were raised in both the 1983/84 and

1990/92 debates centred on the following:

1. Whether the 'Articles of Union' of 1964 provided for a federation, that is three governments (one of Tanganyika, the other of Zanzibar, and a third a federal one) or only two governments as presently existing;
2. As the Union Government is also the government for the Mainland in non-Union matters, does this not give the impression that Mainland is the Union?
3. Does Zanzibar get a fair share in the distribution of benefits coming form the Union?
4. Is Zanzibar well represented in the diplomatic service?
5. Does it get a fair share of foreign aid coming to Tanzania?
6. Since the people of Zanzibar were not consulted at the time of the formation of the Union, should there not be a referendum now to ascertain whether the people wanted the Union or not?

Most of these questions, as can be seen, were coming from Zanzibar, and what surprised many people at the time of the 1983/84 debate, was that they were being aired in the state-owned-and-controlled official mass media.

No such strong feelings were voiced on the Mainland during the debates. Many people who made submissions to the Nyalali Commission said hardly anything about the system of governments that the Union should have.

It was only after the opening up of the political system and the establishment of more political parties that one began hearing very strong views coming form the Mainland on the question of the Union; some of those going even further than anybody in Zanzibar had ever contemplated.

Nyalali Commission on the Union: Agreed to Disagree

One of the major recommendations of the Nyalali Commission was for the replacement of the present Union set-up with a federal one. This was one of the areas that bought about a very heated debate within the Commission and which necessitated members of the Commission having to vote.

Later those who were opposed to the federal idea had to append their own Dissenting Opinion to the main report to explain their position.

But the division in the Commission on this issue almost came to a Mainland/Zanzibar division. Of the 11 members from Zanzibar, 7 wanted the present Union set-up, with some major changes, to remain; 3 wanted a federal and 1 was undecided. Of the same number from the Mainland, 9 wanted a federal set-up and 2 wanted the present arrangement to continue. What is important is that both sides agreed that there were problems within the Union. Even though at the time the complaints form the Mainland were not so loud compared to Zanzibar, it would have been wise if those complaints were addressed and resolved.

The majority of members of the Commission felt that in a federal set-up, both Tanganyika and Zanzibar would retain their identity, federal areas would be clearly defined and the responsibilities of each would be understood, and the federal entity would be distinct from the national ones.

Those holding the minority opinion, on the other hand, were of the view that there was nothing in the 'Articles of Union' to suggest that their framers had a federal set-up in mind; that a federation would be a step backward and might be a prelude to the dissolution of the Union; that corrective measures could be taken, if there is political will, which would define Union matters, list Union institutions and apportion the responsibility of each side on those matters.

Examples were provided from the two Scandinavian countries of Denmark and Finland where entities (Faroe

Islands, Aaland Islands and Greenland) have full autonomy in a number of areas that they exercise within a non-federal state. The Dissenting Opinion in the Nyalali Report pointed out:

* Greenland and Faroe Islands, both of which are part of Denmark, have full autonomy in many matters. For example, a parliament that is not subject to interference form the central government of Denmark, and all political and economic matters agreed upon and even in international relations. The islands of Faroe have their own flag hoisted in all government buildings and on ships registered in Faroe islands. Also Faroe Islands authority issues passports;

* Denmark had agreed to join the European Economic Community. So did Greenland. But later, Greenland withdrew from the Community. Therefore, all EEC agreements and conditionality accepted in Denmark did not apply in Greenland. Similarly, the Islands of Faroe are not a member of the EU.

* In regard to Finland, the islands of Aaland have their own parliament and government. The islands of Aaland also have their own 'identity' for persons born in the islands and who have not lived abroad consecutively for five years or more. The islands have their own flag, issue their own stamps and its citizens are not subject to military service. The islands of Aaland are a demilitarized zone. The Central Bank of Finland must consult the government of Aaland before it takes measures that might harm the economy of Aaland. This, despite the fact that they share a common currency;

* The islands of Aaland, as is the case for Greenland and Faroe, are, on their own right, represented in the Nordic Council that consists of Denmark, Finland, Sweden,

300

Norway and Iceland.

Conclusion: Whither the Union?

As pointed out above, there have been historical links between Zanzibar and Tanganyika long before the coming of the colonialists in East Africa; and colonialism did not in fact stop such interactions from continuing.

During the struggle for national independence, the two main political parties in the two countries cooperated though there is nothing to suggest that the two parties were thinking of merging into a Union of this kind after they came into power.

What they had in mind was to form a federation with Kenya and Uganda. Until the elections of July 1963, ASP still thought that it would win power through the electoral process; and it would appear that their main supporters, TANU, thought likewise.

Now the Union is a fact. Despite a lot of problems, it has brought stability and peace in the region. It is difficult to speculate what would have happened to the Zanzibar Revolution without the Union: whether Zanzibar would have advanced faster or whether a counter-revolutionary force would have taken over and embellished a dictatorship worse than anything the islands have actually experienced especially during the first phase government. What is clear though is that the Union has brought the two peoples much closer together.

I do not believe that the unity of the two peoples can be strengthened by restructuring the present set-up into a federation.

I see movement from the present set-up to a federation as a step towards the dismemberment of the Union; and I do not think that that is to the short- or long-term benefit of the people of Tanzania.

The present problems can be resolved if there is a strong political will on the part of our political class and if the people are told the truth about those problems.

Only when corrective measures are taken, would it be possible to sustain and strengthen the Union. Otherwise if the difficulties inherent in the 'Articles of Union' and the problems arising from implementation are only emphasized and not resolved, the tendency would be towards the withering away of the Union.

In this era of multipartism and openness, it is even more important that matters are discussed and solutions founded on popular will.

Of all the political parties that have been established since the abolition of the one-party system, only one, the Democratic Party led by Reverend Christopher Mtikila, has come out strongly against the Union and called for its dissolution.

Others are prevaricating between 'referendum', 'federation' and modifications within the present set-up. The CCM and its governments which seemed earlier on to strongly accept the Dissenting Opinion in the Nyalali Report, now seems to be torn apart, with a strong group calling for a federal set-up.

The national language, the ethics of equality and human dignity, and the Union of Tanganyika and Zanzibar are what overcame the ethnic hatred, religious bigotry, regional parochialism and national differences and forged national cohesion and unity.

It is these that have made Tanzania an example in a continent beset with secessionism, ethnic violence and religious pogroms.

One hopes that there is capacity, honesty and patriotism within Tanzania that will look beyond the sectarian interests. The alternative is too horrendous to contemplate.

Haroub Othman
Institute of Development Studies
University of Dar es Salaam
United Republic of Tanzania.

The article above was part of a series published in three parts in the *Guardian*, Dar es Salaam, Tanzania, April 26 – 28, 2004.

Appendix II:

Union is a noble entity we should strengthen

Editorial, *The Citizen*,
Dar es Salaam, Tanzania, 26 April 2014

Today, the majority of Tanzanians nearing 50 million are marking a milestone that has dawned a little over two years after the preceding one on December 9, 2011, when we commemorated the fiftieth anniversary of the political independence of Mainland Tanzania.

This time around, the Union between the then Tanganyika and Zanzibar, has clocked 50 years – an achievement of no small measure for which we have cause to be hugely proud. Today's event is indeed more significant, because it represents the survival, for a good fifty years; five solid decades, of the partnership.

It's a huge achievement, primarily because the arrangement entailed each partner surrendering some of its crucial rights and privileges.

In the Mainland's case, the twin-concepts Tanganyika-Tanganyikans vanished. Partnerships aren't easy to sustain, as many rocky human marriages so glaringly show. Yet, the Tanzanian Union is still ticking; that eight foreign heads of state are scheduled to join President Jakaya Kikwete in marking its golden jubilee today, and congratulatory messages pouring in from several well-wishers, speak volumes on its novelty and nobleness.

The Union, and Tanzanians who represent its human face, are saluted for the role-modelling inter-nation partnership, a feat that has eluded several attempts to that end elsewhere in Africa and beyond.

The entity represents a chip in the pan-African spirit of continental unity and fellowship – ideals that the Nyereres and Nkrumahs of yester-years advocated, but which have been persistently elusive. The two-government system is driven by politicians and technocrats from the two sides; and the Union Parliament is engineering the legislative business.

Using constructive debate for positive ends

Plus, Islanders and Mainlanders generally co-exist cordially, save for occasional disruptions of peace by a relatively tiny fringe of troublemakers.

As a member of the Mwananchi Communications Limited family, *The Citizen*, both its daily and weekend editions, salutes the Union, because it firmly believes in initiatives geared at fostering African unity.

In addition to the salutations, the publishers oppose any moves, overt and covert, that seek to weaken and/or wreck the partnership. Granted, the Union is beset by a host of snags that have defied resolution over the years, but which we strongly believe aren't insurmountable, and which it is foolhardy of any person or group to assume can be overcome by wrecking the partnership.

Tanzanians, for whom Tanzanian-ness is a reality rather than a myth, would become a global laughing stock if that were to happen, and the spirits of the pioneers, Mwalimu Julius Nyerere and Sheikh Abeid Karume, would be deeply offended.

Instead, we support and advocate constructive dialogue for resolving problems and misunderstandings; a spirit that extends to regional groupings like the East African Community. We also strongly advocate constructive debate on other critical issues beyond the Union, as well as promoting the interests of the voiceless.

Appendix III:

Katiba: Last hope for future of Union

Salim Said Salim, *The Citizen*,
Dar es Salaam, Tanzania, 26 April 2014

Zanzibar – The United Republic of Tanzania, which is now marking 50 years of its existence, is at a crossroads and has some observers worried that it is headed to a strange, if not an unknown destiny.

The Union has from its formation survived political, economic and social challenges, some of which have threatened to wreck its foundations.

However, the problems promise to evaporate with the start of the Constituent Assembly (CA) meeting in Dodoma. The CA is in the process of paving the way for a new constitution that will meet the demands, hopes and aspirations of all the people of the United Republic.

The Assembly has been meeting for nearly two months now, characterized by a tug of war among its members debating issues of concern and in particular the future structure of the Union.

The manner some of the CA members have been conducting themselves has left a lot to be desired. The tone of presentations has lacked decorum expected of members of a distinguished national body. Instead of achieving reconciliation, such conduct has only served the interest of widening differences.

Many are already questioning the criteria that were used to select some of the members of the CA. Even the role of traditional politicians, mainly those from parliamentary constituencies, is being viewed with some suspicion.

Before the CA is the draft new constitution proposal prepared by the Constitutional Review Commission (CRC) headed by Judge Joseph Sinde Warioba, former Prime Minister and Attorney General.

The CRC draft has recommended, among other things, a three-tier Union. This was on the basis of popular opinions obtained during CRC's nation-wide tours, leading to the proposal for three union governments – the Union (Tanzania), Zanzibar and Tanganyika.

According to the CRC, besides those preferring the three government structure, there were others who had made other suggestions (one or two governments and a contractual Union). However, in its opinion the CRC found the three-tier system as probably the most workable form that would best serve the interests of the Union and allow its strengthening. This is as contained in the draft before the CA.

Unfortunately, this has precipitated what can be described as "organised chaos" in Dodoma.

Instead of dwelling on the proposals in the draft constitution, some of the members have reduced it to a political Ping-Pong, determined to safeguard the interests of political parties.

Members and supporters of the ruling party, Chama Cha Mapinduzi (CCM) appear not to favour the CRC proposal for a three-tier Union, preferring to maintain the two government system - one for Zanzibar and one for Tanzania. Some point to the suggestion attributed to President Jakaya Kikwete during his CA opening address hinting military revolt if the country would opt for three governments.

This has unleashed bitter complaints from opposition politicians and others. Meanwhile, the debate on the Union is sailing through turbulent waters.

The CA is at a point where neither the captain nor the sailors know exactly where the country is headed.

Zanzibar demands more autonomy for Zanzibar under a three-tier government.

They believe that under the present system Zanzibar is losing out on trade and international cooperation which they had gained in 1984 under the President Ali Hassan Mwinyi and Chief Minister Seif Sharif Hamad trade liberalisation policies.

Zanzibaris have also complained about introduction of high taxation by the Tanzania Revenue Authority (TRA) because of losses of revenue by the Zanzibar Treasury and job losses for people in the trade sector.

There is further concern over Union government's withdrawal of Zanzibar from the Organisation of Islamic Countries (OIC) membership because international cooperation is under Union matters. Despite promises that Tanzania would join the OIC under the Union umbrella, more than two decades now this has not happened, even when Zanzibar is 95 per cent Muslim.

International cooperation placed under Union affairs, has only meant denial of Zanzibar power to negotiate international aid, grants and loans.

In his paper on the Health situation in Zanzibar at a seminar to mark 25 years of the Revolution in 1989, Prof Abdul-Aziz Lodhi of Uppsala University, Sweden, said in 1980 Sweden had set aside a 650 million Swedish kroner aid package to Tanzania, but only one million was allocated to Zanzibar. The late Prof Haroub Othman of the

311

University of Dares Salaam had also expressed similar sentiments.

This shows that questions of concern to one side of the Union have not been fully addressed. The architects of the Union, Mwalimu Nyerere and Sheikh Karume, had mixed soils from the Mainland and the Isles in 1964 not only as a symbol of uniting the two countries, but also uniting thousands of families with blood streams from both parts of the Union.

Tanzania must go beyond summoning political will to remain genuinely one and firm in the conviction that the people of either side of the Union cannot contemplate divorce after 50 years of marriage. If that happens, there will be no winner and we will end up as losers all of us.

The on-going constitution-making process offers the best opportunity for a better, fair, united and democratic Union. CA members in Dodoma, taking their tasks responsibly, may well be the last hope for a certain future of the United Republic of Tanzania.

Appendix IV:

Union at 50:
Union's golden jubilee, katiba making process

Kitwana M. Kitwana, *The Citizen*,
Dar es Salaam, Tanzania, 26 April 2014

When I think of our Union and the idea and efforts of its founders Julius Nyerere and Abeid Karume behind it, I see an effort for grim actualisation of the African dream to unite.

Dar es Salaam – It's 50 years since this country became Tanzania! Yes it's half a century since Tanganyika and Zanzibar embarked on the grand project to unite and create a new country in the map of Africa and the world called Tanzania.

This was a milestone even if you belong to the group of Afro-pessimists but this happened and it happened in Africa.

It was a an undertaking to defy the negative doctrine about Africa advocated by people like a famous German philosopher who once put it, "What we properly understand by Africa, is the Unhistorical, Undeveloped

Spirit, still involved in the conditions of mere nature, and which had to be presented here only as on the threshold of the world's history."

The other reasons for the unification might be dozens, commentators and pundits can give explanations behind the dynamics which led to that noble process. For example others would say this was nothing but a product of Western influence to make Zanzibar in the Union to avoid it falling into communism and becoming the 'Cuba' of Africa during the cold war.

I choose to look at it as the initiative to operationalise the Pan-Africanism spirit which is a grand philosophy and came to characterise and define the struggle, efforts, and hope for Africans in the global setting. It is an African attempt to react to miseries of slave trade, occupation, exploitation by outsiders and writing its history.

While the philosophy did well in helping Africans to liberate themselves from colonial occupation in the mid-20th century , it failed miserably in making Africa as one.

The idea of having a united Africa is long overdue and hundreds of meetings which have been held in Addis by our rulers under the Organisation of African Unity/African Union banner have never brought us near that realization.

When I think of our Union and the idea and efforts of its founders Julius Nyerere and Abeid Karume behind it, I see an effort for the grim actualisation of the African dream to unite.

The Union of Tanzania to celebrate its golden anniversary this year is critical, but a very important moment for the history of this country. This country is in the process of writing its constitution and whilst there is a lot to discuss in the on-going Constituent Assembly concerning the proposed draft worked out by the Constitutional Review Commission, the crux of the matter has so far been the Union issue.

It's true there have been ups and downs in the

314

evolvement of the Union and there are different views about how it should be structured. All the differences have to be neutralised by the consensus of people's of both sides of Tanzania. We can talk of the number of governments in the new constitution, but as long as our overarching interests are to have a stronger United Republic of Tanzania that is totally acceptable.

Prof Issa Shivji writes in his book entitled *Let the People Speak: Tanzania Down the Road to Neo-liberalism*:

"Whether such a new Union structure will be based on one, two or three governments; whether the model of the Union would be Canadian, US, Indian, or akin to the European Community or East African Community or some combination of all or some of these, will depend precisely on the outcomes of the process of a national debate....Meanwhile the debate continues. Will it move from Bunge to Buguruni? That is the question."

At times it's hurting that some politicians have been frequently asking about the existence of the Union. For example, there are groups of people in Zanzibar like the famous Uamsho group, which is secretly backed by powerful politicians in Zanzibar seeking Zanzibar's full sovereignty.

The thinking behind the movement is that socio economic problems facing the Isles are a result of its union with mainland Tanzania; hence the need to get rid of the Union and then you have prosperity, a very mechanical way of thinking!

They don't see the Union as the symbol of unity. Rather they see it as Tanganyika's occupation of their country, forgetting that the latter is very fragile if it exists as an independent country, which is a product of history not of the Union. If you choose to see things as they are Zanzibar is deeply divided politically between Pemba and Unguja whereby people in Pemba have sentiments which

315

imply that they have been disadvantaged by the other side of the Isles.

The question is if they want the Isles to be independent, what kind of Zanzibar are they referring to? That of 1963 before the revolution or one after the revolution?

I am asking this because I know there are politicians and their followers who don't believe in the 1964 Revolution and they don't regard it as a revolution per se. To them the revolution was brought about by the 1964 acts of violence.

These negative forces which further widen the fractures which have been existing in our current structure of the two tier government, have demurred to be an Isles affair only. The Mainlanders have decided to reciprocate by crying for their Tanganyika.

The cry for Tanganyika for years had been the policy of the famous controversial pastor and politician Christopher Mtikila and his political party DP and the famous G55 CCM parliamentarians.

Now the club is getting new recruits and there have been nationalistic cries to bring back Tanganyika which existed between December 9, 1961, and April 26, 2014. Those of us born within the Union don't know how Tanganyika tasted and we're therefore bewildered! The debate we have now should be geared towards addressing these challenges rather than escalating them.

We should have adopted a more common sense approach to this problem by having an informed debate and not succumbing to character assassination tactics between those who have opposing opinions in the Constituent Assembly (CA) and those who are supporting.

The noises, diatribes, insults, mocking and the walking out of the CA chamber manifest how we are still immature to take this country in the right direction.

Also we should be ripe enough to grasp that the proposed draft which is now being discussed in the Constituent Assembly (CA) is people's opinions collected and refined by the Constitutional Review Commission headed by Joseph Warioba.

The ad hominem attack from some politicians in the ruling party to Warioba on the CRC proposal of having three tier governments is unfair and it's indeed ridiculous.

One thing which gives me a headache is the evolution of leadership human societies. It's surprising that technology advancement doesn't seem to go hand in hand with development of leadership acumen. It's a worldwide phenomenon that political leaderships are in crisis and Tanzania is not exception.

The level of leadership is diminishing and you have to accept that our founding fathers Nyerere and Karume were ahead of time when they decided to unite these countries. If things proceed as they are in the CA, we will need a Moses to take us to the promised land of the next 50 years!

Mr Kitwana is a political and development analyst based in Dar es Salaam.

Appendix V:

Good intentions underlie union

Richard Mshomba, *The Citizen*,
Dar es Salaam, Tanzania, 26 April 2014

It is no secret that the Union of Tanganyika and Zanzibar was an arranged "marriage" between the leaders of Tanganyika and Zanzibar, Mwalimu Julius Kambarage Nyerere and Sheikh Abeid Amani Karume. Some of the details of their manoeuvres were revealed recently by Pius Msekwa and Salum Rashid who were, at the time, Tanganyika's Secretary of Parliament and Zanzibar's Secretary of the Revolutionary Council, respectively.

Fortunately, Nyerere and Karume had good intentions which are still respected today.

Mwalimu Nyerere was a nationalist, but also an ardent pioneer of Pan-Africanism. He was willing to postpone Tanganyika's independence to wait for Kenya and Uganda, if that meant East Africa would attain freedom as a federation. He saw that the likelihood of a federation after each country had gained its independence separately was slim, at best.

He argued that, "if it is desired to bring about this Federation the right moment to do this is not after each country has separately achieved its own independence but before. ...Surely, if it is difficult now to convince some of our friends that Federation is desirable, when it does not involve surrendering any sovereignty, it is going to be a million times more difficult to convince them later."

History has proven him correct, but that does not necessarily mean it made sense to propose a federation of "unborn" countries. It is hard to imagine that such a federation would have survived when a less ambitious integration, the former East African Community, collapsed after just 10 years.

Nonetheless, the Zanzibar Revolution in January 1964 provided Nyerere a new opportunity. Karume was an enthusiastic counterpart, not so much because he cared about Pan-Africanism, but because he felt that his leadership and the survival of the new Zanzibar needed a strong, geographically close, partner. For Karume, the Union was a "marriage" of convenience, not ideology.

The Union came about the way it did at the time because the two nations did not have nearly the level of democracy that is enjoyed today. Can anyone imagine in a democratic society that two leaders, for example Presidents Kenyatta and Kikwete, would meet secretly and reach a binding deal to unite Kenya and Tanzania? It's unthinkable. But that was what happened regarding Tanganyika and Zanzibar. There was no public referendum or a team like Judge Warioba's that collected people's inputs.

Nonetheless, Tanganyika and Zanzibar are continuing to mature, both as a Union and separately. As a people, Tanzanians have the solemn duty, in a democratic process, to revisit agreements of the framework of the Union, discuss, and even revise them as they see fit. The Union is not static, it is dynamic. It is both hypocritical and an insult to the Father of the Nation to suggest that instituting

320

anything different from what the original leaders put in place is to dishonour them.

Mwalimu Nyerere was a person of high moral principles centred on freedom and equality for all human beings. He had no tolerance for those in public service who took advantage of their positions to amass wealth. If the country truly wants to honour him, it should take a good hard look at income inequality and corruption in the country and fight them with all its might.

Mwalimu was also a great thinker and a pragmatist, highly capable of analysing situations and able to accommodate change. Ascribing to him only one specific way of holding the Union together would be treating him like a mindless bureaucrat.

As the nation celebrates 50 years of the Union, we have a lot for which we should thank Nyerere and Karume. We should thank them not only for the Union, but also because they left us a country capable of maturing to the point where people can now freely debate and execute, as they see fit, the way they want to move forward. Long live the Union, be it with one government, two, or three, as long as the decision respects the democratic process.

The author is professor of economics at La Salle University, Philadelphia, Pennsylvania, USA.

Appendix VI:

Union at 50:
Constitutional Assembly (CA)
won't deliver, says ex-Zanzibar official

Peter Nyanje, *The Citizen*,
Dar es Salaam, Tanzania, 26 April 2014

It is unfortunate that the country has spent a lot of money to finance the CRC (Constitutional Review Commission) while it seems that leaders have their stand on the two governments, says Zanzibar's former chief secretary Salim Said Rashid.

Zanzibar – The former chief secretary of the Zanzibar Revolutionary Council, Mr Salim Said Rashid, is apprehensive over what is going on in Dodoma. After watching the Constituent Assembly members bickering for two months culminating in Ukawa's walkout, Mzee Salim is now sure that the CA will not give the country what it deserves. – (UKAWA – Umoja wa Katiba ya Wananchi – the Coalition for a People's Constitution).

Given the situation in Dodoma, Mr Salim says it is obvious that CA members are not going to agree on the draft constitution. But, this will make the bad situation worse.

He says it is unfortunate that the country has spent a lot of money to finance the CRC while it seems that leaders have their stand on the two governments.

He criticised those who say that three governments will create nationalism, noting that nationalism is already in Zanzibar and that is what has empowered Zanzibaris to stand for their tights within the Union. "They should not tell us that Tanganyika's nationalism will kill the Union while we have the East African Community which is made up of five countries each of which has its nationalism," he says. But he says it is true that there is no nationalism in Tanganyika because people are satisfied because the Union government has been working for them.

Mzee Salim warns CCM, noting that their stand on the Union is going to cost them especially in Zanzibar where majority of people have fallen out of favour with the merger in its current form.

"I have been receiving a lot of CCM zealots here who are against their party stand of two governments... Mr Hassan Nassoro Moyo and I are waiting for (Ismail) Jussa... we are all for full Zanzibar autonomy and there are many people from CCM who support this stand," he says adding:

"Even those who are supporting two governments from CCM here are saying that within that system Zanzibar should have full autonomy."

But he says it is unfortunate that some of the CCM members have taken a different position in Dodoma.

Mzee Salim said also that the debate on the Union structure might also end up severing the Government of National Unity (GNU) in which the two principals support different systems. He notes that while Zanzibar President, Dr Ali Mohammed Shein supports two governments, the first Vice President, Maalim Seif Sharif Hamad, is in favour of a treaty- based Union.

In the beginning

Mr Salim says though many scholars have given different versions as to what prompted the Union, it is true that the merger was not a brain child of the two former leaders, Nyerere and Karume. He says it is the US which forced the merger for its own interests.

This is confirmed by records in the Johnson Library in Huston, Texas. US convinced Nyerere to unite with Zanzibar as a way of blocking communism from entering East Africa. All other reasons that the merger came to strengthen Africa's unity is just nonsense.

And the Union came very fast, according to Mzee Salim. In just one week, the idea was introduced and signed even before many people knew what was happening. Mr Salim says if Zanzibaris were asked then if they were ready for their country to merge with another country they would have refused. Mr Salim says that if they had opportunity they would have told people the effects of conceding their sovereignty. He notes however, that after 50 years their fears have been confirmed given the current demands from Zanzibar.

He says a proposal in the draft constitution that the Union government will now be able to run development activities in Zanzibar does not hold water because the government has no resources to do that.

"The little resources they have are being misused and corruption has dominated. Second, they had all this time to do that, what prevented them from implementing such policies? How are we going to believe them that they are going to do so this time?" he asks.

He says this provision could be used to transfer more

Zanzibar powers to the Union government.

Mr Salim says even himself, despite being a top executive in the Revolutionary Government of Zanzibar, he was not involved closely in the issue;

"I first heard about the plan to unite the two countries when Sheikh Karume brought the proposed Articles of Union. The Union was signed on April 22 and made public on 26th. I only heard about it just a week before when the document was brought from Dar es Salaam.

Mzee Karume asked me to translate it for him and I told him that according to that document, Zanzibar loses its sovereignty. But it seems that he was threatened as he did agree to the plan and did not say anything in protest."

What should be done

Mr Salim says it is very hard to advise what should be done under the prevailing conditions. He says it is hard because various groups, namely political parties, have taken hardline stands on the issue.

But he chided the CCM proposal of establishing a house of representatives for Tanganyika as some of the changes which should free the Union government from being seen as concentrating on Tanganyika's affairs.

"You can't form one and half government and expect things to calm down. Besides, sentiments over the current structure of the Union will always continue in Zanzibar until some tangible changes are introduced," he says.

But he says there is a danger that Tanganyikans after seeing what is going on in the CA as well as demands by Zanzibar, they will also start to demand for their government. This will complicate the situation further in case the authorities stick to the status quo.

The way things stand, Mr Salim says, what Zanzibar needs now is only sovereignty because it has almost all instruments which an independent state needs. He says things will be a bit complicated for Tanganyika which needs to first enact a constitution, something which Zanzibar has already done.

Appendix VII:

Union has grown despite hurdles

Ally Salehe, *The Citizen*,
Dar es Salaam, Tanzania, 27 April 2014

Zanzibar – It is true that the Union of Tanganyika and Zanzibar is this year notching 50 years of existence. It is also true that the Union has forged closer links between the two countries that are geographical neighbours. The merger has strengthened the social and traditional fusion.

The Union idea was born out of Pan Africanism. It was envisaged that smaller unions of neighbours, followed by federations in the regions will ultimately make Africa a one power continent under one strong union.

But that was the first false start made when Tanganyika and Zanzibar united on April 26, 1964. No option under the Articles of Union was provided for any other country to join in and for that reason the dream was drowned.

However, the Union engineered by Julius Nyerere and Abeid Karume, then leaders of the Republic of Tanganyika and the People's Republic of Zanzibar respectively has forged ahead and despite the hurdles and challenges it has achieved a lot.

That the union still stands today is its biggest score point. It has weathered many testing times, but Tanzanians have shown courage and resilience to sustain it because it has benefited both sides of the divide.

The Union which initially brought together two countries of varying proportions - Zanzibar with 300,000 souls and Tanganyika nine million people; and Tanganyika with a size of 960,000 square miles and Zanzibar 2,600 square miles – has not only won praise but also created a powerful country in the region, key at regional level and influential on the world stage.

Tanzania has grown through thick and thin. No effort has been spared to raise the living standards of her citizens across the divide, positively impacting the struggle to reduce poverty and strengthening social services. These policies have paid off with incredible results in lengthening life expectancy, a decrease in child mortality, enhanced education, spread health delivery, among many achievements. Infrastructure, including roads has been extended and communications improved, helping the country catch up with global technological advancement.

The United Republic has so far been led by four presidents, each one of them with his own benchmark s that have helped define Tanzania as the Land of Kilimanjaro and the Zanzibar Isles. The epochal presidents are: Julius Nyerere (1964-1985), Ali Hassan Mwinyi (1985-1995), Benjamin Mkapa (1995-2005) and currently Jakaya Kikwete 2005 to date.

Politically, the Union has been relatively stable. It has been shocked a few times and in some instances threatened a break up. Dissenting voices have been from both sides, and especially from Zanzibar, a partner perceiving that it has been short changed.

The belief in Zanzibar is that the Union is riddled with inherent structural contractions leading to outcries, openly

330

and behind closed doors; Zanzibaris have demanded changes in the Union structure, even to the extent of threatening secession. Nationalist feelings have been aired many times against the few times, especially in the name of G-55 in 1993, demanding a Tanganyika government.

Zanzibaris have contended that they are junior partners in the Union political set up. Tanganyika, on the other hand, has been elevated into a partner-cum-Union government, an arrangement perceived as a ploy made by Union co-founder Nyerere. This has been dubbed as "Tanganyika wearing the Union coat."

There have been many commissions aimed at sorting out issues of concern on both sides of the Union, but to no avail. The commissions have included those of led by Nyalali, Kisanga, Kusila, Amina and Salmin Amour. Almost all the commissions have proposed ways and means to minimize the political wrangles that have sometimes threatened the very life of the Union. Some of the recommendations have been for increased Zanzibar autonomy, stronger economic options and reduction of Union matters from the current 22 because there were only 11 under the Articles of Union.

However, commission recommendations could not be fully addressed for lack of political will. It was not until President Jakaya Kikwete took the big step in 2012 to form the Commission for Constitutional Review (CRC), chaired by Judge Joseph Warioba, that a serious move to right the situation is currently on-going.

The CRC has come up with radical proposals aimed to rest the Union case. The proposals hinge on a three-tier federal system of the United Republic, which it believes is the only solution to address the Union's structural contractions.

It calls for the re-establishment of Tanganyika at par with her original partner Zanzibar, each having powers and jurisdiction limited to their land masses and only being subject to the supreme powers of the United Republic.

331

This and other key CRC draft proposals are now before the Constituent Assembly in Dodoma. The more than 600 members, at most sitting for 90 days, are to determine the direction Tanzania would take in this, the most important decision ever taken by Tanzania.

As Tanzania marks 50 years of Union with over 80 per cent of the population born in the life of the Union, the need for a fresh look could not be more urgent. Departure from the past must be urgently made, otherwise it would not augur too well with the demands of the new generation.

It is important that the Union lives on and this is the wish of most Tanzanians. However, this must also be matched with demands for an equal, just and fair Union, providing for increased independence, control and voice to the people in true Union partnership.

Mr Saleh is a veteran journalist based in Zanzibar.

Appendix VIII:

Secrets of the dead:
Can the union make it to a hundred?

Erick Mwakibete, The Citizen,
Dar es Salaam, Tanzania, 26 April 2014

Mwalimu and Karume are dead. There are things perhaps we shall never really know as to why they formed this political Union.

Dar es Salaam – At one point during his short presidency, ousted Egyptian President Mohammed Morsi was asked in an interview of how he viewed the endless street demonstrations for and against his government which had paralyzed much of state institutions. He opted to be philosophical about it: "We are learning to be free", was his reply.

As Tanzania celebrates 50 years of its existence, perhaps more than at any other time in its history, the moment is nigh to examine the very nature and structure of this political Union.

And with the process of curving out a new constitution

dragging on in Dodoma, characterized by sharp divisions from vested political interests in what the future structure of the Union should look like.

For once, the discussion is showing just how much, like those Egyptians "we are learning to be free" in the sense that this time around we are on our own, and there are no charismatic, feared and respected leaders like Mwalimu to come to the rescue of any side, even though his absence hasn't prevented our representatives in Dodoma to quote him endlessly in their efforts of trying to prove a point or two.

Throughout its history, the ghosts of its past and controversies have, from time to time come to haunt it. And this time around it is no different. The list is long: Confusion surrounding the intended structure, its legality, controversy raised by the Articles of the Union, some high profile political casualties, and the biggest of them all: the demands to revive the government of Tanganyika.

Between them, i.e. the Union government and that of Zanzibar, there have been 21 Commissions/Committees to deal with various issues of the Union, but the issues addressed and the challenges faced have persisted through the years and new ones emerged along the way. To paraphrase Justice (rtd) Joseph Warioba, the country today has "two countries, two governments", even though he said, what we inherited from our founding fathers was "one country, two governments."

So, how then did the Union make it to half a century?

Mwalimu and Sheikh Karume are long dead. There are things perhaps we shall never really know as to why they formed this political Union. Over time, some have come to view the Union as a Jurassic institution. What secrets did they have?

More than anything, the Union owes its longevity to the political setting; domestic and external and more than anyone, to the ingenuity of one of its founders, the late Mwalimu Nyerere.

334

The Union was formed at a time when the world was deeply engulfed by the cold war, which necessitated considerations for strategic reasons in many countries, and the liberation and independence struggles which raged throughout Africa.

Going by this line of argument, then the Union was a product of the cold war as much as it was a product of Pan Africanism.

Domestically, the then ruling parties, Tanu and ASP merged over time to form CCM which went on to monopolize the Union, inadvertently forming the fault lines which came to characterize the Union to this day.

Major issues regarding the Union were from then on decided within the framework of the ruling party. Plainly put, the Union became subservient to the party and not the other way round. This meant that in the event of changed political setting, say a change in the ruling party, the Union was left vulnerable to whims of whichever political party that governs at that time.

Today, this is among the reasons our leaders from the ruling party are using to justify the two governments Union structure. The irony is unmistakable.

Courtesy of this appropriation, systemic problems clogged up, threatening the very existence of the Union. This is why most of the recommendations offered on major issues by the many committees/commissions which were formed by the two governments to find ways to best address the issues which choked up the Union fell on partially or totally deaf ears.

From as far back as 1964, the National Assembly directed the governments to work together to solve the challenges of the day. As global and domestic political settings changed, there were agitations from Zanzibar to reform the structure of the Union, and following the removal of Aboud Jumbe Mwinyi as president of Zanzibar in 1984, there was deep resentment in the Isles.

As the cold war came to a close, in 1991 the

335

government formed the first in the long line of committees and commissions to look into how to best deal with the challenges of the Union.

The solution, for all the teams which came up later has been the same-three governments. And the response from the ruling party has always been the same-flat rejection of that proposal.

As Zanzibar joined the OIC in 1992 and sent political shockwaves throughout the country, the National Assembly directed the two governments to co-operate and work together to come up with the solutions to better manage our Union-and inform it in a year.

Come November 1993, the two governments and CCM rejected the demand by some of its MPs who had passed a motion in the national assembly to re-establish the government of Tanganyika. And the proposals of Shellukindo and Amina Salum Ali committees were never fully implemented. And the ruling party resolved to continue working with two governments towards one- no amendments were made to the Union constitution.

Again the irony in all this is that all these committees and the National Assembly were dominated by people from the same ruling party, but somehow the same party found it impossible to implement the major decisions or proposals offered.

So, here we are today.

President Kikwete's speech to members of the Constituent Assembly in Dodoma aimed at turning back the tide to the political order we have known for the past 50 years. He went out of his way to paint a picture of a political Union whose major challenges had been addressed. He said that of the 31issues raised by the Shellukindo Commission of 1992, and the Joint Commission of 1993, only six issues have remained unaddressed-mainly economic issues and that all were on track of being properly addressed.

This sounded like a promise of a future that would be

better than the past we've gone through. The President was asking Tanzanians to put their faith in the hands of the very people who led us to the current political quagmire! It is a huge leap of faith.

Back in the early 1990s, it was Mwalimu who came to the rescue of the contemporary political order. This time around we are at a crossroads of defining exactly what should differentiate our past and the future we aspire for.

Back in 1962, Mwalimu wrote that in discussions and conversations concerning society at large, it is important to listen to the arguments raised by others, and respond to those arguments by accepting or rejecting them regardless of who raised them; friend or foe. He went on that, those whose arguments have been rejected should accept that what were rejected were their arguments and not themselves.

Without such culture discussions and conversations become meaningless and it is wastage of time.

As the Constituent Assembly is on the verge of collapse in Dodoma, and as the country is trying to find harmony with itself, such words should guide us.

Tanzania has managed to stand out as a political Union for the past 50 years. As we celebrate such achievement we must ask ourselves whether or not we'll make it to another 50 years as a united country. Either way the ongoing process of writing a new constitution, dangerously unravelling at the seams, should help us to come up with a constitution that won't be for the sake of scoring political gains of the moment.

When the sun comes up tomorrow, we should strive to bequeath to our posterity a better country than what we inherited. Oh! The burden imposed by the dead heroes on the living!

Happy Birthday Tanzania!

Mr Mwakibete is a Tanzania socio-political analyst.

Appendix IX:

Adiy: A marked Zanzibari gunning for 'a just union

**Peter Nyanje, *The Citizen*,
Dar es Salaam, Tanzania, 27 April 2014**

He says even in what is going on now results from pressure, but the difference is that now the pressure is from within while in the beginning the pressure was from outside.

Zanzibar – He is a keen follower of Union issues such that he was able to predict what is happening in the Constituent Assembly weeks before the House started its sitting in Dodoma on February 18.

"I predicted what happened in the Constituent Assembly and I addressed a press conference in January to tell journalists what would happen," says Rashid Salum Adiy, who has dedicated his life to Union issues for years now.

His dedication to the Union has seen him branded many labels with some regarding him as a crusader aiming at saving and strengthening the merger which in recent years has been constantly attacked as weak and invalid. But, others regard Mr Adiy as a troublemaker whose sole aim is to see the Union collapse.

"But I am a simple person who like to contribute his views on important issues, especially those on the lives of ordinary people," says the soft speaking Adiy, armed with a number of documents he collected during his years of fighting for a just Union.

Mr Adiy says during an interview with *The Citizen* on Sunday in Zanzibar that many people have been commenting or talking about the April 26, 1964 merger between Tanganyika and Zanzibar without having deep insight into it.

Asked if the Union, which clocked half a century yesterday is still valid, Mr Adiy says an answer to that should be given after reviewing the gains and detriments of the merger. He says, it is true that there are people who have invested immensely in the Union, some of them with their lives. So, to them, negative comments about the Union is something which they would not like to hear.

As opposed to many people who take the Union as a political vehicle, Mr Adiy says, it's a belief in it that is making it strong, as people need to first believe in it for it to be effective. "If people who are supposed to be united do not believe in the Union, we will only be forcing them to come together and that will not give us a strong Union," he stresses. Also, he adds that for the Union to stand, there should be able leader who can defend it. "It is upon our top leaders, President Jakaya Kikwete and President Ali Mohammed Shein to show us the way. If anything happens and the Union weakens or collapses, they will bear the blame," he says.

Mr Adiy warns that some people might not fathom the importance of the Union today, but they should know that cooperation was what was driving the global forces today. He says, the Union is detested today because the Union, since its inception, was built on concepts of selfishness. "But you cannot see this until you conduct a deep research. It seems that though the relations were important, the decision to merge did not originally come from our leaders, they were cajoled into uniting," he says.

He says even in what is going on now results from pressure, but the difference is that now the pressure is from within while in the beginning the pressure was from outside.

Asked what has pushed him to concentrate on the Union, Mr Adiy says his love for his country was behind his dedication. "There is nothing I value as my home. When I am here, I am a Zanzibari and when I go outside the country I am a Tanzanian. There is nothing I value than that," he says.

On shortcomings, Mr Adiy says he started to critically look at the Union in 1984 when the political situation in Zanzibar worsened and then Zanzibar President, Aboud Jumbe Mwinyi was forced into early retirement by his party – CCM. "I was hurt very much when Mzee Aboud Jumbe was forced to resign. I kept on asking myself why a president of a country could be forced out just like that," he says.

He said when plural politics was allowed in the country in the early 1990s, he joined CUF because he believes in opposition. "But many people joined CUF with a view that they will take over the government in the next election," he says, adding, the view made some people in the CUF to regard him as a traitor; then he decided to quit and rejoined the ruling party. But because of his criticism mentality, he fell out of favour with CCM members who also started to suspect him as traitor.

He says, if you look at Zanzibar presidential decree of February 1964 signed by the then chief secretary and agreed to by President Abeid Amani Karume, it stresses on social relations among people of East Africa. He says, after independence, Zanzibar was being governed by Afro

341

Shiraz Party (ASP) policies while Tanganyika was governed by Tanu policies. He wonders what were the policies used to govern after the April 1964 merger between the two sovereign states.

He says that though some people did not like to buy the idea of forming a confederation, the prevailing conditions, from the beginning, would have made the Union stronger through that form of government.

He notes for instance that after the Union, it was Mwalimu Julius Nyerere, as Tanganyika leader, who decreed that all Tanganyika laws and instruments were property of the United Republic of Tanzania.

He says this was wrong because if the idea was to unite the two countries, first there was a need to get a go ahead from the people, who formed the basis of the merger as well as from the governing parties whose policies formed the basis of governance mechanism.

"It was wrong to make laws, policies and instruments from one side become applicable on the other side without the consultation and acceptance by the people from both sides. Because this is the basis of the Union, which is legal, that is why I have also decided to use legal means to counter them. But along them, I have been insisting that if we want to make this Union stronger, let us focus on social relations," he elaborates.

He says by then, Tanganyika was being led by a constitution while Zanzibar was being government by presidential decrees. Though the constitutional governance was seen as more democratic, the Tanganyika Constitution has no provisions which provides for freedom to unite with other countries.

Likewise, there was no provision in the Tanganyika Constitution which allowed the major law to be used as interim instrument for both countries. "If the Union was the idea originating from our leaders, why did they not consider to put that issue in their constitutions or decrees? For, Tanganyika and Zanzibar proximity and social relations were known to these leaders for ages, why did they not provide for the same in their laws after becoming independent," he asks.

Mr Adiy stressed that the way the Union was crafted was wrong and time has come for that to be rectified otherwise the sentiments against the merger will not die. He says his pursuit of the issue has established also that due to the problems, even at international level the Union is not so open. He was referring to the recent demands to have the Articles of the Union shown publicly.

Appendix X:

Karume was jittery over Union before his death

Peter Nyanje, *The Citizen*,
Dar es salaam, Tanzania, 27 April 2014

Mzee Salim Said Rashid says in any institution that has been running for 50 years, stock taking is mandatory. Even those insisting on the status quo would agree that the Union has been problematic. Mzee Salim believes that problems inherent in the Union can only be resolved by making changes to the original idea of the merger.

Zanzibar – Many people have been arguing about the authenticity of the signatures of the Union founders, Mwalimu Julius Nyerere and Sheikh Abeid Aman Karume. But Mzee Salim Said Rashid, who had served as Chief Secretary of the Zanzibar Revolutionary Government when the pact was signed, says this argument is misplaced.

During a recent interview at his Mji Mkongwe home in Zanzibar, Mzee Salim said that Mwalimu Nyerere and Mzee Karume are not alive to defend their signatures, making the argument wanting.

Mzee Salim says that issues of signatures or Articles of Union have no major importance, now that Tanzanians are engaged in improving the Union, which clocked half a century yesterday. Importance must be put in an open debate, involving all people in efforts for a better Union which can benefit the common man in the street.

"There is no doubt that the Union is still as valid today as it was 50 years ago. But the real difference should be in what type of Union the people want under the current conditions and experience over the past 50 years of merger."

In a message to those drumming for the status quo, he says they should look into the history of the Union and they will realize that changes are inevitable. The Articles of Union, for example, had started with 11 Union issues, but now these have increased to 22. This has aroused sentiments questioning how other issues came to be added to those in the original agreement.

He says in any institution that has been running for 50 years, stock taking is mandatory. Even those insisting on the status quo would agree that the Union has been problematic. Mzee Salim believes that problems inherent in the Union can only be resolved by making changes to the original idea of the merger.

Since the Union was crafted by leaders without involving the wananchi, who were not even asked if they had wanted to unite, it is only right that the country works on a people-centred Union, says Mzee Salim.

He further says people on the Mainland might be passive about the Union, but in Zanzibar many people have been questioning the validity of the April 26, 1964 merger.

He notes: "And we have seen it in the on-going Constituent Assembly meetings in Dodoma. We hear sentiments from Tanganyika based on claims that there are many people from Pemba cultivating onions on the

Mainland, but we have not heard how Tanganyikans have suffered under the current Union structure."

"This applies not only to common wananchi, but also ex-Zanzibar presidents – Salmin Amour, Aboud Jumbe, Amani Karume - are on record to have said the Union was not that good and did something to rectify what they regarded as unjust in the Union. But there are no complaints from Tanganyika. It appears that people there are satisfied with the current situation," he adds.

Mzee Salim notes that 80 per cent of these sentiments in Zanzibar relate to social and economic injustices.

He also says that people are overlooking the fact that before his death Karume did not always see eye-to-eye with Nyerere on the Union and they were not on speaking terms for quite some time.

In 1971, he remembers, the entire Zanzibar Revolutionary Council went to see Mwalimu Nyerere to ask him to cede more autonomy to Zanzibar in matters including foreign affairs, defence and security – almost everything which will make Zanzibar sovereign.

In the words of Mzee Salim: "Nyerere told them that he had received their message and he would deal with their request. But, to date no document is available on the issue; and by then no one could oppose Nyerere or Karume and survive."

Mzee Salim concludes that from the outset Zanzibar got a raw deal from the Union agreement and expects little change for the better. Although leaders point to some sticking points that have been resolved, still sentiments keep growing daily.

He points to two major problems in Zanzibar - public opinion, which requires that the people have to be asked what they think. He believes that the Constitution Review Commission rightly concluded in its report that more than 60 per cent of Zanzibaris prefer a contractual Union.

The other problem relates to the age-old issue of governance, between the Union and Zanzibar. He says problems of governance continue to be ignored and asks: "Till when will the Zanzibar sentiments continue to be ignored?"

Similarly, Salim says the problem of employment among the vocal youth (90 per cent unemployed) has not been addressed. He blames this on the Union government investing on the Mainland and ignoring the Isles. He does not expect that the CA meetings, dominated by CCM, will result in anything tangible for Zanzibar. He also dismissed arguments against the three-tier Union proposal, maintaining that priority must be on resolving the governance issue and cost it afterwards.

Appendix XI:

Union at 50:
50 years of Tanganyika, Z'bar philosophy

Dr Azaveli Lwaitama

Dar es Salaam – On April 22, 1964, the presidents of the then Republic of Tanganyika and the then People's Republic of Zanzibar are said to have signed Articles of Union declaring that the two sovereign republics were to unite and form one united sovereign republic that was initially called the United Republic of Tanganyika and Zanzibar.

Four days later, on April 26, 1964, the peoples of these two republics were publicly informed that a Union between Tanganyika and Zanzibar had been formed and that the Articles of Union had been ratified by, at least the Parliament of the Republic of Tanganyika. April 26 has since been marked as the Union Day.

The philosophy of the Union between Tanganyika and Zanzibar would seem to be symbolised by a very important ritual associated with a celebration of this Union. This ritual is none other than the picture of the then President of the newly inaugurated United Republic

349

of Tanganyika and Zanzibar, Mwalimu Julius Nyerere, witnessed by his two vice presidents, Sheikh Abeid Amani Karume, who was also the President of Zanzibar, and Mzee Rashidi Mfaume Kawawa, who had previously been the Prime Minister of Tanganyika, take two sets of soil, and pouring the soil in the two calabashes into a third empty container.

The two sets of soil, one scooped and put in a calabash in Zanzibar and the other put in a calabash in Tanganyika, were poured into a container that was jointly held up together by a man and woman hailing from both Tanganyika and Zanzibar. This was meant to symbolise the mixing of the soils of these two up to then sovereign states into one set of soil, implying that Tanganyika and Zanzibar were from then on one soil, thus, perhaps, one country ('nchi' in Kiswahili), one nation ('taifa' in Kiswahili), and, in international legal terms, one united sovereign state ('dola yenye mamlaka kamili' in Kiswahili).

This philosophy of the Union is reflected in the ideological leanings of the two leaders, Julius Nyerere and Abeid Karume, who signed the Articles of Union, supposedly on behalf of the peoples they both happened to lead.

Both leaders subscribed to and were firm and uncompromising believers in the ideology of Pan African nationalism. Pan African nationalist ideology was a philosophical world view that asserted that in world history being African had emerged as a political identity assumed by people whose ancestry was the African continent.

Most of these were of the so-called of Negro or Black racial extraction, with kinky hair and dark skin, and had been condemned as sub-human by pseudo-scientific anthropological scholarship inspired and funded for material gains derived and engaging in the Atlantic and Indian Ocean slave trade as well as the colonisation of the continent by 19th and 20th century European imperialist powers.

White supremacist pseudo-scientific rationalisations for the trading of Africans like cattle during the slave trade era and the colonial occupation of Africa was meant to influence the peoples of African ancestry to believe that they were sub-human and that their sole calling in life was to be hewers of wood and drawers of water.

In contrast, the Pan African nationalist ideology, first articulated by descendants of peoples indigenous to the African continent who found themselves (as slaves, workers, students) in the Americas, the Caribbean Islands off the Americas and in Europe and those made aware of the traumatic experiences in the diaspora of peoples of African ancestry, asserted that peoples indigenous to the African continent were once a great people who had contributed immensely to human civilisation.

In a speech delivered by Mwalimu Julius Nyerere at Wellesley College, in the USA, in 1960, he summarised the Pan African national utopia sketched out on the basis of the belief in Pan African nationalist ideology by asserting that: "The Africa that we must create must be an Africa, which the outside world will look at and say: If you really want to see free people who live up to their ideals of human society, go to Africa. That is the continent of hope for the human race."

The then presidents of Tanganyika and Zanzibar, sharing this philosophical ideological leaning of Pan Africanism, to the advantage of the geopolitical and strategic situation that prevailed in their two countries to translate age-old trade and social interactions between the peoples of these two countries into a political Union that has now lasted 50 years. Sheikh Abeid Karume and Mwalimu Julius Nyerere were two among the very few post-colonial African leaders of their generation who did not suffer from the political malaise that Mwalimu Nyerere alluded to in his now famous speech in Accra, Ghana, on March 6, 1997: "the glorification of the nation

351

states (that) we inherited from colonialism, and the artificial nations we (have been) trying to forge from that inheritance."

Pan African 'national unity' prompted one to seize every opportunity that presented itself to construct 'united nation- states' across the artificial territorial state borders that the post-colonial African leaders had inherited at independence from colonial rule such as Tanganyika , or those inherited from post- popular insurrectionary states such as post-Revolution Zanzibar.

Believers in Pan Africanism like Julius Nyerere and Abeid Karume take the view that the boundaries of often geographically and ethnically senseless territorial states that were inherited at independence had no future in a globalised world.

To post-colonial African leaders who subscribed to the Pan African nationalist ideology, to paraphrase the late Mwalimu Nyerere in his 1997 Accra, Ghana, speech referred to earlier: "African nationalism outside Pan Africanism is tribalism on an international scale." No wonder, Julius Nyerere and Abeid Karume, in April 1964, may as well have been thinking of uniting Tanganyika and Zanzibar into one unitary sovereign state that later was called Tanzania and whose single state political parties, one for Zanzibar, the Afro-Shirazi Party, and the other for mainland Tanzania, Tanganyika African National Union (Tanu), they also merged into one single political state party, Chama Cha Mapinduzi (CCM) in February 1977!

Fifty years, the Union that aforementioned great Pan African leaders, Julius Nyerere and Abeid Karume formed, is facing some serious challenges. Sheikh Karume is more than 40 years long dead and it is about 15 years since Mwalimu Julius Nyerere passed on.

The Pan African nationalist integration ethos fostered in Tanzania during the Karume and Nyerere era have gradually waned. Neo-liberal economic structural adjustment programmes have been embraced with gusto and these have intensified the integration of the Tanzania economy, on the Tanzania Mainland and in Zanzibar, into the globalised world.

Globalisation, which is the most advanced form of capitalist imperialism characterized financialisation, and militarisation, has worsened the pauperisations of masses of middle class people, and with accentuated de-industrialisation and together with the denudation of basic social services provision, ethnic economic imbalances have increased.

The emerging equity challenges, coupled with the intensification of the competition for natural resources by the advanced and newly advanced capitalist powers, Unions such as the Tanzanian one scripted in period immediately after in independence in 1960s, characterized, as it was by raw Pan African nationalist euphoria, have begun to find themselves under a lot of political strain.

All the efforts spent, in the last 50 years, on what Mwalimu Nyerere characterized as, "Africans trying very hard to be Ghanaians and Tanzanians," seem to have gone to waste. This is partly because, to paraphrase Mwalimu Nyerere again: "Fortunately, for Africa, we (the first generation of African political elite) have not been completely successful. The outside world hardly recognizes our Ghanaian-ness or Tanzanian-ness. What the outside world recognizes about us is our African-ness."

Fifty years on, the philosophy behind the Union of Tanganyika and Zanzibar on April 26,1964, still seems to be Pan African nationalistic but of a more democratic and transparent kind. The current constitutional wrangling seems to demand that the philosophy of Pan African nationalism needs to be reviewed and re-interpreted in the context of twenty-first century globalisation. Perhaps, in the twenty-first century, it is time Pan African nationalism raised its spectrum and embraced a more federalist but wider scope of the boundaries of Pan African nation building.

Perhaps it is time to think more in terms of unifying peoples in the wider Eastern and Central African region in federalist fashion, instead of thinking in terms unifying merely two states like Tanganyika and Zanzibar, whose diversity management configuration may be complicated by viewing the two territories in terms of one being large while the other small in geographical and population terms.

This complication may be eased by having many members seeking to work together in a federal state structures with several being large and several being small! The philosophy seems still to be the right one, Pan Africanist nationalism, but perhaps the scale and scope of integration needs to be widened but in a more democratic and consensus-building manner! Perhaps it is time Tanganyikan and Zanzibari Pan African nationalist decided to abandon trying to build "Tanzania-ness" as a Pan African nationalist end in itself and instead sought to transfer their Pan African nationalist passions to the building a people-centred democratic East African Federation! Only time will tell!

Dr Lwaitama is a lecturer at Josiah Kibira University College of Tumaini University, Makumira in Bukoba, Tanzania. He also taught philosophy at the University of Dar es Salaam.

Appendix XII

Interviews with other American ambassadors accredited to Tanzania during Nyerere's presidency

W. Beverly Carter

Beverly Carter was the first black American ambassador to be accredited to Tanzania. He presented his credentials to President Julius Nyerere on 24 July 1972, six months after the 8th anniversary of the Zanzibar revolution. He served until 14 October 1975.

One of the most interesting aspects of the interview was his assessment of Nyerere as a leader. It was a wide-ranging interview in which he talked about many subjects:

"**Q: Exactly how did you move into the position of Ambassador for Tanzania?**

Carter: (laughs)...Well, I think I did a pretty good job in Kenya at a time just following their independence, and based on that job, I was asked to go to Nigeria as Minister-Counselor for Public Affairs. And at that time, you may recall, Nigeria was involved or about to become involved in a civil war. I got there a year before the Biafran Civil War. And I got there in the summer of '66, and in April 1977, Biafra, the Eastern region, attempted to secede from the Federation of Nigeria.

Our embassy was very active in trying to keep the Federation together when the secession in fact began. There were a number of people in Washington and in the press, politicians who sided with the Biafran Ibos and our embassy found itself in the position of trying to have to explain why we were supportive of the Federal Military Government and not supportive of the break away section of Nigeria.

Ambassador Elbert Mathews, who's now deceased, decided that I would be a person who could best explain that situation in Washington and to the many. politicians and newsmen who were coming out, and so I was both spokesman for the embassy and also did a shuttling job between Lagos and Washington, made a number of appearances on the Hill. And very candidly got the kind of exposure which brought me before the attention of a number of people. And I guess I did that job fairly well.

Then in 1969, toward the end of 1969, when the new Assistant Secretary of State was named, David Newsom, he had observed my work and he asked me if I would come to work for him as Deputy Assistant Secretary of State for African Affairs. David had had prior experience in the Middle East and in North Africa but had had no experience in Africa south of the Sahara. I had both in terms of my Foreign Service career and also when I was a newspaperman.

I guess I did not say that, as a newspaperman, one of my geographical areas of interest was Africa. And so I went to Africa for the first time in 1952 when there were just five of the countries that were independent, and I began to write then about the winds of change in British colonial West Africa, using Liberia and the Gold Coast as points of reference.

So with that kind of background, Newsom asked me to come on as Deputy Assistant Secretary with him, which I did and enjoyed thoroughly, and I think we made a very good team.

And we particularly worked on southern African issues. Dave and I made a trip to South Africa together and I helped to change some of our policies, both in dealing with South Africa on a government-to-government basis, and also in terms of policy changes within our own government about assignments of officers.

We got our first black American officer assigned to one of our installations there; it was the purpose for our visit. We were able to get black South Africans upgraded in positions that other nationals held in the Embassy and consulates.

So with that kind of background ... for three years ... and also having arranged for a ten-nation tour of Africa by Secretary William Rogers, which was at that point in time the first time an American Secretary of State had ever visited Africa, it became fairly clear to the people in the (State) Department that I had some African experience, some African contacts, some African know-how. And Bill Rogers, whom I regarded as one of our very finest Secretaries of State, and David Newsom, said that they would like me to go to Tanzania when that Embassy became vacant, because Tanzania was on the cutting edge of our southern African situation with so many things happening in southern Africa. And I was asked to go, and I was confirmed by the Senate. And we left in June of 1972.

Q: I want to ask about your first impressions of Tanzania, but before you do, you said that you did a number of things to try to keep the Federation together.

Carter: In Nigeria?

Q: Yes. Could you talk about some of those things you did?

357

Carter: Well, I think primarily in trying to maintain a dialogue between the leadership of the people who were responsible for leading both sections of that Federation at the time. Ojukwu, who you recall, was the Governor of the Eastern Region. At that time Nigeria was divided into four states instead of the nineteen that now exist there.

Ojukwu was a very, very popular, very dynamic, very charismatic leader. And Jack Gowon who was the leader of the rest of the country did not begin to have the sort of charisma and political savvy that Ojukwu had. And I think we just tried to backstop him and his colleagues so that they would feel that they could better serve the Federation by trying to accommodate Ojukwu and keep him in the Federation.

We did not realize at that time that there were so many forces outside of Nigeria that were in fact pushing Ojukwu to secede. For instance, the French connection. The Rothschild banking people were financing the secession on the basis of what had become known then as early, early affirmative seismographic discoveries of oil off the Bonny, Calabar and Port Harcourt region of the coast, which region at that time was in the Eastern part of Nigeria.

We tried to keep some of the … Americans who were so enamored with the Eastern Region. We had our largest Peace Corps contingent in the Eastern Region and they were very much spokesmen for trying to tell the U. S. that we should support the Eastern Region and encourage them in their secession. And then the Catholic Church was very strong in the Eastern Region as against the Muslims from the North, and Protestants in the remainder of the country.

So, it was a matter of trying to work with these segments of public opinion in trying to keep focusing on the need for the Federation staying together, using, of course, our own illustration of how much stronger we were as a nation as a consequence of the South and the North remaining, or coming back together after our Civil War.

And, I had, I guess at that point in time the best access to most of the leadership throughout the country, because one of my first assignments as Minister- Counselor was the supervisory responsibility for all of our USIS offices throughout the country.

So I traveled into Enugu, into Port Harcourt, Kaduna and Kano, and Ibadan, as well as working out of Lagos. So I was making a full tour of the Federation and therefore I got to know most of the leaders and most had confidence in me, and so I could talk to them sometimes when they weren't talking to each other.

Q: I see. Shall we move on to Tanzania?

Carter: Yes.

Q: What were your first impressions of Tanzania?

Carter: Well, I had known it because when I served in Kenya, I used to go down to ... the best game parks in East Africa were in Tanzania. And Julius Nyerere was, of course, also one of the early heroes, political heroes, of mine and of many other Africanists. And so I looked forward very much to the, to the challenge -- the intellectual challenge of working with him and with his Government, albeit that some of his economic, political philosophies were somewhat different from those that I had come to know.

But Tanzania is a huge country, very diverse; mountains and with tropical coastline; with over two hundred tribes, but with no tribe being so large that it was a dominant tribe as you had and as you have, for instance, in Kenya where you have the Kikuyu and the Luo, who are the two dominant tribes. And then, as a consequence, there is a great deal of vying between the two. Julius Nyerere, for instance, comes from the very smallest of tribes in Tanzania: about 6,000 people. So you know that he has become leader because of the confidence that the people have in him rather than the fact he simply has more of a constituency than someone else has.

But Tanzania is also a poor country -- without many of

the resources that Nigeria had in rubber and oil and timber; and, without a large infrastructure such as Kenya had from the tourist industry. And yet it also was a headquarters at that time of most of the liberation movements in Africa. The insurgencies that were developing and coming to fruition in Mozambique and Angola, and now in Zimbabwe, were all headquartered in Dar es Salaam.

The capital was the beehive of revolution and liberation, and that was both an opportunity and also a difficulty. Because at that point in time, one of our major NATO allies was Portugal, and the Portuguese did not want us to develop relations with insurgents who were attempting to dispossess them in Angola and Mozambique. So it presented a very delicate political balance.

I'm saying all of this in terms of responding to your question on my impressions, because all of these contributed to the impression that I had, what I was going to. I knew I wasn't going to an easy task (laughs).

Q: How would you describe U. S. policy towards Tanzania at that time?

Carter: Very ambivalent. We, as I said, had this difficulty with Tanzania because it was encouraging a liberation movement by simply giving them a place to ... from which to develop their organization and spread the propaganda.

The Cubans were active in Tanzania; the doyen of the diplomatic corps was a Cuban. Nyerere was an admitted, an avowed and a practicing and proselytizing socialist. We weren't sure what we wanted to do about Tanzania ... we, the United States Government. At that particular time the United States Government was headed by a Republican Administration which added to this, which compounded this problem of confusion. Because while Julius Nyerere was an extremely popular person personally, what he espoused and what his country stood for was just difficult for orthodox and Republican conservatism, and so we did not have a very clearly defined policy.

At the same time, we didn't have a fair policy. Many other countries regarded Tanzania as one of the most important of the developing countries in the world, for instance, the Scandinavian countries. Scandinavian countries -- Sweden, for instance, Sweden's largest economic assistance packages were sent to Tanzania and to India. Great Britain was very supportive economically of Tanzania. So many people that we knew and respected and had associations with -- political associations with -- regarded Tanzania highly. We just at that point in time had, as I say, great ambivalence about what we should be doing. I suspect that ambivalence has not been altogether cleared since then, either, unfortunately.

Q: How did that compare with U.S. policy towards Africa in general, would you say?

Carter: Well, I think that represented a part of the dilemma we had toward Africa. I think that the Tanzanian example most clearly described the horns of the dilemma we found ourselves on in Africa. There were certain countries like Zaire and Liberia and Kenya where we felt more comfortable, and Ethiopia, even at that time, before the revolution.

But those countries where we felt more comfortable were in the minority. Tanzania, Ghana, Zambia, caused us problems, because not only did they do things differently, but they were also in the vanguard of other progressives. They were the bellwether for other progressive African countries. So those countries tended to look to Tanzania for leadership, and Nyerere was never hesitant about offering it and giving it and doing it well.

Q: What were some of the kinds of problems you just referred to?

Carter: Well, I think in fact that Tanzania was supportive of change in southern Africa, in Southern Rhodesia, in Mozambique, in Angola. They kept making us face up to the contradiction of our saying we, I think the phrase is, "abhor apartheid," but we don't do a Goddamn

361

thing about it. And the Tanzanians kept our feet to the fire on that, both in the Security Council and in the General Assembly, and in our bilateral relations. And so there were no really material things to which one could refer, but there were on the world stage of public opinion. It was just that Tanzania was making it difficult for us.

Q: Could you talk a little about the relations between Tanzania and neighboring Burundi?

Carter: I could talk a little about it. Tanzania, Nyerere himself, was very embarrassed about the massacres, about tribalcide that was taking place in Burundi. Tanzania also suffered very much from the refugees who were leaving Burundi because of not only persecution but also because of the slaying of thousands and thousands of Burundis.

But Burundi was a very ... is a very small country. I don't mean to denigrate it because of its size, but the major problem was one of the refugee problem and the one of genocide and tribal conflict. And Nyerere was never a person to turn his back on bad things that other blacks did to other blacks.

He did not only point the finger at whites who were exploitive and destructive of blacks, he would also call a spade a spade, as he did in the Burundi case as well as in Uganda, where he ultimately had to do something which I know very much went against his grain and that was to mount a force to go in to overthrow Amin.

But Nyerere is probably one of the most principled men I ever met in my life. When I say principled, I mean doing things he regards as being right and which, generally speaking, are right by other, by humanitarian, standards.

Q: Could you cite some other concrete examples of it?

Carter: Well, I would say that probably he felt very uncomfortable with General Mobutu in Zaire, because I don't think he felt that Mobutu represented the finest in leadership in that huge country. I think he felt that Mobutu permitted an exploitation and corruption with which

362

Nyerere had difficulty. I think he looked at Kenya as being the worst of what people talk about when they talk about the excesses of capitalism, and that the capitalist sources were in the hands of a few, and that the people in Kenya did not ... the people, the masses of people in Kenya did not ... the standard of living did not go across the board. It was maintained by a few of the Kikuyu elite.

And I'm not a practicing socialist, but I think that an effective capital experience can spread riches up and down the line. I think Nyerere really felt that he didn't see that in Kenya and he didn't see that in Zaire, and he said that. And it's one of the reasons why I think that he and Kenyatta were never the fastest of friends, though Nyerere respected what Kenyatta had done during the fight for independence. But then I think he felt that he became satisfied too quickly with too little for the people of Kenya.

Q: What kinds of problems, if any, did you face, particular problems you faced as Ambassador to Tanzania?

Carter: Well, there are several. I think the first one was with my own country. If an ambassador attempts to, with objectivity, talk about the country into which he is assigned, he runs two risks: one of either being identified as being extremely perceptive and a bright guy who'd really gotten to know the picture well, or having been overcome with what we call provincialism, having become an ambassador for that country back to your own country rather than the reverse.

I talked earlier about my Government's ambivalence about Tanzania. I don't think I made them any more comfortable about this because I described in almost all of my reporting what I saw and the way I analyzed it, and that was not necessarily always what my Government wanted to hear.

I thought that Nyerere should have been treated more like the world leader that he is and that everyone recognized him to be. But you could not even discuss the possibility of a State visit by Nyerere to the United States in 1972, 1973, 1974, because to have done that would have labeled you as being a complete softy or that you'd been taken over by the man and that sort of thing. When in point of fact, Nyerere had not even been in America since President Kennedy had invited him in 1961, I think.

Just unheard of for a man of his... Nyerere's worldwide leadership being treated, I felt, as, not as well as other people who didn't come nearly up to his size. It's sort of symptomatic of the problem I had in dealing with my own Government.

And, of course, I suspect the second problem, and perhaps the one that was most difficult, involved the policy we had about American diplomats not having any association with the insurgent leaders, the liberation leaders like Samora Machel, who became the President of Mozambique and Agostinho Neto, who became eventually the President of Angola, and Joshua Nkomo, and the others from Zimbabwe. We were prohibited from having any association with them, and that didn't cause problems with my colleagues in Nouakchott or in Rabat or in Cairo or some other places because the leaders weren't headquartered there, but they were in Dar es Salaam and so I was... everything I went to, or almost everything I went to, there would be someone from Frelimo or the MPLA or from one or the other, or from ANC, African National Congress, who'd be there.

Not only was I the American Ambassador, but I was also, I think, without attempting to suggest any arrogance on my part, I was also very well liked in Tanzania. I think my blackness did not hurt me. It was known that I'd been active in the civil rights movement before I came into the Foreign Service. I had a track record which people knew. They knew that I had certain attitudes because I was a sincere student of African Affairs and had been for a number of years. And so, I had access and entree.

364

And I was never then, nor would I now, buckle under to instructions to a point where I would, say, if I went into a room and there was the Cuban Ambassador and Samora Michel, ignore them (laughs). Well, I'm just not going to do that (laughs again).

Well, I was there somewhat vindicated because... And this attitude, see, stemmed from our association with the Portuguese and the Portuguese had the same kind of lobby in Washington that the South Africans and the Rhodesians have and some other groups have. They had certain senators, certain congressmen that they knew well. They had access and entree to the NSC, the National Security Council. And I can tell you that if I, in fact, saw someone, it was pretty much known as quickly back in Washington because of these other sources as from my own reporting it. Because I made it always a point of saying that I had done this so that no one would say that I was trying to do it sub rosa.

Well, this put me in a kind of a special ... made me an enigma (laughs) and I didn't, frankly, give a damn. I thought I had a job to do and one of the jobs I had to was to know the country of my assignment and know what was going on in it, so therefore I didn't tend to stay on one side of the street. That was the second problem.

Third problem, of course, is the one which gained much more notoriety, and that was my involvement in the case of the four Stanford University students who were kidnapped while I was there and with a release, safe release I was able to have some responsibility in negotiating. And at that time we had a policy that we did not negotiate with terrorists. That policy conflicted with another policy which said, one of the first things you do faced with Americans who are in jeopardy is to ascertain their health and well being.

So I had to juggle the concern that we have for the health and well being and safety of our citizens with another policy which said you can't do anything about trying to, to rescue them and to save them. I was eventually sacked as a consequence of my action. I was assigned to Copenhagen and that assignment was cancelled as a consequence of my behavior in that situation.

But fortunately a better informed leadership in Washington and certainly the press, almost to a man, or to a publication, and most politicians in Washington recognized what I was trying to do and I was, I guess you might call, rehabilitated and eventually given another assignment. But mine has not been the kind of routine, pedestrian ambassadorial responsibility (laughs).

Q: Could you give us the full story of that Stanford incident, please?

Carter: Well, I don't know the full story. I suppose when I say... Well, let me think about it, what I could talk about it. The reason I hesitate is that there are some aspects of it over which I have no responsibility, which involved the United States Government and which I would have to respect the security aspects of it.

Q : Of course.

Carter: But, it essentially was that Stanford University operated a primate study station in Gombe, G-O-M-B-E, just off Lake Tanganyika and that station was headed by a gal by the name of Jane Goodall. And on the other side of the lake, for a territory about roughly the size of New Jersey, there was a group of, and it still exists, a dissident group in Zaire that opposes Mobutu and they, one night in May of 1975, came across the lake and kidnapped four of the students, took them back across the lake. And they did this essentially to gain publicity for their movement, and gain arms and ammunition to help in their fight against Mobutu.

Their original request for publicity of money and arms and ammunition was addressed to the Tanzanian Government. The Tanzanian Government was obviously not in a position to be responsive, or not so obviously, they didn't ... they were not going to be responsive. Because the students were Americans, we obviously were much concerned and the first thing we are obliged to do in our book of instructions on how to deal with a situation like this is to find out whether the people are alive and well and what can be done to get them out of that dilemma.

The dissident group gave 60 days, I think, in which to ... or gave a declaration of 60 days in which these things were supposed to be done, thirty days passed and we were not able to establish any communication with the dissident group about the Americans. And we were using every device in our power, including sending messages by missionaries, or using the Voice of America, BBC, and other international radio networks. And then we became ... and meanwhile several of the parents of these kids had come out. The University sent its own representative and newsmen began to come into the country obviously because at that time it was a big story.

One day two of the representatives of the dissident movement got on a train and came down from Kigoma, one of the major towns on the lake. Came down on the train from the town on the lake to Dar and walked into our Embassy and had letters from the remaining detainees. One of the detainees had been released first, at the end of the first week. She was released so she could bring the (initial) information about what they (the kidnappers) wanted and then we heard nothing more, until a month later. And while I was, while we were at home having lunch one day with the Assistant Secretary of State for African Affairs, whose name was Nathaniel Davis and who was much concerned about how this was progressing. Again, because of a great deal of Congressional interest and general interest. He was visiting our country and leaving Tanzania that afternoon to go to Kenya (when these fellows walked in).

And while we were having lunch, my deputy phoned me, or my secretary phoned me, yes, my secretary phoned me from the Embassy to say that two men who were French-speaking had come to see me and that they said that they represented the PRP – People's Revolutionary Party -- and that they had information about the kidnapped students and they were there waiting to talk to me.

I asked to speak to my deputy, who speaks some French, and I asked him to get the administrative officer who had served in Zaire and for them to have a quick chat and attempt to verify the credentials ...their credentials, and to see that they were bona fide. And he came back on the phone about five minutes later and said yes, it appeared that they were bona fide representatives, that they not only seemed to be what they said they were, but they also had letters from several of the students, and that one of the parents had been sent for to see if that parent could identify the handwriting of the student.

I then relayed this information to my colleague who was the Assistant Secretary of State for African Affairs. He was elated that we had finally made some contact with the dissidents that we'd been wanting all this time, and it appeared that the three kids were okay. And I said, "Well, Nat, shall we go down and conduct interviews?" He said, no, you're on top of this, go right ahead and see what you can learn, and send me a cable to Nairobi to keep me informed.

That was the first of a whole series of, first, discussions and then negotiations. And in the negotiations we said what we could not do: The United States Government could not, one, provide arms and ammunition; it could not pay money; and it could not carry on The Voice of America any publicity that they wanted us to carry on, but that obviously there were a lot of newsmen in town who were following this and they would certainly be available to even talk to anyone they wanted to on their own, but that we could not have anything to do with it.

The negotiations went on, I suppose, what, for ten days, two weeks in Dar. We went out to the lake for a couple of meetings. One of the parents got involved on the ransom side of it, again, outside of our U.S. Government activity, and completely outside of my involvement and the Embassy's involvement. But again in all honesty, a sum of money was paid, and I'm not trying to extricate myself from any responsibility about this. I'm telling you as it is. I had nothing to do with the ransom or the transmission of the ransom, or the paying of it or anything else. It was done with the knowledge and complicity of others. I don't think that that was necessarily the whole quid.

I'm pretty certain it was not the whole quid, but it was ultimately released that, in fact that happened. Meanwhile there were a number of starts and stops in terms of getting ... there were three girls and one fellow. Barbara Smuts, one girl had been released within one week. We got two girls released later and then the final lad was released in August and that was a very James Bond kind of episode experience again which I can't really talk too much about. Nonetheless, he was gotten out of Zaire across the lake.

Now, in the course of all of this, there were telephone calls and telegrams being sent, not weekly or daily, but three and four, and five times a day, through the night, because of the time change. At four o'clock in the morning I was reading telegrams and sending telegrams just as I would be doing in the morning at ten or twelve o'clock because that's when the State Department was functioning. No one in the State Department was unaware of anything that we were ... everyone in the State Department was aware of everything we were doing. And we had approval up to and including the Undersecretary of Political Affairs, Joseph Sisco.

One of the things that was critical in this whole episode about which not only were we not informed in Tanzania, but most people in Washington were not informed, was that Secretary Kissinger and President Mobutu were going through an exercise regarding adventure with UNITA and

Jonas Savimbi in Angola. And you recall that what we had proposed to do with support of Savimbi in Angola was what led to the Clark Amendment, which now prohibits the U.S. from interfering in, particularly in Angola, or specifically in Angola, because there had come to power MPLA headed by Agostinho Neto. But he was a socialist; he's now dead. And we were ... Henry Kissinger was interested in giving support to Savimbi and he was using Mobutu as his contact person with Savimbi. Zaire and Mobutu were going to be the conduit to Savimbi in Angola.

Now, Mobutu is very sensitive about any dissident movement in his country. He said to the Secretary of State that the American Ambassador ...in Tanzania ... was not only unfriendly but that I was negotiating with the People's Revolutionary Party, which was the party that had kidnapped these four students, and that I had met with them and that I was encouraging them. And since no one knew of Kissinger's conversations with Mobutu or about the Savimbi connection, they did not understand why Kissinger was so disturbed that we were making life difficult for him on one side when he was trying to make it go so well for himself on the other side. I was making Mobutu unhappy because it was alleged that I was doing business with this dissident movement. So Kissinger said to Mobutu, apparently, that he would show this was not only against U.S. Government policy, but that he would have this Ambassador put on the raft.

And so that's when I was ... told that my assignment -- remember I mentioned about this luncheon when we got the phone call, about these two fellows walking into my Embassy? At that luncheon the Assistant Secretary had come to tell me that the nomination had been put forward, my agrément had been requested of the Danish Government but that the (State) Department would like me to stay in Dar es Salaam until the kidnapping (situation) was completed so it would not appear that I was leaving in the midst of this thing, while we were making arrangements about my forward assignment on to Copenhagen.

So the reason that I eventually got a rapping on the wrist was because I was interfering with one of Secretary Kissinger's plans which no one else knew about. Well, it turns out that there ... that I was called back in, I guess, August of '75, and everyone assumed I was being called back to be congratulated and applauded and all that stuff after everybody got out. And that's when I got the word that I was not being applauded but was given my marching orders.

But Larry [Eagleburger], who was Kissinger's special deputy, was very friendly and very supportive and attempted to put all this in perspective for the Secretary and I think was as responsible as any one person in the Department for, for as I said, for my rehabilitation in a matter of months and getting another assignment.

It turns out that Monrovia, the Monrovia Embassy is a much larger embassy than our Copenhagen Embassy and has much bigger responsibility, and I enjoyed it thoroughly. But, in any event, that is as much of the story as I think I can tell right now because so many of the players are still alive.

I think also in just, in sort of completing the story and giving credit to people who were helpful, it would be unfair not to mention the leadership that the Black (Congressional) Caucus took in this whole episode. They seized it; they met with the Secretary about it; and they did not let the issue die. They talked to the members of the press and to other people on the Hill. There was just a tremendous amount of public support, public and political support.

I would guess that it would be a great mistake to try to identify everyone. My wife most certainly was at the focal point of this, because she was back here kind of controlling all the things that were happening. David

Hamburg, who was the Stanford University representative in Tanzania at that time, did yeoman work in trying to contact people and put the story ... cast the story more correctly.

One of the parents of one of the students was a vice president of a major motorcar company and had resources available (laughs). So there are a lot of people who were helpful and. ..I... it's one of the things that I have done in my career, Foreign Service career, that I am ... I don't want to say proudest of -- but I have better feelings about -- than almost anything else I can really cite, because what else have you to remember but what you may have done maybe in saving someone's life? And it was that kind of -- those were the kinds of issues involved.

Q: Shall we move on to Liberia?

Carter: Liberia? Yes.

Q: Tell us about the years in Liberia.

Carter: (laughs) Well, Liberia is very different country from Tanzania, not as large in geography, not as large in population, but where I did not have to start off trying to explain it to my own Government, because my own Government knew Liberia well, had some conceptions of it that I thought needed updating, and of course, the American public had some perceptions of it which continually need updating.

Liberia has probably suffered from the poorest press of any country on that continent, and I think, now, not for the right reasons. It is a country where there's a great deal of American involvement and interest, but a country which had a higher standard of living than many African countries; where the older regime was attempting to involve all of the people in the economy and in the political process; where it was beginning to do that.

If I were going to jump quickly and respond to the question, well then why, if that was so, was there this coup? I would say that I think it's because revolutions occur as people begin to realize that they're making

372

progress. Revolutions never occur when people are completely downtrodden, prostrate and have nothing. The French Revolution is the classic illustration of that and I think Liberia is not as dramatic an illustration but certainly one of the more recent ones.

Almost all Liberians were involved in the cash economy. There are very few African countries where that could be said. I told you that I went to Africa initially in 1952, when I went to Liberia in 1952 it was a place I decided I never wanted to go back to again because it was a very depressing place, depressing country. There was poverty, in terms of customs and exploitation, but I saw, as many Africans say, "with my own eyes" the kinds of changes that have taken place. Not just in road buildings, schools, and hospitals, and clinics and things, but in terms of, of the so-called, and I use this phrase very advisedly when I say "the so-called," the so-called emergence of the countryman in the affairs of the country.

Everyone now talks again about the so-called Americo-Liberian. When I was there that was a no-no. People didn't talk about Americo-Liberians. Western journalists talked about it but Liberians didn't talk about it. The people who went to ... who came back to Liberia were exquisite colonialists like the Portuguese. They became a part of the people and so there were very, very few families that could ever talk about even being completely country families or completely former American families because of the mixture.

Every family had its involvement, its cross-fertilization, if you please. And when I was there in '52 the first so-called countryman had just become a member of the Cabinet and everyone sort of reveled in that. And when I was back there again for Tubman's funeral, in 1971, I guess half the Cabinet was made up of people who could say that they were largely country people. By the time I was back there as Ambassador, there were two or three who could say that they were more Americo-Liberian and less country, and a majority were 'country people.'

But the level of expectation was continuing to rise. There was a great deal of dissatisfaction with the speed of change and I predicted, in my own estimate, that ... that... that there would be a change. But I thought then there'd be a constitutional change. Tolbert was supposed to leave office in '83.

He had himself recommended in the legislation a limit of eight years on the presidency and his eight years would have expired in '83. He made it very clear, I thought, certainly to my satisfaction anyway, but I wasn't the one who made the final decision on this, that he was not going to stand for re-election and I thought that there would be a constitutional change and there'd be more progress as a consequence of this change. Because it's very difficult for a man his age, and to have seen what he saw, not to believe that he wasn't doing a lot for the country. He was doing a lot for the country; it just wasn't fast enough and enough in terms of quantity.

But the Liberians as with Ghanaians and with the Nigerians were far more developed than many of the East Africans because the impact of the West had been longer on them. The West African coast, as you know, has been much traveled for many, many centuries and certainly since the 15th Century, extensively. When you have that kind of exposure, you have a great deal more development than you do in some other places.

So Liberia is a very ... it's very much more developed in many ways than Tanzania and ... but the problem there was not in the vanguard of those nations that were fighting for dramatic change from the past.

Tolbert used to receive Nujoma, Sam Nujoma from Namibia, and he and Sekou Toure got on very well together, but you don't ... you didn't think of Tolbert as being ... a Kenneth Kaunda or Julius Nyerere. He didn't have that capability, was not an intellectual giant. He did not even have quite the quality that Botswana's Seretse

Khama had, who was not a giant intellectually the way I think Nkrumah was or Nyerere is, but nonetheless, you know he was a man with the South Africans surrounding him and almost controlling completely the economy of that country but yet having the courage to have a truly multiracial society and trying to make for change, providing opportunities for South African refugees -- blacks -- to come through on the way north kind of like the underground railroad.

So Tolbert had an image problem which many of the African leaders did not have. But ... and he was not charismatic, and, so he was, I think, in many ways, his own worst enemy. But he was a man who was trying to do good.

Q: What were ... he was a man trying to do good... so I would consider it one of his great strengths.

Carter: Uhm.

Q: Can you think of others?

Carter: I think that's primarily where he ... where one would have to place their need. He was very active in the church. He was at one time you know president of the World Baptist Alliance. I think that was also a part of his problem, his image problem. He was, he was perceived as a man trying to do good but doing a lot of traveling, looking at problems that were worldwide sometimes rather than problems that were in Monrovia or in and around the villages of Liberia and some of the places that needed attention.

I think he also, unfortunately, had made a considerable amount of money over his lifetime because he was a businessman. And sometimes the appearance of ... of ... of your affluence can be a negative. There are many African leaders who have done just as well as he has done, but they haven't done it quite so overtly as he did.

He had one of the biggest rice farms, rice plantations and (inaudible). He was a partner in Mesurado, the big fishing operation. He was a partner in the Bank of Liberia.

All these things he had begun before he became President, but, nonetheless, it helped create the image of a man who-who did... He had some rubber plantations, but there were Liberians who had larger rubber plantations than he had. There are several Liberians, and this is again not to their discredit but just to point out some of the things sometime people are not aware of.

The third largest rubber plantation in Liberia was owned by a Liberian, larger than several of the American firms that had plantations there. Firestone had the largest one and this fellow had the second or the third largest. And he did not acquire it by any corrupt means; he simply was an energetic Liberian who kept adding to his ... reinvesting his profits and doing well: the sort of success story that would go down swimmingly here. But it was perhaps at the wrong time and the wrong place.

Q: How would you describe your work in relations with President Tolbert?

Carter: I think we got on very well together. I think I was lucky in both my relations with President Nyerere and with President Tolbert. They were different kinds of relationships.

With President Nyerere it was ... we used to have great exchanges on issues of economics, he being a socialist and my being a capitalist. Always in a very friendly way, but we used to have very full conversations about that. And then we'd talk about southern African issues. We were often not antagonists, but he knew that I had certain limitations because I represented my government, and he also knew some of my personal views. We had very, very stimulating constructive conversations.

Willie Tolbert and I were much more, much more on a hail-fellow-well-met-peer kind of relationship. We were good friends. And when he talked to me about what he was trying to do and sought my advice and counsel, asked my opinion on things which he was facing, I very often tried to present those views in ways which he could use to try to

376

accomplish what he wanted to do.

I think that I had something of a partnership relationship with all of the Liberians, government and business, because they felt comfortable with me and we were on the same economic, political wavelength.

With Nyerere it was the kind of relationship that you have in a dormitory at night when you're engaging in a good debate (laughs)...

Q: Do you think that it was partly because of the relationship that had existed for so many years between the United States and Liberia?

Carter: Well, I think that certainly was contributory, but there were ambassadors who did not have that kind of relationship. My immediate predecessor did not have that kind of access. He eventually left because he felt that he did not have the access to the Foreign Ministry that he thought an ambassador should have to be able to present his country's views, and asked to be withdrawn.

So I think that there are two things: Yes, countries can have government-to-government relationships, a good relationship, but I think that in the final analysis this either takes off and becomes really effective for the ambassador and the head of government and his ministers get on well. Or in other cases where the chemistry is bad and I could give, if I really had to think about it, a number of illustrations where we'd send people to so-called safe countries and that just didn't work out well because of the relationship.

One that immediately comes to mind is one of the countries in the north, North Africa, where our relations had been traditionally just the best. We sent an ambassador who did everything wrong with the head of government, and we finally had to withdraw that ambassador in less than a year.

Ambassadorial relations become, for good or bad, often very personal... There're certain things you have to do and there're certain things that embassies have to do. But there's another dimension that an individual can make, and I think that's hard. We have to... we countries have to work hard in picking the right people for the right jobs at the ambassadorial level.

Q: Yes. Could you talk a little about that extra dimension.

Carter: I think it's this dimension of one, some knowledge of the country and of the players, of how it fits in our own grand scheme of things, being able to understand how to use the positives from their own experience to match up with our own ambitions and goals. Again, in just talking about Liberia and Tanzania, I'm talking about two countries where I wasn't showing up for the first time.

When I went to Liberia in '52, I developed relationships with people who were head of the bank, the Central Bank, and ministries. One was a lowly person in the Ministry of Information. When I went back, he was Minister of State. When I went there in 1971, to be a part of the U.S. delegation for the Tubman funeral, I was seeing people I had seen twenty years earlier or almost twenty years earlier who were then -- two of them were presidents -- were brothers of the next President: Steve Tolbert, who was later killed (in an airplane accident), and Frank Tolbert, who was executed in that group following the coup. So when I showed up in 1976, I didn't have to start off from scratch.

Tanzania, I was there in ... in 1965 the first time. I went back -- in '70 or '71 when I had returned from South Africa -- and reported to Nyerere on what I had observed when I was in Pretoria and Johannesburg.

And so ... and I guess some of this relates to the inevitable question which arises as to whether black ambassadors in some countries have an advantage or do they have a disadvantage and my view is that an ambassador should have sensitivity and interest in having advantage. And when they're black that doesn't work

378

against them. And when they're white it works for them. It's more a question of sensitivity, *esprit de corps*, concern. Very often we have some identification with this because of our own reference, our own experience, our own similar reference as we've grown up. We tend to know how it feels to be kicked in the shins (laughs). So we start off with some understanding that some others sometimes ... But there are a hell of a lot of white guys that I know who could do my job just as well or better than I can do, and I know a number of blacks who couldn't do it worth a damn. It's not just a question of race; it's a question of these other things which sometimes we have a leg up on; sometimes we don't.

Q: Did you face any special problems in Liberia?

Carter: Yes, I think there are two problems I faced in Liberia. One, the Liberians always felt that we did not do as well for them in terms of economic assistance as the French did, for instance, in Cote d'Ivoire, you know. Every time I saw the Foreign Minister and he'd just left Abidjan, he would talk about, "You see what the French did in Abidjan?" (laughs) I said, I said, "Sure, you know how many Frenchmen there are in Abidjan? There are fifty thousand Frenchmen in Abidjan, not in Cote d'Ivoire, but in Abidjan there are fifty thousand Frenchmen." I said, "Now we have four thousand Americans in all of Liberia. If you want fifty thousand Americans here in Monrovia, we can do the same thing. But you don't want that, do you?" And he said, "no." But nonetheless, they always felt that ...

First of all, you see, Liberia was never a colony of ours, but they had kind of a colonial attitude or mentality, because all of the countries around them had been colonies. The Brits left an infrastructure in Ghana which if it had been better managed could have kept that country so far out in front. I think there was something, and I don't want to be wrong in this, but I'm just going to take the chance.

379

In 1952 there was something like 6-1/2 miles of paved roads in Liberia and when the British left the Gold Coast, Ghana, there must have been 1,800 miles of paved road, maybe more. Just in terms of the most minimal infrastructure, they developed harbors at Tema and at Accra and Takoradi. There's a developed harbor off Monrovia because it was an important harbor for us during the Second World War. We didn't do it because we thought the Liberians should have just a developed harbor. So that was one problem on the Liberian side.

The other problem on the U.S. side was, again, trying to make the point to my government that we should have been doing more. That there are very real reasons for us to do more. One of our largest Voice of America installations (in the world) is in Liberia. Pan American (Airways) serves Liberia and the airport there is a very critical airport.

Liberia has been an ally before. If we ever had occasion to go to war and they'd still be an ally, we'd want to have good use of their facilities and sea facilities.

I don't think we've done nearly enough for Liberia and one of the reasons we haven't is because they've been more passive than they should have been about this. Governments very often will respond to the country that is giving them more hell than someone else is giving.

When I was in Tanzania we ended up having a 65 million dollar economic assistance program. We never spent 65 million dollars in Liberia. Tanzania is larger, need is greater. But in terms of U.S.G. interest, U.S. Government interest, it was very difficult for me having served in both those places to justify spending 65 million dollars in Tanzania where the President's going to be giving you hell at every opportunity (laughs). And Liberia, where we're now I think, back up to 25 million dollars.

Q: I've seemed to focus on the problems you had in these various areas. Are there things you did in Liberia that you feel happiest about?

Carter: Well, I think on the other side of the coin is that I ... we did get our economic assistance program up higher. I think the Liberians felt when I left that we had moved these relations forward more and they were a bit happier with us. We had arranged a visit... an exchange of visits of the Presidents, which not many ambassadors are ever able to achieve. We had President Tolbert here on a State Visit during the Bi-Centennial. We had President Carter stop in Monrovia when every country in the world wanted him to visit. Only two African countries got him: Liberia and Nigeria.

We renegotiated what we had. We had to renegotiate landing rights for Pan American Airways that had been dormant for fifteen years. The Liberians were about to abort these agreements, because the Pan Americans, Pan American Airways, was treating itself differently. And that's a very critical landing agreement, because it was a gateway to all the other countries in Africa down the line: Accra, Lagos, Kinshasa, Nairobi. And that would not have been finally negotiated without my being involved on an eleventh-hour basis.

So it's natural why I think the greatest disappointment in Liberia was that I was not there during the rice riots and I was not there at the time of the coup. Not sure that I could've changed the coup.

I wish that I had an opportunity to go to try to effect some of the changes that many people wanted without the bloodshed that occurred. I don't think anything has ever impacted on me quite as severely as that, because there were so many people who were killed in that change who were not only innocent, should not have died, but who were viable resources that the country will have a long time to try and replace. People like David Neal, who was Minister of Planning and Development. Just one of the great, great personalities of the world. Great planner; man who didn't, who never took a nickel, never involved in any corruption.

Cecil Dennis, who was probably the quintessence of the kind of foreign minister that most developing countries need, he was out there kicking us in the pants when we needed to be kicked in the pants, and, sometimes, much to my consternation, but really an honest man. He was trying to do good for his country.

Clarence Parker, who had offered a very critical study of the Government, what needed to be done to change it who was killed.

Reginald Townsend, who was the first so-called countryman to be brought into the Cabinet who was constantly trying to do good. I could just go on and name ....

There are some names that I have not mentioned and I have not mentioned them deliberately, because I certainly don't think that they should have been killed the way they were.

But I can understand that their involvement was such that it was not likely that they were going to get much sympathy, but there were some very tragic losses in that change. Tragic to the country. None of us can afford to lose talent like some of the talent that was lost in that. I think some of the leaders of that country now realize that. But it's too late. It's like Thurgood Marshall said the other day: "When you convict a man and find that it's a mistake and you've killed him in capital punishment, you don't have a chance to correct your mistake."

Q: One word about your relationship with the other U.S. ambassadors, black and white.

Carter: Well, I guess I had come to the place where I was sort of the doyen of the black ambassadors. I have been around now longer than all of those who are in active service, I guess with exception of Terry Todman. Terry must have been, yeah, I guess Terry Todman may have predated me by a couple of months, but I think, because of my service as Deputy Assistant Secretary where I had supervisory responsibility for ambassadors as well as

382

having that period of time as Ambassador to two countries and then and named Ambassador-at-Large, sort of gave me an elder role, which I don't think of myself as being, but, nevertheless, I guess I am.

And with whites, I got along reasonably well with them. They recognized that I'd paid some dues and it was not sort of a token. So, to answer your question, I did not experience any great problems with them. I think most of them were supportive and helpful and one does not always know what other people think. But I certainly didn't ... I don't recall any episode that I could really cite that would be a negative one.

Q: If you had the opportunity to go back to Liberia as Ambassador today, how would you respond to the invitation?

Carter: Well...I assume you ask that question because ... you guess that there is something to be done, especially there. I don't think that people can generally go back again and be an ambassador in most countries where they've served. It is not a good idea. I suppose if I were asked to go back to Liberia, I would have to think hard and long before saying no simply because, see, I do know that the country is in great need now of help and understanding.

And because I have great sympathy and affection for the Liberians, it would be very difficult to say no. That's about it. I just had never thought about it before. But off the top of the head reaction, I would have difficulty saying no, because I know there is a great need and I think I could be helpful. Whether I'd be willing to go back to being an ambassador anywhere again, I'm not sure I can say yes to that. I certainly would have to think long and hard on Liberia. I have a very warm spot in my heart for that country.

Q: There is one other big question I wanted to ask and that is, of the two posts, which did you like best?

Carter: Uhm...(pause)

Q: And why?

Carter: I really - I'd have to fudge on that. I ... it's ... there're some mornings that I enjoy pancakes and some mornings I enjoy an omelet, and it doesn't mean I don't like pancakes. Each country presented certain values that were very special and I gained from each one of them, and I enjoyed the people in each of them. I was challenged; I was stretched in each one of the situations. I would have real difficulty in deciding which had been the happier or the more gratifying experience.

I think that I was a better ... I think I had learned more about being an ambassador by the time I got to Liberia than I had when I was in Tanzania simply because the longer you do something, if you've got any growth potential at all, the better you do it.

That would be about all, that's about all I think I feel about that at the moment.

Q: All right. I'd like to talk a bit about your work as Ambassador-at-Large, but before we move to that, are there other things you'd like to add about Tanzania or Liberia?

Carter: There's one other subject I think I didn't focus on in talking about Tanzania and that relates to what I've come to develop a keen interest in, and, of course, that's African art. And I guess that that interest began a long time ago but sort of took off when I was in Nigeria and spent a good bit of time in the Benin area where there's a good bit of work done in bronze and terra cotta, and in Ibadan, and then seeing, of course, a number of other things in West Africa -- Guinea, Senegal, Mali -- and then going to Tanzania and seeing some of the art forms that I had never seen before and recognized that they weren't getting the same kind of attention that West African art was getting.

I think a lot of this comes from my wife's interest in the subject area, and spending time with the sculptors and all the painters. And so we came to know a good bit about the Makonde artists in Tanzania who inhabit that northern

384

region of Mozambique, the southern region of Tanzania and who do really an unusual...who do unusual work in sculpture, and also the primitive painters in the area.

And so we decided that it might be useful in our residence there to sort of put in juxtaposition some of the art things we were discovering, as we were resident in that area of the world, with some of the ... with some of the black artists, black American artists. And we had in the residence sort of a little museum, if you please, art exhibit, with a number of black artists. And that was made possible ... some of the works were made possible on loan through what is known as the Embassy and Arts Program in the State Department.

And again as happened so often, in terms of our relations with our own government, while the arts and embassy program was very well developed, it was developed around what was known to most of the people in official Washington. And those people who are best known to official Washington were white artists, not black artists (laughs), and so my wife had to give a little course so that
these people could go out and even acquire on a loan basis some of the artists we felt we'd like to display in our residence.

We got a collection of, I think, very fine pieces together and the collection was of Tanzanian artists and the showings gained such attention that President Nyerere himself came to view the collection. And I gather that that was the first time he'd been in any ambassador's residence in years and years and years, and this was sort of a coup that my colleagues, the other diplomats, were a little disturbed about. But they hadn't thought of this, or they didn't have a wife who thought about it. And he came and spent a very pleasant evening.

And then *Topic Magazine*, which is published by what was then the United States Information Agency, now ICA [International Communications Agency], did a full feature on it. And we were always very pleased, because as people came to the residence, and there were a number of people who were constantly in the residence, they were able to see the reality of Afro-American art, Afro being the African art, and American art being our own black artists. That may have been enough by itself to have made the whole 3-1/2 years in Tanzania (laughs) a very valuable experience. It was also just a delight to be able to live in that kind of an artistic milieu and see the things that were on display on the walls and on platforms throughout the house.

There is a follow on to that, and that is, we obviously had to return the American artists' pieces because they were on loan, but we have subsequently given to the Museum of African Art in Washington, a large portion of our collection, which has now become a part of their own permanent collection.

And we're pleased because there is not much ... there is nothing much displayed or written about or talked about of the East African artists, and so this has been a small contribution we were able to make toward the understanding of African art in general terms." – (Ambassador W. Beverly Carter interviewed by Celestine Tutt, *The Association for Diplomatic Studies and Training (ADST), Foreign Affairs Oral History Project*, 30 April 1981, copyright, 2008 ADST, pp. 4 – 22).

James W. Spain

James W. Spain served as the American ambassador to Tanzania from 8 January 1976 – when he presented his credentials – to 21 August 1979. He covered a wide range of subjects in the interview. And this is what he said about Tanzania, President Nyerere and other subjects:

"Q: Going to Tanzania. Did you have any problems getting approved? Were there White House candidates in the bidding?
Spain: No. As far as I know, in Henry Kissinger's early days at State there wasn't any of this. What Henry said, went.

There was a Congressional problem, however. I always thought I got along well with politicians. Fulbright had retired the year before but the Foreign Relations Committee was still mostly the old committee with John Sparkman chairing.

There was a marvelous woman from somewhere in the South, an older woman, who was the NEA congressional liaison type--Kay Folger. She took me over, as was the habit then, to meet the chairman as soon as the nomination was announced. The chairman asked two questions, figuratively patted me on the head, and said, "It will be a pleasure to have you with us next Tuesday, Mr. Ambassador." Well, On the way back to the Department Kay said, "You're in. He called you 'Mr. Ambassador.'"

I appeared at the Committee meeting right behind someone who was going to some fairly important European post. There were six or seven senators present. When that nominee was heard, they all cut and ran, except for Sparkman, Clifford Case of New Jersey, and a newly elected Senator from Iowa named Richard Clark.

Clark had an aide who was just out of college. She knew something about Africa and had gotten the impression, understandably, that this anonymous character (me who had never had a thing to do with Africa)) was Kissinger's hatchet man put in to replace that great and good American Black, Beverly Carter. (He was the ambassador Kissinger had pulled out for allegedly negotiating with terrorists.) She had also learned about my years with ONE in CIA. Clearly her concept was that the silly State Department was sending out a spy to deal with the great and good neutralist, Julius Nyerere, President of Tanzania.

Clark started his questioning along this line. "Do you not think that your record with CIA, etc......?" Fortunately, the newspapermen had gone out when the important ambassador and the rest of the senators had. I did the best I could to answer, "No I do not think it would have any effect..." But it didn't go over with Clark, who was a freshman senator eager to show how alert and bright he was.

At this point Hubert Humphrey walks in. He has a staff aide with him that I knew was engaged to be married to Clark's staff aide. Humphrey sits down and listens for five or ten minutes. Then he says, "Senator, do you know Julius Nyerere? Well, I do. I have seen a lot of him. What do you think he thinks the Chinese ambassador is, a

Confucian scholar? What do you think he thinks the Soviet ambassador is, a rug merchant? What do you know about ONE and Sherman Kemt?" He suggests that he hasn't heard language like Clark's in the Senate since Joseph McCarthy.

Sparkman smiled benignly and said, "Thank you Mr. Ambassador." I was confirmed a couple of days later. But for 45 minutes to an hour I was in a bad sweat.

Q: Because we are trying to pick up various things about the Foreign Service, you alluded to what happened to Beverly Carter. What was the alleged problem?

Spain: Let's see if I can condense that Gothic tale to just a minute or two. There was a chimpanzee sanctuary run by a famous woman named Jane Goodall out on Lake Tanganyika. I'm talking about the spring and summer of 1975. There were a number of graduate students in biology and zoology there, including two Americans, an Australian, I think, and a few Europeans. Just across the lake in Zaire there was a rebel movement against Mobutu. One night the Zairian rebels came across and grabbed some foreign students. They were taken back across the lake and ransom was demanded.

Kissinger had just formulated the U.S. Government policy of not paying ransom for or negotiating about hostages. The parents of the two Americans, who were connected with Stanford, showed up in Dar es Salaam wanting to pay the ransom. The money was in London and they couldn't get it transferred. They convinced Beverly Carter to let it be sent through the pouch.

Then, one of the rebel leaders showed up in Dar es Salaam. By coincidence an American missionary who had spent his life out in Ujiji near the preserve and where Stanley found Livingston was also in Dar. The parents made arrangements with him to be the go-between with the rebels. He would take the money across the lake and bring the kids back. To keep everybody in touch an

389

embassy communications officer would go to Ujiji and stay there.

The night the missionary was supposed to go across the lake he lost his nerve and refused to go unless the communications officer came with him. The Foreign Service person agreed. The money was handed over. They didn't get the kids right then but they all were sent back within a few days.

No one ever told Bev Carter that one of his people had actually crossed the lake. Still, that should have been the end of it with rejoicing everywhere. But almost simultaneously Kissinger and Mobutu came together at some international meeting. The life President gave the American Secretary of State hell for violating his own no ransom policy and supporting rebels against his government. He insisted that an officer from the American Embassy in Dar was present when the money was handed over.

On the day of the rescue Kissinger sent Carter a commendation for the successful recovery. After he talked to Mobutu he pulled him out for having been party to a hostage negotiation. This was less than fair. Bev knew there was a communications officer in Ujiji, but it was only long afterwards that he found out he had crossed the lake.

Q: Before going out to Tanzania, in many ways you were the new boy on the block.

Spain: Very much so.

Q: You were there from when to when?

Spain: From 1975-59.

Q: Okay. Julius Nyerere was a renowned leader in African terms and was the darling of particularly the socialist bloc--the Swedes, and socialists in England and Germany, etc.-- What were you being told about Nyerere before you went out there?

Spain: As I recall, I was briefed particularly on ujamaa scheme, collectivized farming. There were no policy

390

problems between the U.S., and Tanzania, other than their constant voting on the other side of issues in the UN. Tanzania's uniqueness in Africa was one thing that was emphasized to me. I only had a week in the Foreign Service Institute. The briefing was entirely adequate. There was someone to give me a crash course in Kiswahili.

It was explained that Nyerere was the big man among radical--as opposed to 'good'-- Africans. He was a radical and a socialist, generally hostile to American policy, a strong supporter of rebel movements in Rhodesia, Namibia, and South Africa. The country was under real threat from the large number of Soviet and Chinese advisers. The Chinese were building the Tanzam railroad. There were 20,000 of them there.

Q: You arrived there in 1975. What was the political situation there at the time?

Spain: Nyerere had ruled the country since independence in 1960-61. It was a one party state. Its democracy was not representative. The only thing that could be said was that it was that Nyerere's rule was relatively benign. I am quite sure he never ordered anybody killed. There were a few people in jail but not many. Some were from Zanzibar, under sentence of death there but kept alive on the mainland.

The country struck me as radical in its international policy and downright stupid in its economic theory, but pretty moderate in human terms. People didn't get killed. They might get relocated under the ujamaa system of farming, but Nyerere never even thought of 'liquidating the kulaks.'

Q: Was this ujamaa a relocation system?

Spain: In Tanzania the land to people ratio is very good. It is a big country with relatively few people. The traditional African rural society was a couple of huts, a family and extended family on top of a hill with its own few coconut palms and a casaba patch. On the next hill there was another family. It was not really village life. Nyerere's great aim was to bring education and medical facilities to his people. That was pretty hard to do it when they were scattered like that.

So he set up the idea of ujamaa, the family village, and the people were all ordered in. Government would dump a truck load of cement blocks and a few pipes and say here, build it. It was a pretty inefficient operation and a lot of the people sneaked away to their old homesteads to harvest their coconuts, etc. Sometimes when they were brought back or even when they were first ordered into these collective villages, some of them didn't get on the trucks fast enough and got a rifle butt on the side of the head. It was not without brutality, but nobody was ever killed that I know of. And Nyerere did bring educational and medical facilities to the villages, far better than those in rural Kenya at the time.

I got there not long after the first round of ujamaa. Food production had gone straight down. Typically, Nyerere, instead of ordering, "shoot the capitalist pigs," said "Well, all right, we have the people in villages now where they have medicine and education. Rearrange the land system so that there are private plots and each family can keep what it grows."

The next two years food production went straight up. Then he insisted on going back to doing things "the right way," and collectivized again. After I left they had to do decollectivization again.

Q: What was the role of the American ambassador there?

Spain: In a public sense it was very modest. The US wasn't popular. I saw my job as knowing Nyerere and seeking possible areas of cooperation with him. When I showed up the assumption was there were very few, if any, of these.

He was a hopeless socialist full of silly slogans, such as "No man should have an automobile until every man has a bicycle." Still, he was clearly a very sincere and humane man.

I thought times were changing. I and DCM Herb Levin one day came to the conclusion that we mind find common ground with Nyerere on Rhodesia and the Namibia. We started reporting and analyzing his views on these issues, selectively but I think accurately. Lo and Behold and behold! Henry Kissinger got interested. He came to visit Dar three times in 1976. David Owen, the British Foreign Secretary, joined him for a couple of his meeting with Nyerere. The "Anglo-American" plan for the independence of Rhodesia began to evolve. Nyerere was more cooperative than Kissinger expected.

He made no bones that he would give all the support he could, including arms, to the Namibian and Rhodesian rebels. That was to end "colonialism." But he saw the situation within South Africa differently. That was a fight between Africans and Africans. The Boers, as he always called the Afrikaners, were Africans too, bad Africans, but Africans. As he told an American visitor, "Unlike the British in Rhodesia, they have no place to go home to."

From 1976 on Tanzania became more important in US thinking. Nyerere was Chairman of the "Front Line States," Zambia, Mozambique, Angola, Botswana and one or two others, who were dictating the African position on Rhodesia and Namibia. Kissinger's visits were the first real policy contact with the US. Then in 1977, literally a week after the inauguration, who shows up but Andy Young, our new UN PermRep. A lot of Tanzanians took to him immediately. The first African chief of state that Carter invited to the United States after his inauguration was Nyerere and he developed a great empathy with our president.

During the visit I could easily see why. I was amazed that Carter, a former naval officer from Georgia, president for only a few months, faced with multiple world challenges, knew the names and numbers of all the players on the Southern African scene. He carried on five hours of discussion with Nyerere as competently as anyone in the State Department could have. I met Nyerere a few times in later years and he never failed to praise Carter as "a good man and a true democrat."

One of our problems on Rhodesia was British Foreign Secretary David Owen. Despite his Labor Party background, he rubbed most Africans the wrong way. And, even when he made a concession, he did it grumpily and grudgingly. Still progress was made. There was a real dialogue with Nyerere. Andy Young visited Dar five or six times in 1977. Cy Vance came for one important meeting with all the insurgent leaders. Out of it all came the Anglo-American plan for Rhodesia.

When a Conservative government came back to power in London, Owen was replaced by Peter Carrington. Strangely, the radical Africans found this smooth aristocrat much more compatible than "red brick" Owen. Carrington, of course, had a good deal of personal experience in Africa and I think he used it to "pull the wool over" Margaret Thatcher's very conservative eyes in her early days in office. He perhaps made it up to her by throwing us out of the negotiations and the "Anglo- American Plan" became just "Anglo." But expected blood baths were avoided and Zimbabwe got its independence.

Q: What was your role?

Spain: If I did anything useful, it was to convince Washington that Nyerere was not a brutal African dictator and a Communist stooge and to persuade Nyerere that the U.S. was a decent democratic country and not merely the world's bully.

It helped that I found Nyerere fascinating. He had an MA in English from Edinburgh University and loved word play. I never read a book that he hadn't read.

He translated Shakespeare into Kiswahili. He had the same Catholic secondary education at a mission school that I had.

394

I recall going in to see him one day and being confronted with the question: "Mr. Ambassador, do you remember what the ultimate sin is?" I said, "I think it is despair." "Yes, it is despair. You are dying and you are in despair of God giving you mercy." I agreed. "Isn't there something else," he asked, "final impenitence?" I agreed again. "You are dying and you don't ask God for forgiveness because you are convinced He wouldn't give it to you if you did." "Yes Mr. President."

He delivered his punch line. "I am on the verge of despair about Ian Smith. Will you please tell President Carter that. If he doesn't do something about him soon, we're all going to be dammed!" I passed the message along, although I left the intricate theology out.

Another story. Nyerere came back from an OAU meeting in Addis or Khartoum during the war with Uganda. I went in to see him and said, "Well, how did things go, Mr. President?" He replied, "You know how they went, you read the newspapers. They all condemned me for warring with my African brother, Idi Amin. I told them, let me tell you about my African brother. He is a murderer, a pervert, a monster. Then my fellow heads of government called me names. They said I was a rampaging elephant. That didn't bother me. You can see I'm a little guy, barely 100 lbs. Then they called me a mad buffalo. I shed that too. But finally one of them called me a mischievous little black monkey. That hurt! Look at me and that hurt. Look at me. I jump around and I talk with my hands. I do look something like a monkey."

You can see why I am very fond of Julius Nyerere.

Q: Well he seemed to have had particularly good relations and charmed money out of the Swedes and other socialists. He would call up and seemed to get whatever he wanted. Did you find this was true?

Spain: Most Western development aid to Tanzania came from Scandinavia, particularly the Swedes. They liked the intellectual socialist, the benign father of his

395

people who didn't kill or imprison people, while trying to create a new way of life with better prospects. The fact that it all didn't work very well didn't bother them.

Q: Were you able to at any point sit down and have a good discussion with him about the effects of a lot of this socialism, that it was cutting down on a lot of opportunities and that maybe a more capitalist form of government might make some sense, to unleash the mercantilistic energies of the people?

Spain: I must confess that I really didn't try. For one thing, unlike other parts of Africa, no one was starving or dying of uncontrolled disease in Tanzania. For another, despite Nyerere's close identification with radical socialist theory, I don't think he cared much about economics. He was basically a humanist with a keen sense of both tribal traditions and modern politics, a social science type.

Besides, our AID program in Tanzania was very small and I didn't have much to bargain with. Above all, the primary US interest at the time was a peaceful settlement in Rhodesia, Namibia, and South Africa. I was much more interested in promoting that than in arguing economics.

Come to think of it, there was one time just before he came to the US on his official visit. He told me he wanted to try to make clear the "north-south" problem between the "haves and the have-nots." He asked what I thought about his proposed approach. He talked about a Tanzanian man and wife out in a village who sew and reap a hundred kilos of sisal. As always happens in dealing with sisal, they cut their legs. Sooner or later they are likely to get skin cancer. It is a pretty miserable life. They earn enough to have 3 ounces of carbohydrates and 1 ounce of fat a day. (I forget the exact statistics.)

That sisal is sent off to the United States. The shipping cost is controlled by the Westerners who make a profit on it. What originally cost 5 cents, when it arrives costs 15 cents. An American company buys it and makes it into a ball of twine. It sells it to a stationery store 65 cents. The stationery store sells it to a customer for 98 cents. Part of the difference between 98 cents goes in wage to the unskilled clerk behind the counter. Her weekly wages enable her to buy new clothes, go to movies, take a vacation. My people don't get enough out of the process to do any of these things. "That is what I mean by north-south inequality!"

I told him that he should try his explanation. Incidentally, he was much more precise and eloquent than I have just been. He put the idea into a speech in San Francisco. I don't think anyone understood what he was getting at.

Q: Was there concern at all during this that Nyerere would become a tool of the Chinese and Soviets? Henry Kissinger was seeing so many things in East-West terms.

Spain: Yes, there was some concern, particularly because there were a great many Chinese there, 20,000 at one point when they were building the Tanzam railroad. Such military equipment as Nyerere had was Soviet supplied. Russian diplomats and technicians were fairly much in evidence. Press and public opinion favored both Russians and Chinese. I personally didn't share it.

As far as I could see, if anybody was trying to take over the country, they weren't doing a very good job of it. And, also, with the Tanzanians, as with the Egyptians and the Afghans and every other people I had known in Asia and Africa, there was a real nationalism. Just taking aid from a country didn't mean they were going to be absorbed by it. The Chinese put in an enormous amount of money for the Tanzam railroad and their numbers were of some concern at the time. But as we can see now, all they achieved was building a railroad.

Q: What about Zanzibar? One of our concerns has been the communists getting a foothold on the Indian Ocean and Zanzibar being a traditional port and all that. Did this play any role?

397

Spain: After the Zanzibar revolution when the Africans overthrew the Sultan just a year or two after independence, the Russians and particularly the East Germans were very active there. The latter provided apartments buildings, a color television station and receiving sets, etc. When the island joined with Tanganyika to form Tanzania, Nyerere was, I think, a restraining influence on Communist penetration. By the time I got to Dar there was little reason to fear a Communist take-over. It seems to me that our mistake in Africa and Asia during this period was not in fearing sinister Communist intentions but in not taking into account local ones. No country wanted to be a Communist satellite—any more than it did to be an American one.

Q: I think one of the themes has been much of the Cold War that back in Washington the political leaders and congress were sometimes reflected in the Secretary's statements, were seeing communist menaces around and all, where those in the field were seeing these things self-contained and these were people take opportunities to get a little extra arms or aid. Did you see this split at all?

Spain: I certainly did. In the case of Tanzania there was much more concern in Washington than there was in the field. One of the amusing sidelights of Henry Kissinger's second or third visit was this. He stayed in the Kilimanjaro Hotel. When the party was clearing out to go to the airport, I was told that the Secretary wanted me. I went upstairs. People were carrying away files and suitcases.

In the middle of a table there was a "bug" protector that was still making weird electronic sounds. Henry gets both of us hunched over this thing. He said "Thank you very much. This visit has been useful. Your arrangements were fine, but I want to warn you about one thing. This fellow Nyerere is not on our side." This was a pretty accurate reflection of the spirit of the times. The fact was that Nyerere certainly wasn't on our side, but he wasn't a tool

398

of the Chinese or the Russians either.

Q: What about the situation with Uganda? Could you explain for someone who wouldn't be familiar, what had happened in Uganda that caused it?

Spain: Idi Amin was a monster. He jumped in to grab a piece of northwestern Tanzania. He send his army down without notice and occupied it. Why? God knows. Tanzanian forces mobilized and started getting in there, but before any real fighting took place, the Ugandans withdrew. You could make an argument that whatever it was it was over.

But Nyerere took the position, probably correctly, that Idi Amin remained a major threat to Tanzania. If something wasn't done about him, he would come back in and do the same sort of thing again. He had started the war, and, by God, the Tanzanians were going to finish it. Personal enmity between Julius Nyerere and Idi Amin was enhanced by philosophical differences. There really wasn't anything economic or political at stake.

Q: How did that work out?

Spain: The Tanzanians chased them all the way to Kampala. Nyerere replaced Amin with Milton Obote, a previous Ugandan prime minister who had bee in exile in Tanzania for some years. He ran the grocery store where we bought out food supplies. He was another intellectual socialist but without Nyerere's charm, humanity, or intelligence. He started killing people just as soon as he got back to Kampala and was overthrown again. I really have no idea of what has gone on in Uganda since.

Q: Was there a difference between the Tanganyikans and Ugandans and the Kenyans?

Spain: If you look at it from an anthropological standpoint I don't know if you would really find much difference. Uganda had had this complicated thing of Buganda where there was actually a monarchy and one tribe that had the history of ruling. Tanzania's great blessing was that it had a hundred or so tribes, none of them were anything like a majority in the country. I think the biggest tribe in all of Tanzania was 6 percent of the population. Nyerere himself came from a small tribe up near Lake Victoria which had only 5,000 or so people. Kenya is more evenly split between Kikuyus and Luos, tribes of almost equal size which are intensely jealous of each other.

Q: It would seem to me that a place like Tanzania where the Americans were not, although we were talking to them in polite terms, but they were not with us on UN things and that type of things. What would you do when you got your yearly shopping list of things to do? Would you go around and say, "Please vote this way," knowing they were going to stick their thumb in your eye? Could you make any grounds or was this a proforma thing?

Spain: Sometimes I didn't even due it pro forma. I went in twice a year on two issues. One was Puerto Rico; the other was nuclear non-proliferation. Nyerere would sit there grinning, not reflecting hostility but really not hearing me either. At one point Kissinger sent out a demarche that included the phrase "for Tanzania to vote for Puerto Rico independence would be an unfriendly act."

I remembered my international law courses which taught that "an unfriendly act" was one just short of war. Nyerere had had a few courses in international law, too. I figured throwing that at him would just make him furious.

But I also knew that the Secretary felt strongly. So I said, "Mr. President, I know you strongly favor Puerto Rican independence, but I want to stress that the people of the United States feel strongly about the subject too. They become unhappy when they see countries that really have little interest in the matter constantly voting against us. They think acts like that are unfriendly." I added that I would really like to brief him on our view of Puerto Rico sometime. He politely agreed.

The subject was up again in the UN a few months later.

Before instructions went out to beat everyone who disagreed with us about the head, I asked for briefing material from the Department. I got an armload. When I went to see Nyerere this time, he had his foreign minister and three or four others present. We had our little seminar, very conscious of the fact that on this occasion at least we weren't engaged in a confrontation. All I got out of Nyerere was a comment that "Yes, some of this is new and interesting. Next time we face this face this issue, I will be better prepared."

Before very long, of course, we had to face it again and this time, according to Washington, the Tanzanian vote may be critical. I never really understood this use of words. It might be critical to the UN vote in the Committee of 77 but that really didn't make a damn bit of difference to what we would do. However, I went back to Nyerere and said, "You remember how we discussed Puerto Rico. I'm told your vote is likely to decide the outcome this time. Do you really want to be the country that faces the U.S. with a demand for Puerto Rican independence?"

He asked a number of questions and called up his foreign minister. Then he said, "I don't think we would be the single vote that puts it over, but I will make you this promise. My representative will be instructed that if it comes to that, she is to excuse herself to go to the bathroom." Actually, the independence issue was defeated by several votes that year, so Tanzania felt free to vote it favor of it. Not a great achievement, was it?

Nyerere's standard answer to my pleas for Tanzania to sign the non-proliferation treaty was that it was an "unequal treaty." Some countries had to sign it and some did not. "Mr. Ambassador," he told me one day, "you come in and tell me that the U.S. has signed it; bring it with you and I'll sign it then and there." Obviously I got nowhere with him on the subject--except that he occasionally teased me: "When are you bringing me your nonproliferation treaty?"

Q: I would think that in a country such as Tanzania that as the ambassador one would feel very leery about having the CIA around there because anything they did would...in the first place it wouldn't have any bloody effect. But almost anything they did could get into the papers and be blown up all out of proportion and we would just have egg all over our face, etc. How did you find this?

Spain: We had a small CIA station there. Two of the three station chiefs I had were pretty good citizens. They understood that covert collection had more prospect for loss than gain. Unfortunately, they were under constant pressure from their headquarters to collect at any cost.

Q: We are talking about rogue elephants, somebody going out...

Spain: They weren't cowboys, but I saw no need for them. State political officers produced better information on Tanzanian affairs. The Agency people claimed they were tracking Soviets and Chinese through the port and airport. They also had "high priority requirements" for information on Zimbabwean and Namibian rebel leaders. Andy Young and I were in regular contact with all of these and I never saw the Agency come up with anything that we didn't know already. I did see some stuff they produced that was plain inaccurate.

Q: We had full relations without restrictions on talking to these people?

Spain: Yes. The only restriction was that no American official could go into Rhodesia. Later the one exception to that was Steve Low, who was ambassador in Zambia. He was designated a roving ambassador or something like that and actually visited Rhodesia. There were no restrictions at all, even during the Kissinger days. And, after Carter, Young, and Moose came into the picture, it was talk, talk, and talk. My wife gave Sam Nujoma the first American social event that he ever attended, a birthday party for him in the house in Dar es Salaam in 1977.

The CIA's problem, incidentally, was in Washington. The White House asked for all available information on the rebel leaders and the Agency set out to get it by hook or crook. Equal priority was give to collection in Tanzania, Zambia, Mozambique, and four or five other places, including South Africa. I tended to be somewhat skeptical of the hair-raising stuff that came out of the last. When I raised a question about this scatter shot approach, suggesting that they might look for information about Mugabe in Maputo (where he spent most of his time) and about Nkomo in Lusaka (which he made his headquarters), I made a lifetime enemy of a swashbuckling spook named Clair George.

Q: Clair George being?

Spain: The chief of the Africa covert division of CIA. He told me once that I was the worse ambassador of the whole crop. Simply because I had said, "For God's sake, fellows, don't risk getting blown trying to recruit a drunk who was once Robert Mugabe's driver, Robert Mugabe has been long gone from Dar." I didn't shed many tears when George, having ascended very high in the Agency, was convicted of felony in federal court a few years ago-- and I didn't break out the champagne when Bush pardoned him.

Q: Were there any other areas we should cover?

Spain: On Tanzania, I don't think so--other than the interesting aspect of diplomacy when you come back with an official visitor to the United States. As I said Nyerere was the first African chief of state that Carter invited back. I accompanied him.

Only twice in my life have I been in substantive sessions in the White House. I was with Carter and Nyerere, Vance, Moose and Brzezinski for something like five hours. Then too, five or six days are allotted for the distinguished visitor to see the US. We took our own plane out to Chicago, San Francisco and Los Angeles, and the rural Midwest and South. Nyerere didn't play bridge but his foreign minister (now President of Tanzania) did. ....weekend and apparently is the likely new president.

Such visits are very useful in terms of getting a feel for what people in the field often tend to forget. One is that the American people, while polite and interested, simply don't care all that much about foreign affairs. Another is Washington meetings, hordes of people tripping over their own feet; everybody serving his personal interest; nobody ever willing to make a decision. I couldn't help thinking how great it would be if I had no one but Carter, Vance, and Moose to deal with. But governments don't work that way.

Q: What would President Carter and his Secretary of State Vance be doing talking to Nyerere for five hours? That is a lot of time.

Spain: Rhodesia and Namibia were high priority issues at the time. Kissinger had devoted three or four days to them in 1976. We were in the middle of the negotiations for an independent Rhodesia.

The personal chemistry between Carter and Nyerere was great. Toward the end of the discussions Carter shuffled his papers and said, "Well, I think that is all Mr. President. It has been very useful."

His National Security Adviser who had been sitting down the table and hadn't said a word coughed pointedly. "Oh, yes," said Carter, "There is the matter of the Cubans in Angola." "Yes, indeed Mr. President," Nyerere responded. "I thought we were going to agree on everything, but that is something that we can disagree on. Let's talk about it." Carter didn't seem very eager. He said, "We feel that's bad." Nyerere gave his standard reply: as soon as the South Africans get out of Angola the Cubans will get out. "How can you guarantee that?" "Because the President of Angola has promised me and I will see to it that he lives up to his promise!" There isn't.

Brzezinski broke in. "Mr. President, are you aware that

the number of Cubans in Angola compared to the total population of Angola is larger than the number of Americans who were in Vietnam at the height of our involvement?" "Oh, really, how interesting," replied Nyerere. Carter started folding up his papers. "And, Mr. President," asks Brzezinski," Are you aware that the number of Cubans in Angola compared to the total population of Cuba is very much larger than the number of Americans in Vietnam at the height of our involvement compared to the total population of the United States?"

This time Nyerere didn't say a word. He waved his hand with a condescending smile. Carter grabbed his papers, stood up, and announced "Well, it looks like we really are finished!"

As is obvious, I was personally very fond of Nyerere-- not necessarily a good thing for a diplomat. He was a very remarkable man and, I think, a very constructive element in the peaceful solutions to the problems of Southern Africa that eventually emerged.

Q: What was your impression of Andrew Young? He came out right afterwards. Andrew Young was a well-known civil rights leader but one gets the feeling that he was in a way over his head in the diplomatic world.

Spain: In terms of professional diplomatic knowledge and technique, he might have been. But he was very charismatic, a public leader with vision. Nyerere was very fond of him. So were most of the rest of the African Front Line leaders. They may well have trusted him more than we professional white diplomats. Andy putting his foot in his mouth in New York in the very sophisticated ambience of the UN is one thing. Andy going off and buying Makonde carvings, eating cassava or leading "Happy Birthday To You" for Sam Nujoma was a very real asset. I can't think of anything that he ever did or said in Africa that was negative. I was very fond of Andy. That's how I ended up as his deputy at USUN for a brief period.

While in Tanzania, I was asked by a top Washington official "Is it true that now that Don Easum has retired you are the only Foreign Service officer that Andy Young can stand?." I hedged, saying "You might better ask him." There was a chuckle. "Well, that is not the real question any how. Is it true that you are the only Foreign Service officer that can stand Andy Young?" I said, "I like him." "Good! Go be his deputy in New York."

Q: When did this happen?
Spain: June, 1979.
Q: So, this is your next job?
Spain: It lasted six weeks.
Q: Could you tell the story of what happened?
Spain: I came back and was confirmed by the Senate...
Q: This was a deputy...?
Spain: As Deputy Permanent Representative. Jim Leonard, I think, held the job before me. I asked Andy "What do you want me to do?" "Run this place," was the reply. I am told you are a Middle Eastern type. We need more dialogue with the Arabs. We have to talk to the PLO. We can't do it in Washington, but we can do it here. Get to know the Arabs here at the UN and maybe eventually we can get something started."

I paid a month's rent on an apartment in New York and went back to Tanzania for ten days to pack out. We got all our household effects and airfreight on the way to New York. The night before we were due to leave Carter fired Young. There were frantic calls from Washington. Warren Christopher told me "Look, we don't know who the President is going to choose. Whoever it is, we don't want to present him with a pre-packaged deputy. Can you stay in Dar a while longer?"

I told him that I had said goodbye to the president and the foreign minister. The protocol chief would be waiting at the airport in the morning to see me off. I added that I didn't care whether I went to New York or not, but I really thought I should get out of Tanzania. He said, "OK. But take a while getting home. Take some leave."

We went to Fiji where our daughter was in the Peace Corps and spent a couple of weeks with her. I got another call in Fiji saying that it looked like the President was going to appoint the president of Notre Dame, Father Hertsburg. Would I be willing to be his deputy? I didn't know him from Adam, but it was the same sort of thing with a public figure, so I said yes.

By the time we got home Carter had appointed Don McHenry, previously number three on the USUN staff. He knew infinitely more about the UN than I did. I thought that what was needed now was a political deputy. Don was very nice. He said that as far as he was concerned my appointment held. We mulled it over for a while and I decided that I didn't want to. Looking at a computer run later I found that I was listed as Acting PermRep for a few days between Andy's formal resignation and confirmation of Don's appointment. That was my USUN experience.

Q: Well, then what happened to you?

Spain: Everybody in the hierarchy at the time said, "Don't worry, take your home leave." (We had waived it for the assignment in New York.) The situation was complicated by the fact that my wife had discovered a lump in her breast on the way back from Tanzania. She had a modified mastectomy. After that the doctors were so sure that everything was all right that they didn't recommend radiation or any other additional therapy. While awaiting a medical clearance for her, I spent the better part of a year serving on a promotion board and doing performance reports on FSOs assigned out of the Department.

Then Edith's cancer returned. There was another operation. While we were awaiting the doctors' verdict, Director General Harry Barnes telephoned me to tell me that I had been promoted to Career Minister and to warn me that I could expect a call from the Secretary asking if I wanted to go to Turkey.

I had served twice in Turkey and spoke Turkish. It was the one job in the Foreign Service I really wanted. Harry clearly expected a shout of joy and an instant yes. Instead I asked if I could let him know next week. In a few days after the doctors operation, I came back with another "all clear" verdict. State Med said it would clear her for overseas in sixty days. When the call came I was able to say a happy yes. But, of course, the doctors were wrong again. The cancer appeared again after a few

years and finally killed her. But meanwhile, we were in Turkey.

Q: You served in Turkey from when to when?

Spain: From 1970-72 as consul general in Istanbul; 1972-74 as DCM in Ankara and 1980-81 as ambassador.

....Q: What was the situation when you got to Sri Lanka at the end of 1985?

Spain: The Sinhalese-Tamil conflict had been brewing for some time....By 1985 much of the north and east was out of government control but few yet realized that the country was in a state of civil war....

Q: Were you involved much with UN votes?

Spain: No. Sri Lanka usually voted with the moderate commonwealth. I can't recall a single controversy, unlike Tanzania, with whom we had conflicts on almost every UN issue." – (Ambassador James W. Spain interviewed by Charles Stuart Kennedy, *The Association for Diplomatic Studies and Training (ADST), Foreign Affairs Oral History Project*, 31 October 1995, copyright, 2008 ADST, pp. 29 – 43, 48, 51).

Richard Noyes Viets

Richard N. Viets was the American ambassador to Tanzania from 18 October 1979 to 16 May 1981. In his interview, he covered various subjects about Tanzania including its policies and its main leader, President Nyerere:

"Q: Today is January 14, 1993 and this is continuing the interview with Dick Viets. After Israel you get your first ambassadorial assignment. Could you tell me how this came about?

Viets: Well, one never, of course, knows the full story behind any decision of this nature. But during my posting in Israel I think over forty percent of the time my Ambassador, Sam Lewis, was traveling to or from Washington. And he had a certain amount of regional travel to boot. As we have discussed earlier, this was an intensely active diplomatic period leading up to the Camp David agreement and, following that, all the negotiations related to the Egyptian-Israel peace treaty. This required Sam's physical presence in Washington for a great number of meetings, consultations, etc.

So I was left minding the store for long periods of time and very frequently. Because life did not stop while Sam was away, there were still lots of things going on in Israel and there were high level meetings almost every day of the week with the Prime Minister, the Defense Minister, etc. We had terrible problems up on the Lebanese border at that point with Israeli incursions into Lebanon...sound familiar?...to which President Carter was adamantly opposed. So we were constantly hammering the Israelis to stay on their side of the border.

In consequence I suppose I developed a higher than usual profile for a Chargé in Washington. I can remember indeed getting phone calls from the Department saying that the President has called the Secretary on your meeting with Begin and wants to congratulate you, etc. It was all very heady stuff for a guy who still didn't have a totally white head of hair. I also, of course, during this period got to know Secretary Vance fairly well because he was coming through regularly and I, myself, was going occasionally back to Washington.

The sum of all this being that one's name got to be known fairly well. In 1979 you will recall that we were in the final phase of our negotiation with the British, with the Rhodesians and with the soon-to-be Zimbabwean independent state.

The US was extremely active in this negotiation. In fact, in retrospect, I am not sure that historians have yet really given the credit I think due to the Carter administration, particularly Secretary Vance and his immediate subordinates...people like Chet Crocker and Steve Low, etc...for the extraordinary efforts they made that culminated in this peaceful transfer of power from whites to blacks in what was seen to be one of the more insolvable of the world's standoffs between whites and blacks.

At that time in mid-1979, the so-called front line states in Southern Africa, I think there were five of them ...the organization was chaired by Julius Nyerere, the President of Tanzania, a very remarkable gentleman. Nyerere really towered over the other four heads of state and this organization in many respects was a one man operation. Because of his long association with the independence movements in East Africa and throughout Southern Africa he was highly respected. Nyerere is an intellectual of very considerable dimensions, an extraordinarily articulate person. So the leadership of this group was essentially his without any challenge. He was offering almost daily advise to the Zimbabwean leadership on tactics, strategy, etc. in their negotiations with the British and the Americans and the others involved.

We had a very competent Ambassador named Jim Spain in Tanzania at that time who had been there for about five years. Jim had played a remarkable role in counseling, advising, pressing, pulling Nyerere in an attempt to shape his views, not always successfully. There was a strong view in Washington and I think the Secretary, himself, felt strongly about it, that Nyerere needed a good bit of handling and Jim's time had come to an end. So I was the designated hitter. I think, as far as I know, it was Secretary Vance who decided this. I knew Carter fairly well at that point and he went along with it. So off I went.

Q: Were there any problems with confirmation?

Viets: None. This was almost a pro forma hearing.

Q: You obviously had not been in the area. What were you getting from the Desk, the African Bureau and maybe in the corridors, about Tanzania? Being in the Foreign Service and not in the area, to me the word was out that here is this guy Nyerere who is brilliant, a great speaker, but ruining his country. That he had got caught up in the British left wing social thing and was a disaster. This was the impression I heard. What impression did you go out with?

Viets: Well, I went out with a lot of impressions of that nature. I should say that from the moment I was first alerted that I was selected as Ambassador, while I was still in Israel, I made arrangements with the Department to receive all of the important cable traffic between Washington and Dar es Salaam as well as some of the regional cable traffic relating to the negotiation. I did that to try to get a running start while I was still in Tel Aviv.

There was a second reason for this. Sam Lewis would not let me go from Israel and had a commitment from the Secretary that I would not be released until after a successor had been designated who Sam approved of. There is a rather amusing anecdote behind all that. My first candidate was someone whom Sam Lewis had never met. A gentleman by the name of William Brown with whom I had served in India back in the early sixties.

Bill was a Chinese language specialist, a hydra headed monster. He was both a Chinese language specialist and Russian area specialist...a very rare bird, and an exceptionally capable officer. It seemed to me that Bill had a great many of the qualities that would serve Lewis very well and more importantly the United States government and the Embassy in Israel well. Bill at that point was in Taiwan running that curious organization, whose name I don't even remember, which was in fact...

Q: A liaison office.

Viets: Well, we didn't even call it a liaison office. It was a fancier name. But in effect it was our Embassy. I called Bill on the transpacific telephone from Tel Aviv, tracked him down, and after the pleasantries I told him in three or four sentences why I was calling him. And there was a long pause and then a kind of giggle over the phone and he said, "Dick, do you know where I am taking this phone call?" I said, "No, I don't." He said, "Well, I am lying on a chaise lounge beside one of the most beautiful swimming pools in the world. I am waiting for my Chinese butler to bring me one of the best Chinese meals you will find anywhere in the world, cooked by one of the best Chinese cooks anywhere in the world. I probably will put in at least an hour of work today and the rest of the day I am going to spend reading and perhaps play a little tennis, have a couple of swims. This is the best assignment and the best kept secret assignment in the world. And if you think I am going to trade this to go to Israel and work my butt off, you are absolutely crazy, so get off the line and let me get back to my snooze."

I said, "Well, Bill, we all have moments when we have to do things that we don't like and you are going to come to Israel." "Well, the hell I am. It is nice talking to you Dick and just forget it. There is no way I am going to be moved from this place."

I had by then sold Lewis on the fact that Brown was the man. And Sam Lewis, who is one of the world's greater behind the scenes operators, without Bill Brown knowing what had happened, arranged to have Bill brought back to Washington on consultation at a time when Sam, himself, would be in Washington on consultation. He backed Bill Brown up against the wall and said, "You are coming to Israel." Well, in fact, Bill came to Israel. And, indeed, to finish off the story, Bill served out two or three years as Deputy Chief of Mission, went on to Thailand as Ambassador and a couple of years later returned to Tel Aviv as the US Ambassador to Israel. So I always felt that I made a fairly good choice.

Sam, having got all of this finally lined up, let me depart in September, 1979. I still remember that series of farewells in Tel Aviv. It is probably the only country in the world, of substance, where you can just turn out the entire government to see you off. A lot of that was testimony to my very remarkable wife who had made a great hit in Israel.

In any case, off we went. I do not frankly recall at this point when I got to Dar. It seems that there was a delay in Congressional hearings due to recess or something, but we got there in the Fall.

Q: Before you went out you were going to focus on

413

the area. How did you manage that?

Viets: I realized in my preparation for the assignment that the major focus in preparation should really be in learning everything I could about Julius Nyerere. The historical side of the preparation was fairly easy to do. Tanzanian history is not that complex. I decided that one of the ways to do this was to go around and see every American Ambassador who had ever served in Dar es Salaam.

I did this because I realized firstly, as I just said, that Nyerere was the key to my success, or lack of success, in that assignment and secondly, because as I read Jim Spain's reporting cables back to Washington it became increasingly clear to me that he had developed a remarkably close personal relationship with Nyerere. They had become very, very good friends. As a consequence I think Jim had had a great deal of influence on Nyerere. Nyerere had been trained by the Jesuits as a young man and so had Jim. They were both strong, practicing Catholics. That was an immediate bond.

And they had developed a wonderful game. Every call on Mr. Nyerere, which usually was at Nyerere's seaside house and not at his office...he preferred to do business out on the porch of his house...one or the other would open the conversation with a quotation of some renowned Catholic philosopher or a Biblical quotation and before the end of the conversation the other person was supposed to complete the quotation and identify its genesis.

Well, this had gone on for five years. The bond between these two men was very strong. Obviously I had studied a lot of school boy Latin, but I was not Catholic and I was not steeped in Church history and my memory of biblical quotations, to say nothing of Latin quotations, is pretty thin. I realized if I wasn't going to be able to do that, I had better have some alternative intellectual horsepower that could compensate for it.

And that was the reason why I decided I needed to

414

know more about Julius Nyerere than anybody else on the face of the earth.

And, as I was saying to you earlier, it was the first and last assignment I ever had in the Foreign Service that I did start with a sense of confidence that after a period of settling in I could get on top of the job relatively well. I strongly believe that no Foreign Service officer is worth his salt if, irrespective of his lack of regional knowledge of an area, he can't operate well after an initial start-up period. But for the first time because of Jim's intense and close relationship with Nyerere, who was effectively the key to our influence in East Africa, and more importantly, the key to influencing the Zimbabwean leadership it was important I be able to develop quickly a strong personal relationship with Nyerere.

The last American Ambassador to Tanzania that I saw before departing for Dar was a gentleman who is no longer living, but I think should go nameless because of the nature of the story I am going to tell you. I remember he was posted in Washington at that time in a sort of nonsense job. He was getting ready to retire. I recall walking into his office...he was a great tall, imposing man. He got out of his chair and came around his desk. I introduced myself, we had never met, and sat down.

I candidly told him that for the first time in my life I was starting an assignment with some lack of confidence. I knew that he had also enjoyed a strong relationship with Nyerere and had served there during a very tough period...there had been a kidnapping of some Americans and he was involved in negotiating their release. But I said that the man who had clearly set the standard was Jim Spain and I went into the Latin quotation business, etc.

This gentleman sat there with a grin growing on his face as I went on explaining why I felt so
ill prepared to go down and deal with this great fellow. I finished and he looked at me and he said, "Dick, let me tell you something. Jim Spain and I and all our other

predecessors, all developed the world's greatest relationship with Nyerere. Why? Because it was Nyerere who developed the relationships. He is a very shrewd man and knows that he is going to need to develop a very close relationship with any American who is sent down as chief of mission in that country. You don't need to worry. Nyerere will make sure that a different game is found. You are going to find that you are going to do just as well if not better than any of your predecessors. This is a lot of bull shit that Jim Spain has handled it better than I did or anybody else. So don't think that it won't go well."

And, indeed, I have to say that when I left Dar es Salaam I was absolutely convinced that I had a better relationship with Julius Nyerere than any American Ambassador who had ever set foot in that country!

But, going back to your original question on Nyerere, he was, he is, because he is still living, a most remarkable figure in contemporary African political history. I always said, and others who knew him well I think shared this view, that if Nyerere had been born in Western Europe or the Far East or even in North America, he would have been an exceptional figure in public life. He was a superb politician.

He had an acute brain, the memory of an elephant, intellectual horsepower that was second to none.

He was cunning. He could be warm-hearted one moment and cut you off at the legs at the next if it met his political or personal needs. He had, of course, been the principal political figure behind the Tanzanian independence movement in the 1950s.

He had been the great hope, I think, of the British when they were departing East Africa. Here was the man exceptionally well prepared to take over political power in a country that was endowed with extraordinary resources ...physical resources, a beautiful country...very rich in natural resources. It had an agricultural base at the time of independence that was second to none in East

Africa. A wonderful deep water port, etc. And a stable political environment.

Alas, for a variety of reasons, Nyerere, while he continued to maintain a stable political society...there was none of the Mau Mau type of operation that ever developed in Tanzania...went in the same direction that many other African political leaders did at that point, namely, that government always knew best and everything should be operated by the government, everything should be nationalized, and the people simply weren't ready to conduct their own affairs and the government would always know best. In consequence the economy went into a tailspin and even to this day, 1993, the Tanzanian economy is a vastly poorer economy then it was on the day of independence about 30 years ago.

Part of Nyerere's economic developmental philosophy surely was shaped by the Fabian socialists. Various LSE professors (London School of Economics) used to float in and out of Dar es Salaam offering advice to him. Also, I think he was genuinely convinced that given time his particular formula for the development of Tanzania would turn out to be right. He believed what he first had to do was to educate the population because at the time of independence it was essentially an illiterate society. As I recall, other than three or four doctors there wasn't a Ph.D. in the country. There was still a big British and other expatriate population that ran everything from the water works to the railroad, etc.

Nyerere simply concluded early on that his first moves toward bringing Tanzania into the second half of the 20th century must be (a) to establish a national educational program, which he did; (b) to break up the big estates which had been by foreigners and to divide the land among the peasantry, which he did, and (c) to nationalize all the limited industry in the country so that the profits derived from these organizations would go into the national treasury and not turn up as dividends being

417

repatriated to the tea or coffee market in London or the gold market in Zurich. This he also did.

Alas, as I say, all of these moves turned into an economic disaster primarily because he did not have the trained cadres to run any of these things. Pretty soon the Tanzanian economy developed into a basket case. The international organizations such as the World Bank, IMF, etc. came to Tanzania's rescue. There was one point when Tanzania was getting more international donor assistance per capita then any country in the world, billions of dollars.

Q: By the time you got there in 1979 the structure had shown where it was going. There was no doubt about it. What was the reading you were getting from the people you talked to why Nyerere didn't say, "Gee, maybe this isn't working"? Was he an ideologue or was it a matter of political control? What was our reading for his stubbornness in driving his country to economic disaster?

Viets: You put your finger on the principal reason. He was an enormously stubborn man and he did not want to admit that he had been wrong. But having said that I do remember the last several months of my posting there...I was only there for a year and a half because suddenly the telephone rang and I was told that our masters wanted me to go as Ambassador to Jordan...I do remember the last several months of my posting there...by then I had developed a pretty solid relationship with Nyerere and used to frequently go out to his home and sit on his back porch facing a beautiful Indian Ocean lagoon and swat the mosquitoes away as he sat there in his Gucci loafers and safari suit and talked about the world and Tanzania.

As his confidence and trust grew in this foreign ambassador he would open up more and more about his own views of the way things were going. I began to pick up threads of tacit or implicit admission that he had taken some very bad turns over the years and that things had to

418

be put right. And, indeed, a couple of years after I departed he left office voluntarily. That was already written on the wall. I remember sending cables forecasting he was going to retire. He resigned first from the office of the Presidency, but very shrewdly kept control of the political party apparatus and he kept himself on as chairman of the party.

Perhaps the most influential person around Nyerere was a very interesting, extremely intelligent English lady name Joan Wicken who had gone out to Dar es Salaam as a young woman shortly after independence, or just at the time of independence, and had moved into the YWCA and had volunteered to help in the launching of this new East African state.

She was a gifted writer and Nyerere, who himself remains as far as I know the principal translator of Shakespeare from English into Swahili and one of the most gifted orators I have ever heard in English, and himself a marvelous drafter of the English language, spotted her right away and took her into his inner circle. She remained with him all those years as an inside, very private and confidential advisor.

Joan was a born socialist, not an economist but very well read in economy and she held some very strong views on developmental economics, etc. I think, on looking back, that she had helped, if not shaped his views. Certainly she buttressed many of his own views.

Q: During your time there when the economy was obviously in a shambles were they blaming anybody for it? Was it a capitalist plot?

Viets: By the time I left one clearly had developed enough relationships, not simply with Nyerere, but with others so you could hold very candid conversations in private. It wasn't difficult to get a conversation going in which people were very open in saying that this was a mistake and that was a mistake, there was corruption, etc. Overall I think there was the universal view that for

419

whatever reason, the international markets were rigged against the interests of the third world.

Nyerere constantly hammered at this theme. I can remember listening to him rail hour after hour against the IMF and the prescriptions the IMF was demanding of Tanzania that he argued would send it further into poverty, etc. He would cite how many pounds of tea in 1953 it took to buy a truck and how many tons of tea it took in 1979 to buy a truck.

So there was certainly a sense of while Tanzania had made mistakes, and most people were perfectly prepared to admit that...Nyerere not publicly, but privately...there was also a strong feeling that the first world, Western Europe, Japan and the United States, had very carefully rigged the game so that so-called third world economies would never become competitive, that they would always be at the end of a leash that would be controlled by these major primary commodity markets, at that point raw commodities were all that Tanzania had in terms of exports.

I can't say there was a bitterness about this. It was, as you find so often in societies of that nature, an almost quiescent, benign acceptance of this as fate...we were born in the wrong place at the wrong time.

Q: Trying to get Rhodesia in a situation where the blacks could take over was one of your assignments, but other than that did you feel that you as the ambassador was under any obligation to put the Tanzanians on the right course as we saw it or was it any of our business?

Viets: No, it wasn't all Rhodesian independence. There were three or four principal issues that I got involved in. One was the Rhodesian independence issue and that was my primary focus in the early months.

The second issue was the estranged relationship between Tanzania and Kenya. For economic reasons this was an extremely difficult period for Tanzania because the borders were closed and no commerce was flowing back and forth. Thirdly, we had next door in Uganda the famous Idi Amin. You will recall at one point the Tanzanians sent half the Tanzanian army to get rid of Idi Amin. Julius showed in that venture a little bit of the imperialist in him. He wanted to play the kingmaker in Uganda and poured a lot of Tanzanian treasure into his efforts to dominate the political process and formation of the new political leadership in Uganda.

One of the side benefits to this was the impact on his army which became very accustomed to living very well as armies of occupation always do and they came back to Tanzania to a much poorer economy. One of the immediate repercussions was a sudden spurt in vicious crime, of lawlessness and the society was buffeted seriously. I think to this day the domestic security situation of Tanzania is more dangerous than it was prior to the incursion into Uganda.

Lastly, there were serious political problems in Mozambique, the country to the south of Tanzania. Nyerere was not physically involved in the sense of having an army down there, but politically he was deeply involved in trying to resolve the conflict between Michel, the then leader of Mozambique, and the forces that were financed by South African interests who were trying to destabilize and overthrow Michel.

There was also the Namibia problem in which Nyerere was involved in as president of the front line states. That became increasingly a problem on my plate.

Angola, yes we became involved in that but more peripherally. And always looming over the horizon was South Africa. Nyerere had black South African revolutionary groups training in southern Tanzania and there was financial assistance to them, etc. So in that part of the world there was a fair amount going on.

In addition to all these external problems that the American Ambassador by virtue of being the American

Ambassador constantly became involved in the role of advisor, hand holder, message deliver, and idea generator, we also had a major involvement in the dreadful Tanzanian economy. There was a substantial AID mission in Tanzania. We also had restarted a Peace Corps operation there. It was my lot to wind down the major part of the AID effort primarily because I felt we were simply wasting our money. I told Nyerere so, and told his Finance Minister so, etc. So that did not make me a very popular figure.

Q: Let's deal with various parts of this. How about the Zimbabwe thing? Was there much of a role to play or was it pretty much on course at that time?

Viets: There were just a lot of bumps on the road, but there was no driving over the cliff. In the final months of the negotiations, Nyerere became increasingly helpful and less skeptical of the long term objectives of the Americans and the British. Therefore he was more amenable to influencing his Zimbabwean brothers to take more moderate positions on various aspects of the negotiations. I think by the end we all gave Nyerere pretty solid marks for the role he had played. It was a positive role. It was a beneficial role on the whole. In the earlier part of the negotiations, I think Jim Spain had many more problems to deal with than I did on Rhodesia.

Q: What you haven't mentioned is the role of the British. Had the British sort of blotted their copy book? What was the role of the British Ambassador as opposed to the American Ambassador?

Viets: The British were the senior partner in this negotiation, there is no question of that. But because of that, there were aspects of the negotiations and moments in the negotiations when the Americans were a much more acceptable intermediary than were the British. More trusted, I think. We had no axe to grind.

Q: No constituent pressure.

Viets: We had relatively minor investments there to

protect. But we had no population there that we had to worry about.

It is interesting that the current British Ambassador in Washington was the principal Foreign Office staffer in the negotiation. The British Ambassador in Dar es Salaam, or High Commissioner as he was called because Tanzania was in the Commonwealth at that point, and I worked very closely on this issue. We traded information and very often harmonized our demarches to Nyerere and reported to one another on our conversations and reactions. I would not wish to characterize which of us was the more effective with him. You can go talk to Julius about that.

Q: What about the problems with Kenya, Uganda, and Mozambique? Did we have any particular involvement in these?

Viets: Well, the Kenya thing I really took on as a personal project. I very often got well out ahead of Washington which wasn't very interested in this problem. For the record I don't want to suggest that I was violating any policy, but I sure as hell was making policy in Dar es Salaam and not espousing made-in-Washington policy in my discussions with the Kenyans and occasionally their neighbors over how to resolve all this.

I also was working very closely with the World Bank representatives at that point trying to figure out ways to alleviate tensions between the Kenyans and the Tanzanians. And we made quite a lot of progress. By the time I left the major breakthrough hadn't occurred, but things were pretty well set so that my successor was able to finish it off. Of course, let's not forget that the Kenyans and Tanzanians themselves finally settled things, but they were helped a lot by the Americans.

Q: For somebody in the future looking at this, our role was one of facilitation, sort of an honest broker, because of a lack of major commitment there, but we had a moral commitment there.

Viets: Surely the diplomatic history of the United

423

States, especially in the last 15 years, I think will play that very theme over and over around the world. This is possible because (1) we are what we are...a huge powerful giant of a country with all kinds of resources at our command and (2) I think with some notable exceptions, the quality of the chiefs of mission we had representing us were people who had the intellectual capacity and experience to play this type of role. We were not High Commissioners or Field Marshals. We worked by in large very quietly behind the scenes.

Often few people knew what we were up to, sometimes not even people on our own staffs. Most of us, I think, were able to develop, again not because of our scintillating personalities, but because we represented what we did, most of us were able to develop very close relationships with the head of state and principal advisors and play very influential behind the scenes roles in the countries to which we were accredited.

Unfortunately, the official diplomatic history of the United States probably will not cover all this in the terms I am describing it because many times I know we didn't report all that we were up to.

Q: This, of course, is one of the fun things about being in a place such as Africa. What about the African Bureau? What was your impression? This was not your bailiwick.

Viets: With exception of the Rhodesian negotiations, which was very high on Vance's list of priorities...during the last part of my tenure in Dar, Chester Crocker had come on board as Assistant Secretary. By all odds he was one of the most capable men I ever worked with. So superb leadership came out of the Bureau.

In general, our missions in Africa were staffed by very young, relatively inexperienced diplomats. It was a training ground. I don't know whether it still is, but it certainly was in those days. There were very few, it seemed to me, at least in East Africa, trained, regional

424

specialists. The physical stress and strain on employees and their families was such that people would do a tour in Africa and then usually rotate out into something less damaging to livers and blood streams. There certainly were devoted Africanists, but they couldn't be compared for the most part with the specialists you would find in Asia or Eastern Europe, etc.

I also felt that the competence level was not as high as what I had encountered in other parts of the world. I had the impression the personnel people used Africa as a dumping ground for people who were in the B and C+ category. I don't wish to suggest that all our embassies were filled with B and C+ people. But the average embassy in Africa that I saw, and I saw only a fraction of the total number, never seemed to me to be up to what I had been accustomed to elsewhere in the world. It was my first assignment in Africa below the Sahara Desert. I had been in North Africa early on where we had a highly skilled staff, or so I thought.

Q: Did you find that you were comfortable doing things such as trying to promote connections between Tanzania and Kenya, etc., without over informing the Department? You didn't feel that anybody in Washington would get their nose out of joint?

Viets: Well, the truth of the matter is that I got bored towards the end. When I arrived, as I have said, there was this one burning, diplomatic negotiation going on. So one had quite a lot to do. Secondly, there had been a long hiatus of Chargéship. Spain had left many months before for another assignment. Frankly, the Embassy I inherited was a very sleepy and inefficiently run operation, I thought. Remember I had just come from this big time Israeli experience.

I probably piled into the poor staff in Dar es Salaam with a little more horsepower than needed. But by the time I left I thought we had a pretty sparkling Embassy and I think the Department did too. But I always called that assignment to Tanzania as my sabbatical. I had a couple of times been headed for the War College and Senior Seminar and each time had been diverted off to something else, so this was my year and a half away from the front lines.

Q: Now to the AID business. Obviously the country doesn't like you to yank AID out, but also even more important from an American Ambassador's point of view, AID hates to go out. You are breaking a very large rice bowl in one of the nicer countries to serve in.

Viets: I don't want to get into the details of this even for the historical record, but AID was rather poorly served in Dar es Salaam during the latter part of my tour there, which was when I began to wind things down. So we had two problems. We had very poor leadership, which ultimately ended up in legal difficulty. Secondly, we had a Tanzanian government which was simply wasting American taxpayers' money, in my judgment.

We were involved in a great number of peripheral programs that had grown up over the years and nobody had paid much attention to them and we just kept pouring money and people into them. There were various university contracts that had gone on well beyond the time when they should have been terminated.

It was I think the classic scene in the third world of time to pull things up by the roots and either throw them over the fence and move on to other things or close down. I might add that there were also some legal difficulties that arose between the government of Tanzania and the United States government, namely that the Tanzanians were frequently missing their debt payments and under public law after a certain period disbursement of AID funds has to be frozen. So we had that to contend with as well.

My successor in Dar es Salaam was a political appointee, a young businessman who had been working for an American multinational corporation in Nigeria. He had a lot of business experience and I think he finished off what I started. I understand today, however, we are back

426

giving various types of assistance to Tanzania. But I don't think it is of the magnitude that it was in the sixties and seventies.

Q: I have this very strong impression that so many of these AID projects were matters of bright ideas with very little follow through or else they were not suited for the society but beneficial for the Ambassador, the AID Administrator for living in the country. But the overall effects were either nil or almost pernicious. Did you have this feeling?

Viets: A final point on this. As I earlier stated, the magnetism of Nyerere's personality...and he was an internationally known figure, he wasn't simply a political figurehead in East Africa...he was highly respected outside of Dar es Salaam, especially in Western Europe and particularly in Northern Europe in the Scandinavian countries. He had a lot of supporters in the World Bank, less so in IMF. But he managed over his career to bring into Dar es Salaam several billion dollars in economic assistance.

The United States government bilateral contribution was a fraction of all that. So we, in fact, were quite small time players, at least during my period as Ambassador there, in comparison to the Swedes, the Danes, the Germans, etc.

Q: He had Socialist connections.

Viets: Indeed he did. The point that I want to make was that I will go to my grave gnashing my teeth over a mental picture I have of Swedish, Danish, Norwegian, German aid employees spending every afternoon at the Dar es Salaam Yacht Club sailing their yachts, scuba diving in those beautiful reefs, living lives of considerable wealth and position, lives most of them I doubt could undertake at home.

They were paid enormous salaries, paid much better than their American counterparts, and doing fairly well nothing in my judgment to earn their salaries. It was just a

427

dreadful picture of the worse of the excesses of the donor world.

I think the single most effective aid program that I ever encountered anywhere was in Tanzania and that was conducted by the Dutch. The Dutch knew exactly what they were doing and then got their money's worth. They were very generous in terms of the size and scale of their economy, but then kept a very tight hold on expenditures.

On the other hand, it was a running sore of mismanagement, corruption, incompetence, sloth, indolence on the part, I think, of most other aid representatives.

The Chinese learned their lesson faster than any of the rest of us when they built the famous Tanzam railway in the 1970s between Zambia and Dar es Salaam. They spent hundreds of millions of dollars on this project and before it was finished it was already rusting and deteriorating with bridges washing away, etc.

The Chinese became very disillusioned with the capacity of the Africans to absorb their hard earned assistance in an effective manner.

Q: This was at a time of great tension with the Soviet Union. The Soviets had moved into Afghanistan to prop up a Communist government. The Carter administration had done a tremendous flip flop because they had been betrayed; the Brezhnev Doctrine was in full force, not allowing any Communist country to change its form of government. Africa was considered by many cold warriors to be probably the one open battle field... What was your impression of this during the 1979-81 period?

Viets: The Russians were minor players in Tanzania at least during my period there. They had learned their lesson earlier on, that this was a kind of open ended hole into which you tossed money and got really very little back in return for your investment.

They were, of course, supporting a number of

428

revolutionary groups operating on the periphery of Tanzania. They were active in Mozambique and surely were supporting with arms and funds some of the South African groups...SWAPO was one of their favorite beneficiaries.

But Julius Nyerere had by then I think pretty well concluded that the Soviets were not the best game in town and while he maintained cordial enough relations with them, he didn't spend a great deal of time worrying about enlarging his relationship with the Soviets.

The other Eastern European representatives who were in Dar, and they were all there...remember this is a time when they were essentially taking orders from Moscow...all had small aid programs and all were active. But you had to ask yourself whether their governments realized these were peripheral role operations at best. They probably would have done better to go elsewhere.

The one burning issue which isn't related to the Russians that we haven't mentioned occurred when our hostages were being held in Tehran. I can remember demarche, after demarche, after demarche that I had to make either to Nyerere or to the Foreign Minister for assistance with the Iranians on releasing these hostages.

I remember the last major demarche I made. Nyerere was off in Zanzibar on a political tour and I was instructed to deliver this damn demarche within two hours. I had to hire a plane and fly over there and insist on seeing Nyerere. I interrupted some important discussion he was having with island political leadership to deliver it.

I remember he sort of quizzically looked at me and I recall thinking "Oh God, Washington has once again kind of lost its perspective on the importance of all this."

But he was helpful to a degree. He didn't have any influence with Tehran to speak of, but he did maintain relations with Iran and did send messages once or twice.

Q: At one point when we were issuing our human rights reports and all, Nyerere was called a hypocrite.

Human rights were big during the Carter time and you were there during most of that time.

Viets: I do recall some strain on this issue. In particular there was some discriminatory imprisonment and even torture, I think, of some of the Indian-Pakistani community. As I remember there were several instances when some of Nyerere's own political opposition found themselves in jail and there was some question about mal-treatment, etc.

But on the whole I think the Nyerere regime's record is...in the human rights arena when one is talking about imprisonment and torture, or loaded legal shenanigans against opposition, I think his record is remarkably good. If human rights includes the right to a job, an education, hospitalization, etc., then you have to give him pretty good marks.

Q: How about UN votes? Did you have to trot in and ask for their vote in the UN?

Viets: I did quite a bit of that. In the final months of my tour the Foreign Minister of Tanzania was a gentleman named Salim Salim, who nearly became the Secretary General of the United Nations. I think he would have had it not been for George Bush.

Bush remembered Salim Salim as the Tanzanian delegate who came and danced in front of his chair in the General Assembly the day the Chinese were admitted to the United Nations. And Bush never forgot Mr. Salim Salim. I found Salim Salim, who I think is now Secretary General of the OAU, to be a very, very bright, interesting man whose revolutionary zeal had long since cooled.

But the Tanzanians were always a part of the Third World nonaligned group. This was a period when they didn't break ranks.

One could bring all the rational arguments you wanted to in making a demarche, but I don't ever remember turning more than one or two votes.

Q: What about Zanzibar? What I understand is

that it was really an Arab trading place. Do we still have our station there?

Viets: No. We had closed it down.

Q: At one time we had a satellite station there for our space effort and all.

Viets: We totally closed down there. I think Jim Spain had closed it down. After I left one of my successors was John Shirley. He was a senior USIA career officer who had a great interest in USIA activities. He reopened the USIA installation in Zanzibar.

During my time we had no one there. I used to go over, of course, from time to time to meet with the leadership of the island and press the flesh as it were. It is a fascinating island to visit, but a very sad scene. The clove export market was still a major source of foreign exchange for the Tanzanian government, but the Zanzibar government saw very little of it. It all disappeared on the mainland.

There I think Nyerere has to be judged by history. He treated the Zanzibareans as second class citizens in the Tanzanian Commonwealth, as it were. There was a lot of strain and tension between the two entities and I think it exists to this day.

Q: You are talking about people who have really international trading instincts in the blood.

Viets: Yes, they are very different genes." – (Ambassador Richard N. Viets interviewed by Charles Stuart Kennedy, *The Association for Diplomatic Studies and Training (ADST), Foreign Affairs Oral History Project*, 14 January 1993, copyright, 1998 ADST, pp. 55 – 68).

432

David Charles Miller

David C. Miller was accredited to Tanzania when Nyerere's long tenure as president was coming to end. He served as the American ambassador from 4 November 1981 to 28 February 1984. He had the following to say about the years he spent in Tanzania and about the country's policies and leadership whose embodiment was none other than Nyerere himself:

"**Q: You were talking about Philips Brooks House. What sort of work were you doing there?**
Miller: Philips Brooks House is the largest undergraduate institution at Harvard. It typically has about one out of every four Harvard students involved in it. It is entirely devoted to social service. There is a mental health program, a prison teaching program, a community development program. When I was there we launched a program to start teaching in Tanganyika. Little did I know I would end up going to Tanzania later on....

A White House Fellow friend of mine, Peter Krogh, was dean of the School of Foreign Service at Georgetown. I had always stayed in touch with Peter, and when I was

433

hiring some new employees for Westinghouse, got permission from the corporation to hire some youngsters out of the Georgetown School of Foreign Service. Frankly, I thought the corporation needed some leavening in its electrical engineering pie.

Peter introduced me to a fellow running the master's program at Georgetown's School of Foreign Service, named Chet Crocker. The rest is history. Chet was selected by Secretary George Shultz and the President to become the Assistant Secretary of State for African Affairs. And Chet asked me to become our Ambassador to Tanzania....

Don Easum (the American ambassador to Nigeria) was such a good friend that when the Tanzania opportunity came up, Don was back in the United States and I called him. I said, "Don, I have this opportunity to be an ambassador but I don't want to take it if you think it's wrong. I want to talk to you about a responsible way for a political appointee to behave."

I went up to New York and Don laid out a game plan. It was wonderful. That's how political appointees ought to do it. Don sat down and said, "Are you curtailing the tour of a career officer?" "Nope. It's a normal rotation. A new ambassador is going to go out." "Okay, that's okay." "What skills do you bring to Tanzania? How does Dr. Crocker explain this to the career officers." "Well, we want a political guy next to Nyerere because Nyerere is the leader of the Frontline States with whom we are negotiating to implement UN Resolution 435. We want to get South Africa solved. He's going to have a hard time understanding Reagan. He's going to have a hard time understand Crocker. We want a personal friend of Crocker's out there."

And so we went through this whole checklist. That was the first step toward making my six State Department years very productive. I learned a lot from that embassy in Lagos and I think Don Easum's a giant, as does everybody else who's ever worked with him. That's not an unusual observation.

Q: What happened after Ronald Reagan was elected?

Miller: Chet Crocker was appointed Assistant Secretary of State. He called one day and asked me to meet him at the old hotel across from the State Department, the one next to the Foreign Service Officers club. Over a bowl of chili, he said, "I want you to be an ambassador." You could have knocked me over with a feather. I said, "I'd love to be an ambassador." He said, "I'll tell you where I want you to go. I want you to go to Tanzania because Julius Nyerere is going to be very important to us and he's got to understand us better. I want you to do that." I was thrilled.

Q: You were in Tanzania from when to when?

Miller: '81-'84. Here is the cable announcing my arrival on November 3, 1981.

Q: While you were getting ready to go there, what were you getting from Tanzania from the briefings and your reading and all?

Miller: Little. Here is what happened, which was very difficult for us in the sense that Chet's nomination was put on hold by Senator Helms because Senator Helms wanted Chet to fire a career officer who was the principal deputy in the Africa Bureau at that point, Lannon Walker. Chet would not do that. He would not tell Senator Helms that he was going to name a different Principal Deputy. Over that issue he put a hold on Mr. Crocker's movement toward hearings.

Now, the Miller family had already sold their home in Baltimore on the assumption that it couldn't take more than five months for confirmation. A bad judgment. We ultimately ended up living at the Kenwood Country Club in two rooms. Ambassador Negroponte was also in residence at some time with the same problem. John and his wife and Mollie and I were sitting around at Kenwood waiting to get confirmed. During that time, my wife, a

435

linguist, went to work on Swahili and I sort of went down to the Department every day. I was able to work around the Department for three or four months.

Because Chet's nomination got held up, my nomination got held up. I got to know all the Deputy Assistant Secretaries, the office directors, and the culture of the building. And more importantly, they got to know me. You never know. Political appointees, like career officers, come in all different shades and colors and sizes. Some of them are great; some of them are catastrophic. But political appointees are almost by definition an unknown quantity. So, those three or four months around the building in which people figured out that I was not a jerk and not a crazy ideologue and in fact really liked Africa and had done a lot of work in Africa turned out to be really important.

It was one of the things I've counseled new political appointees to do··· try and spend as much time in the building as you can. The Foreign Service works. These are people that want to make things work. If they don't know who you are, they don't know quite how to react. It's like any other culture. GM is getting a lot of credit for bringing outsiders on to the GM system to try to reform General Motors right now. I'm sure those people are greeted with a lot of skepticism at GM headquarters. Well, your political appointee ambassador has done a lot of things that offend the career FSO and he doesn't really know it. Most importantly, the political appointee has taken a job that could have gone to a career officer.

Most Foreign Service Officers know that there are going to be hundreds of competent career officers who never get to be ambassadors. Being an ambassador is not a be all and end all, but it allows you to get a seat at a nice restaurant. Being a Deputy Assistant Secretary is more important than most ambassadorial tours. But the maitre d' doesn't know that.

So, if you pitch up at Nathan's and say, "I'm a Deputy

Assistant Secretary," the maitre d' is going to say, "Yeah, that and five dollars will get you a good table." Well, if it's Ambassador Miller coming to dinner, that's just so swell. So, you've got to understand that when you're coming into this system, it's better to try to come in and be friends and understand that they're just a little offended by how you got there.

That first three or four months allowed me to make the point that I was less of a jerk than I might have been.

Q: What was Helms after?

Miller: He was after getting Lannon Walker removed from the job as the principal deputy, which Chet was going to do anyway in time, but he was not going to be blackmailed by Senator Helms. Chet brought in Frank Wisner but Dr. Crocker is a real statesman and one of the things about Dr. Crocker is, you do not do things that are ethically or morally wrong. It is wrong for a U.S. senator to use leverage to move a career officer. If the political appointee wants to do that, that's fine. That's up to Dr. Crocker. But it was wrong for Helms to go after Lannon that way and Chet wouldn't have it.

Q: Sometimes these moves are made because a staff member is upset. Did you get a feel for what set this off?

Miller: No. And I went around my own loop with the Helms staff people and clearly his staff people played a very critical role. I do not know what their problems with Lannon were.

Q: What were you getting about Nyerere? Had he peaked by this time?

Miller: No. This was our "problem." I thought it was a real opportunity. He was on his way to the Cancun summit, the only head of government from Africa among the 13 presidents at Cancun. He was the leader of the frontline states in the negotiations over Resolution 435, which was the Namibian independence resolution passed by the UN. In terms of national power at home, he was at

437

quite a peak. Physically, he was old enough to be wise and young enough to be vigorous. He was a great guy to work with. He lived up to every expectation I had.

I can't remember who had served there before me, but this chap said, "You know, there's never been an unsuccessful ambassador in Tanzania." I said, "That's wonderful." This guy said, "Nyerere makes sure that every American ambassador succeeds because he wants to have a dialogue with the United States." I couldn't have been going into a nicer job.

Q: I interviewed somebody who was going there and was worried because he said the ambassador he was replacing had had a Jesuit education and that he and Nyerere used to make quips and all that and the ambassador said, "Don't worry, he'll find a way to beat you."

Miller: Absolutely. He was a biology teacher. He was a Jesuit. He went to the University of Edinburgh in Scotland. He was from upcountry. He had been to Cancun. Julius would find a hook somewhere like all great political leaders. He would look at you and say, 'Hah! This man wants to talk about the NFL games.' Julius was a great man.

Q: How about confirmation?

Miller: It didn't amount to a hill of beans.

Q: When Crocker got in, you got in.

Miller: Yes. You live in terror of confirmation hearings. First of all, it was held on Monday morning at 9:00. If you know the Senate, which I didn't at that time, Monday morning at 9:00⋯ there is not a senator to be found who is awake. Nancy Kassebaum arrives in the hearing room where Ambassador Pickering (going to Nigeria). Ambassador Brown and I were waiting at the table. Nobody had turned the lights on in the Foreign Relations Committee hearing room. There was nobody there.

At 9:00, Senator Kassebaum arrives, sees none of her colleagues, says, "Well, I've been told I can go ahead and have this hearing. I'll learn more if I just ask general questions about Africa. I'm really very interested in Africa. And you can just answer questions that you're interested in." Pickering and I had made the following observation. He had been in Tanzania as a junior officer. I had been in Nigeria. He spoke Swahili. I had worked for four years in Nigeria. Tom and I said, "Hey, we really ought to answer questions on each other's countries. Tom said he would be happy to talk about Tanzania, and I responded that I'd be happy to talk about the Nigerian problem." That was the first time I had met Tom Pickering, but I knew that Tom Pickering was a great player in an instant. The three of us had all of a 45-minute hearing. Nothing occurred. No problem at all.

The second time confirmation came up, regarding the Zimbabwe appointment, I had no hearing at all. Senator Kassebaum called me in to her office in the Senate and said, "Everybody knows you've done a good job. I'm going to circulate your name for approval. We won't even schedule a hearing." That was the sum totals the dreaded confirmation process, allowing me to serve almost six years as an Ambassador.

Q: Today is February 20, 2003. Tanzania 1981. What was the situation in Tanzania as had been described to you and what you had been expecting?

Miller: The descriptions were pretty accurate. Nyerere had been a world leader of the non-aligned movement for a long time. His economic policies were well-known and the impact of his economic policies had been apparent for some period of time. In a nutshell, on the domestic front, Tanzania had succeeded in integrating itself as a political entity. At independence, there was Zanzibar and there was Tanganyika.

But there was also Julius Nyerere's belief that it was important for every citizen of Tanzania to move forward roughly together economically and to integrate themselves socially and that over a period of time his approach to the economic management of Tanzania would produce a more coherent, unified country than, as he was fond of pointing out, Kenya, his next door neighbor, which was our favorite country.

So, domestically, he had succeeded with a single party approach to governing Tanzania and thought that that had worked well for him. Economically it was a mess. It had not succeeded. Ujamaa, this approach to state socialism, had not worked well for him. The United States had been a large AID donor and so I had a large AID account and wrestled with Nyerere about the issues of domestic economic policy.

On the international front, Julius Nyerere had just returned from Cancun, where he had been with President Reagan and 11 other heads of government discussing a range of issues typically described as the north-south dialogue. Nyerere, a man of some humor, said to me when we had our first private meeting in his library in his home, "You know, I've just returned from Cancun. There was only one real ideologue at Cancun." I said, "Yes, let me guess." He said, "It was Ronald Reagan."

That set the tone for three years of discussion about economic ideology and the international community, which I enjoyed immensely. He was a competent, honest, wonderful guy. He was, most importantly from a diplomatic assignment standpoint, chairman of what was then the Frontline States, a group with which we were negotiating to implement UN Resolution 435 to bring independence to Namibia, at that point Southwest Africa. On that issue, Julius and I really did disagree but had any number of candid discussions.

Our approach to 435 was that we had to get the Cubans out of Angola, where they were resident in substantial numbers. We had to convince the South Africans that they would be secure in their own country as apartheid was dismantled. So, we spent a good deal of time working with the Frontline States to try to get the Cubans out of Angola, reduce the threat as the South Africans saw it, which then allowed for elections in Namibia. That worked well. Ultimately, Namibia achieved independence and apartheid came to an end in South Africa. But on the diplomatic front, Julius and I spent a lot of time talking about the tactics and strategies of trying to get Namibian independence.

Q: How did you see Nyerere as a person?

Miller: Wonderful, warm, friendly, smart, honest, brave, humble. He was as great a head of government as Africa has seen as evidenced not by his ability to do the little day to day things of running a country but on the big accounts, the most important being his lifestyle, which remained humble throughout his whole time as head of government. Most remarkable, was his retirement from the presidency at a time when he was perfectly capable of going on physically.

Then, of course, he returned to his village upcountry as one of the few heads of government in Africa who behaved the way George Washington behaved here and said, "We do not need presidents for life in Africa and I don't intend to be one."

Frankly, he was probably happiest when he was back home in Butiama with his wife and grandchildren in a very humble home. It was hard to get to by vehicle. So, for me, he stands out in stark relief to the failed public leadership in Africa that can be found in almost every country.

Q: I've interviewed people who were ambassadors in Rwanda and Burundi and all this somewhat the period you were there. They would get incensed by that the Scandinavians and the United States were lavishing funds on a failed economic system and here we're trying to bring these other countries, which are more with it in American terms··· You're saying the Nyerere charm worked wonders for getting support but when you get right down to it, if your country is an economic

disaster, it's an economic disaster however nice a person you are.

Miller: Well stated.

Q: How did you see it at the time?

Miller: I think that's correct. I don't mind that argument. I think it goes like this. Julius Nyerere because of his global leadership – and this is the thing that you have to remember: nobody in their right mind today can tell you who was president of Burundi or Rwanda 20 years ago – Julius was an international author, an international statesman, and used that effectively as a head of government to gain support for Tanzania well beyond either its objective importance or its internal economic performance. To a great degree, that's what a head of government in a developing country ought to be trying to achieve. Julius achieved that.

Then you say, "Well, did that make any sense for the United States taxpayers to support that," which as a Republican appointee is always my litmus test. The interesting thing about it is that in the world of realpolitik, the answer is yes. Here are the reasons. Zanzibar was a hotbed of extreme Marxist radicalism in the early '60s. You go there today and you can still see East German public housing projects that are appalling. Zanzibar was a real threat. We had very competent officers in Zanzibar, including Frank Carlucci and Tom Pickering.

Q: Most of them seem to get PNGed out of there.

Miller: Yes, In fact, the story of Carlucci's being PNGed is interesting. It occurred during the national day celebrations on Zanzibar when he got on the phone with the Embassy and said, "This is really an important celebration. I want you to send a lot of big guns [some important people from the embassy staff]." That was intercepted and Carlucci was PNGed in short order over English colloquialisms.

When you look at some of the things Julius did, one of them was stopping the radicalism on Zanzibar. Secondly, when somebody had to invade Uganda and get rid of the Idi Amin and his brutal regime, Julius put Tanzanian troops into that battle. Third, when we had refugees coming out of the Hutu-Tutsi disasters which were going on even back then, he volunteered a good piece of Tanzanian territory for the refugees, supported by UN money, but an awful lot of people fleeing from that conflict found refuge in Tanzania.

Then the last thing on the global account is that he put aside a great deal of the country and protected it in national parks. This is really fascinating when you wonder why Julius captured the imagination of so many people. He took large pieces of Tanzania and rather than doing nothing with them, just letting them be overrun by scrub settlements and agriculture that never would have been successful, he turned them into not parks but reserve areas where there were no roads built, where people were not allowed to go in and farm.

The Selous wilderness area, which has been written about in a book called *Sand Rivers*, is a marvelous example of Julius saying, "Tanzania has an international trust. Even though we're poor, I intend to live up to that."

The long and short of it is that those of us who were in the aid donor business kept trying to get Julius to add two and two and get four. He would always add two and two and get some other number. For example, when you got down to privatizing game lodges, the service at game lodges was poor in Tanzania. The service at game lodges in Kenya was good. Hence, Kenya got more tourists than Tanzania.

So, Julius proudly announced one day that he was going to privatize some of the major game lodges. I said, "Well, Sir, I have a simple question for you. Will the workers be allowed to accept tips?" He said, "Oh, absolutely not. That would fly in the face of the socialist principle that people should be treated equally." I said, "But, Sir, in a service economy, people get tips because

443

they perform well for the people they're taking care of."
He was not able to deal with that.

So, did the economy ever work perfectly? No. Did it achieve what he wanted? Yes, it did. It produced a level economic base that is now producing a solid Tanzanian economy without the disasters that befell Kenya. If Julius were here today sitting with us, he would say, "I told you, David. Kenya turned into a corrupt mud hole. Tanzania is now slowly taking off the ground with responsible leadership in a country that's socially unified." I'm happy to make that argument for him.

Q: The Germans and then the British had a fairly good coffee or tea –

Miller: You have coffee up on the slopes of Kilimanjaro.

Q: How was this going when you were there?

Miller: Poorly. Almost everything was going poorly. Everything was going poorly because of the following issue, Julius Nyerere gave a great speech in which he enunciated the principles of Ujamaa, a Swahili word for "shared ownership." Julius argued that the state should own and operate the "commanding heights of the economy." That was the phrase from that speech.

It was my argument to Julius that the Chama Cha Mapinduzi, the CCM, his party, had taken the doctrine of Ujamaa and moved economic control from the commanding heights of the economy down to the level of the local bus companies, which didn't work because government parties shouldn't be running bus companies.

Julius and I spent a lot of time on the realities of implementing a program that ended up crippling things like the coffee and tea industries or the sisal industry or the cashew industry or any of a number of things because he took socialism down from "Let the government run the ports. Let the government run the rail lines." To the sad state of – "Let the government replace individual entrepreneurship and run smaller things."

444

Q: Could you talk a bit about Joan Wicken? I've heard that Fabian socialism was far more disastrous to Africa than Marxism. Could you talk about Nyerere's background, Joan Wicken, and the coterie around him?

Miller: Julius was a biologist and was a biology teacher after graduating from the University of Edinburgh in Scotland. I don't know exactly where Julius ran into Joan Wicken, but Joan was clearly out of the London School of Economics Fabian socialism group and was with Julius forever throughout his tenure as president.

In fact, Joan is still alive in England and we still trade cards at Christmas and so on.

There were other people like Joan, but Joan was the kindest Rasputin you've ever seen. The thing that was remarkable about Joan was that she, like Julius, lived the life that she espoused. Joan lived at the Salvation Army camp in Dar es Salaam. She lived in what was hardly even a private home, in a very small room or two in the Salvation Army camp, something the size of the office we're sitting in today.

Unlike many ambassadors, I decided that Joan was important and interesting. I saw no reason to ignore Joan and I asked if I might pay a courtesy call on her Salvation Army camp, which I did. I think Joan found it pretty strange to see the American official car with a flag on the fender.

My wife, Mollie and Joan and I became good friends. Joan and Mollie continue to exchange notes up to today. Joan was clearly, by my sense, 30 years out of date economically and was the ideological backbone to a lot of Julius' economic ideas.

The reason that I came to admire Joan personally, and enjoyed working with her is that she lived her principles. The problem that I've always had with a lot of socialists was the staggering hypocrisy of their lives...presuming that they should live well but that other people should live

445

nobly motivated by something other than greed.

So as I can tell, Joan was never motivated by greed in her whole life. So, when you discussed ideas with her, you at least knew that she was doing what she believed in and I thought that was good. Her ideas were wrong. They were poor for Tanzania. But as a human being, she did what she thought was right, which is better than most people do in their lives.

Q: Did you find an influx of Fabian types from Scandinavia and from the SPD?

Miller: Sure. We had odd people that would arrive from the London School of Economics that you thought really came from Mars and not from the LSE. But this was their hope, their dream, that Tanzania was going to work, that socialism was indeed the ideology that was closest to African traditional concepts of the common ownership of land, of consensus decision making, and many of them thought that with Nyerere they had a president of a country that would make socialism as they dreamed of it work. It obviously didn't...but they tried.

Q: How about the Swedish influence?

Miller: There was a lot of Swedish influence, a very competent Swedish ambassador. Probably the best ambassador was a Dutch ambassador. They both had a very large aid program, as did all the Scandinavians, as did Canada, as did the United States. We were all involved in trying to figure out how to introduce a little bit more rationality in the economy.

It was an outstanding diplomatic world simply because of Nyerere's presence and who he was and the importance of having Julius' support when he was head of the Non-Aligned Movement, of having Julius' support when he was running the Frontline States. When Julius Nyerere spoke or traveled, people listened to him. So, countries that were playing in that environment wanted to have a good mission in Dar es Salaam.

Q: You came out of a business background, a

446

Republican   background,   under   a   Reagan administration –

Miller: And I was ideologically motivated.

Q: This was early Reagan.

Miller: How did it feel to be a Republican ideologue in King Arthur's court?

Q: Yes.

Miller: I loved it. One of the most interesting experiences was greeting a small Senatorial delegation. The group included Paul Laxalt, who was very close to President Reagan and clearly an ideologue and Mark Hatfield, not as close to Reagan and clearly not so much an ideologue. Senator Laxalt, knowing I was a Republican appointee in Tanzania, got me in the library of the residence and said, "What are you doing here?" I said, "I'm having a wonderful time." He said, "Why would you want to come here?" I said, "Because this is where we ought to be."

Let me make some sense out of that. I think that market economies work. I deeply believe that. In general, governments fail. One of the key reasons that we beat the Soviet Union was simply that a greater percentage of their economy was in the government and a lesser percentage of ours was in a government. Recognizing that there are some functions that only a government can perform, in general the governments don't do many things efficiently.

But in general the more of your economy that is managed in the public sector the less rational economic management you have. I was having the time of my life in the sense of being an economics major at college and spending a lot of time in the private sector. I had an opportunity to work with one of the brightest socialists that the world had seen.

He was running a country. I had an opportunity to spend a lot of time talking with him in his library about things that worked and things that didn't work. We really enjoyed each other's company. We would frequently end

447

up with him saying, "But you care so much about people, how could you be in the Republican Party?" I'd say, "Because it works."

Q: Did he seem to understand American politics?

Miller: Yes. He was a political master and clearly wanted to get his messages back to the administration. Although he didn't know it, he took the advice of the 29ᵗʰ Commandant of the Marine Corps, Al Gray, one of whose rules in life is "don't make any more enemies than you already have." Julius Nyerere knew that he didn't want the United States for any kind of an enemy.

He just disagreed with President Reagan. He understood that heads of government would disagree. So we had a remarkably civilized dialogue through the veto of his candidate to be the Secretary General of the UN, though awkward times. We got along just fine.

Q: Let's talk about the veto of his candidate. Who was that?

Miller: Salim Salim. That was really very difficult. It was a very difficult and poorly managed situation. As I was going to post, it came time for the African countries to get to nominate for the first time an African candidate to be Secretary General of the UN. They picked Salim Salim, who had been Tanzania's Ambassador to the UN. He had been Zanzibar's first Ambassador to the UN when they were independent. A remarkable man, became an ambassador at the age of 28. He had gone on to become foreign minister of Tanzania and was their nominee to be Secretary General, supported by the African group of countries.

As I was going to post, Secretary of State, Alexander Haig whispered in my ear that, "oh, by the way, we were going to veto the Salim Salim candidacy." I knew that that was really going to make my opening weeks, months, or years in Tanzania very difficult.

The veto occurred as I was en route to post. I arrived to present my letters of credence to a head of government whose foreign minister's public career had just gone down in flames before the world. We had just embarrassed the Organization of African Unity that was supporting Salim Salim. In general, we had made a complete diplomatic mess out of an issue where any reasonable diplomatic management would have come up with a different approach. As I went in to present my letters to President Nyerere, I said, "I hope this is a cordial meeting" because this was literally two or three weeks after this debacle and Nyerere had agreed to withdraw Salim's candidacy. It was just a terrible mess.

Q: Did you see this as the heavy hand of Jean Kirkpatrick?

Miller: It was alleged to be the heavy hand of George Herbert Walker Bush, who was alleged to have become quite annoyed when (Mainland) China finally gained admission to the UN General Assembly.

Salim Salim was alleged to have danced in the aisles··· and it certainly looked like that in the photographic records of the event. Salim ultimately said he really didn't mean to dance in the aisles. He was going up and down shaking hands with the delegates who had supported the admission of China.

Those who have reviewed the videotape say he was dancing. Those of us who know Africans well thought he was engaging in a "victory walk..." going up and down the aisle shaking hands. It probably looked like a dance to the average Caucasian. To the average African, it probably looked like an exuberant walk. That said, there was no instant replay and George Herbert Walker Bush did not like Salim Salim and that was the end of it.

That was the first time I came to understand what a fine man Nyerere was. I was young. I was inexperienced and could have easily spent a miserable time in Tanzania and been knocked off base by Nyerere. In the presentation of credentials we had a wonderful, long conversation about a ton of interesting issues, quite a substantive conversation which was out of character for the initial meeting.

He obviously knew that I liked Africa a lot and we had a wonderful time. He did not bring up the Salim nomination nor did I. I left his office that day unscathed.

But about three days later, a call came in requesting me come out to his beach residence and see him in the library, which is where he had all serious conversation. I looked at my DCM, David Fischer, and said, "Gosh, isn't this great? I'm getting to go out to Nyerere's home and chat in the library." David said, "I'm willing to bet you a year's pay that what you're going to hear about is Salim Salim." Of course, I did.

Nyerere's take on it was that it had been horribly managed by the United States. He said, "Here we had an African candidate we all liked. If you had in any way signaled to us that Salim would not be acceptable, we would have found another candidate. We desperately wanted to have an African running the General Assembly." As it turned out that time, an African was not picked. We did not have a black African until we had Kofi Annan today.

Boutros Ghali qualifies as an outstanding Egyptian. Kofi Annan has proved to be a tremendous Secretary General.

There is an argument that Salim Salim would have proved to be a very effective Secretary General, but that was not to be. Nyerere was very upset that he had been embarrassed, that Salim had been embarrassed, that the OAU had been embarrassed needlessly by the incompetent diplomatic management of this account by the United States. I heard that in no uncertain terms.

It's not that Julius was ever rude. Julius would not have been rude to somebody with a gun at his head. But you knew that among gentlemen, Julius was upset. And yet once that was done, that was it. This issue never stood between our friendship.

The performance by Salim Salim was equally

450

remarkable when he returned as Foreign Minister. I figured that perhaps he wouldn't be as gracious as Nyerere had been. It turned out that he was. He said that he knew clearly that I had not been involved in arguing for a veto of his candidacy, that he looked forward to working with me, and that he learned as a young man that public life was like this, that he thought he would have made a good Secretary General but it was not to be. Very much like Julius, he set about to help me, which I thought was fascinating.

You have to remember what I looked like. I was 39. I had no previous diplomatic experience. I could have either been a terrible failure and embarrassed my country and myself or I could have been helpful to the people I was working with. For example, Salim Salim said to me, "You know, David, that you can hand write me a note and that's not viewed as an official transmission. If you wish to communicate with me on some issues that are troublesome but you don't want to come down and leave me with a typed message, feel free to write me a handwritten note and neither one of us will treat that as an official communication. Furthermore, my home is not far from here. Given the importance of the U.S., if you need to see me at home and you don't want people here to know, I'll have you and Mollie over to dinner very quickly. I want you to know my wife. If you need to see me, come knock on the door at home and tell them you want to come see me."

We developed a great relationship. Another example involved the air conditioner in his office. The air conditioner in his office didn't work...and it was made by an American manufacturer. We had similar air conditioners in the mission. I said, "You know, Sir, I can fix your air conditioner." He said, "Yes, and it would probably broadcast all the way to Zanzibar." I said, "Well, you'd have to take it apart to find the transmitter." He said, "Yes, but it's so hot in here I'm going to take the chance."

451

So, we got along fine. We laughed about everything in the world. Of course, he went on to head the OAU. I've seen him recently in meetings. We get along great.

Q: Speaking of this, I've talked to other people who served as ambassadors to Tanzania and Nyerere would consult with the Americans. They would have this relationship. Since Nyerere was off on almost a different track on the socialist non-aligned, why was he giving so much time to the Americans?

Miller: He wanted us to represent him effectively in Washington, which we all did. He had a position on the world that's like Pat Moynihan...he was first and foremost an intellectual and an ideologue.

Pat was accidentally a senator, a White House staffer, a professor at Harvard. Pat could have sat in a cornfield in Iowa and talked to people about the world and it would have been wonderful.

Julius Nyerere was an intellect. He wanted to talk to people about his ideas and what worked and didn't work. The American ambassador was somebody that could act as an amplifier for his views and a contributor to new ideas. So, as somebody said to me when I had not gotten to post, I was, of course, worried about getting along with the president of Tanzania, they said, "Are you kidding? Nyerere will find some way to relate to you. He finds a way to relate to everybody. He loves talking to American ambassadors." That proved to be the case. And he did it because it was fun. He wanted us to know that he thought in the long run his system was going to be okay.

Q: You said your DCM was David Fischer. Did he or anybody else when you would come back from these meetings with Nyerere say, "Okay, let's get out of the clouds?" Did you find that anybody on your staff was concerned about the Nyerere charm?

Miller: No. One, because everybody had been charmed. Two, because while half of the messages were transmittable, half of the exchanges were simply an intellectual dialogue. So, when you'd get that, you'd simply sit down with the DCM or the political officer or the station chief and say, "Hey, Julius is really interested in x, y, and z today. Didn't say anything worth sending back to Washington."

There were some times he just wanted to talk. The best illustration of Julius as an intellectual partner involved organic agriculture and Rodale Farm and Press in Emmaus, Pennsylvania.

Bob Rodale and his family were the pioneers in organic agriculture in the United States. Before we went to post, my dear wife, Mollie, who has been very active in studying organic farming and sustainable agriculture, drove us up to Emmaus, Pennsylvania, and we bought what must have been 50 books from the Rodale library. We shipped all those books over to Tanzania.

When we got there and my wife got to know the president, she concluded that he would enjoy some of these books because he was a biologist and he cared about agriculture. So, she sent him a few of the books on sustainable agriculture. That resulted in a meeting about two weeks after that in which my AID director was called out to the library at Julius' house and the president said to him, "See these books on organic agriculture? They come from Mrs. Miller. Why aren't you doing that here in the country?"

Well, my AID director was appalled, stunned, upset, and off the roof because he was a fairly traditional AID program manager. He got me on the phone and said, "What's your wife doing?" I said, "She's exchanging ideas with her friend, Julius Nyerere." He said, "This is outrageous. He's telling me I'm supposed to get out of dry land farming with these giant tractors. He wants to do sustainable organic agriculture." He was quite upset. But I said to Mollie, "I tell you what. You go out and see the president." So, she went out to see the president. He said, "I want to have Bob Rodale come to Tanzania and talk

453

about sustainable agriculture at the Morogoro Agricultural College."

The first result was that our AID mission sort of announced that they would boycott that whole thing. Then Mollie talked to Bob Rodale and he said, "Of course I'll come out to Tanzania." Julius Nyerere then opined to me in a moment of truth, "Organic farming is no different than what the Africans have done for the last 3,000 years. In the last 20 years, all of your AID missions have been here telling us that we have to use these giant tractors and all this fertilizer. We can neither afford the fertilizer nor the tractors. But we clearly can use animal manure, bring it in, use it for compost, collect and keep the animals. But most importantly, if I got up and said that my citizens would think that I was going backwards and that this was not a world-class approach to agriculture. But if Mr. Rodale comes here and we have a big seminar, then my citizens will think that the United States thinks that organic farming is a good idea and that's why we're having Mr. Rodale."

I said, "That's really good."

We literally had this wonderful program at this agricultural college. It was just terrific. Bob Rodale came out, talked about organic farming, and organized a lot of test plots. I have not a clue what the long-run impact has been, but he had the Chama Cha Mapinduzi, all the district people came in to learn about this, were sent back out to talk to people to say, "This is a responsible way to farm."

Because of my wife's involvement and the involvement of a minister in Tanzania named Gertrude Mongela, we raised a number of interesting issues. For example, the length of the handles of farm instruments. The AID programs were all run by men and administered by men and the implements were designed by men, but as you know, in Africa, the people that do the farming are the women.

So my wife and Gertrude Mongela were going through

454

the agenda for the meeting and they looked at all these implements and said, "Here we go again. We're getting hoes that have 5-foot handles and that's all wrong. They should be shorter and easier for the women to use."

So, not only did we get into organic farming but we got into the fact that women ought to be involved in the design of agricultural implements and guys ought to stop buying instruments that were good for them for the two hours that they hoed as a test before they sent 10,000 hoes out to the countryside, all but one of which would have been used by an African woman. It was a wonderful thing.

Q: Let's go on to foreign policy. Before we get on to African policy, the period you were there was the height of our engagement in Central America, which was arousing the wrath of all the left around the world. This was on the Sandinistas in Nicaragua, the civil war in El Salvador. How did that play with Nyerere in Tanzania?

Miller: Not as much as you might think. It played more with Robert Mugabe in Zimbabwe, as I was to learn during my tour in Harare. Nyerere in some ways was Afrocentric. While he had been very active in the non-aligned movement and made a lot of pronouncements about north-south inequality and so on, he understood that his political capital was nowhere near as valuable outside of Africa as it was inside Africa. So, we really did not spend much time on issues outside of Africa.

Robert Mugabe, in contrast, was quite upset about our Central American policy.

Julius was very upset that we saw the Cubans in Angola as a greater threat more than our support for Jonas Savimbi. Julius did not believe that the whites in South Africa really perceived that Samora Machel in Mozambique, and the Angolans, led by Dos Santos and so on, would be such a threat that we couldn't unwind apartheid until we convinced the Afrikaaners that they weren't going to be overwhelmed by this group of African

455

Marxists on their border. So, the ideological dialogue about Marxism, non-Marxism, Cubans, non-Cubans, etc., occurred very much in the context of southern Africa.

Q: You had spent Ph.D. time and business time··· You had been involved with Africa for some time. What about the Reagan administration coming in and talking about constructive engagement? Did you see this as being something constructive or did you feel that this was an excuse for supporting the white government?

Miller: Oh, heavens no. I wouldn't have supported an apartheid government. And neither would Dr. Crocker. The concept was that you could not beat the Afrikaaners out of the rat hole into which they had crawled. Rather, you had to induce the Afrikaaners into the sunlight, and I think that proved to be correct. They are quite independent, difficult, strong-minded people. That's how they survived and prospered.

Dr. Crocker was a remarkable statesman who will never get the kind of credit that Nelson Mandela will for bringing about the end of apartheid in South Africa with no bloodshed. But Chet understood that with luck he would have an 8-year run with George Shultz to unwind the problems in Southern Africa with a minimum of violence. That was achieved. That was quite remarkable.

The fundamental construct was that at the time that Dr. Crocker took over the account, there were a very substantial number of Cuban troops in Angola, perhaps something in the range of 20,000 Cubans. And Samora Machel in Mozambique, on the other side of South Africa, was clearly a socialist. While there weren't as many armed troops in Mozambique there were an awful lot of intel types from East Germany and so on.

When you were a white South African and who had been fed a dose of "the ANC is a communist front" and the communist side of the ANC, the African National Congress, was run by Joe Slovo, a white South African, and you got to be very, very defensive. And that led to a defense of racial supremacy as the only way to defend yourself.

The only way to get the South Africans to release, to give up, control over the military in their country would be to say, "We will make your neighborhood benign. We are going to set out to make it so that you can worry about your internal problems" and that's what we did.

So, I thought that Constructive Engagement worked quite well. I was opposed to economic sanctions on South Africa. I think that was a bad decision. But you had to have been deeply involved in the issue to understand that. I had already been talking with the young Nationalist Party politicians about the fact that apartheid was going to come to an end because young whites in South Africa saw the world changing. So, you knew apartheid was coming to an end, but a patient approach was hard to defend. It was very hard to defend the orderly demise of something that is on the face of it a moral disaster of many, many years.

Yet to produce a functioning society at the other end without violence, without a lot of deaths, with a functioning economy which would allow the ANC to come in and take over a very advanced country, took tremendous intellectual stamina and courage.

Crocker's children were picketed at Sidwell Friends. He was, of course, described as being some horrible racist. This is a man who has devoted his entire life into working on African issues, still does. He knew that the way to end apartheid without violence was to create the right stage, which he did. It took a lot of patience.

Q: Were you the carrier of messages? Were we asking things of Nyerere?

Miller: Sure.

Q: What sort of things?

Miller: The messages were all around the basic theme. The message never changed much. Dos Santos is a frontline mate of yours and Machel is a frontline mate of yours and so on. As long as Dos Santos has 20,000 combat trained Cubans in Angola, we're going to have a hard time getting the South Africans to implement Resolution 435.

The obvious dialogue that went on for years was, of course, Julius would reply that if you got Savimbi to do less, then you could have fewer Cubans.

Savimbi was a very hard account to manage.

Sam Nujoma, who came out of the bush to become Namibia's first president, also made a lot of pronouncements that weren't very helpful when you were trying to convince everybody here in Washington that Sam would be a good president, which he has largely become. Sam Nujoma has been a very responsible president.

But back to the question, "What were you doing with Julius?"

You were trying to get these messages across to Julius. For example, you would show Julius examples of satellite photography of Angola. And then point out that the overhead photography keeps turning up baseball diamonds all over Angola. We know that they're Cubans playing baseball. And the South Africans are going to know they're Cubans playing baseball. They're going to continue to send their troops illegally through Namibian territory into Angola. We're going to continue to have a war. We're going to continue to slaughter each other. We have a policy that will lead to this ending," which we did.

So, your basic message with Julius was to get your points across and listen to Julius saying, "If Savimbi keeps doing blank, there's a problem. If the South Africans keep sending covert raids into Dar es Salaam, you are going to have a problem." We had covert South African activities running around in the region. That was bad. You were trying to get these two sides to disengage and trust each other.

Q: Did the white South African government have any representation in Dar es Salaam?

Miller: The first time I really saw an official was in

Harare. They had a trade office in Harare. In Dar I don't think they had anybody official. But everybody was trying to do what we should be trying to do on the Iraq account today and that is, to defuse a situation.

The problem in Southern Africa was like almost all others in the world. If you listen long enough, you will find some common room to move the ball forward, hence Dr. Crocker's term Constructive Engagement. So I basically sat there and said, "If we in the United States are helpful and if the frontline states are helpful and if the South Africans are helpful, we can unwind this thing without a disaster." That was my job and that's what happened.

Q: How did you react to the resignation under pressure of Alexander Haig and the arrival of George Shultz? What was your feeling and that of the embassy?

Miller: It made little or no difference. Frankly, the only thing that made any difference to me was that George Shultz and Chet Crocker were then and are now best of friends. Secretary Shultz gave Dr. Crocker all the backing in the world for the whole run. That was important to us that we had a Secretary who understood what we were trying to do and stuck with it throughout all the political difficulties in the United States. He understood where we were going. We had bad times in the United States politically and good times in the United States politically.

Q: Did you find statements in Congress? Were they for the most part helpful or unhelpful? Were you trying to put out fires?

Miller: No.

Q: I think Nyerere was sophisticated enough to understand the players in Washington.

Miller: Sure. We had no flaps whatsoever. It just was not like Zimbabwe. We really just had no difficulties at all.

Q: How about the Black Caucus in Congress? Did they appear at all?

Miller: No, not much. The thing to remember is, I have a very strange history. John Lewis and I started working together when John was not too long out of SNCC and I was living in Bedford Stuyvesant. I had some credibility with black congressmen from the outset.

Q: John Lewis being what?

Miller: The now Congressman Lewis, but at one point head of the Student Non-Violence Coordinating Committee before he lost out to Stokley Carmichael, who came into SNCC with a much more violent approach. I still see John today. I hired John at Westinghouse as a consultant in 1972. As soon as I got there, I was asked to work on the issues of race relations in Westinghouse.

So I called John and said, "We've got a lot of problems with black and white folks in Westinghouse. Do you think you can come up and lend us a hand?" That is one of the things that has allowed me to be as direct and candid as I have working with Africa. The little house in Bedford-Stuyvesant that gave me the background to work with both blacks and whites··· and of course many senior black leaders knew of my background.

Q: Was there any racial feeling in Nyerere or his government or his country?

Miller: I don't think so. As some of my friends will tell you, I'm probably as oblivious to some things as anybody you'll ever meet. Somebody has to work pretty hard to convince me that there are racists before I go looking for it. I've always felt that if you reached out to people and presumed they were decent, that seems to induce decent behavior on the part of many people.

I never had any racial problems in Tanzania.

Clearly when we got down to Zimbabwe there were problems of race. There had been a war in Zimbabwe between blacks and whites. There was still some tension there. I had only one black officer. I went back to the Department and said, "It would be a little helpful to me if I could get another black officer." I had one black guy, Jim

Spit, who was a colonel in the Army. In one meeting when we were discussing racial tensions, Jim piped up and said, "I don't have any problem getting along with people here." I said, "I think there's a message here, folks." This is a country in which race was important. This was six years after a black-white war. But in Tanzania, there had been few whites even during the colonial period.

Q: How did you find the role of women?

Miller: For an African society, it was quite progressive. The CCM had a lot of women in positions of leadership. In that sense, it was better than "average." In general, women in Africa are not treated as well as any American would expect they should be. I've never quite understood that, but that's certainly the way it is. In those days, we really did not have any programs targeted to that issue, leaving out things like maternal and child health care, which was obvious then and is obvious today. You have a terrible infant mortality rate that you're wrestling with and you lose way too many mothers in childbirth.

Q: What was home life, social life, for you all?

Miller: It was our first diplomatic post. There was a period of time in which it was exciting, odd, and different to be entertaining officially for the United States. That was fun. My wife worked very, very hard at that at that assignment...and its importance should not be underestimated.

Before going out to post, she found both books on protocol. There were only two books on protocol in the world. There is the United States book and there's a British book. She bought those. Going to cooking classes and just making sure that we did everything right. That was fun for a period of time. After a while, as you know, it becomes a little tiresome. For the family, they had been in Nigeria for four years and so to the kids it was another international school in Dar es Salaam which was not a particularly good school.

But the Embassy obviously brought a lot of extra

461

excitement. It was fun for them to have the Marines around. It was fun for them to go to the Marine Ball as little kids. It was fun for them when they got old enough to try to run some of the physical fitness tests, some of the PFT stuff, for the kids. I think that was probably the most enjoyable time for the family because everything was new and exciting and different. Frankly, by the time we got to the last year in Zimbabwe, we had done enough entertaining and enough dinners and we had had enough of dealing with the house staff issues.

Q: How did the island of Zanzibar play?

Miller: Not a lot. Zanzibar in my mind loomed two or three different ways. We started our initial Peace Corps program in Zanzibar. When I got to post they were coming back our direction so we were reaching out to them again. We had a home in Zanzibar, so we'd get out there and work. Zanzibar was the home of the first U.S. diplomatic mission to East Africa, with our first officer arriving in something like 1822. Some poor chap from Boston sat out there pretty far from home.

Q: He ended up as a deckhand. He set up his treaty with Muscat to include Zanzibar.

Miller: That's right. We had some of the Gulf fiefdom principalities working on Zanzibar. We had an old, old building in the old part of Zanzibar which amazingly enough, we managed to lease for our AID program in Zanzibar. So, we had the same building that the chap pitched up in 1822 or 1823.

But there was a Peace Corps program that was important to us. There was a malaria eradication program that we were sponsoring. We worked a lot on trying to get the incidence of malaria down.

Then we had political leadership of Zanzibar that was a little bit different than the political leadership of Tanzania, not at the government level but at the working level. So, you wanted to get out there and look at textile factories and other economic development programs. For example,

462

tourism, a terrific opportunity that they should have been hitting the ball out of the park on and they were doing nothing, a small national park that should have been attractive that was not.

The Zanzibaris would want you to come out and say, "Why don't we get more of your aid money? Why don't we see more of you? Why don't you have officers stationed out here permanently? Why don't you speak Swahili better? This is our native tongue."

That was about the whole account other than the fact that I found out that as a former Westinghouse employee the archives of Zanzibar were collapsing – literally, the paper – because all the air conditioners had broken and they were all Westinghouse. It was the first time I sent a rocket back to Pittsburgh corporate headquarters in the diplomatic post saying, "Equipment is broken. Please send replacements."

So my old boss, Tom Murrin called and said, "What are you talking about?" I said, "Tom, all the air conditioners are stopped. The Zanzibar archives are falling apart." He said, "What do you need?" Westinghouse shipped out air conditioners. They stood up to the plate and hit the ball.

Q: Did the neighboring countries play much of a role? Was there any Hutu-Tutsi problem or Uganda or Kenya?

Miller: Tanzania had closed the border with Kenya for a while. We had tensions between Presidents Moi and Nyerere. When I crossed the border, frequently there were only diplomats crossing the border. A lot of smuggling was going on. It was just a tense time. The two countries were not getting along. I can't even recall all the issues.

The things that were sticking in people's craws at the time were an unfair allocation of tourist revenues, the smuggling of goods from one country to another and not paying duties on them. Those were the larger issues. It was classic. It was unproductive for both countries and it got resolved.

It did acquaint me with one of the most ingenious programs of smuggling I have ever heard of. That is, in Arusha, there was an American company that had a very small tire plant, a plant of which the Tanzanians were very proud. Kenya had a shortage of tires. The group that crossed the border up there were Masai, but if you were caught smuggling tires it was a problem. So, the Masai tied the tires onto their animals and they turned their animals loose on one side of the border and the animals generally wandered across to the other side of the border, where the Masai collected the tires from their cattle. If the animals were caught, it wasn't anybody's fault. It was quite an ingenious scheme. I was very impressed with the Masai.

Q: How about Uganda?

Miller: Things were okay. There was some violence up there. Things still were not perfect. We sent some of the Marines up there to augment the Marine security guard detachment in Kampala. But we didn't do a lot of regional stuff in general.

Q: You left there when?

Miller: Sometime in '84. I went down to Zimbabwe.

Q: You were in Zimbabwe from when to when?

Miller: I think 1984 to 1986." – (Ambassador David C. Miller interviewed by Charles Stuart Kennedy, *The Association for Diplomatic Studies and Training (ADST), Foreign Affairs Oral History Project*, 6 January 2003, and 20 February 2003, copyright, 2004 ADST, pp. 11, 37, 41 – 42, 45 – 62).

John William Shirley

John W. Shirley served as the United States ambassador to
Tanzania from 28 July 1984 to 18 July 1986. He had a lot
to say in the following interview:

"**Q: I think we've probably pretty well covered now
your period of time in USIA, and I guess you'd like to
go on now to your experience as an ambassador in
Tanzania. When you discuss this, not only would I like
you to discuss many of the situations that came up with
which you dealt, but also to the extent in which you feel
your prior USIA experience was a value to you as an
ambassadorial appointee.**

Shirley: A lot of people who have been ambassadors
will tell you that being one is not everything it is cracked
up to be. I differ. I think being ambassador is great fun. I
liked being in charge. I liked having all the elements of the
embassy working for me, and I enjoyed the fact that I had
to think about AID problems, and Peace Corps problems,
and other sorts of problems that I had not been asked to
confront in the past.

I enjoyed the fact that during my tenure in Dar es

Salaam Julius Nyerere was still President of Tanzania. I found him an interesting and extremely intelligent man. And since South Africa was in turmoil at the time, and because Nyerere was, to say the least, not particularly sympathetic to the policy of constructive engagement, my meetings with him were frequent, animated, sometimes sharp, but never acrimonious. It was as intellectually stimulating to deal with him, as it was to deal with Prime Minister Salim Salim.

Did my experience as USIA officer help me be a better chief of mission? Insofar as I was a good chief of mission at all, yes. A USIA Foreign Service officer who has had senior assignments abroad in USIA, and senior assignments in the Agency, is as well prepared to be a chief of mission as a political cone ambassador. If he is an intelligent man, a thoughtful man, a well-read man, if he knows history, and if he is a political animal, the USIA officer is as prepared to be a good chief of mission as the fellow who has spent his entire life in the political cone.

In some respects, he is better prepared because he will have managed large amounts of money and large numbers of people, whereas plenty of political cone officers become ambassadors with virtually no management experience at all.

Q: While you were dealing with Nyerere, what language were you dealing with? French?

Miller: No. Nyerere's English was every bit as good as mine. He had been educated at the University of Edinburgh." – (Ambassador John W. Shirley interviewed by G. Lewis Schmidt, *The Association for Diplomatic Studies and Training (ADST), Foreign Affairs Oral History Project*; initial interview date: 21 November 1989, copyright, 1998 ADST, p. 30).

Notes

1. Colin Legum, *Pan-Africanism: A Short Political Guide* (New York: Frederick A. Praeger, 1965), see texts of declarations of the Ghana-Guinea union, and the Ghana-Guinea-Mali union, appendices 6 and 12.

2. Haroub Othman, "The Union with Zanzibar," in Colin Legum and Geoffrey Mmari, editors, *Mwalimu: The Influence of Nyerere* (Trenton, New Jersey: Africa World Press, 1995), p. 173.

3. Frank Carlucci, quoted by Haroub Othman, "The Union with Zanzibar," ibid.

4. Haroub Othman, ibid., pp. 173 - 174.

5. Benjamin Mkapa, in his national broadcast on Radio Tanzania, Dar es Salaam (RTD), announcing the death of Julius Nyerere, quoted by the Associated Press (AP), October 14, 1999.

6. Benjamin Mkapa, quoted in "Tanzania: IRIN Focus on the Union," October 28, 1999.

7. Ali A. Mazrui, "Nyerere and I," in *Voices*, Africa Resource Center, 1999.

8. Julius Nyerere, in *The New York Times*, December 19, 1961; Ali A. Mazrui, *Towards A Pax Africana* (London: Weidenfeld & Nicolson, 1967), p. 77.

9. Julius K. Nyerere, "Nationalism and Pan-Africanism," in *WAY Forum*, No. 40, September 1961; and

in Paul E. Sigmund, Jr., editor, *The Ideologies of the Developing Nations* (New York: Frederick A. Praeger, 1963), pp. 208, and 209.

10. Julius Nyerere, in Tanganyika *Standard*, Dar es Salaam, November 1964.

11. Julius Nyerere, in an interview with James McKinley, "Tanzania's Nyerere Looks Back: Many Failures, and One Big Success – Bringing A Nation to Life." *The New York Times*, and the *International Herald Tribune*, September 2, 1996.

12. Julius K. Nyerere, Julius Nyerere, "Freedom and Unity," *Transition, Volume 0, Issue 14, 1964*, Kampala, Uganda, pp. 40 – 45. This was a republication of what he wrote earlier in June 1960 before he led Tanganyika to independence the following year. For an analysis of cooperation among the three East African countries of Kenya, Uganda and Tanganyika, see also Donald Rothschild, *Politics of Integration: An East African Documentary*, Nairobi, Kenya: East African Publishing House, 1968.

13. *Intelligence Study: Zanzibar: The Hundred Days' Revolution (ESAU XXX), Directorate of Intelligence, Central Intelligence Agency, No. 18, RSS No. 0013/66, 21 February 1966*, pp. xiii, xiv.

14. Helen-Luoise Hunter, *Zanzibar: The Hundred Days' Revolution*, Westport, Connecticut, USA: Greenwood Publishing Group, 2010, pp. 95, 96, 98.

15. Mohammed Ali Bakari, *The Democratisation Process in Zanzibar: A Retarded Transition*, Hamburg, Germany: Institut für Afrika-Kunde, 2001, pp. 118 – 119.

16. Nyerere, quoted by Bakari, ibid., p. 119. Nyerere also, cited by Bakari, quoted by Martin Bailey, *The Union of Tanganyika and Zanzibar: A Study in Political Integration*, Syracuse: East African Studies, 1973, p. 3.

17. Ambassador Donald Petterson interviewed by Charles Stuart Kennedy and Lambert Heyniger, 29 –30 November 2000, *The Association for Diplomatic Studies*

and Training (ADST), Foreign Affairs Oral History Project, p. 50; copyright 2002 ADST.

18. Ambassador Robert T. Hennemeyer interviewed by Charles Stuart Kennedy, February 1989, *The Association for Diplomatic Studies and Training (ADST), Foreign Affairs Oral History Project*, pp. 8 – 20; initial interview date: 15 February 1989; copyright 1998 ADST.

19. Ambassador Donald Petterson interviewed by Lambert Heyniger, 29 – 30 November 2000, *The Association for Diplomatic Studies and Training (ADST), Foreign Affairs Oral History Project*, pp. 27 – 37, 38 – 40, 42 – 48, 50 – 57; initial interview date: 13 December 1996, copyright 2002 ADST.

20. Ambassador Robert C.F. Gordon interviewed by Charles Stuart Kennedy, January 1989, *The Association for Diplomatic Studies and Training (ADST), Foreign Affairs Oral History Project*, pp. 16 – 18; initial interview date: 25 January 1989, copyright 1998 ADST.

21. Ambassador Frank Carlucci interviewed by Charles Stuart Kennedy, *The Association for Diplomatic Studies and Training (ADST), Foreign Affairs Oral History Project*, June 1997, pp. 28 – 38; initial interview date: 1 April 1997, copyright 2000, ADST.

22. Robert Henneyer, interview, *The Association for Diplomatic Studies and Training, Foreign Affairs Oral History Project*, ibid.

23. Ambassador John Howard Burns, interviewed by Charles Stuart Kennedy, May 1995, *The Association for Diplomatic Studies and Training, Foreign Affairs Oral History Project*, pp. 18 – 27, copyright ADST 1998.

24. Ambassador Claude G. Ross interviewed by Horace G. Torbert, February 1989, *The Association for Diplomatic Studies and Training, Foreign Affairs Oral History Project*, pp. 62 – 71; initial interview date: 16 February 1989, copyright 1998 ADST.

25. Julius Nyerere, in an interview with Ikaweba Bunting, "The Heart of Africa," *New Internationalist*,

Issue 309, December 1998.

26. Julius K. Nyerere, "Policy on Foreign Affairs," in J.K. Nyerere, *Freedom and Socialism: A Selection from Writings and Speeches 1965 – 1967* (Dar es Salaam, Tanzania: Oxford University Press, 1968), p. 369.

27. Ann Talbot, "Nyerere's Legacy of Poverty and Repression in Zanzibar," in "World Socialist Web Site: WSWS: News & Analysis: Africa," International Committee of the Fourth Internationale (ICFI), London, November 15, 2000.

28. Abdulrahman Mohamed Babu, "The 1964 Revolution: Lumpen or Vanguard?", in Abdul Sheriff and Ed Ferguson, eds., *Zanzibar Under Colonial Rule* (Athens, Ohio: Ohio University Press, 1991). See also, A. M. Babu, *African Socialism or Socialist Africa?* (Dar es Salaam, Tanzania: Tanzania Publishing House, 1981).

29. Jorge Castañeda, *Compañero: The Life and Death of Che Guevara* (New York: Alfred A. Knopf, 1997), pp. 326 – 327, and 328.

30. Gamal Nkrumah, "The Legacy of A Great African," in *Al-Ahram Weekly*, Issue No. 452, Cairo, Egypt, 21 – 27 October 1999.

31. Jim Lobe, "Tanzania: Restiveness in Zanzibar," in *Foreign Policy Focus: Self-Determination*, 2 May 2001.

32. Averill Harriman, "Telegram from the Embassy in Nigeria to the Department of State/1/," Lagos, Nigeria, March 25, 1964, 7 p.m., in US Diplomatic Archives: Nigeria (1964 - 1968), *Foreign Relations of the United States 1964 - 1968, Vol. XXIV Africa*, US Department of State, Washington, D.C. Source: Johnson Library, National Security File, International Meetings and Travel File, Africa, Box 31, Harriman's Trip, 3/64. Confidential; Priority; Passed to the White House.

Averill Harriman, in *Foreign Relations of the United States 1964 - 1968*, op. cit.; Kevin kelly, "How Communism Affected US Policy in East Africa," in *The East African*, Nairobi, Kenya, December 6, 1999.

33. US State Department document, 7 February 1964, in *Foreign Relations of the United States 1964 - 1968*, op. Cit.

34. Julius Nyerere, in the *East African Standard*, Nairobi, Kenya, February 13, 1964; quoted by Ali A. Mazrui, *Towards A Pax Africana*, op. cit., p. 153.

35. Ronald Aminzade, "The Politics of Race and Nation: Citizenship and Africanization in Tanganyika," Department of Sociology, University of Minnesota, December 2, 1998. See also *Tanganyika Standard*, Dar es Salaam, Tanganyika, January 22, 1964; *Tanganyika Standard*, January 23, 1964, on the mutiny.

On the incendiary debate on Africanisation in the preceding years, which led up to the mutiny in January 1964, see also, *Mwafrika*, Dar es Salaam, Tanganyika, October 4, 1960, a newspaper published in Kiswahili. The Minister of Labour Derek Bryceson, a British who settled in Tanganyika in 1951, said in parliament that Tanganyikans of Asian and European origin should also be considered as Africans, and defined as such; to which leaders of the opposition African National Congress (ANC) responded: "The meaning of Tanganyikans is Africans with black skins."

See also Tanganyika Council Debates (LEGCO – Legislative Council – Debates), speech of Bhoke Munanka, October 13, 1960: "Africanisation means Africanisation, it does not in any way suggest localisation (to include local Asian and European Tanganyikans and other non-blacks together with African Tanganyikans)"; *Ngurumo*, Dar es Salaam, Tanganyika, 3 - 4 November 1960, another Kiswahili newspaper containing reports on the heated debate on Africanization, and definition of "Africans."

Besides Zuberi Mtemvu, leader of the opposition African National Congress (ANC) and others in parliament, another ardent and uncompromising advocate of rapid Africanisation was Christopher Kasanga Tumbo, former trade union leader and member of parliament who resigned from his position as high commissioner (ambassador) to Britain and returned to Tanganyika in August 1962 to form the People's Democratic Party (PDP). The PDP's leading and founding members included several ANC activists, and the party advocated racial policies on citizenship, Africanization, and on minorities - Asians, Europeans, Arabs and other non-blacks - contrary to what TANU said, and objected to clauses of the new republican constitution, "which made the president a virtual dictator." See *Tanganyika Standard*, Dar es Salaam, Tanganyika, January 9, 1963.

In early January 1963, the PDP leaders met to discuss plans to merge with the ANC. See *Tanganyika Standard*, Dar es Salaam, Tanganyika, January 4, 1963; *Tanganyika Standard*, January 18, 1963, in which it was reported that the opposition parties, including AMNUT (All-Muslim National Union of Tanganyika), demanded a referendum on the one-party system.

See also Julius Nyerere, in a letter to all the cabinet members and their ministries, January 7, 1964, against Africanization: "The nation must use the entire reservoir of skill and experience.... The skin in which this skill is encased is completely irrelevant.... This means that discrimination in civil service employment as regards recruitment, training, and promotion must be brought to an end immediately.... We cannot allow the growth of first and second-class citizenship. Africanization is dead." In the *Tanganyika Standard*, Dar es salaam, Tanganyika, January 8, 1964.

Trade union leaders objected vehemently to this directive from President Nyerere. Teendwa Washington, leader of the Local Government Union, accused Nyerere of taking Tanganyika "back to the colonial days." See *Tanganyika Standard*, Dar es Salaam, Tanganyika, January 9, 1964.

Almost exactly two weeks later, on January 20, after

Nyerere issued his policy directive against Africanisation, the army mutinied over this very policy, demanding higher salaries and the replacement of British army officers by black ones in pursuit of full Africanisation of the armed forces.

36. Kevin Kelly, "How Communism Affected US Policy in East Africa," *The East African*, Nairobi, Kenya, 10 December 1999; US State Department background paper, February 7, 1964, in *Foreign Relations of the United States 1964 - 1968*, op. Cit.

37. Ulric Haynes, in a National Security Council memo, June 8, 1966, in *Foreign Relations of the United States 1964 - 1968*, op. cit.

38. Julius Nyerere, "Principles and Development," in J.K. Nyerere, *Freedom and Socialism: A Selection from Writings and Speeches 1965 – 1967* (Dar es Salaam, Tanzania: Oxford University Press, 1968), pp. 202 – 203.

39. Julius Nyerere, "Rhodesia in the Context of Southern Africa," in *Foreign Affairs*, New York, April 1966; J.K. Nyerere, *Freedom and Socialism*, op. cit., pp. 143, 154 - 155, and 156.

40. J.K. Nyerere, on the Warsaw Pact invasion of Czechoslovakia, August 1968.

41. Colin Legum and John Drsydale, eds., *Africa Contemporary Record: Annual Survey and Documents 1968 – 1969*, London: Africa Research Limited, 1969, pp. 221, and 614.

42. J.K. Nyerere, "Policy on Foreign Affairs," in Nyerere, *Freedom and Socialism*, op. cit., pp. 370, and 371.

43. J.K. Nyerere, ibid., p. 203.

44. Ibid., p. 202.

45. Mohammed Ali Bakari, *The Democratisation Process in Zanzibar: A Retarded Transition*, *The Democratisation Process in Zanzibar: A Retarded Transition*, Hamburg, Germany: Institut für Afrika-Kunde, 2001, p. 122.

46. Mwesiga Baregu, quoted by M.A. Bakari, ibid., p. 123. See also, cited by Bakari, Mwesiga Baregu, "In Defence of Closer Union and Greater African Unity," *The African Review, Vol. 22, No. 1 and 2*, 1995, p. 82.

47. Benjamin Mkapa, quoted in Benjamin Mkapa, quoted in "Tanzania: IRIN Focus on the Union," 28 October 1999; CNN, Dar es Salaam, 20 November 2000, "Tanzania's Mkapa pledges to act on Zanzibar, fight corruption."

48. Samir Amin, "The First Babu Memorial Lecture," in honour of the late Abdulrahman Mohammed Babu (22 September 1924 – 5 August 1996), London, 22 September 1997. See also Samir Amin, "The First Babu Memorial Lecture on 22 September 1997," *Pambazuka News, Issue 451*, 8 October 2009; Abdulrahman Mohammed Babu, "A New Europe: Consequences for Tanzania," in the *Review of African Political Economy*, Vol. 18, No. 50, Spring 1991, pp. 75 – 78. Mohamed Suliman and A.M. Babu, "Face to Face with A.M. Babu," in the *Review of African Political Economy*, vol. 22, No. 66, December 1995, pp. 596 – 598.

49. Ali A. Mazrui, in "Africa's Mwalimu: Ali Mazrui Pays Tribute to Julius Nyerere," in *Washington Magazine*, Washington, D.C., Vol. 12, No. 4, Fall 1999; Ali A. Mazrui, "Mwalimu Rise to Power," in the *Daily Nation*, Nairobi, Kenya, October 17, 1999; Ali A. Mazrui, "Nyerere and I," in *Voices*, Africa Resource Centre, October 1999.

50. Ali A. Mazrui, "Witness to History: Interview with Ali A. Mazrui," *The Gambia Echo*, 25 July 2008.

51. Julius K. Nyerere, in an interview with M.A. Novicki and B. Boorstein, in *Africa Report*, November 30, 1985, p. 10. See also Pal Ahluwalia and Abebe Zegeye, "Multiparty Democracy in Tanzania: Crises in the Union," in *Africa Security Review*, Vol. 10, No. 3, 2001; Martin Bailey, *Union of Tanganyika and Zanzibar: A Study in Political Integration*, Syracuse, New York: Syracuse

University, June 1973.

52. Julius Nyerere in his speech during the 40th anniversary of Ghana's independence, Accra, Ghana, March 1997.

53. Julius Nyerere, quoted by Austin Ejiet, "Kwa heri, Mtukufu Rais Julius K. Nyerere," in *The Monitor*, Kampala, Uganda, October 17, 1999. See also A. Ejiet, Ibid.:

"Three things sum up Mwalimu Julius Nyerere for me. Sometime in the mid-sixties (sic) a Swiss bank wrote offering to keep his money in a secret-coded account at extremely generous interest rates.... But far from jumping at the offer, the president published the letter in the national newspapers with the memorable declaration that he had no money to hide and that the little that he had could only be banked in Tanzania where it belonged....This action underscored the president's faith in his country and spoke volumes about the extent of his sincerity.

Shortly after this, a type of precious stone was unearthed in Tanzania. The country's parliament unanimously resolved to name this gem the 'Nyeretrite' in recognition of his stature as a statesman locally as well as internationally. The president thanked his countrymen for their kind consideration but politely declined the honour. Instead he proposed that the stone be named the 'Tanzanite.' Tanzania, he aruged, was more important than individuals.

Just one more. Mwalimu Julius Nyerere paid a visit to Ghana shortly after his retirement in 1985 and reportedly berated the leadership of that country for the shabby way in which the republic's founder, Kwame Nkrumah, had been treated."

54. Julius K. Nyerere, in "The Heart of Africa: Interview with Julius Nyerere on Anti-Colonialism," in *New Internationalist*, Issue 309, January-February 1999.

The interviewer was Ikaweba Bunting, an African-American who had lived in Tanzania for 25 years when he interviewed Nyerere. As he stated:

"In recognition of Nyerere's passing, I present his last great interview. The first issue of *The Internationalist* in 1970 had as its cover story an interview with President Julius Nyerere of Tanzania, then at the very centre of the new movement for world development. Three decades on, Nyerere is, Mandela aside, Africa's most respected elder statesperson, still active in attempts to resolve the current conflicts in Burundi and DR Congo. No one is better placed to look back on the anti-colonial century....

It has been my privilege to be associated with Mwalimu Nyerere for the past 25 years. During a visit to Harlem, New York, in the late 1960s Mwalimu extended an invitation to Africans in the Diaspora to come to Tanzania and participate in building a socialist African state. I came over through a new organization called the Pan-African Skills project and have lived in Tanzania ever since, for a quarter of the century.

Nyerere's Tanzania was a magnet for anti-colonial activists and thinkers from all over the world. Uganda's President Yoweri Museveni, for instance, was deeply influenced by his time as a student at the University of Dar es Salaam. Museveni belonged to a study group led by the Guyanan Walter Rodney, who wrote his seminal book *How Europe Underdeveloped Africa* while he was a professor there.

The University of Dar es Salaam became the centre for the guerrilla-intellectuals and activists of African liberation movements. FRELIMO of Mozambique, the ANC and PAC of South Africa, ZANU and ZAPU of Zimbabwe, the MPLA of Angola and SWAPO of Namibia all had offices and training camps in Tanzania. The country also gave safe haven to US civil-rights activists, Black Panther Party-members and Vietnam War resisters.

It was an exciting place to be. Under a head of state who valued equal rights, justice and development more than pomp and power of office, Tanzania was at the heart

476

of the anti-colonial struggle.

Over the years I have often been able to sit with Mwalimu and reflect on Africa's struggle for self-determination and development. Now, in December 1998, prompted by the *New Internationalist* special issue on the Radical Twentieth Century, Mwalimu Nyerere and I sat down over two days at his home in Butiama, Tanzania, and reflected on his role over the past 50 years as an activist and statesperson in the anti-colonial cause."

Nyerere's awakening started early when he was a student at Makerere University College, Kampala, Uganda, which was then and for many years the most renowned institution of higher learning in colonial Africa, attracting students from all parts of the continent. As he stated in the same interview:

"At Makerere in 1943 I started something called the Tanganyika African Welfare Association. Its main purpose was not political or anti-colonial. We wanted to improve the lives of Africans. But inside us something was happening.

I wrote an essay in 1944 called The Freedom of Women. I must be honest and say I was influenced by John Stuart Mill, who had written about the subjugation of women. My father had 22 wives and I knew how hard they had to work and what they went through as women. Here in this essay I was moving towards the idea of freedom theoretically. But I was still in the mindset of improving the lives and welfare of Africans: I went to Tabora to start teaching.

Then came Indian independence. The significance of India's independence movement was that it shook the British empire. When Gandhi succeeded I think it made the British lose the will to cling to empire. But it was events in Ghana in 1949 that fundamentally changed my attitude. When Kwame Nkrumah was released from prison this produced a transformation.... First India in 1947, then Ghana in 1949.... Under the influence of these events,

477

while at university in Britain, I made up my mind to be a full-time political activist when I went back."

Nyerere was 27 years old in 1949, and 21 when he founded the Tanganyika African Welfare Association at Makerere University College in 1943.

55. Donald Petterson, "The Zanzibar Revolution."

56. D. Petterson, ibid.

57. Donald Petterson, "The Association for Diplomatic Studies and Training Foreign Affairs Oral History Project," interviewed by Charles Stuart Kennedy and Lambert Heyniger on 30 November 2000; initial interview date: December 13, 1996, pp. 50, and 55.

58. D. Petterson, ibid., pp. 37 – 38.

59. Ibid., pp. 40, 42.

60. Ibid., pp. 49 – 50.

61. "Declaration of Federation by the Governments of East Africa" signed by Julius Nyerere, Milton Obote, and Jomo Kenyatta, Nairobi, Kenya, 5 June 1963.

62. CIA, *Intelligence Study – Zanzibar: The Hundred Days' Revolution (ESAU XXX), No. 18, RSS No. 0013/66, 21 February 1966*, pp. 1 – 2, v, xiii – xv, 9 – 10, 63 – 64, 118 – 119, 120 – 121, 122, 123, 125, 136.

63. *Intelligence Study: Zanzibar: The Hundred Days' Revolution (ESAU XXX), Directorate of Intelligence, Central Intelligence Agency, No. 18, RSS No. 0013/66, 21 February 1966*, pp. 126 – 127.

64. Robert Conley, "Tanganyika Vote Completes Union," *The New York Times*, 26 April 1964.

65. Ronald Aminzade, *Race, Nation, and Citizenship in Post-Colonial Africa: The Case of Tanzania*, New York: Cambridge University Press, 2013, pp. 99 – 102. See also, cited by Ronald Aminzade, Amrit Wilson, *U.S. Foreign Policy and Revolution: The Creation of Tanzania*, London: Pluto Press, 1989; Anthony Clayton, The Zanzibar Revolution and its Aftermath, Hamden, Connecticut, USA: Anchor Books, 1981, p. 70; Abdulrahman Babu, "I Saw the Future and It Works," in Haroub Othman, ed., *I Saw*

the Future and It Works: Essays Celebrating the Life of Comrade Abdulrahman Mohamed Babu 1934 – 1996, Dar es Salaam, Tanzania: E&D Limited, 2001; Godfrey Mwakikagile, The Union of Tanganyika and Zanzibar: Product of the Cold War?, Pretoria, South Africa: New Africa Press, 2008; Julius K. Nyerere, "The Union of Tanganyika and Zanzibar," Freedom and Unity: Uhuru na Umoja: A Selection from Writings and Speeches, 1952 – 1965, Volume 1, Dar es Salaam, Tanzania: Oxford University Press, 1967, p. 292).

66. Julius K. Nyerere, Freedom and Unity: Uhuru na Umoja, Dar es Salaam, Tanzania: Oxford University Press, 1969, p. 292.

67. Andrew Nyerere, in Godfrey Mwakikagile, Nyerere and Africa: End of an Era, New Africa Press, Fifth Edition, Dar es Salaam, Tanzan, and Pretoria, South Africa, 2010, pp. 125 – 126.

68. Donald Petterson, "Nine Hour Revolution."

69. Foreign Relations of the United States 1964 - 1968, pp. 610 – 611.

70. Averell Harriman, Johnson Library, National Security File, International Meetings and Travel File, Africa, Box 31, Harriman's Trip, 3/64. Confidential; Priority; Exdis. Passed to the White House. See also, US Diplomatic Archives: Nigeria (1964 - 1968), Foreign Relations of the United States 1964 - 1968, Vol. XXIV.

71. Averill Harriman, in a report to President Lyndon B. Johnson, 28 October 1964. See Foreign Relations of the United States 1964 – 1968; Kevin Kelly, "How Communism Affected US Policy in East Africa," The East African, Nairobi, Kenya, 6 December 1999.

72. US State Department background paper, 7 February 1964, in Foreign Relations of the United States 1964 – 1968.

73. Julius Nyerere, quoted in the East African Standard, Nairobi, Kenya, 13 February 1964; cited by Ali Mazrui, Towards A Pax Africana, op. cit., p. 153.

74. Ronald R. Aminzade, "The Politics of Race and Nation: Citizenship and Africanization in Tanganyika," in Diane E. Davis, ed., *Political Power and Social Theory, Vol. 14*, Amsterdam: Elsevier Science, 2001, pp. 53 – 90; Ronald Aminzade, "The Africanization Debate, The Failed Army Mutiny, and a Restructured State," in Ronald Aminzade, *Race, Nation, and Citizenship in Post-Colonial Africa: The Case of* Tanzania, New York: Cambridge University Press, 2013, 79 – 89.

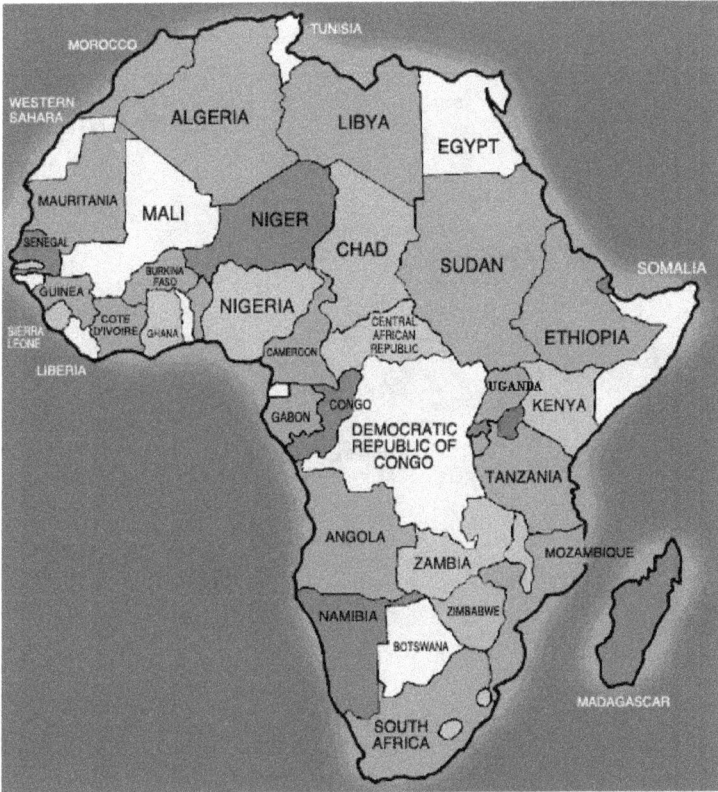

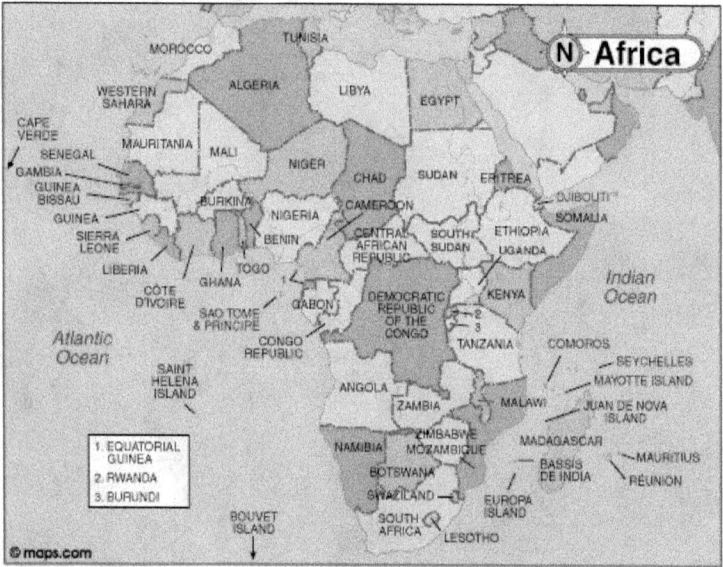

N Africa

TUNISIA
MOROCCO
WESTERN SAHARA
ALGERIA
LIBYA
EGYPT
CAPE VERDE
SENEGAL
MAURITANIA
MALI
NIGER
CHAD
SUDAN
ERITREA
DJIBOUTI
GAMBIA
GUINEA BISSAU
GUINEA
BURKINA
NIGERIA
CAMEROON
SOMALIA
SIERRA LEONE
BENIN
CENTRAL AFRICAN REPUBLIC
SOUTH SUDAN
ETHIOPIA
UGANDA
LIBERIA
TOGO
GHANA
CÔTE D'IVOIRE
SAO TOME & PRINCIPE
GABON
DEMOCRATIC REPUBLIC OF THE CONGO
KENYA
Indian Ocean
Atlantic Ocean
CONGO REPUBLIC
TANZANIA
COMOROS
SAINT HELENA ISLAND
ANGOLA
ZAMBIA
MALAWI
SEYCHELLES
MAYOTTE ISLAND
JUAN DE NOVA ISLAND
ZIMBABWE
MOZAMBIQUE
MADAGASCAR
MAURITIUS
NAMIBIA
BOTSWANA
SWAZILAND
BASSIS DE INDIA
RÉUNION
EUROPA ISLAND
BOUVET ISLAND
SOUTH AFRICA
LESOTHO

1. EQUATORIAL GUINEA
2. RWANDA
3. BURUNDI

© maps.com

482

www.ingramcontent.com/pod-product-compliance
Lightning Source LLC
Chambersburg PA
CBHW050448270326
41927CB00009B/1650